CELEBRATING
DR. BEN-JOCHANNAN

CELEBRATING
DR. BEN-JOCHANNAN

From Eternity to Eternity

FREDERICK MONDERSON

SUMON PUBLISHERS

FREDERICK MONDERSON

SuMon Publishers
PO Box 160586
Brooklyn, New York 11216

sumonpublishers.com@sumonpublishers.com
fredsegypt.com@fredsegypt.com

Copyright SuMon Publishers, 2012, 2023 All Rights Reserved. No part of this book may be reproduced, stored in a retrieval system, or transmitted by any means without the written permission of the author.

ISBN – 978-1-61023-041-4
LCCN - 2012944050

In the **Tribute to Professor George Simmonds**, "Unsung Hero," Dr. Fred Monderson sat at the feet of his heroes, Brother X, Michael Carter, Dr. Leonard Jeffries, Elombe Brathe, Dr. Lewis, Prof. George Simmonds, Dr. ben-Jochannan, Sister Camille Yarbrough, among others.

INTRODUCTION:

CELEBRATING DR. BEN-JOCHANNAN

DR. BEN, "OUR FATHER"
By
Dr. Fred Monderson

Dr. Ben is "Our Father," our intellectual father, who in travelling the road, first encountered then pointed out the pitfalls systematically arrayed against the African, as Marcus Garvey proclaimed, "Those at home and those abroad." The little man stood tall and illuminating, withstanding the intellectual, religious, educational and disguised economic assaults America and the West have perennially launched against African men of substance whose knees refuse to bend! Very early he grasped the significance of ancient Nile Valley civilization as advancing humanity's development within the context of state formation and the enlightenment of metaphysics as well as the African's origination, development, consolidation, expansion and spread of consciousness and knowledge enabling the world's people to advance religiously, culturally and scientifically.

Mirroring the actions of great black men challenging oppressive behemoths, viz., Hannibal and Rome; Shaka and the Boers; Nat Turner and American enslavement; Frederick Douglass as an abolitionist; Samori Toure halting the French advance in West Africa as part of the continent's nationalist assertion; Martin Delaney and Biblical distortion and the black man's place in early world history; Booker T. Washington and the exclusion of blacks from the industrial development of the nation; Menelik II repelling the Italians at the Battle of Adowa; W.E.B. DuBois and the significance of the struggle for Pan-Africanism; Marcus Garvey, the UNIA and the importance of black symbolism and motifs; Carter G. Woodson and the dangers of mis-education; Paul Robeson as a voice in the "wilderness;" Malcolm X as a grassroots

FREDERICK MONDERSON

visionary; and Dr. Martin Luther King, Jr., hewing "a stone of hope from a mountain of despair;" Dr. Ben dazzled as a principal star in constellations of intellectual and moral giants who spoke truth to power.

In the spectacular journey of his life, Dr. Yosef Alfredo Antonio ben-Jochannan raised a loud and consistent voice against Western and American hypocrisy, falsity, bigotry, distortion, omission and maligning of the African, his heritage, its legacy and the destiny of Africa's sons and daughters at home and abroad. He meticulously analyzed and challenged the writings of pseudo-scientific proponents and others as Father Placide Temples, M.W.D. Jeffries, Basil Davidson, Flinders Petrie, Wallis Budge and James Breasted, among others.

Possessing no pistols, canons or warships, Dr. ben-Jochannan "went to war" to recapture the African rightful place in the intellectual development of the human spirit. Encountering many obstacles, he still persevered despite the odds and opposition. Very early he made the connection between the ancient African and the evolution of scientific study and religious practice, metaphysics and spiritualism. In intellectual analysis of Western holy books, he critiqued propagators of the "curse of the black man" syndrome, the stealing of the African's intellectual heritage claiming to be its originator, then denying the victim access to the educational opportunities this knowledge promised. Conducting penetrating research, he discovered ancient commentators who were contemporary with Egyptians and other ancient Africans and who presented a different version of present history colored by the machinations of imperialism, racial discrimination and an indiscriminate propensity to propagate views of Western standards that purport the African to be inferior. He frowned upon the devastating and long-lasting psychological and social scarification of the slavery experience. He recognized ancient

CELEBRATING
DR. BEN-JOCHANNAN

African man and cultures contributed more than recognized today towards the development of the same Western standards of learning, religion, technology, architecture, science, and so much more. He railed against religious bigotry and surprisingly his efforts threatened the pillars of Western falsity that suppressed indigenous cultures in Asia, Africa and the Americas.

As an anthropologist and archaeologist, he early discovered the conspiracy against ancient Egypt, recognized the mechanisms of the strategy of ancient artifacts acquisition and misrepresentation of such treasures in museum displays and other fields of publication. He took students to view Egyptian collections at museums and pointed out the positives and negatives in the displays. He also took students to his Harlem apartment showcasing his library to reinforce their realization of the existence of diverse and not easily disclosed sources of referents.

To counter the intellectual and cultural assault against the African personality, he began advocating, lecturing, teaching and writing and publishing correctives to standard negative portrayals. He initiated the concept of self-publishing because established publishing houses recognized the dangers of his enlightening the people. Becoming tremendously pro-active, he began Tours of Egypt and encouraged others to so engage the yearning masses with the intent of unleashing intellectual uprisings that would educate and uplift Africans long denied the real advantages of constructive and systematic learning. Contacting Dr. Leonard James, a longtime educator Emeritus of New York City Technical College of CUNY and admirer of Dr. Ben's courageous intellectual challenge, he reminded: "Dr. Ben is an unsung hero and a great African scholar who produced unbelievable scholarship." The strength of Dr. Ben's thrust was revealing the wide diversity of referents for research and encouraging young scholars to "Get the earliest materials and work from there." In Egypt, he always laid down the law, "Now that you've been to Egypt, seen what you have seen, what are you going to do with the knowledge?" He consistently advocated travel to Egypt, "Let the Monuments Teach," to better grasp the industriousness of the ancient African and the lasting effect of his contributions. Thus, he admonished, "Publish or Perish!" Dr. James continued, "Every modern African and African-American Egyptologist owes Dr. Ben a debt." Equally and even further, "Each and every African and African-American studies department in college owes Dr. Ben a debt."

As time and toil took its toll, Dr. Ben faced and fought many health issues. Still, he persevered. In his glorious march of fame, he "talk the talk" and "walk the walk" and "talk the walk" and "walk the talk!" He often boasted, "I took Egypt to combat racism and misrepresentation." This was particularly evident in Egypt where Dr. Ben's work among poor Egyptians and indigenous Nubians was tremendously significant. The construction of the Egyptian "High Dam," the "Damn Dam," displaced untold thousands of Nubians and submerged many Nubian temples and cemeteries containing important cultural evidence. In response, Dr. Ben adopted and worked with the village of Daboud, the operational center of the displaced Nubian villages.

Actually, such a collaboration was fostered because, on one 1980s tour going from Luxor to Aswan, the bus broke down on the outskirts of Daboud Village and as the Americans stood in the steaming desert sun waiting for repairs, the villagers came to their assistance. Flabbergasted that "Nubian Americans" would come to their land, they extended their meager hospitality, cherished at the time! Thenceforth, Dr. Ben would stop at the village, to great fanfare, each time he passed through. He encouraged brothers and sisters on tour to bring

CELEBRATING DR. BEN-JOCHANNAN

medicine, school supplies for the children, new clothing and other essentials. He helped build a school, a hospital and playground, worked with the Council and adopted and educated several students at university level. Any donations collected at the village he would match twice over, give it to the mayor who would then disperse the money and essentials to different villages. Dr. Ben's actions emboldened Nubian resistance sweltering under Egyptian yoke! Through bribery of travel agents his efforts were undermined. In no uncertain terms, he was told "Stop it!" Decades later, Nubians welcoming their "Nubian-American brothers and sisters" would ask "How is Dr. Ben?" "Is he still alive?" "How is he doing?"

An outstanding trait of Dr. ben-Jochannan has been his unselfishness and lavish praise and uplifting of Africans globally. Everywhere Dr. Ben traveled in Egypt he helped people. Every hotel his group stayed at in Cairo, Luxor and Aswan, people were rewarded. Housekeeping, food-service, gardeners, baggage-handlers, bus-drivers, musicians and gatekeepers at sites all got remuneration. Everyone benefitted. Each group received an envelope. He really distributed the wealth!

On the "farcical 2003 trip," Dr. Ben was very sick. When I saw him in the Lobby of the Oberoi Hotel, and approached, I said a silent prayer for Dr. Ben! Then I thought, "Thank God he will die in his beloved Egypt!" Rushed home and thanks to the efforts of Dr. and Mrs. Lewis of Harlem, Dr. Ben was up and about and dancing within months. Subsequently, he was enstooled at **National Action Network** in Harlem by the Reverend Al Sharpton.

FREDERICK MONDERSON

On November 15, 2010, the day Dr. Ben again (*Daily Challenge* March 1, 2000, Centerfold) recognized and endorsed my work, as a longstanding student of his, while having lunch at his favorite Harlem Restaurant, Dr. Ben said to me: "Monderson, can you take me back to Egypt one last time. I don't want to go to the sites, just to sit in the hotel lobby. The people will come to see me!" That is, the Oberoi Hotel Lobby at Aswan! Contacting his lawyer, he told me, "The Court will not permit me to allow Dr. Ben to travel."

Dr. Ben led an exceptional life. He expended great energy, time and resources in defending and upholding things African. He paid a price for his outspokenness! He was especially proud of and adored the African woman whom he placed as on an obelisk pedestal. He was in the forefront of the "black is beautiful" movement; initiated wearing African clothing and insignia in America; greatly admired African heroes and heroines; he shined the light for all to see; and directed the focus of African intellectuals, encouraging their research on Egypt, Africa, as well as championing Africa's place in universal history. He pioneered use of indigenous names as *Alkebu-Lan* for Egypt and *Denk Nesh* for Lucy! and frowned on such disgusting appellates as "Negro," "Nigger" and all such offensive names. He devoted his life to teaching African people to "Be proud of your color, culture and history!" Dr. Ben has always been and will remain a "great light in the African pantheon of heroes" from Eternity to Eternity!

MAKING DR. BEN'S DAY

On Thursday September 6, 2012 at 9:00 AM, I visited Dr. ben-Jochannan to show him the book I wrote in his honor. Once Dr. Lewis gave me directions to the Bay Park Nursing Home in the Bronx, I worked my way there from Brooklyn, thru Manhattan and into the Bronx. I found him sitting having coffee in the dining room. Once we began examining the book in color on

CELEBRATING DR. BEN-JOCHANNAN

my computer along with the black and white version of the book sitting on the desk, I was impressed with how sharp Dr. Ben's mind still is. He told me he will be 95 years old on December 13, 2012! As we began to examine the first photos of the book, he said, "There's Dr. Jeffries and Dr. Clarke and Ben Carruthers." Then he said of the two, "They're dead!" He noted Professor "Simmonds was a good man. He died before Gertrude." He constantly checked his watch, staying abreast of time at it passed. In the book, he instantly recognized the Old Cataract and then the New Cataract Hotels at Aswan and talked about the Nubian Village on the opposite bank. He recognized the Aga Khan Mausoleum in the distance across the Nile River.

As I began to show him the covers of some of his authored books that he autographed for me, he remarked: "I don't know where my books are!" I reassured him the-some-30-books in their mostly original covers shown in this one will all be enshrined in the Library of Congress.

Dr. Ben's Photo 1. Dr. Leonard Jeffries and Erik Monderson give the "Black Power Salute" at Medgar Evers' **Black Writers Conference** – "Gathering at the Waters," 2017.

FREDERICK MONDERSON

Dr. Ben's Photo 1a. Dr. Fred Monderson showing Dr. Yosef ben-Jochannan the book *Celebrating Dr. Ben-Jochannan: From Eternity to Eternity* (on the desk) and on the computer in color on Thursday September 6, 2012, when he autographed the book in his honor.

When we got to the book on Kwesi Adebisi he instantly recognized him as "The fellow from Ohio that died in 1975." "I am waiting to go home," he mused, believing he will return to his apartment soon as he waited on his lawyer Mr. White and another person.

Showing him images of black Gods and kings in the Oberoi Hotel dining room, he remarked: "It's a black culture in all of Africa. Europe came down in Africa, that's what cause the big rift." Showing him the Nubian Museum photos, he remarked, "That's up in Aswan." He remembered the Old Cataract is "a brown building" and you "walk down the steps to the water."

Speaking about Paul Coates the publisher of Black Classic Press, he remembered, "He moved from Baltimore to

CELEBRATING DR. BEN-JOCHANNAN

Washington, DC." On Curtis Alexander he remembered he's "The tall, thin fellow in the Virginia" (State U).

Dr. Ben's Photo 1b. Cover of Celebrating Dr. Ben Jochannan (left) and **Title Page** showing Dr. Ben's signature after he examined the book and was not only pleased with it but enthused about his book covers within and the photographs that took him back to the famous monuments of Egypt he visited, spoke of and wrote about for decades.

He asked about Brother Abdul in Karnak and when I told him Brother Abdul has retired, Dr. Ben told me "Abdul must be about 85 years old." He asked about Egyptian Guides Shawki and Farouk. Then he asked about "The lady who lived down the street from the Mena House Hotel in Cairo" and wondered if she is still alive.

Showing him the fallen statue of Rameses II at Memphis Museum, he remembered "You have to go up the stairs and walk around to see the statue properly." He was surprised you

FREDERICK MONDERSON

can't use cameras in the Valley of the Kings or in the Cairo Museum. I told him they repaired and opened the "Sphinx Road" between Karnak and Luxor Temples and he was surprised and pleased. He remarked about the African features of the Sphinxes beside the Temple of Luxor and wondered about the replacement and was very pleased about the upgraded Plaza at Karnak Temple. We enjoyed a good morning before he had to go to lunch and I left knowing I had raised his spirits and happily **Made Dr. Ben's Day!**

Dr. Ben's Photo 1c. Erik Monderson on the Upper Terrace near a statue of Queen Hatshepsut at her Deir el Bahari Temple.

CELEBRATING DR. BEN-JOCHANNAN

TABLE OF CONTENTS

Introduction   3
1. Poem to GOD RA   18
2. Poem to GOD PTAH   26
3. Poem to GOD AMON-RA   36
4. Poem to KARNAK TEMPLE   47
5. DR. YOSEF BEN-JOCHANNAN – A TRIBUTE   60
6. DR. BEN'S LETTER RECOGNIZING DR. FREDERICK MONDERSON, March 1, 2000   77
7. DR. BEN'S LETTER RECOGNIZING DR. FREDERICK MONDERSON, November 15, 2010   78
8. DR. BEN'S LETTER AUTHORIZING TRIBUTES, SEMINARS, CALLS FOR PAPERS, June 5, 2010   80
9. "PRAISING THE BLACK WOMAN"   82
10. DR. FRED MONDERSON PRESENTS HIS SECOND MEMORIAL DAY TRIBUTE TO Dr. Yosef A.A. ben-Jochannan "LET'S LIBERATE THE TEMPLE!"   103

FREDERICK MONDERSON

11. THE EGYPTIAN TEMPLE — 106
12. CELEBRATING DR. BEN I — 149
13. CELEBRATING DR BEN II — 162
14. CULTURE AND SPIRITUALITY IN ANCIENT AFRICA — 177
15. SPIRITUALITY IN ANCIENT EGYPTIAN TEMPLES — 225
16. "MYSTICAL NATURE OF AFRICAN SPIRITUALITY" — 255
17. MOUNTAIN VIEW OF AFRICAN SPIRITUALITY — 267
18. BLACK GENESIS I — 274
19. BLACK GENESIS II — 284
20. HAITI "BY THE GRACE OF FAITH" — 297
21. HAITI – "EYEWITNESS TO DISASTER" — 312
22. AFRICA: "MOTHER OF WESTERN CIVILIZATION" — 323
23. THIRD ANNUAL MEMORIAL DAY TRIBUTE TO DR. BEN-JOCHANNAN — 330 / 331
24. AFRICAN ORIGINS OF THE "MAJOR" WESTERN RELIGIONS — 331
25. BLACK MAN OF THE NILE AND

CELEBRATING DR. BEN-JOCHANNAN

HIS 0FAMILY	333
26. RELEVANCE OF EGYPTOLGICAL STUDIES TODAY	342
27. DR. FRED MONDERSON PRESENTS FOURTH MEMORIAL DAY TRIBUTE TO DR. YOSEF BEN-JOCHANNAN	384
28. ETERNAL, YET CHANGING EGYPT 2005	385
29. EGYPT 2008	416
30. EGYPT 2010	433
31. WHO WERE THE ANCIENT EGYPTIANS?	447
32. THE CONSPIRACY AGAINST ANCIENT EGYPT	528
33. Comparing EGYPTIAN Chronology	614
34. THE MAGIC OF KING TUTANKHAMON	618
35. IMMORTAL Distortions and Omissions in Ancient Egypt	637
36. BLACK EGYPT AND THE STRUGGLE FOR INCLUSION	643
37. RED – COLOR OF THE GODS	653

FREDERICK MONDERSON

38. CELEBRATING IVAN VAN SERTIMA	679
39. INTELLECTUAL EXPRESSION FOR HUMAN AND SOCIAL PROGRESS	696
40. GOLDEN AGE-WEST AFRICA	704
41. HONORING A GIANT	716
42. PRAISE OF DR. BEN	722
43. INDEX	723

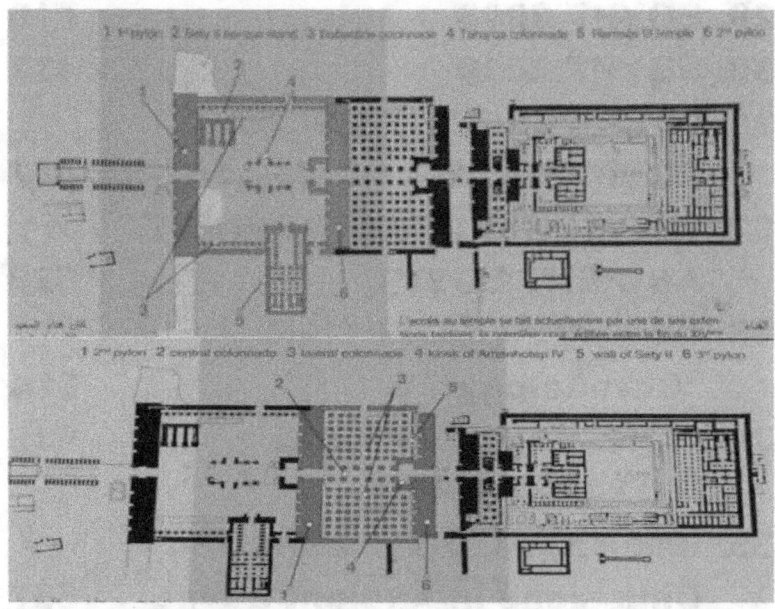

Dr. Ben's Photo 1d. Highlighted in red, Karnak Temple's Great Court (above) and Hypostyle Hall (below), a "Holy Place," where Dr. Ben, was considered "a Master of Karnak."

CELEBRATING
DR. BEN-JOCHANNAN

Dr. Ben's Photo 1e. Dr. Yosef Antonio Alfredo ben-Jochannan and a friend. Bending over in the rear is the future Governor of New York David Patterson.

Dr. Ben's Photo 2. Dr. Fred Monderson stands before and joins "Warrior Scholars" – Dr. Leonard Jeffries, Professor Scobie, John Henrik Clarke, Dr. Ben-Jochannan, and Prof. James Smalls, of which several influenced him tremendously.

FREDERICK MONDERSON

1.   Poem to GOD RA

O Ra, King of the Gods, you enjoyed a prominence matched by few divinities. You emerged at Heliopolis, and absorbed, you extended your significance throughout dynastic times. Father of the Gods whose soul is exalted in the hidden place with symbols of the Disk of the Sun, encircled by the serpent Khut with ankh, scepter and tail from your waist. Self-begotten and Self-born creative vigor, Power of Powers with two uraei, you are a doubly hidden and secret God. Lord of Eternity, Sovereign of the Gods, you exist forever, Lord of Souls.

Dr. Ben's Photo 3. At a 1990s New York City ASCAC Conference at City College, where Dr. Jeffries applauds **Dr. John H. Clarke in the Chair**, as Dr. Jacob Carruthers gives the **Icon** his full and respectful attention and the **Immaculate Sisters** lend their support.

CELEBRATING
DR. BEN-JOCHANNAN

Sekhem, begetter of his Gods, from Heliopolis, your priests influenced political developments in the Old Kingdom when Pyramid builders incorporated your name into theirs, becoming "Son of the Sun," hence the title Son of Ra. These kings built sun temples with names as Favorite Place of Ra and Satisfaction of Ra all in Praise of the Lord of Rays. Self-Created, King of Heaven, Great Duration of Life, Lord who advances, you are the Soul that do good to the body. Governor of his Eye, Lord of Generation, invisible and secret, you are Governor of the Tuat, Double Obelisk God.

Dr. Ben's Photo 4. Dr. Ben and daughters Nabila (l) and Magda (r). Daboud Nubian Village, Nubian Resettlement Villages, Aswan Governorate, Upper Egypt.

Governor of your circle, Aged One of Forms, Memphis received endowments in the Old and Middle Kingdoms in Praise of thee, King of the World. The Priesthood of local

FREDERICK MONDERSON

Gods linked their deity to the Sun Gods name Ra, Mighty in Majesty, Vivifier of Bodies. The Theban triumph merged Amon with Ra assuming all of the ancient Gods' attributes as Maker of Heaven where you are firmly established. God One from the beginning of time, Mighty One of myriad forms and aspects, Creator of Laws Unchangeable and Unalterable, Lord of Truth whose shrine is hidden, you are the Soul which gives names to his limbs, Body of Khepera, God of Souls who are in the Obelisk.

Judge of Words, the glory of Ra manifested in Amon at the Temple of Karnak. During the New Kingdom, Thebes gloried in the imperial age, and you were Opener of Roads in the Hidden Place. The Ruler of all the Gods, more-strong of heart than all those who are in your following, you are maker of Gods and men, Creator of Heaven, Earth and the Underworld. Divine Man-Child, Heir of Eternity, you are Chief of the Gods, Supreme in their Districts, being Crowned King of the Gods, Ram, Mightiest of Created Things.

Dr. Ben's Photo 5. Abu Simbel Temple of Rameses II. Four seated colossal statues on the façade of Abu Simbel with females between the statues' legs, as the King offers to Ra-Horakhty above the doorway between the statues and with baboons on the Cornice.

CELEBRATING
DR. BEN-JOCHANNAN

Dr. Ben's Photo 6. Abu Simbel Temple of Rameses II. The two left seated colossal statues of the King with female members of his family between the legs. Prisoners are illustrated at the sides of the statues base. The head of the statue to the right lies in the foreground.

Provider of the Sovereign Chiefs, Governor of the Holy Circle, Ra as Amon brought victory and fame to those who followed his teachings and praised his name. Proclaimed King of Earth, Prince of the Tuat, Governor of the Regions of Aukert, Souls in their Circles ascribe your Praises. Beautiful Being, Rays of

FREDERICK MONDERSON

Turquoise Light, you are Personification of Right, Truth and Goodness, O Mighty One of Journeys, Lord of the Gods, Light of the lock of hair.

Dr. Ben's Photo 7. Abu Simbel Temple of Rameses II. The two right-side seated statues with female figures between the legs and miniature hawks at the base above cartouches of the King.

Creator of Hidden Things, Lord of Heaven, Lord of Earth, for untold ages men praised the Exalted of Souls. The Maker of Eternity, Ra you sail a Boat of Millions of Years. In all your glory, you emerge in a Morning Boat *Matet*, becoming strong

CELEBRATING
DR. BEN-JOCHANNAN

at Midday. The day's work done, becoming weak, you ride the Evening Boat *Semktet*. Confronting your mortal enemy *Apep*, fishes *Abtu* and Ant swim before the Boat of Ra with its defenders aboard. United in Numbers, Destroyer of Darkness, Night, Wickedness and Evil, on the dawn of a new day, there are Acclamations of your Rising in the Horizon of Heaven.

Lord of Fetters of your enemy, Protector of hidden spirits, you conquer the fiends of the underworld. Souls of the East follow thee, Souls of the West praise thee, Support of the Circle of Amenta, God of Life, King of Right and Truth, you are the World Soul that rested on his High Place. The Soul who moves onward, Opener of the roads in the Hidden Place, Ra, you are the Great God who lifted up his two eyes.

Fifth Annual
Dr. Yosef A.A. ben-Jochannan Banquet

Saturday, April 24, 1993

Minisink Town House
646 Lenox Avenue -
(142nd Street)
New York, New York 10037
Banquet Complex

7:00 p.m. - 12 midnight

Dr. Ben's Photo 7a. The Flier from a Banquet given in Dr. Ben's Honor at Minisink Town House on Saturday, April 24, 1993, given by Dr and Mrs. Lewis and others.

FREDERICK MONDERSON

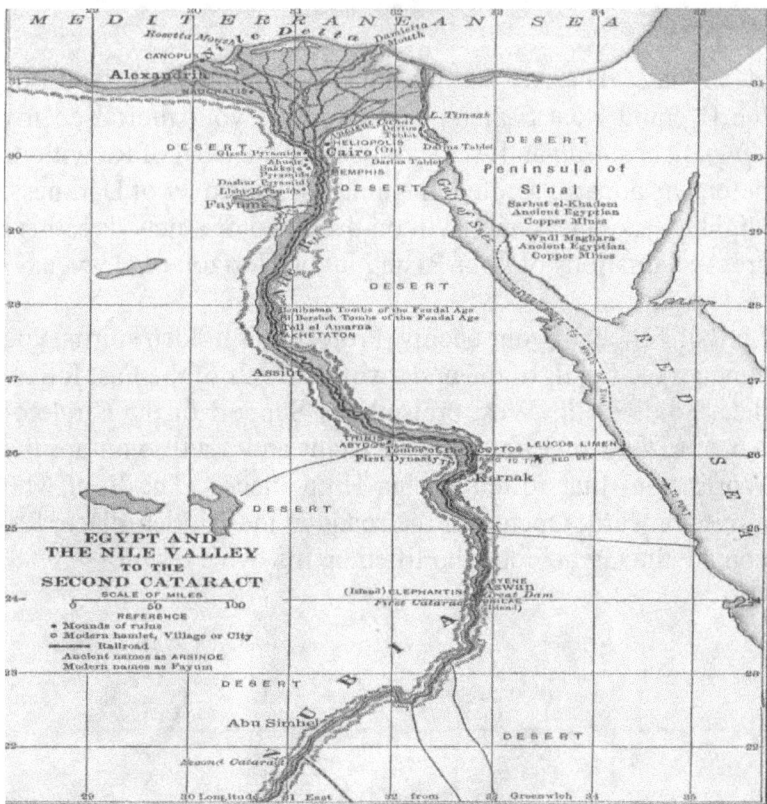

Dr. Ben's Map 1. Egypt and the Nile Valley to the Second Cataract.

Hidden Face, Glorious Creator of Eternity, you make being come into existence in your creations in the Tuat. You rise like unto Gold, Great Light Shining in the Heavens illuminating darkness. Oldest One, Great One, you are Self-begotten, Self-created and Self-produced, the Soul who Departs at his Appointed Time. You existed forever and would exist for Eternity, Illuminer of light into his Circle. Source of Life and Light, Glorious by reason of thy Splendors, you are Joy of Heart within your Splendor. Mighty One of Victories, Ra, how wonderful was your manifestation among early Africans.

CELEBRATING DR. BEN-JOCHANNAN

Generator of Bodies, True Creative Power of Divine attributes, Sender of Light into his Circle, Ra you rise in the Horizon, and are Beautiful. So too, Rat, Mistress of the Gods, your female counterpart, Lady of Heaven, Mistress of Heliopolis. Mightier than the Gods, Glorious Being, Lord of Love, Double Sphinx God, you are Ruler of Everlastingness. God of Motion, God of Light, Lord of Might, you destroy your enemies. Protector of hidden spirits, the Soul that Mourns, the God that Cries, you are the Soul One who avenges his children.

Aged One of the Pupil of the Utchait, Ra, Lord of the hidden circles, creative force who gather together all seed, you are manifold in your holy house. Lord of Wisdom whose precepts are wise, Lord of Mercy, at whose coming men live, you make strong your double with Divine Food, Creator of Hidden Things and Generator of Bodies.

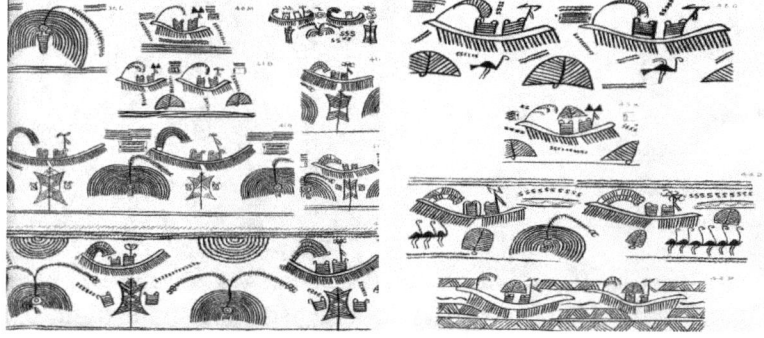

Dr. Ben's Illustration 1. Prehistoric pottery markings of 2-deck boats with sails plying the Nile River(left); and, more Prehistoric pottery markings of 2-deck boats with sails. Notice birds along the river (right), in W.M.F. Petrie's *Prehistoric Egypt* (1920).

FREDERICK MONDERSON

2. Poem to GOD PTAH

Ptah, Great Architect of the Universe, you were among the earliest African Gods. At Unification of Kemet, Narmer founded the White Wall as his capital in Aneb-Hetch, the first Nome of the Lower Kingdom. The King built a temple, Hat-Ke Ptah at Khut-Taui, Horizon of the Two Lands and established worship of your triad Ptah-Sekhmet-Nefertum, later worshipped at Thebes. While the fortunes of other Gods rose and fell, yours as Patron of Artists, Artisans and Artificers remained not paramount, but consistent, and your festival was celebrated on March 21.

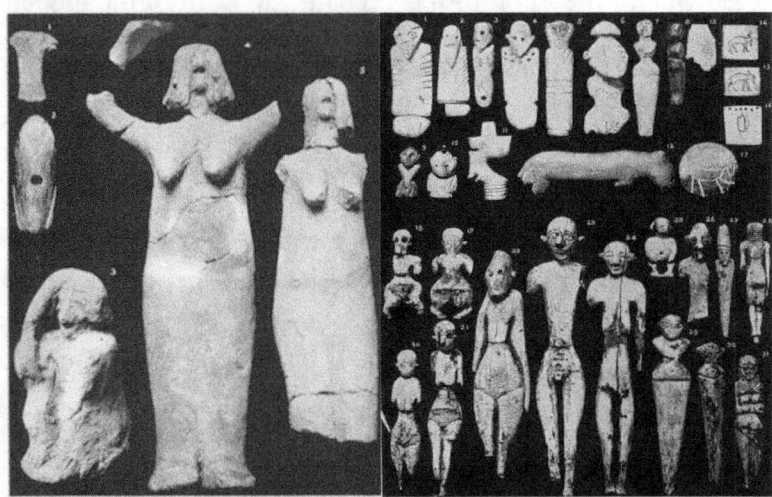

Dr. Ben's Illustration 2. Prehistoric female figurines with pendulant breasts (left); and, Prehistoric Ivory figures of humans and animals in W.M.F. Petrie's *Prehistoric Egypt* (1920).

Lord of the Hidden Throne, whose hidden form is unknown; Powerful One, at Memphis, your High Priest, Great One, Commander of Workmen, was the chief artist of the court.

CELEBRATING DR. BEN-JOCHANNAN

From here, the Great Chief of Artists played a prominent role in state politics, as you Ptah established Ma'at throughout the Two Lands. Father of Fathers, Power of Powers, you are the Master Architect and Designer of Everything which exist in the World and was employed in the Construction of the Heavens and the Earth.

Ptah, Disk of Heaven, you illuminate the Two Lands with the Fire of your Two Eyes. The Theban triad dominated the Middle and New Kingdoms and you, Great Chief of the Hammer, resided in the palace of their abode. As emblems of your majesty, a close-fitting garment, and from an opening in front project your two hands with scepter, ankh, and Tet as power, life, stability. The *Menat*, symbol of pleasure and happiness hangs form the back of your neck.

Fire God, while little evidence of Middle Kingdom temples remain, the 18th Dynasty embellished your sanctuary at Karnak and Memphis, the City of Walls. Ramesside kings were your most ardent champions, O God who Stand upon the Ma'at Pedestal. Rameses II erected two great sandstone statues at Memphis, one over 10 feet high. God of the Beautiful Face in Thebes who created his own image, and fashioned his own Body, you oversaw the construction of that great city, Chief of All Handicraftsmen and of all Workers in Metal and Stone, God of Wisdom.

FREDERICK MONDERSON

Dr. Yosef A.A. ben-Jochannan

Yosef A.A. ben-Jochannan, son of Julia and Krastan Jochannan, father of 12 biological and 6 adopted children, husband of Gertrude M. England, was educated in the public schools in Brazil, S.A.; U.S. Virgin Islands (St. Croix) and Puerto Rico, Ph.D. in Cultural Anthropology in Cuba and a PH. D. in Moorish History in Spain. He has also received a L.L.B./Law Degree. Dr. Ben is an architect.

"Dr. Ben" as he is affectionately known, has practiced law as an assistant Prosecutor in Puerto Rico and has worked as a Civil Engineer in both Puerto Rico and the United States.

From 1945-1970 Dr. Ben was the Chief of the African Desk of United Nations Education Scientific Cultural Organization (UNESCO) dealing with cultural, anthropological, historical and archaeological information. He also served as the civilian advisor to the Permanent African Missions to the United Nations from 1957 to 1964. Dr. Ben has taught at numerous Universities in Africa, the Caribbean, North America and South America.

Dr. Ben has taught at Al Azar University, Cairo, Egypt, recently retired from Cornell University in Ithaca, N.Y.

Dr. Ben is Chairman of the Alkebu-Lan Foundation and Alkebu-Lan Books and Educational Materials. He is the author of twenty-eight (28) published books, sixteen (16) unpublished books and a six (6) volume encyclopedia on Africa.

Dr. Ben is presently conducting educational tours to Egypt and the Nile Valley and has conducted archeological digs in Aswan, Egypt. Dr. Ben recently celebrated his Jubilee year in Egypt (March 1939 - March 1989). Dr. Ben is the Special Advisor for the Festival in Aswan, Egypt 1991, the 1st African Nubian Festival in Egypt.

We are most fortunate to be in the same time and space with this multi-genius.

Dr. Ben's Photo 7b. Brief Biography of Dr. Ben prepared for his guests at the Banquet referenced above.

Very Great God who came into existence in the earliest times, you are the blue-collar God, Master-workman of the Universal Workshop, the Supreme Mind. Mind and Tongue of the Gods, all things proceeded from you Ptah, Lord of Ma'at, King of the Two Lands. As a form of the Sun God, Father of Beginnings, you are the Creator of the Eggs of the Sun and Moon. In this you are the personification of the Rising Sun, artificer in metals, smelter, caster, sculptor, great celestial workman and architect preparing the primeval elements of earth and water.

God the Father and Son, Lord of Justice, Divine Sculptor, you gave and still give forms to all things and being on earth. Opener of the Ways, you fashion the Souls of the Dead to live in the Underworld. As Ptah-Seker, with crook, whip, scepter,

CELEBRATING
DR. BEN-JOCHANNAN

crown of disk, plumes, horns and uraei with disks on their head, the Office of your High Priest existed form the time of the Second Dynasty. Great God who came into being in the beginning with two feathers of Ma'at, you rested upon the darkness as King of Eternity, Everlastingness and Lord of Life. You bring the Nile from its source to make flourish the staff of life and to make grain come forth aged one of Nu. In same manner you make fertile the watery mass of heaven.

Dr. Ben's Photo 8. Abu Simbel Temple of Rameses II. Close-up of third statue from left with Rameses in Blue Crown offering image of *Ma'at* to Ra-Horakhty above the entrance.

FREDERICK MONDERSON

Dr. Ben's Photo 9. Abu Simbel Temple of Rameses II. Close-up of Rameses, in Blue Crown, offering his name as *Ma'at* to the Temples Titular deity, Ra-Horakhty.

CELEBRATING
DR. BEN-JOCHANNAN

Dr. Ben's Photo 10. Abu Simbel Temple of Rameses II. Feet of the statues, the females and hawks in the foreground with prisoners at the base, all before the entrance.

Dr. Ben's Photo 11. Abu Simbel Temple of Rameses II. At the feet of the right-side, pair of Statues female figures, standing officials and hawks.

FREDERICK MONDERSON

Dr. Ben's Photo 12. Abu Simbel Temple of Rameses II. View from the platform at the statues' base where the figures wear crowns.

Ptah-Tanen, Disk of Heaven, in peace you light up the world with your brilliant rays. Of multitudinous forms, with the Sun and Moon as your eyes, you pass through eternity and everlastingness. Builder of your own limbs, maker of your own body, your upper part is heaven; the lower part is the Tuat. Maker of the Tuat with all of its arrangements, you make to come forth the water on the mountains to give life to all men

CELEBRATING
DR. BEN-JOCHANNAN

and women in your name Ari-Ankh, Lord of Justice. Aged one traversing Eternity, Prince of Annu, you judge the dead and give them access to the Field of Peace, Field of Reeds, Field of Grasshoppers.

Ptah, you make all land and all countries. As you mold Gods, men and everything that is produced Great God who stretched out the heavens, you make your disk to revolve in the body of Nut as you fashion yourself without the help of any other being. Fully equipped you came forth fully equipped and the Company of Gods of your Supreme Company Praise You.

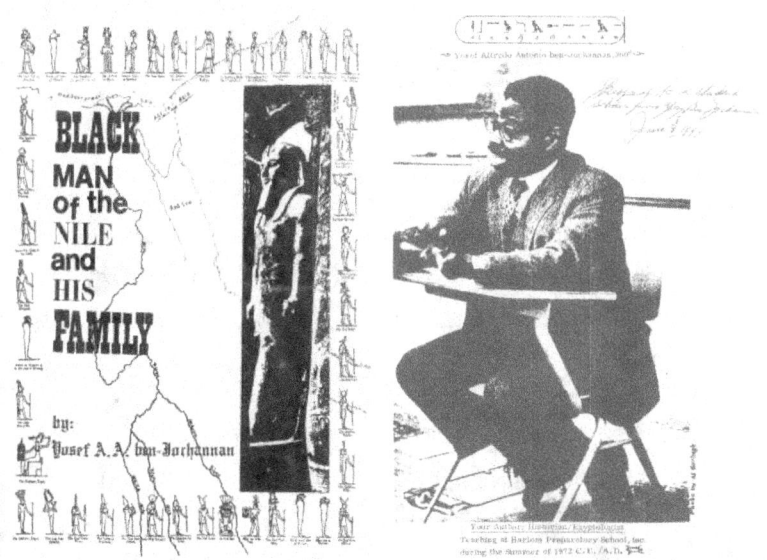

Dr. Ben's Books 1. BLACK MAN Of the NILE and His FAMILY (1972, 1981). Note, this and so many others of Dr. Ben's books he autographed to Dr. Fred Monderson.

FREDERICK MONDERSON

Ptah-Seker-Asar, Triune God of Resurrection you Dwell in a Secret Place. Lord Ta-Tchesetet, pygmy with large bald head and thick limbs, beetle and plumes, you are the Governor of Everlastingness. Begetter of Men, Maker of their lives, Creator of all the Gods, you are the Father of the Father of the Gods. Ptah-Tanen, Babe Born Daily, Aged One on the Borders of Eternity, Lord of Life, Giver of Life at Will, you hear the prayers men make to you.

Dr. Ben's Photo 13. Abu Simbel Temple of Rameses II. Close-up of the two ride-side undamaged statues busts.

Dr. Ben's Photo 14. Abu Simbel Temple of Rameses II. Close-up of the other two on the other side, with one damaged head.

CELEBRATING DR. BEN-JOCHANNAN

Dr. Ben's Photo 15. Abu Simbel Temple of Rameses II. Kashida Maloney of Brooklyn, New York, stands before the entrance to the King's temple with the head of one of the broken statues lying to the left.

The Hapi or Apis Bull, incarnate of Ptah, emerged as the Ptolemaic Serapis in the Memphis Mausoleum or Serapeum of the Greeks, where the great Imhotep was recognized as your son. From this House of the Aged One, your temple *Aneb-Abt* in Memphis, *Men-nefer*, you maintain the Balance of the Two Lands. In this City of White Wall, Persea and Acacia trees bloom and here reside your female counterpart Sekhmet, sister and wife, mother of your son Nefertum. This great African Goddess, the Great Lady, Lady of Sa, Queen of Ant, is mighty, strong and violent. O Holy One, the Lady of Flame, Mighty Lady, Greatly Beloved of Ptah, Lady of Heaven, is Mistress of the Two Lands. You Gods of Holiness, Bless and Protect African people in the many challenges they face, O Divine Artificer of Creation.

FREDERICK MONDERSON

Dr. Ben's Photo 16. Abu Simbel Temple of Rameses II. The Cornice with Cartouches, Uraei and Baboons.

3. Poem to GOD AMON-RA

O mighty Amon, the Greatest of the Black African deities, ithyphallic, you were from primeval times, Lord of Gods. Your creativity radiated over an age, father of the Gods, when worshippers praised your hidden nature. Conquering peoples and places, they brought light and civility to the world, in your immortal name, multitudinous, more numerous, not known. The vanquished contributed wealth filling your treasury and your subjects, victorious in their imperial exploits, erected mansions in glory and praise of your being, Chief of the Great Ennead of the Gods, Self-Begotten, Lord of Heaven, Lord of Earth. O Dweller in Anu, the Gods ascribe praise to you maker of things celestial and things terrestrial, for you illuminate Egypt, President of the Apts.

Beautiful child of Love, from relative obscurity you emerged in the Middle Kingdom and sat on your Sacred Mound of Creation. That first time, seeking to complete the task of previous Gods fallen short, you Created Brilliant Rays, Thunder in Heaven. Black African rulers of that age imbibed

CELEBRATING
DR. BEN-JOCHANNAN

in your inspiration, Lord of the Two Lands. Mighty in Power, Lord of Awe-inspiring terror, they similarly manifested resolute courage, wisdom, intellect, and creative prowess. They gained success as Warrior pharaohs, with mighty souls, all in your name, Fashioner of the Beauty of Kings, Priests and Artisans, O Lord of the Throne of Egypt. All the Gods are three, Amen, Ra and Ptah and none like thee. Amen is his hidden name; Ra is his face, Ptah his body.

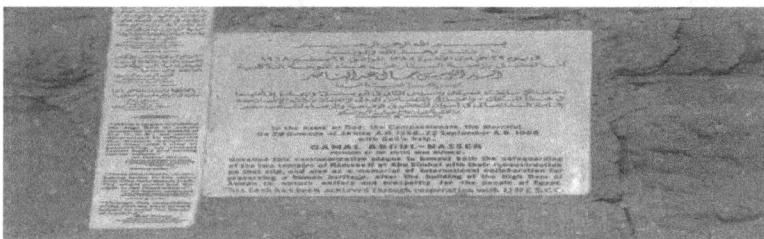

Dr. Ben's Photo 17. Abu Simbel Temple of Rameses II. A Plaque unveiled by President Gamal Abdul-Nasser September 22, 1968, commemorating reconstruction and removal of the temple to higher ground as a prelude to building the High Dam at Aswan.

Dr. Ben's Photo 17a. Abu Simbel Temple of Rameses II. Carmen Monderson with the river at her back.

FREDERICK MONDERSON

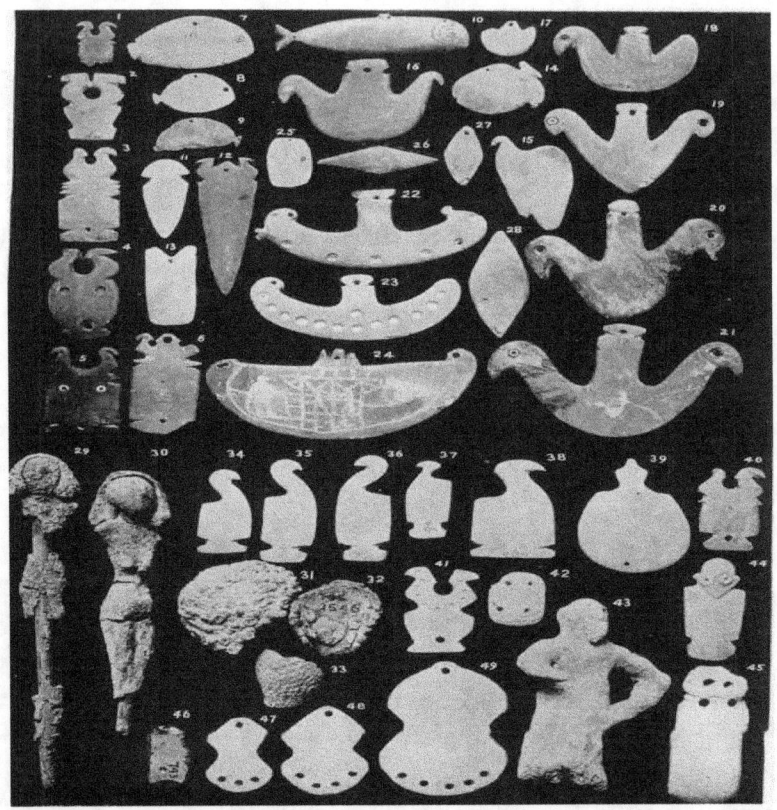

Dr. Ben's Illustration 3. W.M.F. Petrie's *Prehistoric Egypt* (1920) - Prehistoric Magic Slates, figures and spacers.

Power made by Ptah, Bull of Heliopolis, kings architects shaped a society whose blueprint you encouraged in manifold manifestations. Lord of Scepter and Ankh, Frog, and Uraeus, Couchant Lion, your symbols include Beautiful Tiaras, Lofty Plumes, and *Ureret*, *War*, *Nemes* and *Atef* crowns. The prosperity you endowed your adherents generated artistic, scientific and linguistic creations, Lord of the Apts. These first beneficiaries of your generosity toward mankind, erected temples as chapels simply to glorify your great name, Amon Lord of Thebes, Lord of the Two Lands, Lord of Might, Lord

CELEBRATING DR. BEN-JOCHANNAN

of Food, Bull of Offerings, Kamutef at the Head of his Fields. Lord of Victuals, Bull of Provisions, the Gods beg their sustenance from you, Lord of Fields, Banks and Plots of Ground.

Lord of Truth, Father of the Gods, Maker of Men, Creator of all Animals, Black African Kings, men of vision, fortitude and tenacity, benefited from an earlier age of African creativity. They synthesized, experimented and with vision and bellicosity bequeathed a creative era where craftsmen, philosophers, priests and kings, were motivated to extol your name to greater heights. Lord of Radiant Light, you Exist into Eternity as Lord of Heaven, Lord of Earth, Lord of the Gods, Lord of the High Lands and Mountains, Lord of the Joy of Heart, mighty one of crowns. Your Loveliness is in the Southern Sky and your Graciousness is in the

Northern Sky. Your name is strong and your will is heavy. Mountains of ore cannot withstand your might, for you set in order the kingdom of eternity unto eternity.

Lord of Eternity, Creator of Everlastingness, you arise in the eastern horizon and set in the western horizon. Born early every day, you overthrew your enemies, steering oar, Pilot who knows the waters, Lord of the ship of the morning and ship of the evening, Master of two stems. Beautiful form fashioned by Ptah, Ox with strong arm who loves strength; you are first in Upper Egypt, Lord of the Land of the Matoi and Prince of Punt. Lord of Perception who speaks with authority, Lord of the Gods whose shrine is hidden, you are Lord of the Double Crown, Great Hawk who makes festive the body, and fair body that makes festive the breast.

FREDERICK MONDERSON

Dr. Ben's Papyrus 1. God Shu separates Goddess Nuit (Sky) from God Geb (Earth). Note all the symbols of power associated in the illustrated frame (left); and, the Psychostasia depicts a deceased female, with Isis to her rear, standing before Anubis who adjusts the scales as Osiris sits enthroned awaiting the results of the Judgment.

Beneficent God, you presided over a world as King of Kings. Lord of the Thrones of the Two Lands, Bull of your Mother, New Kingdom monarchs competed trying to outdo predecessors praising Amon, Greater than Great of the Primordial Deities, who continued to bless his champions. Chief of Egypt, territorial conquests, ensuing wealth, architectural constructions, and religious and philosophical sonnets, extolled the name of Amon, Presider of Karnak, who dwells in the Most Select of Places, in Power and Glory, Invisible and Creative. As Chief of all the Gods, you fashion the deities, One in his actions as with the Gods. Stablisher of all things, Lord of things that are, you Create all Life, Lord of the *Sektet* Boat and of the *Antet* Boat.

Firstborn Son of the Earth, Chief of Mankind, your Sanctuary at Karnak is a splendid piece of divinely inspired architecture. Master of the Double Crown, you receive the *Ames* Scepter. Lord of the *Makes* Scepter and whip, your precinct befits the Eternal Spirits of the Theban Triad, Amon, Mut, Khonsu, whose reigns encompassed millennia. Priests manifested political and theological power from this sacred abode, constructed in stone while similar Mansions of Millions of

CELEBRATING DR. BEN-JOCHANNAN

Years profess Amon's august name, as Source of all Light in Heaven. Lord of Karnak, King of the South and North, Lord of Things which Exist, Stablisher of All Creation, You Last Forever, equip all lands, Fashioner of all that exists, Just One, Lord of Thebes.

Dr. Ben's Photo 18. Abu Simbel Temple of Rameses II. A look into the deep recesses of the temple, past the 8-colossal standing statues wearing the White Crown in the Hypostyle Hall, and towards the Sanctuary with deities Ra-Horakhty, Rameses II, Amon-Ra and Ptah therein.

FREDERICK MONDERSON

Dr. Ben's Photo 19. Abu Simbel Temple of Rameses II. Close-up of one of the standing colossal statues in the Entrance Hall in light and decoration.

CELEBRATING DR. BEN-JOCHANNAN

Dr. Ben's Photo 20. Abu Simbel Temple of Rameses II. Rameses smites a kneeling enemy held by the hair, as Queen Nefertari stands at his rear, all before Amon-Ra with raised scepter to the left.

Beautiful boy whom the Gods praise, maker of men and stars who illuminates the two lands, you are great of strength, Lord of Might, Chief who made the two lands, the Gods rejoice in your beauty, Amen-Ra, venerated in Karnak. Lord of the Deeds Case who holds the flail, you are the Heliopolitan, first of his Ennead, who lives daily on truth. The Gods love to gaze at you when the Double Crown rests upon your brow, hawk in the midst of the horizon; you are beloved in the Southern Sky and pleasant in the Northern Sky, Possessor of Praise, the Sun of Heaven.

Lord of Things that are, acting as Judge, Vizier of the Poor Who Takes No Bribes, your intellectual majesty enlightened the world in knowledge of arts and medicine. Your inspiration pioneered astronomy, quarrying, navigation, stone-transportation, agriculture, mathematics, and all gifts of the African mind. Generations of Black men and women worship and praise you mighty Amon, King of the Gods, First Born, and Resting upon Ma'at. Amenemenes, Sesostris, then Ahmose, Amenhotep, Thutmose, Hatshepsut, Seti, Rameses, Merenptah and Piankhy, Shabaka, Shabataka, Taharka, were greatest adherents, physical Father of these kings, Power of the Gods. Amen-Ra the Justified, you give your hands to those you love and assign those you hate to fire.

Dr. Ben's Photo 21. Abu Simbel Temple of Queen Nefertari. The King in White Crown (left) and Red Crown (right) guards the portal while Nefertari offers flowers and a sistrum to enthroned Hathor (left) in horns and disk and flowers to Hathor (right) in Double Crown.

Dr. Ben's Photo 22. Abu Simbel Temple of Nefertari. Upper portions of two statues of the King before the entrance of the Queens temple with Rameses cartouches in the center. Notice, while the Kings nose is disfigured, his breast and beard are intact.

CELEBRATING DR. BEN-JOCHANNAN

Dr. Ben's Papyrus 2. An Old Kingdom painting shows geese or ducks in different attitudes.

Dr. Ben's Photo 23. Abu Simbel Temple of Queen Nefertari. Kashida Maloney of Brooklyn, New York, stands in the Plaza of Nefertari's temple as other visitors pause to admire the entrance statues.

FREDERICK MONDERSON

The Gods love to behold you and they rejoice in your beautiful acts. These divinities acclaim you the Great House and Crown you with Crowns in the House of Fire. Homage to you, Dweller in Peace you are Successor to Ra. Fashioner of Kings and Queens, sole king among the Gods, your collective wisdom schooled the Greeks and Romans, the newest converts. They immersed in your wonderful cultural heritage, and praised you with equal zeal and vigor. Chief of all the Beings of the Underworld, Lord of the Nubians, Governor of Punt, King of Heaven, Amon the Great African God, we beseech you, Lord of Eternity, today make enlightening the Black culture of Kemet/Egypt, land of the ancestors. Pour forth your salvation and ingenuity to inspire our people even more as they meet challenges in a new Millennium.

Dr. Ben's Photo 23a. Abu Simbel Temple of Rameses II. Seated in the Sanctuary are (left to right), Ptah, Amon-Ra, Rameses II, and Ra-Horakhty.

CELEBRATING DR. BEN-JOCHANNAN

4. Poem to the Temple of Karnak with its two axes, oriented east to west and north to south.

O, mighty Temple, Hatshepsut affirmed Karnak is the horizon on earth, the august ascent of the beginning, the sacred eye of the All-Lord, the place of his heart, which bears his beauty, and encompasses those who follow him. Everlasting, you are a great dwelling of myriad years that is Shining like the horizon of heaven, and established as an eternal work. Like the heavens, abiding upon their four pillars as a monument, great, excellent and useful for the Lord of Eternity, you are a favorite place of the Lord of the Gods, Amon and his consort, Amunet. One whose hands are many, Suspender of the sky, you're the living lamp which rises out of the Ocean of Heaven, to support all things, for the Master of the Apts, the beloved One!

Stela reveal New Empire furniture and utensils restored by Ahmose with gifts of gold rosettes, lapis lazuli, and vases of silver, malachite, and vessels for the Ka. Jars with ointment, ebony, gold and silver houses, granaries, and gardens, all given when he established Amon, father of the Gods, as Lord of Heaven. From the beginning, this House of Amon, Throne of Keb, with the serpent-diadem, is proclaimed the horizon on earth and horizon of heaven. It is the Throne of Horus before the Splendors of the Great House, whom the Great Ennead of Gods has brought up to be Mistress of the Circuit of the Sun. This is the Splendid Place in which Amon loves to be, flourishing and established, with dark complexion, as ithyphallic Min, strong in his might.

FREDERICK MONDERSON

At your City of the All-God, in the resplendent ascent from the Quay, two small Obelisks and Avenue of Ram-Headed Sphinxes stand before the Ethiopian Pylon, built during the XXVth dynasty, in Praise of the Beloved of the South and North. At the entrance into the Open Court, French Savants chronicled the dimensions of your revered Enclosure standing as a Seat of Truth, emblem of Ma'at. The Great Court centrally houses the surviving column of the colonnaded Kiosk of Taharka. The Shrine of Seti II abuts the Pylons inner face at the west of the Northern Colonnade, while the Temple of Rameses III to the Southeast is east of the Southern Colonnade. Sheshonk's sculptures are nearby, in this place of the Lord of Truth, *Ipit Isut*, great in glory.

The statue of Rameses II, usurped by Pinudjen, and gateway to the Open-Air Museum, are also majestic features of your Court. Southwest, a mound and unfinished column provide evidence of colonnade and pylon construction techniques evolved in your expansion. Within your holy seat, all foundation ceremonies began the day of the Feast of the New Moon. A later altar and sphinx in this Court celebrate first entrance into your sacred precinct, with its trapezoidal mud-brick enclosure wall, where Amon is Lord of Thebes. As Lord of all Gods, he commanded and all the Gods came into being, and they fall down awestruck at his feet when they recognize his majesty their Lord, Great One of Souls, Mighty One of Victory, his love brings the Nile.

Further in, older the temple, thus, as Amon looks out, not second but fifth Pylon of Rameses II encloses the Hypostyle Hall to the West. It is a splendid and majestic philosophic expression of Kemetic/Egyptian architecture. Its manifestation indicates structures of theological, philosophic, cosmological, epistemological, and scientific foundations of learning. How profound, ben-Jochannan recommends six visits to comprehend this primeval forest of 12 processional

CELEBRATING DR. BEN-JOCHANNAN

and 122 flanking columns, where Amon-Ra is king of the Gods. This Lord of Wisdom, Lord of Mercy, Lord of Magnanimity, is strong in apparel, of Beautiful face, coming from the Nubians. He is Ra, whose word is Truth, and whose rulings Thebes loves.

Sacred enclosure, Amenhotep III built your Processional Colonnade and Horemheb conceived the Great Hall. Begun by Rameses I, built by Seti I of fine sandstone and decorated by Rameses II, the walls portray Amen and other Gods, worshiped in mysterious splendor. He sits on the Horus Throne of the All King, like Ra, forever established and Karnak is content. Seti's sculptures are to the north and Rameses to the south, in this domain. Here Amon the Beautiful Bull, Creator of Everlastingness, Giver of Life is living in Truth, Forever in this beautiful divine resting-place. Mysterious Lion, a Bull for his city, a Lion for his people, the Bright God, excellent of counsel, he is the Good Protector in every truth.

Dr. Ben's Photo 23b. Abu Simbel Temple of Queen Nefertari. The King and Queen are depicted in a number of attitudes.

FREDERICK MONDERSON

Dr. Ben's Photo 24. Abu Simbel Temple of Queen Nefertari. Visitors admire the statues on the entrance façade showing Rameses, Nefertari, their children and Hathor.

Dr. Ben's Photo 24a. Abu Simbel Temple of Queen Nefertari. Rameses offers two bouquets to enthroned Hathor while Nefertari stands behind him in her temple.

CELEBRATING
DR. BEN-JOCHANNAN

Dr. Ben's Photo 25. Abu Simbel Temple of Queen Nefertari. Wearing horns, disk and feathers, Nefertari offers a Bouquet and Sistrum to enthroned Hathor in the Queens Temple. Notice her long flowing dress.

FREDERICK MONDERSON

7

Dr. Ben's Photo 26. Abu Simbel Temple of Queen Nefertari. Rameses offers a bouquet of flowers to Hathor while Nefertari, at his rear, offers flowers and rattles her sistrum, Hathor's symbol.

CELEBRATING
DR. BEN-JOCHANNAN

Dr. Ben's Photo 27. Abu Simbel Temple of Queen Nefertari. Hathor, Ptah and Horus on columns in the Queens Temple (right to left).

Lord of Praises, the modern third, ancient fourth, pylon of Amenhotep III, the "magnificent," enclose the central court. Today's fourth and fifth or first and second ancient pylons of Thutmose I enclose the first or 18th Dynasty colonnade.

FREDERICK MONDERSON

Thutmose I, Horus Mighty Bull, Beloved of Truth, Shining-in-Beauty, in his petition for the God to recognize Hatshepsut's kingship as he had his, erected four Granite obelisks for Amon, Presider of Karnak, who is Lord of Eternity, Lord of Heaven, Ruler of the Gods, Ruler of Thebes. Amon, the Bull of Godly countenance, darling in Karnak, Chief of the Great Ennead, is the Judge of Horus and Seth in the Great Hall.

Splendid dwelling, your second 18th Dynasty colonnade abuts Thutmose IIIs sixth or fourth pylon enclosing the Hall of Records listing his 17 campaigns. All stand on hollow ground, before the divinity with lofty plumes who looks out from his Sanctuary or Holy of Holies, and whose hidden shrine is the repose of the Lord of the Gods. There is divine presence in the great seat and Amon, resting upon his great throne, is enduring in his temple forever and ever. Chief of the Great Ennead of the Gods, sustainer of all things, maker of things below and above, he is Lord of Wisdom, Lord of Mercy, Treasurer of the Celestial Heights, Lord of Gods who lives on truth.

Beyond this "Throne of Thunder," the Middle Kingdom court esplanades the *Akh Menou*, Festival Temple of Thutmose III. To Paris, Prisse D'Avennes removed the *Karnak Tablet* from its revered Hall of Ancestors. Thutmose III built this temple at Karnak for his father Thutmose I, and as a monument to the kings of his fathers. In the rear of the *Akh Menou*, a Temple of Rameses II faces the eastern gate, before a **Kiosk of Taharka**. All this, in the name of the sole one with many hands, Maker of Beams, Maker of Light, whose adherents in oath swore, If Amon permits me to live. Shield of the Bowmen and owner of all ships, Lord of the Highlands and Mountains, Chief Creator of everything on Earth, his disputations are greater than those of every God. Great of strength, there is none other that is like him.

CELEBRATING DR. BEN-JOCHANNAN

Divine House, your eastern expansion at a limit, Hatshepsut conceived the Eighth Pylon, usurped by Thutmose III, defaced by Amenhotep III, and restored by Seti I, that initiated the north/south axis with the Seventh Pylon to its north enclosing the first or "Cachette Court" with its rich hoard. Furthest east along the east/west axis, Taharka's Temple stood facing Hatshepsut's now fallen obelisk. A summit in Cairo, another completely disappeared, her standing obelisk, the last of two pairs, with that of Thutmose I, are towering sites in the surrounding area. Senmut, Prophet and Steward of Amon, Queens architect, erected his majesty's obelisks of red Aswan granite, with pyramidions of electrum to radiantly illuminate the lands, like the Sun disk of the Good God, Calf of the Heavenly Cow. The dweller in heaven, Amon whose name is hidden from the Gods is a sweet breeze to him that calls upon him who preserves the weary.

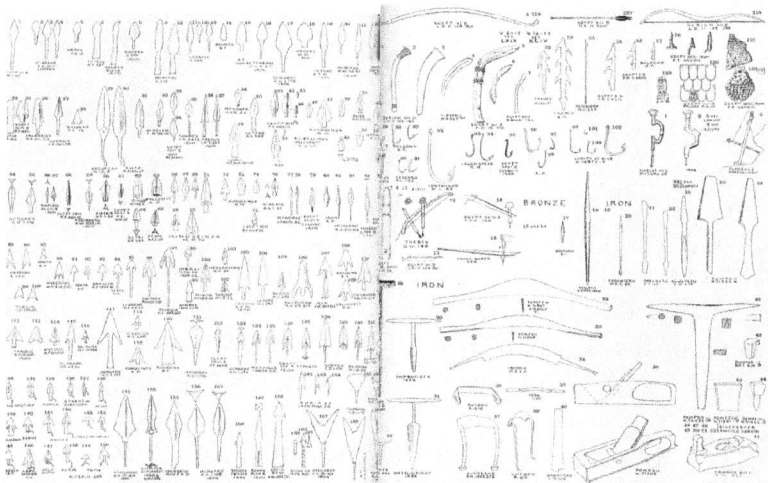

Dr. Ben's Illustration 4. Arrows and Darts in Bronze (left); and, Egyptian and Foreign - A. Bow and Arrow; B. Throw Stick, Harpoon, Armor, Fish-Hook; C. Boring, Planing in W.M.F. Petrie's *Tools and Weapons* (1917).

FREDERICK MONDERSON

August Abode, the Sacred Scarab of Amenhotep III, moved a tad to the west, rests near the Seventh Pylon and perpendicular to your Sacred Lake, where sacred Barques floated at festive time, and priests washed as admonished Let everyone who enters here be pure. In the southwest corner of your enclosure, an east/west Ptolemaic Opet Temple perpendicularly abuts Rameses IIIs north/south Temple of Khonsu. On this axis, Hatshepsut built the Eighth Pylon, erected before the Seventh and enclosing the Second Court, while Horemheb built the ninth and tenth pylons enclosing third and fourth courts. In this last Court, the Heb-Sed Festival Temple of Amenhotep II celebrates the Beautiful Countenance of the God, the Only One who has no second, Father of the Father of the Gods. Your revered master is the dweller in the Horizon, Amon, Lord of him that is silent and Gods obey his majesty and extol the might of their creator.

Light of the World, beyond or south of the Tenth Pylon, an Avenue of Sphinxes connected the Temple of Mut and its Sacred Lake. The Temple of Khonsu Pa-Khered built by Rameses III is in the preceding Fourth Court of the Karnak enclosure. Nearby were Bark Stations of Thutmose III and Hatshepsut, and Sanctuary of Amen-Kamutef and Temple of Nectanebo II. North of your main axis is the Chapel of Osiris Hekadjet, Temple of Ptah, Temple of Thutmose, and the Precinct of the War God Montu. A nearby Tomb of Osiris, together with exquisite gardens, all rest within your sacred abode of the Theban Triad Khonsu – Son; Mut – wife; and Amon – father and husband; the most-mighty of the Gods.

Mighty Karnak, Mountains yield stone to make your gateway great. People of Punt bring Perfume to make festive Amon's temple. Your Lord of All is a glaring lion with raging claws and a bull, firm of back and heavy of hoofs upon the neck of his foe. He is a bird of prey; flying high and seizing on him

CELEBRATING DR. BEN-JOCHANNAN

that assails him. The mountains are moved beneath him at the time of his terror.

Creator of Heaven, eldest of earth, Lord of what exists, Amon, the Double Crown is established on your head. Your Love passes throughout Egypt/Kemet when you send out light and rise with your two beautiful eyes. Your beauty seizes Upon Hearts. Your Loveliness makes heads more creative. Your beautiful operations make the arms Weak and hearts become weak at the sight of you, Great Hawk making the body Festal. Sole One and Only, with many hands, while men sleep good herdsman, you find fodder for your creatures. Jubilation and reverence to you, for you created and care for mankind.

Praise is given in this Great House, *Ipit Isut* palace where the fashioner of all Gods and Ennead dwells, alongside the Lord of Earth, Sole King among the Gods. Karnak, you espouse thoughts and philosophical paradigms of Black African creativity in knowledge, enlightenment and inspiration. These principles issued forth from you are all part of Africa's gifts to the world in arts and architecture and metaphysics, theosophy, and religiosity. Beacon of Light, inspiration and hope; continue to radiate your blessings of health, prosperity, stability and purposeful vision to African families, men, women and children, who strive to make the world more loving and humane for humanity.

FREDERICK MONDERSON

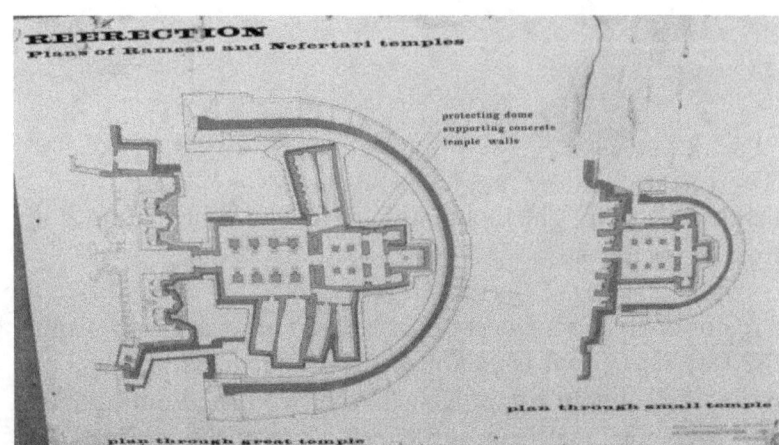

Dr. Ben's Plan 1. Abu Simbel twin temples of Rameses and Queen Nefertari dedicated to Ra-Horakhty as well as Ptah, Amon-Ra, the King, Hathor, etc.

Dr. Ben's Photo 28. Abu Simbel Temple of Rameses II. The Sanctuary with its four Gods from right to left, Ra-Horakhty, Rameses II, Amon-Ra and Ptah. The first three were bathed by the sun on the Kings birthday but Ptah was not!

CELEBRATING
DR. BEN-JOCHANNAN

Dr. Ben's Photo 29. Abu Simbel Temple of Rameses II. At the base of a statue, the Nile Gods unite the land under the Kings Cartouche *User-Ma'at-Ra*.

Dr. Ben's Photo 30. Abu Simbel Temple of Rameses II. One side of the pedestal displaying "prisoners" beneath feet of the "Two Ladies" title of the King.

FREDERICK MONDERSON

Dr. Ben's Photo 31. Abu Simbel Temple of Rameses II. Beside the entrance, Rameses in Sobek Crown (left) and Blue or War Crown (right) smites kneeling enemies before Amon-Ra wielding scepter; and below, the King kneels in an attitude of humility and again holding a scepter.

5. Dr. YOSEF A. A. BEN-JOCHANNAN: A TRIBUTE
By
Dr. Fred Monderson

Sitting and listening recently to one of Dr. Ben's lectures given back in 1997, I realize he is near 95 years old, at least! Equally and considering he has had more than half a dozen strokes, and as a student of his, I thought he certainly deserves a tribute from me, before its too late! Dr. Ben is an extraordinary man of many talents, but principally a man who held the African woman in the highest esteem. He taught us in the beginning was the African woman! Creation came out of the African woman! As the obelisk is a small pyramid on a tall base, this is the pedestal upon which Dr. ben-Jochannan placed the African woman. He honored the Black Woman who is the source of the Black Family! He taught us the Black Woman is a Goddess! He also led the light to the Nile Valley. He "took Egypt to challenge and destroy white supremacy!" Its

CELEBRATING DR. BEN-JOCHANNAN

like Marcus Garvey said, "the cubs are running free out there," and thanks to Dr. Ben, intellectual cubs are challenging the distortions, omissions and putting Africa in its proper place in world civilization history given its accomplishments in Nubia and Egypt, Nile Valley cultures, that gave so much to the world.

Dr. Ben's Temple Site Ticket 1. Philae Temple of Goddess Isis at Aswan. Then and Now. The Western Colonnade with its 32 columns to the left, rear of the Eastern Colonade with its three Chapels of Harendotus, Mendulese and Imhotep, and the Pylons with the river to the rear.

FREDERICK MONDERSON

The Twentieth Century has been blessd with great African and African-American writers and historians. These include Dr. W.E.B. Du Bois, Dr. Carter G. Woodson, Dr. Kwame Nkrumah, Dr. Ivan Van Sertima, J.A. Rogers, Cheikh Anta Diop and Dr. Leonard James, Emeritus Professor of New York City Technical College of the City University of New York, among others. This collection of brainpower equally extends into the Twenty-First Century. However, none of these giants singularly surpass the literary production, commitment, tirelessness, and sincere dedication of Dr. Yosef Alfredo Antonio ben-Jochannan. Outspoken visionary, above and before his time; controversial and not afraid to take an iconoclastic and individual if a somewhat idiosyncratic point of view; Dr. Ben was always prepared to defend his position, irrespective. His friends and students, affectionately call this father, teacher, historian, friend and Egyptologist, "Doc Ben." In fact, back there in the early 1970s when even "Black folks" did not readily accept "Dr. Ben," ever wonder how he got his name? It was a young man named "Barney" and this writer who first started calling him not "Dr. Ben" but "Ben Jo" and the name stuck. Finally when a fellow student Curtis Dunmoodie picked it up and said we must be more respectful, we began calling him "Dr. Ben" in defiance of those "feather bedders" who said "Dr. Ben has no PhD!"

Ever cried for Dr. Ben? This statement once made me cry at New York City (Community) Technical College. I hurriedly took the A Train to 125th Street to their second floor office on Lennox Avenue across from the **Choc-Full-O-Nuts** Coffee Shop in Harlem. There Prof. George Simmonds calmed me down, showing me **Dr. Ben's Doctorate in Anthropology** on the wall. That is what some of the "false prophets" still do today in academia to him and others! And so, you ask them to match their literary production with their in-clandestine vituperativeness and they cannot! Period!

CELEBRATING DR. BEN-JOCHANNAN

Here is a serious scholar, Dr. ben-Jochannan, who spent a lifetime researching, writing, and defending the integrity and intellectual capabilities of African people worldwide. Dr. Ben pioneered in indigenous ancient African terminology. Imagine a European-American scholar discovered the bones of a fossilized African woman in Ethiopia and named her *Lucy* after an Englishmans song "Lucy with Diamonds" then playing on the radio. Dr. Ben said no! Her name is *Denk Nesh* not Lucy!

In 1989, Doc Ben celebrated fifty years of visiting ancient Kemet, Ta-Merry (Egypt) and the Nile Valley cultures. This prolonged involvement has under-girded the basis of his researches, speeches, writings and educational tours. Equally, he began and for some time maintained archaeological digs on the Island of Elephantine and elsewhere. Alas, these have been discontinued.

Dr. Ben's Photo 32. Dr. Yosef ben-Jochannan giving a lecture at the Dempsey Center in Harlem with some of his books owned by the author that were signed by the Master-teacher.

FREDERICK MONDERSON

Dr. Ben's Papyrus 4. The "Tree Goddess" offers libation sustenance as Hathorand Ma'at back up kneeling figures as Isis stands beind an enthroned figure with Thoth while and Ammit stands at the ready.

Dr. Ben's Photo 33. Prof. George Simmonds, "Unsung Hero," Dr. Ben's Associate who Co-Authored *The Black Man's North and East Africa,* Spoke at an event at the dempsey Center in Harlem.

CELEBRATING DR. BEN-JOCHANNAN

Dr. Ben's Photo 34. Dr. Yosef A.A. ben-Jochannan and Dr. Fred Monderson with some of the author's books in first edition Monderson acquired over the years in which he supported the Master-Teacher who autographed them all.

This writer was happy to be a part of that epoch making tour that marked Doc Bens Fiftieth Anniversary visiting the ancient African "holy-land" and the next year for the First Nubian Festival. More importantly, I met "Doc Ben" in early 1972. This was right after the publication of his seminal works, *African Origins of the Major Western Religions* (1970), *Africa: Mother of Western Civilization* (1971), and *Black Man of the Nile* (1972), later *Black Man of the Nile and his Family*. The style of his writings, copious nature of referents employed to defend things African, and his Afrocentric pioneering approach made Doc. Ben, a very well-respected elder, and later a sought after speaking attraction, a man who "tells it like it is!"

Dr. ben-Jochannan has compiled an impressive thirty odd publications. He helped set the stage for a whole new approach in interpreting Africa's contributions to civilization and its legacy. He lit the fire of intellectual and cultural consciousness in Africans worldwide. The Diasporan style of dress with an Afrocentric flavor is also credited to him. Establishing connections between Africans in America, Africa, Asia and Europe are all attributed to Dr. ben-Jochannan, a man of vision, seer, and intellectual giant. Many of his books challenged the distortions of Europeans in writing, publishing and disseminating knowledge about the arts, sciences, religion, etc., of the ancient people today called Egyptians. Dr. Ben has rightly included omissions and corrected distortions systematically implanted and perpetrated by racist Western, European and American historiography that has falsified the historical past with a prejudiced interpretation against African people. Many of his books challenged the distortions of Europeans in writing, publishing and disseminating knowledge about the arts, sciences, religion, etc., regarding ancient Africa as representation and modern interpretation. Dr. Ben dared to expose the hypocrisy of western scholarship. He attacked the foundational pillars upon which a false legacy rests. Naturally, he paid a price!

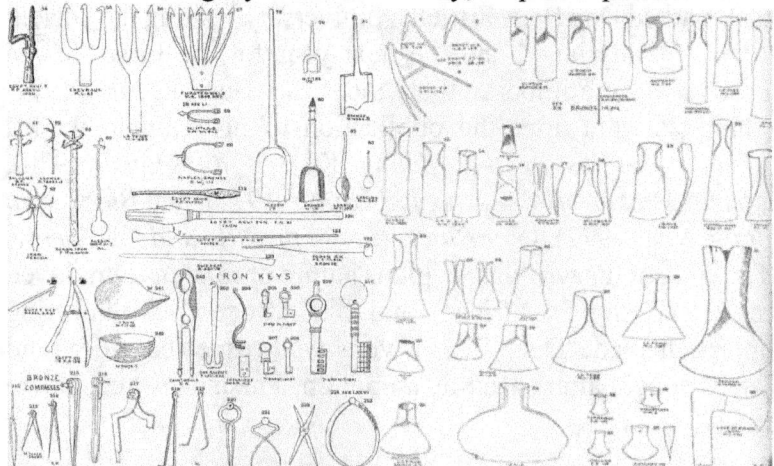

Dr. Ben's Illustration 5. Egyptian and Foreign – Fish Spear; Flesh Hook; Shovel; Key; Compasses; Casting (left); and, Egyptian and Foreign - Metal Hoes (right), in W.M.F. Petrie's *Tools and Weapons* (1917).

CELEBRATING DR. BEN-JOCHANNAN

Very early he also expressed the view some scholars are confused because they were taught from a wrong premise. In his own right, and as a result of his teachings, he had no choice but to produce, publish and distribute his works without the aid of major publishing firms. He was thus a pioneer in self-publishing, launching Alkebu-Lan Publishing Company and appealing and winning the support of many upcoming nationalists as they purchased his books in first edition form!

Initiating a new approach to history and the end result was an exposition and critical analysis of dynamic forces of Europe and Africa in struggle to claim heritage of the ancient and modern historical record. Dr. Ben addressed professionals, laymen, clergy, students and educators. He stressed vitality, resilience and creative expressions that shaped the modern African personality and worldview. Such an approach found ready ears among a people yearning for enlightening factual information about their illustrious African past in effort to free their minds shackled by ensklavement, racism and the debilitating effects of white supremacy and its arrogance. These young and old minds were enthused by the positive nature and potency of their cultural African heritage as "Ben" outlined it. He also took great pains to explain that there were lusterless pages in Africas past. Nevertheless, his concern fueled their emerging aspirations. This outlook brought Dr. Ben the adulation and respect of a grateful people, he so long deserved. They understood and welcomed his contributions among the litany of great African-American literary artists.

Dr. Ben's writings, lectures and educational tours over the years have stressed two essential themes. The first is that the "emergence of civilization, viz., science, religion, government, architecture, agriculture, philosophy, and the arts, began in Africa." The messages in these utterances became the foundation of todays Egypt and the Nile Valley

FREDERICK MONDERSON

accomplishments. In his approach, Dr. Ben has shown how the structural foundations of western civilization developed from discoveries and scientific applications in this ancient African land. Lastly, he took great pains to show the writing and teaching of modern history has been distorted to elevate Europe and degrade Africa, which is clearly wrong and must be rectified. This fundamental view helped establish the need for African historical reconstruction and interpretation particularly as we navigate this new century and millennium.

The second of Dr. Ben's themes has been that "Africans worldwide should be proud of their ancestors accomplishments. The arts and sciences that today govern the world are Africas legacy. African-Americans should show great pride and dignity in their history and heritage." They must respect themselves and carry themselves with dignity and pride. Those who know can teach the young how to identify with Africa. In so doing, they must form study groups and visit Africa. Yet, they must also be aware of the machinations of cultural imperialism and cultural genocide constantly at work. Further the young must immerse themselves in an African-centric perspective and research, write and teach others in turn. They must study languages, French, German, Swahili, Greek, Latin, Coptic, Arabic and *Medu Netcher* or Hieroglyphics. They must struggle to correct the recent distorted history of Africas past. In this way, future leaders would help to better the lot of humanity and save the world from its impending moral, spiritual and scientific destruction. To accomplish these objectives the good doctor has supplied a reservoir of information from his lifes researches in the arsenal of published works he has created. Of course, these works must be read, ingested and digested and returned to time and again. This is important for as Dr. John Henrik Clarke once said, "People buy but never read Dr. Ben's Books." Herein then is the dilemma.

CELEBRATING DR. BEN-JOCHANNAN

The Author's major thesis of his *African Origins of the Major "Western" Religions* is that African religious practices were denigrated and called "fetishism" and "paganism." In fact, these early thought processes he showed are necessarily the fundamental bases of Judaism, Christianity and Islam. He argued that these ideas were first developed and nurtured in Central Africa among indigenous peoples and then migrated down the Nile and extended throughout the Nile Valley. Such ideas and influences found greatest fruition in Kemet (Egypt) and were preserved by its civilization advances and the nature of its geography. The early knowledge, particularly that of a religious nature, was first written down in such selections as the "Book of Gates," "Book of Knowing Ra," etc. These were associated with the "Pyramid Texts," then "Coffin Texts," and the later *Book of the Dead* or *Book of Going Forth By Day*, and equally the "Mysteries of Sais" (Egypt). The fortunes of geography enabled Africas second cultural daughter, Kemet to rise to greater prominence than did the eldest, Ethiopia, Dr. Ben explained! He stressed and still maintain to this day, despite all the "new evidence," that civilization began to the south of Egypt! Much of this is borne out through discoveries as at Qustol and Nabta Playa and in the Eastern Desert. As such, despite modern falsification of history and the insistent propagation of such falsity, his thesis is as credible as ever.

Another of Dr. Ben's seminal works is *Africa: Mother of Western Civilization*. Its major thesis holds that "the fundamental laws, principles, philosophies, ideas, arts and crafts that educated the west, are indigenous to Africa through the Nile Valley cultural experience." For critical teachers who face this dilemma he has some advice. As such, he wrote, "the only credentials necessary in the experience of African history, otherwise mis-nomered the Black Experience and Black Studies are the documented proofs and the sources from whence they are taken."

FREDERICK MONDERSON

For this reason, *Africa: Mother of Western Civilization* is an enormous compendium of facts, sources, illustrations, and analyses that challenge laymen and scholars alike. It suggests all educators and lay persons alike become involved in reclaiming the stolen heritage of Africa. This *magnum opus* opens new vistas for historical investigation and provides a wide array of references relating to the significance of Africa in world civilization.

Black Man of the Nile and His Family marks the third of the "trilogy of Dr. Ben's seminal works." This particular source represents the maturity of his thoughts and presentations for it focuses on the role Black men and women have played in bequeathing science, religion, arts, metaphysics, agricultural method, boat building and river navigation to the world through Africas conduit in Egypt and Nubia. It also contains a number of objectives the author seeks to accomplish.

The first of these objectives is, "an attempt to create in young African, African-American (Black person), and all other African people, a sense of belonging in the great African heritage." It is, writes Dr. Ben, "specifically directed to those who have criminally demasculinized, denuded, and otherwise denigrated the Africans of their CULTURAL, ECONOMIC, POLITICAL, SCIENTIFIC, SPIRITUAL, and all other forms of their heritage and human decency." To this we should add the intellectual heritage as represented in Egypt; that is, through "acquisition methods," and teaching, writing and misrepresentation of the artifactual evidence.

It also presents: "AFRICAN ORIGINS OF EUROPEAN CIVILIZATION" in a manner whereby, "scholars can find interesting use for it in their research; as much as the layman can for processing information."

CELEBRATING DR. BEN-JOCHANNAN

Dr. Ben views his role as gadfly presenting, "pertinent information needed in the African peoples RE-IDENTIFICATION with their great ancestral heritage." Lastly, he continued, the "major desired accomplishment this volume seeks to achieve, is to provide anthropological evidence in the ancient heritage of the Africans" and their contributions all over the world.

Abu Simbel to Ghizeh: A Guide Book and Manual is in itself a useful piece of writing. But, there are other books.

In the acquisition of knowledge, Sir Francis Bacon (1561-1626) told us: "Some books are to be tasted, others to be swallowed, and some few to be chewed and digested." This much can be said of the trilogy of Dr. ben-Jochannan's works, *Black Man of the Nile and His Family, Africa: Mother of Western Civilization* and *The African Origins of the "Major" Western Religions*. The others are equally interesting! Everyone must buy and read these books and pass them on to others particularly their sons and daughters.

Finally, as a student of his, and based on observations and analytic critique, this writer would like to add a 15-point summation of how all can view Dr. Yosef Alfredo Antonio ben-Jochannan's contribution as an unselfish and fearless elucidation of the historical record systematically distorted to elevate Europe and denigrate Africa while wrecking psycho-social debasement of the African spirit and persona. Without question, whether through omission, distortion and even false presentation, the urban youth across America have most seriously been victimized in the systematic alienated educational process they have been subjected to. As such, the potent cultural lifeline Dr. Yosef Alfredo Antonio ben-Jochannan has provided is today critical in rescuing these young people adrift in the academic and intellectual cosmos of these modern times going forward. The prescription therefore is as follows:

1. We must praise and show thankfulness for the man who, for more than half a century challenged the behemoth of western intellectual oppression of Africa and her offspring while enlightening many to the wonders of a creative African cultural heritage.

2. We must commend Dr. ben-Jochannan for the humanitarian work he did among the Nubians in Egypt and Sudan, viz., Aswan, Daboud, Wadi Halfa, Dongola Province and Fashoda.

3. We must recognize his call to action in the cultural genocide in the African American studies curriculum predating the Afrocentric insistence on multi-culturalism.

4. We should continue to emulate his style of critical analysis of contemporary developments, whether it was historical omissions in Alex Haley's *Roots*; misrepresentation in King Tut's exhibition that is again taking place in America today; taking to task T. Eric Peet's "The Problem with Akhenaton;" Criticism of Father Temples' *Bantu Philosophy*; challenge to another writers description that Rameses II had "badly abscessed teeth," and so forth.

5. We can appreciate his identifying "They all look Alike, All," thus linking African peoples across the globe who were victims of racial hatred and cultural aggression.

CELEBRATING
DR. BEN-JOCHANNAN

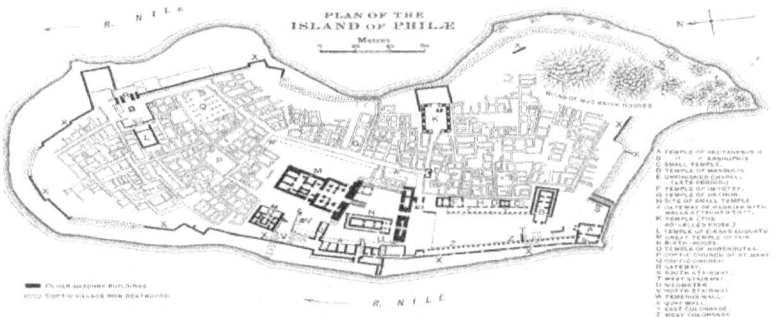

Dr. Ben's Plan 3. Plan of the Island of Philae.

6. His early clarification of the differences between the *Black Nationalist and the Black Marxist* was very timely and inspiring and still is.

7. First to outline the *History of the Bible*, he challenged the *Black Clergy Without a Black Theology* and offered *A Black Bible for Black Spiritual and Religious Consciousness*.

8. We must acknowledge as a human he may have made some mistakes, miniscule, as they were, outweighed by the foundational reservoir of ethical and cultural Ma'at he implanted in the consciousness of African people worldwide.

9. His insistence that all African Americans visit the Nile Valley to imbibe in the cultural heritage and grow from the intellectual exposure, but more particularly their dress code and mannerism among the people must not be construed as the "arrogance of Ugly Americans," was and is still timely and insightful.

10. His outspoken nature, love for Marcus Garvey and his *Philosophy and Opinions*, praise of Black Goddesses, critique of Academics who are "fifth columns" made him anathema to people with ill-intentions toward African people.

FREDERICK MONDERSON

11.   Dr. ben-Jochannan had little respect for people in high positions who never promoted the aspirations of their Black subordinates.

12.   A staunch Pan-Africanist, he aspired to see accomplished sustained and measurable economic, political and educational empowerment for people of African heritage worldwide.

13.   He said, "I took Egypt to show our people the proper way" and to challenge its misrepresentation, in white supremacy, racism and religious bigotry.

14.   He insisted we not just read books, do research but also form study groups that debate and discuss these important issues raised by him as well as personally critique status quos positions.

15.   He asked us to standardize our learning and take responsibility for our own history. He stated: "Until African (Black) people are willing, and do write their own experience, past and present, we will continue being slaves, mentally, physically and spiritually to Caucasian and Semitic racism and religious bigotry." This latter we must never allow to happen, for as Dr. John Henrik Clarke has admonitioned, "African people must write their own history."

Therefore, we must recognize that Dr. Yosef A.A. ben-Jochannan has made a major contribution to African intellectual growth. He created a cosmological vision over time that allowed us to see the light. His work has been seminal! In fact, he was our light! He taught us how to persevere to persevere! He asked that we establish and maintain a standard for our behavior, and dont fear, dont fear defeat, dont fear death!

CELEBRATING DR. BEN-JOCHANNAN

THE NEGATIVE CONFESSIONS

1. I have not done Iniquity
2. I have not robbed with violence
3. I have not done violence to any man
4. I have not committed theft
5. I have not slain man or woman
6. I have not made light the bushel
7. I have not acted deceitfully
8. I have not purloined the things which belongs to God
9. I have not uttered falsehood
10. I have not carried away food
11. I have not uttered evil words
12. I have not attacked any man
13. I have not killed the beasts that are the property of God
14. I have not acted deceitfully
15. I have not laid waste the land which has been ploughed
16. I have never pried into matters to make mischief
17. I have not set my mouth in motion against any man
18. I have not given away to wrath concerning myself without a cause
19. I have not defiled the wife of a man
20. I have not committed any sin against purity
21. I have not struck fear into any man
22. I have not encroached upon sacred times and seasons
23. I have not been a man of anger
24. I have not made myself deaf to the words of right and truth
25. I have not stirred up strife
26. I have made no man to weep
27. I have not committed acts of impurity, neither have I laid with men
28. I have not eaten my heart
29. I have abused no man

30. I have not acted with violence
31. I have not judged hastily
32. I have not taken vengeance upon the God
33. I have not multiplied my speech over much
34. I have not acted with deceit, and I have not worked wickedness
35. I have not uttered curses on the king
36. I have not fouled water
37. I have not made haughty my voice
38. I have not cursed the God
39. I have not behaved with insolence
40. I have not sought for distinctions
41. I have not increased my wealth, except with such things as are justly mine own possessions
42. I have not thought scorn of the God who is in my city.

Dr. Ben's Photo 34a. Isis Temple at Philae.
Pharaoh makes a Presentation to Isis as Hathor wearing horns and disk with Nephthys at her side wearinrg the Queen mother crown also with horns surmounted by the Red Crown with feathers.

CELEBRATING DR. BEN-JOCHANNAN

6. DR. BEN'S LETTER RECOGNIZING Dr. FREDERICK MONDERSON, March 1, 2000

AMON-RA

LETTER TO THE EDITOR

Today I recognize Brother Frederick Monderson as a stalwart in the field of Egyptological Nile Valley research.

Fred Monderson has been a student of mine since 1972. He possesses many of my works in First Edition, that with the deepest appreciation, I subsequently endorsed. Having read my books and traveled to Egypt/ancient Kemet with me on several occasions, Brother Monderson has written nearly 400 pieces on African History and local social, political community matters. These were published in your New York City's Only Black Daily newspaper the Daily Challenge. In this pyramid of Black social consciousness he has enlightened the Black community on the efficacy and significance of African history and culture. The Afro Times and New American newspapers were also vehicles in this undertaking. In manner reminiscence of my efforts and with a style that I endorse, Brother Monderson has borne the torch of Black enlightenment in New York, with dignity and a revolutionary fervor that I admire.

Years ago at one of Dr. Lewis' Dinners honoring my efforts, I'm reminded of Fred Monderson's statement: "Dr. Ben, as you move along life's path and your vision becomes cloudy and you look for someone to pass the baton to, look for Brother Monderson for I'll be there." On my tour of Egypt in the summer of 1997, participants were given an assignment in Karnak Temple. Mr. Monderson's assignment had been to locate and report on the name of Rameses III in that enclosure and elsewhere on the tour.

While somewhat disappointed with the reports or lack thereof from the other students, I was impressed with Brother Monderson's studiousness and attention to historical detail of his assignment, Rameses III. My response was, "Everybody fail except Mr. Monderson. Well, perhaps you and you." There is a typed recording of this statement.

The author of several books on ancient Kemet/Egypt, consistent with the dynamics of African historiographic reconstruction, I endorse the efforts of Fred Monderson's continued research and his endeavors as a Tour Guide to the land of ancient Kemet. It is my firmest belief he will continue to educate and enlighten our people regarding the strengths, significance and utility of the ancient Nile Valley heritage.

With respect and warm affection I close.

Dr. Yosef-A.A. Ben-Jochannan is a Researcher, Black African nationalist, author, lecturer and Tour Guide, Ehler Harlem, NY.

Karnak Temple. On the wall, Thutmose III raises hands in adoration before Amon... notice the king's dress.

Karnak Temple. On the wall, Thutmose III offers Ma'at a feather of truth to Amon.

Dr. Ben's Illustration6. Dr. Ben's letter to the *Daily Challenge* endorsing the work of Dr. Frederick Monderson published March 1, 2000. It should actually be Rameses II offering the "feather of truth."

FREDERICK MONDERSON

Dr. Ben's Illustration 11. Tarkhan. Ptah Bowl, Sa Case, Scarab, Fling Armlets, Zebra Drawings (left); and, Graves 1034 with "goods;" 1035 - the deceased in the "contracted position;" 170 and 1007 with "goods" and the "contracted position" with bones dismantled.

7. DR. BEN'S LETTER RECOGNIZING DR. FREDERICK MONDERSON

Dr. Yosef A. A. ben-Jochannan
Lennox Terrace
40 West 135th Street
New York, New York
November 15, 2010

Greetings,
Today I recognize Dr. Frederick Monderson as an outstanding scholar, researcher and writer of Egyptological studies and expresses confidence in his ability to defend Egypt as African!

CELEBRATING DR. BEN-JOCHANNAN

As our people move forward, the history and significance of Egyptian - Nile Valley civilization remains crucial to black-African intellectual development. To sustain this effort requires the best researchers and writers to continue the tradition of excellence established by many including myself and Dr. John H. Clarke of Hunter College of the City University of New York.

Dr. Monderson is a product of that "Hunter School." As a student of mine who has traveled to Egypt with me on several occasions and possesses all my books, he has admirably answered the age-old question I posed decades ago: "Now that you have come to Egypt and seen what you have seen, what are you going to do with this knowledge?" As an African historian and Egyptologist, Dr. Monderson has responded admirably by writing hundreds of articles and dozens of books on this vital field of interest.

I thankfully praise his writings on my behalf, welcome his Memorial Day Tribute to my work and endorse his efforts as a tour guide to Egypt. Encouraging him to choose one of fifty countries in Africa to specialize in and he choosing Egypt, Im pleased with his development as an outstanding Egyptological researcher and writer. As such, I recognize the valuable role he has, can and will play in educating our people about the wonderful resource of Egyptian history, culture, science and spirituality. Therefore, I unequivocally give my blessings to Dr. Frederick Monderson's work in Egyptian studies and feel confident he will continue to educate and enlighten many, particularly the young, about the glorious African past in the Nile Valley.

Dr. Yosef A.A. ben-Jochannan
Harlem Resident, historian, lecturer, writer and Egyptological Master Teacher.

FREDERICK MONDERSON

8. DR. BEN'S LETTER AUTHORIZING TRIBUTES, SEMINARS, CALLS FOR PAPERS

Dr. Yosef A.A. ben-Jochannan
Lennox Terrace
40 West 135th Street
New York, New York 10030
June 5, 2010
Subject: Permission to conduct tributes, seminars, calls for papers, in my name!

Greetings to All!

Dr. Frederick Monderson has been a student of mine for nearly 4 decades and has traveled to Egypt with me on several occasions. On one such occasion, he demonstrated a particular excellence that has remained indelibly imbedded in my memory. He possesses practically all my books in first edition; many of which I affectionately autographed.

Dr. Monderson has consistently demonstrated the highest standards of academic scholarship, proficiency in research techniques, is a prolific writer and staunchly defends Egypt as African. For nearly two decades he has written extensively on ancient Egypt, African history and local events, in New Yorks black press, and this deserves the highest praise. His work as a researcher and Egyptological scholar deserves recognition in the excellent tradition in which he was taught. I commend his commitment to the education of African people!

Mr. Monderson has written extensively in praise of me as an elder, Egyptologist, historian and scholar. He has held seminars in tribute to my efforts to educate African people and

CELEBRATING
DR. BEN-JOCHANNAN

this is commendable. As a result, I give Dr. Frederick Monderson permission to continue sponsoring academic tributes, calls for papers and any intellectual pursuit in my name that reflects the highest standards demonstrated in interest of African people. As such, I am confident, any tribute, calls for papers, sponsored tours of Egypt conducted in my name will reflect the high standards he has consistently demonstrated and will be a credit to the African people we both love and serve diligently. Again, I endorse the work of Dr. Frederick Monderson that reflects the highest standards of academic excellence and feel confident he will continue to be a credit to my name and the African people he serves.

Thank you. My love and respect to all!
Dr. Yosef Antonio Alfredo ben-Jochannan, Harlem, New York - June 5, 2010

Dr. Ben's Photo 34b. The majestic Western Colonnade with its 32 illustrated columns at Isis Temple at Philae.

FREDERICK MONDERSON

9. "PRAISING THE BLACK WOMAN"
By Dr. Frederick Monderson

As we celebrate Womens History Month in March this year, commentary and praises are due to Black women who for so long have given so much, from the earliest times up to now, giving birth, been companion, leader, visionary, perfectly planned, a dish of the Gods, who improves with love, and so much more.

Science, utilizing DNA reconstruction, has demonstrated that the earliest surviving progenitor of the human race has been a woman who roamed the plains of East Africa over two hundred and fifty thousand years ago. Earlier, a palaeo-anthropologist named Johanson discovered the most complete human fossil. It was of a woman in the Hadar region of Ethiopia, who was subsequently, nicknamed "Lucy," and dated to more than two million years old. Science has also confirmed, again through DNA reconstruction that the individual thought to be "Eve" and most probably the mother of all humanity was an African woman who roamed the plains of East Africa about 200,000 years ago. From her all races, as we know it, trace a lineal descent. Thus, together with the "Black Madonna," this puts the Black woman in the most sacred and divine company. Perhaps this is why the respected elder, historian, Egyptologist, tour guide, etc., Dr. Ben-Jochannan in praising the Sacred Womb of the Black Woman, began the Keynote Address at ASCAC's *Second Annual Ancient Egyptian Conference* from February 28 through March 3, 1985 by saying: "Brothers of the Craft and Sisters of the House: Heaven is between a Black Womans Legs." In this,

CELEBRATING DR. BEN-JOCHANNAN

Dr. Ben argued, she has given life, been supportive and played a role of great distinction as woman, warrior, entrepreneur, supportive as always being told "woman behold thy son." Sometimes witty, tactful, sometimes a pain or a pleasure, always a treasure, lovely in her bones, faithful; Sparrow says "using guile with a pretty smile;" assertive often with a tigers heart, the womans work is never done.

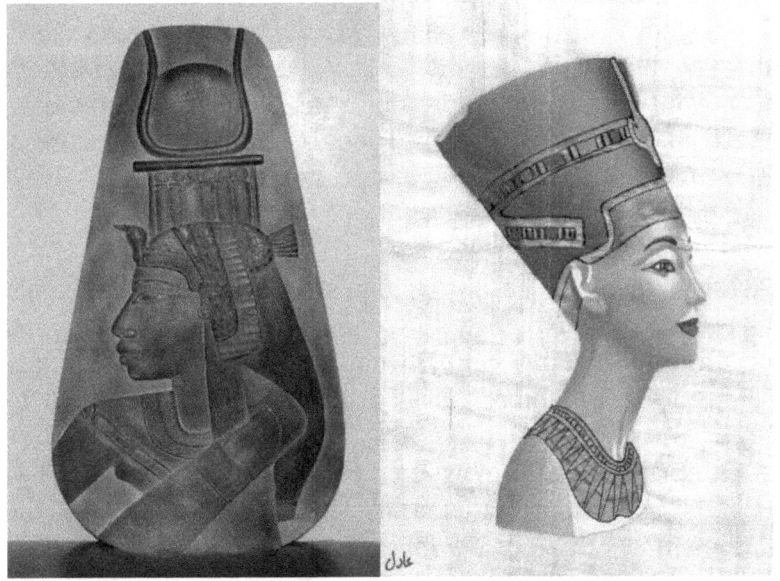

Dr. Ben's Photo 35. What a remarkable contrast of the Egyptian woman made of clay (left) and Papyrus (right). Even though made for the modern tourist trade, not original in any way, one of them reinforces a false interpretations as to who these African people were! So, I ask, "You do the math!"

That essential element of Len Jeffries' complimentarity "Male-female principle" is equally what Marcus Garvey said in his *Philosophy and Opinions* that woman is: "What the night is to day, is woman to man. The period of change that brings us light out of darkness, darkness out of light, and semi-light out of darkness are like the changes we find in woman day by day. She makes one happy, then miserable. You are to her kind, then unkind. Constant yet inconstant. Thus we have **WOMAN**. No real man can do without her." Its as Shakespeare said, "She is a woman, therefore may be wood; She is a woman, therefore may be won." And this is what we strive for. Of course, let us not go where Hipponax (570 – 520 B.C.) said, "There are two days when a woman is a pleasure: the day one marries her and the day one buries her." Still, let us not forget as Longfellow said: "As onto the bow the cord is, So unto the man is woman, Though she bend him, she obeys him, Though she draws him, yet she follows, Useless each without the other."

As such then, in the chronological development of female assertion, the next great flowering of African womanhood occurred in the Nile Valley, where, as Nornelia Otis Skinner said in 1901, a "womans virtue is man's greatest invention."

As a result, the role of women in ancient Egypt/Kemet has been essential, appreciated, respected and necessary. From the earliest times the indispensable position of Egyptian women has been depicted in the graves of the prehistoric period and in the tombs of deceased nobles. Their roles as Goddesses, queens, princesses, mothers, and plain old folks, were demonstrated and the impact on numerous pharaohs as well as Egyptian society has been recounted.

Many women have ruled as queens of Egypt but Hatshepsut of the Eighteenth Dynasty has been the significant woman bold enough to rule as King or Pharaoh of this ancient land.

CELEBRATING
DR. BEN-JOCHANNAN

Dr. Ben's Photo 36. **Aswan**. Tombs of the Nobles as viewed from the Oberoi Hotel, now closed.

Dr. Ben's Photo 37. **Aswan**. The Oberoi Hotel as seen from across the Nile.

The female principle in Egypt, as in Africa, is divine in nature. In Egyptian cosmogony and religious beliefs, female divinities have played important roles. They have featured prominently in triads, and in a number of instances, shapely as a swan, females were a part of pharaonic triads.

The Goddess Nuit or Nut was, from the earliest times, a water Goddess who formed part of a divine company of eight. The males were Nu, Hehu, Keku and Kerh. The females were Kerhet, Keruit, Hehut and Nut. Not much is known about the other Goddesses but, in the New Empire, Nut was represented as a woman and as a cow.

According to the *Book of the Dead* or the Hieratic Transcript of the *Papyrus of Ani*, translated by E.A. Wallis Budge, there were a number of female deities in the Egyptian religious drama. The male Shu and the female Tefnut were children of Ra, the Sun God. Tefnut formed the third member of the company of Gods of Anu. Tefnut is sometimes shown as moisture and at other times as sunlight. This Goddess originated in the Nubian Desert. She had a lion head and wore a disk or uraeus or both. She drank her enemies blood and had fire in her eyes.

The next female divinity of importance was Isis or Auset. She was the seventh member of the company of Anu, wife of Osiris and mother of Horus. She is usually depicted as a woman with a headdress in the shape of a seat. Her temple is located at Philae, now Agilka Island. Some early names ascribed to her are "the great Goddess, the divine mother, the mistress of words of power and enchantment." In later times she is called mother of the Gods and the living one. Isis is sometimes shown as a cow and has a solar disk between her horns with a throne or seat, and she also has plumes or feathers. Her most famous depiction is as the mother suckling her child Horus. The original Madonna and Child concept is based on this depiction. Naturally, she was Black like the sky, hence, associated as the Black Madonna.

CELEBRATING DR. BEN-JOCHANNAN

Nephthys was Isis sister and wife of the evil God Seth. "When the sun rose at the creation of the primeval waters Nephthys occupied a place in his boat with Isis and other deities; as a nature Goddess she either represents day before sunrise or after sunset, but not associated with night. Her hieroglyphic name means "lady of the house." Plutarch tells of a legend that said she was the mother of Anubis by Osiris, who later became judge of the dead. She is shown as the companion of Isis and was grieved during Osiris murder.

The next female divinity was *Ma'at*, the female counterpart of Thoth. The Heliopolitan tradition makes her a daughter of Ra. She was the wife of Thoth, the God of writing. A feather symbolizes her name and she also holds a scepter in one hand and an ankh in another. The name *Ma'at* means straight, right, genuine, righteous, just, real, truth, balance, order, steadfast, unalterable, etc.

Hathor, the "House of Horus," was the Goddess of the sun where the sun God rose and set. Hathor is depicted as a woman with a disk and horns on her head. She is also shown as a cow with a disk between her horns. Budge says, as a "Cow-Goddess she is probably of Sudani origin." That is Africa proper, to the south of Egypt.

Neith has been called "the divine mother, the lady of heaven, the mistress of the Gods." She is mentioned in the *Pyramid Texts* as the mother of Sobek, the crocodile God. Neith was believed to be self-produced and an ancient Saite tradition made her to be the mother of Ra, the Sun God. She is depicted in the form of a woman, having upon her head the shuttle or arrows, or she wears the Red Crown and holds arrows, a bow and a scepter in her left hand.

Sekhmet was the wife of Ptah, and the mother of Nefer-Temu and of I-Em-Hetep (Imhotep). She personified the terrible heat of the desert. "When Ra determined to punish mankind with death, because they scoffed at him, he sent Sekhment, his Eye to perform the work of vengeance; illustrative of this aspect of her is a figure wherein she is depicted with the suns eye for a head." Bast was a sort of opposite to Sekhmet. She personified the gently and fructifying heat of the sun. She is usually pictured as cat-headed.

Nekheb-ka is the name of a Goddess represented by a vulture and Uatchit a serpent. Uatchit and Nekhbet were very special Goddesses. They personified Upper and Lower Egypt and comprised the Pharaohs *"Two Ladies"* name. Uatchit, a form of Hathor, is depicted as a woman with the crown of the north and a scepter. Nek-habit was the vulture Goddess, tutelary deity of Upper Egypt from the city of Nekheb. Mut, the earth Goddess, was wife of Amon-Ra the Sun God and mother of Khonsu the moon God. She was an essential part of the Theban triad, of Amon Ra, Mut and Khonsu. She too is sometimes shown as a vulture.

As a result, female roles in the divine cosmogony and religious drama of the Egyptians gave them a special place in the social fabric of the society. Whether, wife, mother or sister, females were respected, cared for, and had equal status before the law. They could inherit property, become literate and were able to conduct business.

The graves of the Badarian and Naqada I burials show much evidence of some association between the dead and women. What we call female paraphernalia can be found in many graves of the time. These include combs, rings, bracelets, and studs for the nose, jewelry of shells, carnelian and coral around the neck. There, earrings and dresses are also included. These

CELEBRATING DR. BEN-JOCHANNAN

early people utilized dyes with green malachite and castor oil for cleansing and softening the skin.

By the time of the Gerzean culture or Naqada II, figurines of the fertility Goddess are found in graves. Carved bone and ivory figurines of women are also found in graves. They were designed to accompany deceased men into eternity for purposes of pleasure and companionship.

Female jewelry was made from a wide variety of materials including amethyst, button-pearl, amber, agate, onyx, and glass. The jewelry included necklaces, girdles, bracelets, and a circlet or diadem for the head. Therefore, in the pre-dynastic time, before 3200 B.C., the role of women was considered important enough to receive the attention indicated in the graves.

From the time of the First Dynasty, 3200 B.C. onwards, the position of women seems advanced and appreciated. On the Narmer Palette Hathor is featured, while on the Macehead the king is shown beneath a pavilion. His wife, Queen Neithhotep is represented also seated and facing him. Some feel this is probably a marriage ceremony. However, it clearly shows an elevated position for his wife. They had a son named Aha, who succeeded his father to the throne.

While Narmer was buried in a regular sized mastaba tomb at Abydos, Aha built an elaborate tomb for his mother, Queen Neithhotep. The indications of this are that the husband and son, in ancient Egypt, loved and respected the wife and or mother. The same care and concern could be found for the daughter and for the sister.

FREDERICK MONDERSON

In this respect, the basis for the love, respect and proper consideration of women or females in Egypt is clear. This treatment is evidence by the roles of and respect accorded the Goddesses, queens, mothers and princesses. It stands to reason that the ordinary woman also enjoyed some of these special considerations. However, it must also be pointed out, there were women who held positions as household help and enslaved, as in many societies of the ancient world.

The significance of women in Egypt is further indicated by their status before the law. The Supreme Court, according to an inscription on the walls of a tomb at Sakkara, upheld a certain womans right to inheritance. Schafik Allam's *Everyday Life in Ancient Egypt*, argues that women could "inherit moveable things, house and landed property."

Even more, and equally with consideration, women were held accountable for their actions in the society. Important, they could also engage in business or represent their husbands in business transactions. They could receive loans, mediate between two parties and were allowed to bear witness in many judicial proceedings. Women had the legal right to conduct legal affairs without the prior authorization of their husbands.

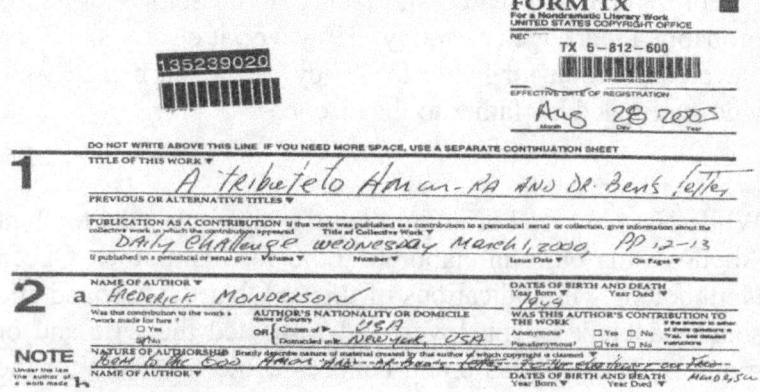

Dr. Ben's Photo 38. Library of Congress Registration of Dr. Ben's Letter endorsing Dr. Fred Monderson's work.

CELEBRATING DR. BEN-JOCHANNAN

Dr. Ben's Photo 39. Aswan. Landing for the boats hierd to take visitors to the Temple of Isis on Philae, now Agilka Island. The new location was chosed to relocate of the temple to preserve it from the flooding of the Nile.

As an example of womens status before the law, an inscription at Sakkara tells of a woman named Ornero, who was "designated by the courts as representative for a group of heirs and who consequently had to administer on trust all the property in question." Women could sue in court. Many wives of officials were "responsible for regulating their husbands affairs and looking after their husbands interests." Many were authorized to act in his absence. Therefore, its clear, a number of dynamic African women have impacted on the three thousand years of socio-political-religious cultural expression experienced in dynastic Egypt.

The Third Dynasty began the first "golden age" in Egypt. It also began the Old Empire or Old Kingdom.

FREDERICK MONDERSON

Dr. Ben's Illustration 13. Tarkhan. Burials 902, 217, 208, 234, 286 and VI Dynasty (left); and, Graves, 216 and 207, Unopened and Opened in W.M.F. Petrie and A.H. Gardiner - *Tarkhan I and Memphis V* (1913).

The accomplishments of the preceding Pre-dynastic and Archaic periods set the stage for the new era. The Step-Pyramids and the great mastaba tombs became prototype for the true pyramids of the Fourth Dynasty.

The pharaohs who dominated the Fourth Dynasty were Snefru, Khufu, Khafre and Menkaure. The first built two pyramids at Dashur and Meydum. The other three built the famous Giza group. What is significant, however, is the role Queen Hetep-Heres played in influencing these four great African kings. Queen Hetep-Heres was the wife of Pharaoh Snefru, mother of Khufu, grandmother of Khafre and great-grandmother of Menkaure. What a progeny! She must have been a powerful African woman.

CELEBRATING DR. BEN-JOCHANNAN

Dr. Ben's Photo 40. Aswan. Billboard for "Sound and Light" show.

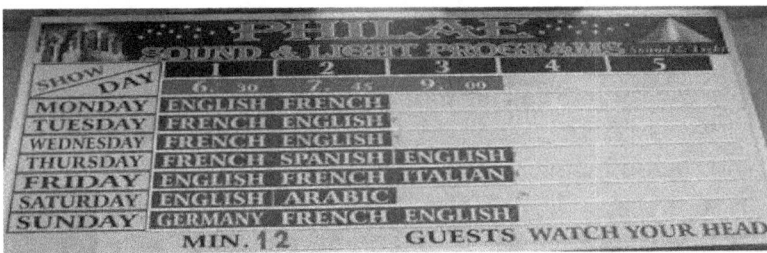

Dr. Ben's Photo 41. Aswan. Languages of shows on specific nights.

In 1925, excavators in an expedition from Harvard University worked at Giza. Behind the pyramid of Khufu, they discovered the "only intact tomb chamber from the Old Kingdom" found up to that time. According to J.E. Manchip Whites *Ancient Egypt: Its Culture and History*, a "wonderful collection was unearthed." In this discovery, Archaeologists found, "there was a canopy, a bed, two chairs and a carrying chair, all sheeted in gold. There were alabaster vessels, a copper and gold manicure instrument. There was a toilet box with cosmetics contained in eight little alabaster pots, and a jewel case with twenty silver anklets inlaid with lapis lazuli, carnelian and malachite. Inlaid gold hieroglyphs on the ebony panels of the carrying chair carried the fourfold inscription:

FREDERICK MONDERSON

"Mother of the King of Upper and Lower Egypt, follower of Horus, guide of the Ruler, favorite whose every command is carried out for her, daughter of the God (born) of his body Hetepheres."

In the tradition of powerful African women, Hetepheres was one of the greatest. The bust of Pharaoh Khufu is so African with his broad nose and thick lips; one can only wonder what his mother and father looked like. During the Eleventh Dunasty and start of the Middle Kingdom, Intef challenged Mentuhotep for Theban supremacy. In one encounter, coming out of the pass on to the Plain of Thebes, he encountered Mentuhotep with a superior force waiting for him. Thereupon he called upon his motter Queen Achtotes to broker a peace treaty with Mentuhoteps mother, Queen Aam. This shows the influence these women exerted in their sons' lives.

Whos better than the greatest? The answer is Teti-Sheri!

The Eighteenth Dynasty was the most remarkable of all others. This was so because of the females who provided the progeny and inspiration for this greatest golden period. Teti-Sheri was the wife of Sekenenra II. In *Temples, Tombs and Hieroglyphs*, Barbara Mertz wrote: "Teti-Sheri survived him; she lived to see her daughter marry her own brother, Sekenenra the Brave. Her granddaughter Aahmose-Nefertari also married her brother, Ahmose .... Ahmoses queen was a lovely woman, and a great lady, who was deified in later times." Sekenenra was killed with an axe-blow to the head in the war of liberation against the Hyksos, Asiatic invaders.

The family relationship of Teti-Sheris progeny is important for it clearly reinforces the Blackness of the Eighteenth Dynasty. In *The Splendor That Was Egypt*, Margaret Murray describes Ahmose, the founder of the dynasty as a "strongly built man, broad-shouldered, and with curly brown hair; he was not

CELEBRATING DR. BEN-JOCHANNAN

good-looking for he had projecting front teeth, and his portraiture suggests an admixture of Negro blood."

From her portrait in the British Museum the beautiful Aahmes-Nefertari leaves no doubt about her Black Ethiopian origin. Her granddaughter Queen Hatshepsut had to contend with the fact of her "Ethiopian blood" as the heiress to the throne after her father Thutmose Is death. This equally remarkable woman challenged male dominance and ruled for two decades. Senmut, her favorite and architect who built the magnificent Deir el-Bahari temple at Thebes, headed her personal circle.

In his role as principal architect, Senmut also quarried and erected two obelisks for the queen. Another architect, Amenhotep, erected two others. Two have disappeared while one still stands at Karnak and another lies beside the Sacred Lake. Two others were thought to be erected east of the **Akh Menou** before the East Gate. The standing obelisk measures 105 feet and is the tallest in Egypt. This queen; who described her-self as "beautiful to look at above all things; her voice was that of a God; her frame that of a God; her spirit was like a God," maintained the prosperity of her nation but succumbed to male rage, revenge and dominance. Her name still ranks as one of the most beautiful and powerful of African heroines.

Queen Tiye was the wife of Amenhotep III and the mother of Amenhotep IV. Her husband ruled Egypt at the height of the New Kingdom's "Golden Age." She played a prominent role in events of her time. Amenhotep III treated her as an equal and built a palace called Malcata for his beautiful Black Queen Tiye as well as a Lake for her to sail the Royal Barge. She exerted a significant impact on her son Amenhotep IV. He changed his name to Akhenaten and ushered in a new religious movement. Also, the art of the time was probably influenced by his ideas. Critics have credited her with influencing the rebellion her son introduced.

Nefertiti, Dushrata's daughter Thadukippa, was a Mitanni princess who came to Egypt to marry Amenhotep III but married he and Queen Tiyes son Akhenaton or Ikhnaton instead. She came into a powerful family and played a significant role in her husbands rule. She bore him five daughters and visibly displayed her love for him in a number of representations.

In the Nineteenth Dynasty Rameses II, the great builder and warrior Pharaoh built the Abu Simbel temple in Nubia. He married Nefertari, a Nubian princess and built her a temple next to his at Abu Simbel. This was the supreme test of love, which clearly indicates the power of this African woman. Tausert, buried in the Valley of the Kings was the last ruler of the Nineteenth Dynasty.

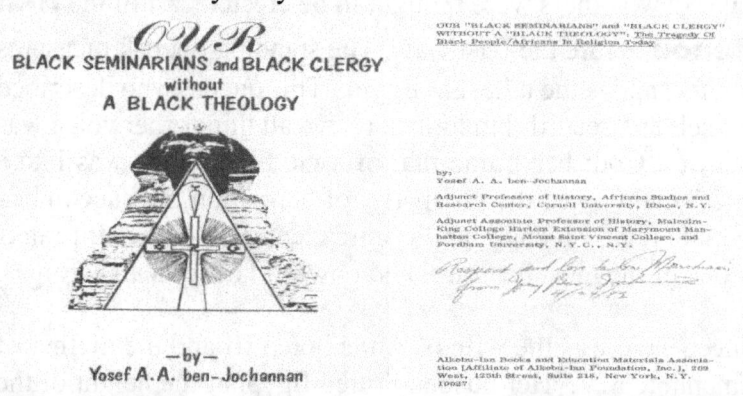

Dr. Ben's Books 2. OUR "BLACK SEMINARIANS" and "BLACK CLERGY" WITHOUT A "BLACK THEOLOGY" : *The Tragedy of Black People/Africans In Religion Today* (1978). Notice the Author's autograph for Dr. Fred Monderson.

CELEBRATING DR. BEN-JOCHANNAN

This selection seeks to highlight the majesty, power, beauty and everlasting testimony of the greatness of African and African-American womanhood. Clearly, no nation on earth can boast such a splendid line of outstanding women as Egypt who have influenced their states and the world. They remain to be admired and serve as role models of integrity and female accomplishment for an entire race of people. These were indeed great African women and they set powerful examples for progeny of the African race.

Queen Amenardis, sister of Piankhy of the Twenty-Fifth Dynasty was a beautiful woman who became Gods wife to Amon-Ra at Thebes following the Ethiopian conquest of Egypt.

Queen Cleopatra was beautiful and had to contend with the changing realities thrust upon her nation and she rose to the occasion. Ethiopia produced a strong line of queens called Candace who were warrior Queens and represented their nation and people with distinction. These followed in the tradition of Queen of Sheba, who while not a warrior, was Black and beautiful and a lover as well.

In West Africa the role of Queen and Queen Mother was significant contributing much to that culture cluster of the Ghana, Mali and Songhay empires. The descendants of these women were later dragged off to be slaves in the New World. One of the first of those was Angela who disembarked from the Dutch Man O War in 1691 and Isabella who, in 1624, gave birth to the first Black-African child born in the New World. Tonya Bolden in *The Book of African American Women* mentions 150 crusaders, creators and up-lifters of Black men in America. These women were in every walk of life, from slave to plantation owner. Some were entrepreneurs, preachers, abolitionists, activist-lecturers, thinkers,

FREDERICK MONDERSON

conductors of the Underground Railroad, writers, singers, mothers, nurses, spies, real estate investors, playwrights, cooks, poets, journalists, educators, civil rights activists, doctors, pharmacists, aviators, army officers, judges, lawyers, anthropologists, historians, dancers, psychologists, politicians, athletes, mathematicians and even more. Some were lynched and there were the "Four Little Girls," victims in a Birmingham Church bombing during the Civil Rights era.

In looking at James Allens exhibit on "Lynching across America" a grandmother in the line said: "I must get my grandchild to come over to look at this" as she viewed the Black woman Laura Nelson who was lynched in Oklahoma in 1911. That day both mother and son were lynched! Recently, the Equal Justic Initiative in Montgomery, Albama, chronicled some 4040 lynchings in the South from 1870-1950 No one was held accountable in these many murders. Interestingly enough, there is no question, in the more than one hundred slave rebellions Herbert Aptheker chronicled in this hemisphere, women played a significant role, and we can add to this Angela Davis, Joann Chesimard and Assata Shakur as "bucking the system."

Recognition is due the dignity and accomplishments of the ancient "sheroes" mirrored in the struggles and untiring efforts of many modern women. Today, Queen Mother Moore, Joyce Dinkins, Adelaide Sanford, Marilyn James, Winnie Mandela, Coretta Scott King, and Mrs. Jessie L. Jackson stand for the same principles of African achievement. We should also not forget Phyllis Wheatley, Harriet Tubman, C. Virginia Fields, Leticia James, Sojourner Truth, Mrs. David Walker, Mrs. Henry Highland Garner, Mrs. Frederick Douglass, Mrs. Booker T. Washington, Mrs. W.E.B. Dubois, Mrs. Marcus Garvey, Driscilla Dunjee, Mrs. Carter G. Woodson, Mary McLeod Bethune, Fannie Lou Hamer, Septima Poingette

CELEBRATING DR. BEN-JOCHANNAN

Clarke, Gemma Grigsby and Anna Arnold Hedgemon. Miriam Wright Elderman founded the Childrens Defense Fund. Lets also mention Dorothy Height, Barbara Jordan, Patricia Harris, Cybil Holmes, Orleane Williams-Brooks, Juliet Plummer Cobb, biologist, Alice Walker, and Zora Neal Hurston, writers, Johnnetta Cole, educator and Rev. Elizabeth Lott, mother and member of the CME Church. Then there is Jean Leon, Marjorie Matthews, Kathie Rones, Mrs. Benjamin, Jacqueline Lennon, Kadiatou Diallo, Mary Acevedo, Audrey Phillips-Caesar, Mrs. Steil, Mrs. Parris, the Auxiliary Ladies at Kings County Hospital Center, and Betsy Youman, Katie Harrell, Renee Morgan, Deborah Souvenir-Tinsdale, LaRay Brown, Renee Rowell, Jermaine Berger-Gaskin, Debra Lasagne, Mrs. Mock, Josephine Brathwaite, Renee Smoke, Marilyn Washington, Ruth Green and Carmen Rudder.

Betty Dopson of **CEMOTAP**, Ella Fitzgerald, Carmen McRae, Vonetta Price, Bessie Smith, my aunts Edith Maude Graham and Mavis Hill, then Aretha Franklin, and Philippa Duke Schuyler, Haidee Ildefonsa Galan, and Cybil Williams-Clarke and Gertrude ben-Jochannan, Shirley Chisholm, Una Clarke and Diane Choyice Robinson, are only some of the names.

Then there "Moms Mabley". "Me Moms" Mitta Monderson, "Me grand-Moms" Cherise Preville, "Me Sister" Cherise Maloney, Enid Graham, Mavis Hill, Carmen Monderson, Audrey Monderson, Sarah Monderson, Keisha Monderson, Queen-Tiy Monderson, Bridget Ann Monderson and Bridget Monderson-Duncan, Emma Merneith-Mitta Monderson, Kashida Maloney and we could add contemporary woman educators, Rhonda Hurdle, Mrs. Purdie, Hyacinth Rowe, Marisela Alcantara, Kathy Sharpton, Lucille Lang, Mrs. Ilene Loncke, Hessel Woolcock, Mrs. Harper, Mrs. Elizabeth

FREDERICK MONDERSON

Buckman Jones, Suhail Pena, Mrs. Virginia Jackson, Mrs. Jane Roberts, Estelle, Valma and Lorna Browne, Ayesha Monderson, Sheba Monderson, Rhonda Mormon Harris, Merimba Ani Donna Richards my teacher, Winna Allette, Sophie Williams, Ethel Foy, Melinda Melbourne, Mrs. Murray, Bernice Wiley, Evelyn Castro, Debra Brathwaite, Mrs. Angela Jitu Weusi, and so many more. Still, we cant forget Kiatdou Diallo, Agnes Green, Mrs. Haggler, Linda Bascombe, Osela McCarty, philanthropist, Sarah J. Hale, humanitarian, Venecia Sanchez, Annette Robinson and Mary Pinkett, former City Councilwomen, Darcell Anderson, Andre Pennix Smith, Lois and Ruth Goring and Gwendolyn Harmon community minded.   Marcia Melbourne, Toni Morrison, Madame C. J. Walker, Mary Church Terrell, Ava Stagger, Pura Belpre, writer, Bessie Coleman, Aviator, and other women in music, Pearl Bailey, Mariam Anderson, Condoleezza Rice, Susan Rice, Michelle Obama, Carolyn Moseley Braun, Ketanji Brown-Jackson, Vice-President harris, Marlon Williams, Sarah Vaughn, and Lena Horne, Rosetta Dunning, Nzinga, Yaa Asantewaa, "Bottom Belly" and Queen Mary, as well as Crystal lying beside the Runaway Slave Samuel Carson at Anson Manso in Ghana. Let us pay a special tribute to Pan-Africanist Joycelyn Loncke and her sister Yvonne Loncke-Waite, Veronica Corbett, Doris Alexander and Priscilla Maddox, Bernice Green and Viola Sanders, all the School Nurses. They are all so beautiful and its so hard to snub a beautiful woman. As Winston Churchill said: "It is hard, if not impossible, to snub a beautiful woman – they remain beautiful and the rebuke recoils." Let us remember the Bible says: "A virtuous woman is a crown to her husband." George Meredith (1829-1909) believed: "A witty woman is a treasure; a witty beauty is a power" and Wordsworth opined as so many here recounted: "A perfect woman, nobly planned, To warm, to comfort and command." So, to coin a phrase from Charles Farrar Browne (1834-1867), "The female woman is one of the greatest institutions of which

CELEBRATING
DR. BEN-JOCHANNAN

this land can boast." The black man can echo similar sentiments as he cherishes, appreciates and is thankful for his woman, lover, heart throb, charming companion and fine specimen of nature. And, here we can insert Barack and Michelle Obama. Of course, dont ever cross them, for as William Congreve (1670-1729) affirmed: "Heaven has no rage like love to hatred turned, Nor hell a fury like a woman scorned."

The African-American male is therefore fortunate to have such powerful women to stand with, beside and behind him, to help guide his endeavors. Perhaps William Dean Howells (1837-1920) was right when he said: They were Americans, and they knew how to worship a woman." Therefore, this tribute to these women is well deserved. There are conduits in the tradition of strong Black women bequeathing the strong yet tender and ferocious African womanism so essential in the American experience. Its been said in this year of the tenth anniversary of the **Million Man March** we must have women this time for they were so essential in the March on October 16, 1995. Black men, make your women proud, they understand!

Dr. Ben's Photo 41a. Aswan. Erik Monderson on the Cornice at Aswan in 2018.

FREDERICK MONDERSON

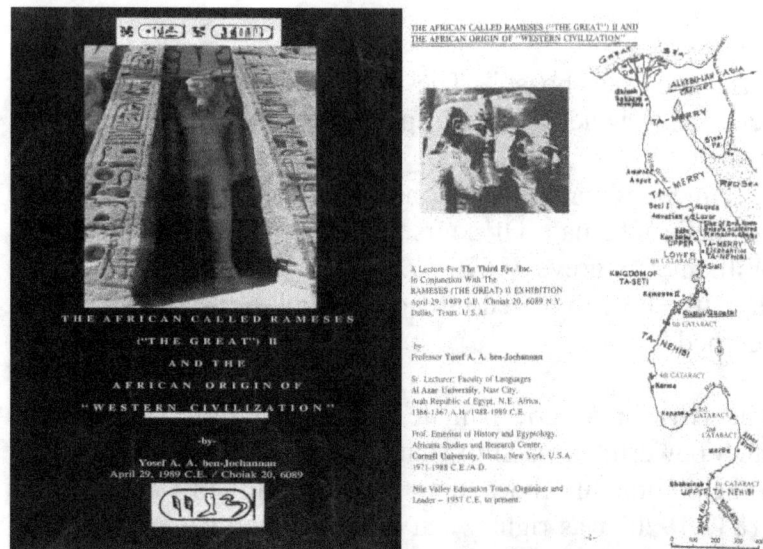

Dr. Ben's Books 3. THE AFRICAN CALLED RAMESES ("THE Great") II AND THE AFRICAN ORIGIN OF "WESTERN CIVILIZATION" (1990).

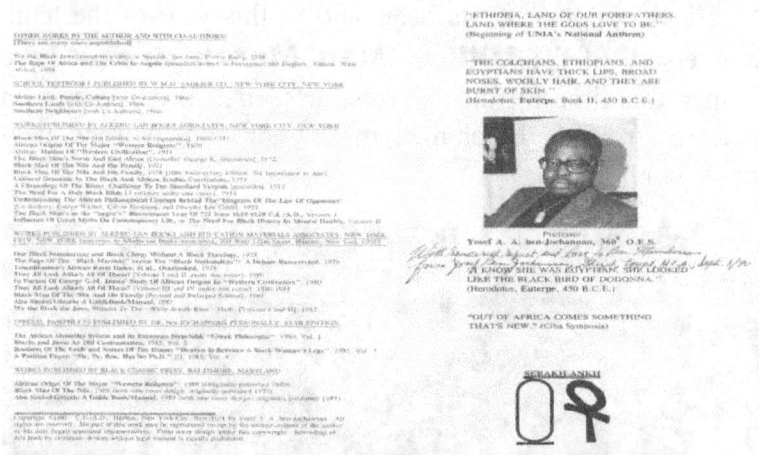

Dr. Ben's Books 3. THE AFRICAN CALLED RAMESES ("THE Great") II AND THE AFRICAN ORIGIN OF "WESTERN CIVILIZATION."
Overleaf. Notice the Author's autograph for Dr. Fred Monderson.

CELEBRATING
DR. BEN-JOCHANNAN

10. DR. FRED MONDERSON PRESENTS HIS SECOND MEMORIAL DAY

TRIBUTE TO Dr. Yosef A.A. ben-Jochannan "LETS LIBERATE THE TEMPLE!"
SUNDAY MAY 30, 2010 - 3:00-6:00 pm}
MONDAY MAY 31, 2010 - 3:00-6:00 pm)
TRUE SOUTH BOOKS
492 Nostrand Avenue (Halsey and Hancock)
truesouthbooks@aol.com

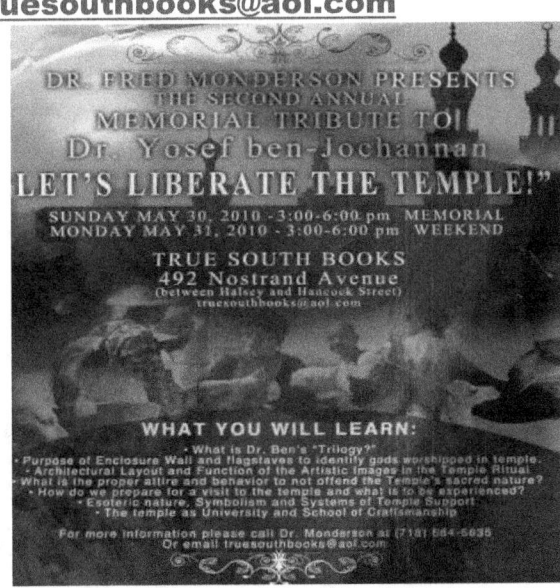

What You Will Learn:
- What is the proper attire and behavior to not offend the Temple's sacred nature?
- How do we prepare for a visit to the temple and what is to be experienced?
- What is Dr. Ben's "Trilogy?"

FREDERICK MONDERSON

- Purpose of Enclosure Wall and flagstaves to identify Gods worshipped in temple.
- Architectural Layout and Function of the Artistic Images in the Temple Ritual
- Esoteric nature, Symbolism and Systems of Temple Support
- The temple as University and School of Craftsmanship For more information please call Dr. Monderson at (718) 564-5635 Or email truesouthbooks@aol.com

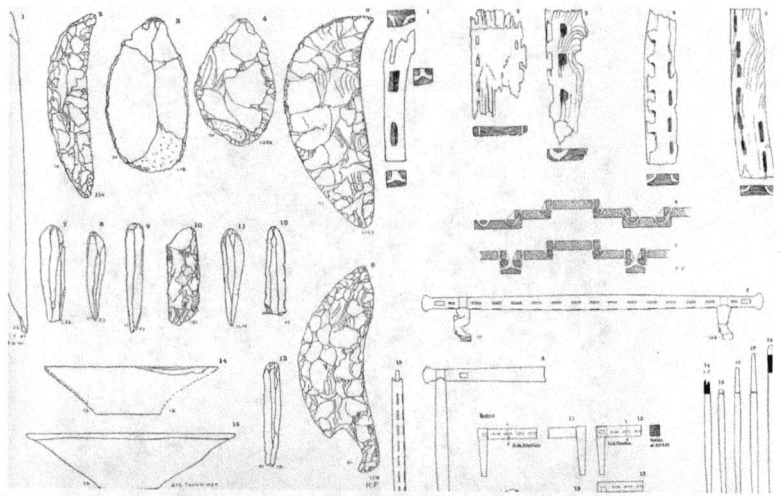

Dr. Ben's Illustration 14. Tarkhan. Worked Flints, Copper Bowls (left); and, Tarkhan. House Timbers, Bed Frame, Arrows in W.M.F. Petrie and A.H. Gardiner *Tarkhan I and Memphis V* (1913).

CELEBRATING DR. BEN-JOCHANNAN

Of my own knowledge, "An Education Is Not Necessary What One Must Ingest, Very Often It Is Mostly What One Must Expel" [a paraphrasing of Marcus Mozaiab Garvey's Philosophical Concept on "Education"]. Everything I have written in this "Guide Book/Manual" has nothing to do with any type of "Degree" from any study within "Western Academia". This work is for an "African Reading Audience" -- check yourself by the "Mirror Test". Remember , "We came from the beginning of the Nile [Blue and White] River Valley where God Hapi Dwells, at the foothills of the Mountain Of The Moon".

The Author [1]

Yosef A. A. ben-Jochannan, 360° O.E.S.

[1]. Professor of History and Egyptology, First World Alliance School of African Thought; Adjunct Professor of History and Egyptology, Africana Studies and Research Center, Cornell University; and Adjunct Associate Professor of History, Malcolm-King, Jr. College Harlem Extension.

Dr. Ben's statement about his intent and purpose for writing *Abu Simbel to Ghizeh Guide Book and Manual.*

FREDERICK MONDERSON

11. THE EGYPTIAN TEMPLE
By
Dr. Fred Monderson

Dr. Ben always emphasized, when on trips to Egypt and at other time, that his students pay particular attention to the architectural features of the temple. This way, with the right preparation, visitors get a deeper understanding of the esoteric and spiritual meaning of some of the divinely inspired structures. At Karnak Temple in particular, he advised his students visit the Hypostyle Hall some five or six times to really comprehend the true significance of this important hub of the temple. He insisted we ask questions of the Guides and in the after-site lecture he would explain much that was not explained and still remained mysterious. As such,

The Egyptian temple was one of the most fascinating structures of the ancient Nile Valley civilization of Kemet, Tawi (the two lands), and modern Egypt. Not simply a repository for the God worshipped therein, but its religiosity also shaped the beliefs and practices of the culture that has impacted heavily on the consciousness of man throughout history. The temple helped expand architectural designs, the extraction and transportation of building stone and the ancillary crafts that decorated and made livable the enclosure. The attendant great occurrences connected with the temple depended heavily on the Nile River whose foundational gifts flowed as cultural effluence from the bosom of Africa. Thus, this phenomenal Nile Valley experience was an African and by todays standards, Black culture, first of its kind to become conscious of its intellectual, philosophical, esoteric, religious and spiritual creativity. Africans of ancient Kemet along the Nile unquestionably enlightened the world through religious thought and practice, theosophy, theology, metaphysics and

CELEBRATING DR. BEN-JOCHANNAN

social, scientific and material accomplishments! As much, argued the great African intellect Cheikh Anta Diop in systematic, interdisciplinary, erudite, irrefutable and well thought-out scholarship entitled *African Origin of Civilization: Myth or Reality*. A number of dedicated African and African-American writers including Martin Delaney, W.E.B. DuBois, Carter G. Woodson, George G.M. James, Yosef ben-Jochannan, George Simmonds, malana Karenga, Ben Carruthers, John H. Clarke, Theophile Obenga, Molefi Asante and Ivan Van Sertima, after many years of research and teaching, have asserted the exact idea. This then, is the idea to advocate!

Dr. Ben's Photo 42. Aswan. Panoramic view of the Nile River and sailing boats, crews ships and highlands in the background.

FREDERICK MONDERSON

Dr. Ben's Photo 43. Aswan. Panoramic view from the balcony of the Old Cataract with the Oberoi Hotel far in the background.

Dr. Ben's Photo 44. Aswan. Another view from the river, this time the entrance to the Old Cataract Hotel.

CELEBRATING
DR. BEN-JOCHANNAN

Dr. Ben's Photo 45. Again, from the Nile, the "Old" and "Old" New Cataract, Hotels.

Dr. Ben's Photo 46. **Aswan**. The Mausoleum of Aga Khan on the highland across the river.

FREDERICK MONDERSON

Dr. Ben's Photo 47. Aswan. Feluccas moored across the river as others ply the majestic Nile scenery, with the Mausoleum far off in the distance.

The great achievement and gift of this North-east African culture was its theosophical, religious, architectural and moral genius embodied in the ancient Egyptian or Kemetic temple whose equilibrium was dictated by the profound social and philosophical principle of Ma'at. The Egyptian temple, therefore, was creative process, a work of art! This creation, unlike the Jewish synagogue, Greek or Roman Temple, Muslim Mosque, or Christian Cathedral uniquely manifested principles, principalities and powers that still evokes and exudes profound theological and cosmological spiritualism, posing thoughtful questions for scholars to this day seeking to define it. It was an edifice essentially erected by a king in honor of some divinity. Sometimes it was in his honor to be worshipped as a divinity upon his death, or dedicated to a triad of divinities, to whom he wished to pay special homage. This is either in return for benefits received or for some future favors. In the sculptures and paintings on the wall panels and columns of various temples, the king is shown as the principal figure. He is shown waging war with the enemies of Egypt

CELEBRATING
DR. BEN-JOCHANNAN

who were brought home as captives. At other times of peace, he offers gifts and sacrifices. The prayers are said in his name. He leads the procession in which are carried the statues and emblems of the divinities. Therefore, whether cult, mortuary, sun, rock, valley, or processional temple, even "birth houses" and "Soul houses" that deserve mention, these structures were an integral part of the Nile Valley culture that helped shape the morality and religious beliefs and practices of these ancient African people. The temple therefore came to play an important part in fostering much of civilization development we associate with ancient Egypt.

Dr. Ben's Papyrus 5. A priest in leopard skin pours a libation and holds an incenser before a "Table of Offerings" to enthroned Queen wearing a Queen Mother Crown (above); and below, a funeral scene with Anubis administering to the deceased as his bier is being drawn by bulls.

All this notwithstanding, the idea of the Egyptian temple is an evolved concept dating to the time of the emergence of the Gods who needed to be sheltered on earth and they instructed their adherents of the specifications and dynamics of their homes. Their priests, in turn, were active and inspired creators of the civilization and by the time of the Old kingdom had begun to play an important role not simply in religious, mortuary but also in civic and social matters. So much so, for that time, Indus Khamit Kush in *The Missing Pages of "History"* (1993: 25) quote Robert Forest Wilson in *The Living Pageant of the Nile* (The Bobs Merrill Company, Indianapolis, 1924, p. 31) who wrote, by this first great flowering of Egyptian culture: "She had refined her system of law and government, invented taxation, developed an intricate economic system, vastly expanded the tastes and needs of her individuals, gone into foreign trade, applied state aid to agriculture, made a start with most of the common sciences, produced philosophers, erected some of the mightiest buildings the world has ever seen, discovered beauty in art, and done a thousand other things – and over the face of the rest of the earth the primeval darkness yet rested." In all this unfolding the temple played a crucial role for the priests were the great teachers and philosophers of the society.

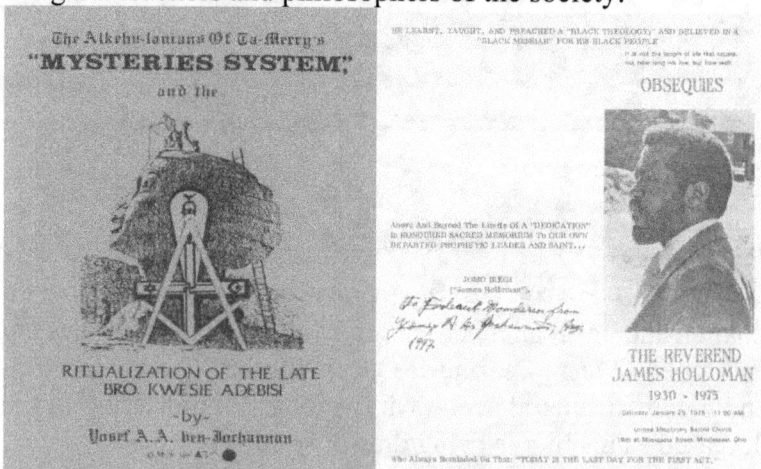

Dr. Ben's Books 4. **The Alkebu-lanians of Ta-Merrys "MYSTERIES SYSTEM" and the RITUALIZATION OF THE LATE BRO. KWESIE ADEBISI** (1981). Note Dr. Ben's endorsement of most of his books to his early students and a scholar, Dr. Monderson.

CELEBRATING DR. BEN-JOCHANNAN

As the art of temple building developed, unfolding within the sacred enclosure, no public worship was performed, the faithful did not congregate for public prayer, and no commoner was admitted into the inner portals of the temple except the priests who performed temple business. Individuals high in the social orders were welcomed into the Great Open Court, but no further! Nonetheless, writes Maspero, the "Temple was built as an image of the world, as the Egyptian imagined it to be." Importantly, Erman (1907: 6) in commenting on the temple in this early age of the world or in the consciousness of the ancient Egyptians as early as of predynastic times, notes: "Their temples were huts with walls of plaited wicker work; the front of the roof was adorned with projecting wooden beams. A few short posts and two high masts in front of the building were added to provide shelter decoration. The altar consisted of a reed mat, and for the celebration of festivals, simple bowers were erected."

Dr. Ben's Papyrus 6. A female deceased female before the "Scales of Justice;" before Thoth as a Baboon; and presenting an offering to Osiris in White Crown with Isis and Nephthys at his rear as the vulture with Uraeus soars overhead.

FREDERICK MONDERSON

Dr. Ben's Photo 48. Aswan. In the Oberoi Hotel dining room replicas of the Gods Amon and Horus are as shown. What do these Upper Egyptian, Nubian natives know that most others, especially in Europe and America, don't?

CELEBRATING
DR. BEN-JOCHANNAN

Dr. Ben's Photo 49. Aswan. Oberoi Hotel. Perhaps the Natives know something that Cairo folks and others do not!

FREDERICK MONDERSON

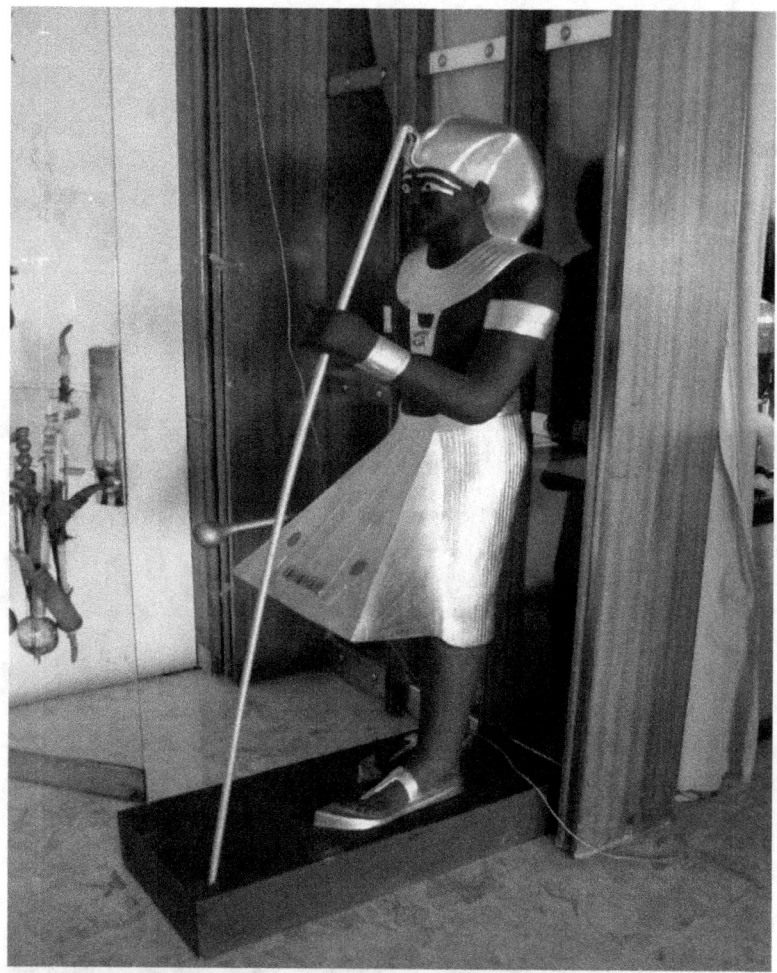

Dr. Ben's Photo 50. Aswan. Oberoi Hotel. An image of the Tutankhamon statue found guarding the Kings body into the Afterlife!

Additionally, Aldred (1980: 144) wrote: "The Egyptian temple, the God's house, had its origins in the prehistoric reed or palm-leaf both, similar to the maize-stalk shelter that the peasant even today erects in his fields to shield his beasts and himself from the cold winds of winter and the burning heat of summer. In the beginning, the God had arisen on the primeval

CELEBRATING
DR. BEN-JOCHANNAN

mound above the waters of Chaos, and by magic the shrine was built around him with a fence to keep off intruders, and a rag of cloth on a pole to show that the place was sacred and taboo. As the work of creation continued and light appeared on the face of the waters, the God of the Void lifted the sky from the new marshy earth, and kept it in position on its four pole-like supports. Thus the temple as the abode of the God grew to its final form, not as an architectural concept so much as myth made tangible in stone. This finite model of the universe at its beginning is visible in the primal Egyptian temple, and determines its decoration. The sanctuary, housing the image of the God, is built on the highest point of the ground, on a sort of hillock representing the primeval mound, and is a stone interpretation of the prehistoric reed hut, which is clearly discernible as a small house within larger dwelling. Except here in the elemental darkness prevailing before the First Time."

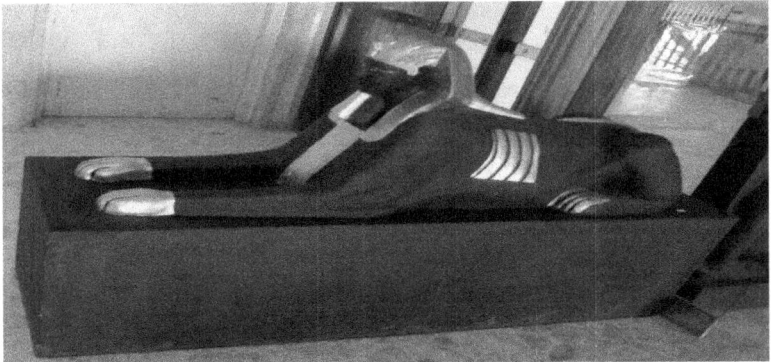

Dr. Ben's Photo 51. Aswan. Sphinx and Pedestal bear same color.

Sauneron in Posener (1962: 281) offers another view: "The Egyptian temple was a functional building, devoted to the most essential work of earthly life, namely, the maintenance of the creation. Obscure forces of chaos existed before the world was created, and, although they were cast away to the outer edge of the world, they nevertheless continued to threaten it; the equilibrium which maintained the visible world and the various forms of life was the fact of a creation daily renewed. Every evening, in the darkness, the world again was in danger of falling into a sleep from which there would be no awakening, the return of the sun the next morning happily drove away the risk. Only the Gods, by their ceaseless efforts, preserved the precarious existence of this essential vulnerable universe. These Gods, universal forces in different places under different forms, lived on earth in their "houses" – the temples. The function of this building and of its personnel was to protect the Gods from attacks by hostile forces, to nourish them and keep them in perfect condition, in order to facilitate their cosmic task and to keep from them any influence which could impede their action."

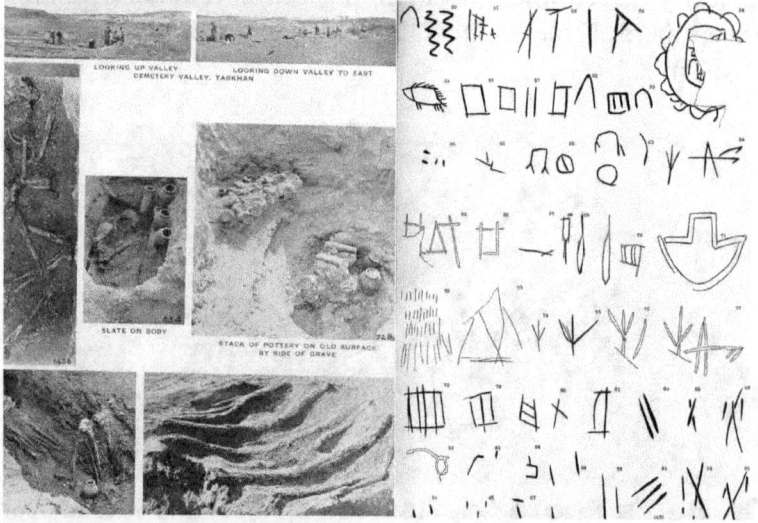

Dr. Ben's Illustration 15. Tarkhan. Different views of the Cemetery Valley at Tarkhan showing men at work, slate on body and stacks of pottery on old surface by side of grave, etc. (left); and, Pottery marks from the 1st Dynasty in W.M.F. Petrie's *Tarkhan II* (1914).

CELEBRATING DR. BEN-JOCHANNAN

Aldred says further (1980: 145) in his explanation: "By the time of the New Kingdom, most of the local divinities had become solarized under the influence of the theologians of Heliopolis, and had attached to themselves the name of Re Horakhty, the active aspect of the sun-God, so that forms like Amon-re, Sobek-re and Mentu-re are now found. The sun God, however, was worshipped at an altar set in a colonnaded court under the open sky where he was lord. The architecture was divinely inspired and with space for the principal Gods, the buildings became complex with small rooms for secondary Gods, statues, dim lights, maze of halls, and arrangement of trick doors, as well as stairs to the roof. There were also side rooms for keeping garments, jewelry, and cult objects for the religious ceremonies on altars."

Erman (1907: 40-41) again offers his view regarding the temple structure within the enclosure and the principal gateway with its propylon or pylon entrance. "Behind this gateway lay the first large space, an open court surrounded by colonnades. Here the great festivals were celebrated, in which a large number of citizens were entitled to take part. Behind this court there was a hall supported by columns, the place appointed for all manner of ceremonies, and behind this again lay the holy of holies, the chamber where the statue of the God had his dwelling. In adjoining apartments were the statues of the wife and son of the God. This was the essential part of the temple, naturally there would be various additional chambers to contain the sacred utensils, and for special purposes of the religious cults. A further characteristic of every temple is that from front to rear each apartment was less lofty and light than the preceding. Into the court the Egyptian sun blazed with uninterrupted splendor, in the halls its light was admitted to a modified extent through the entrance and through the windows in the roof; in the holy of holies reigned profound darkness."

FREDERICK MONDERSON

Dr. Ben's Photo 52. Aswan. Nubian Museum. Image of Khepre pushing the "Dung of Life."

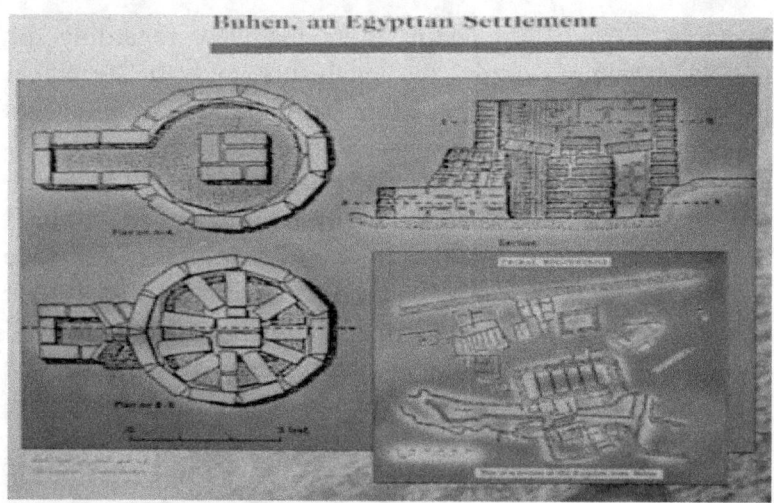

Dr. Ben's Photo 53. Aswan. Nubian Museum. Replica of an Egyptian Settlement at Buhen in Nubia, from the Middle Kingdom onward.

CELEBRATING
DR. BEN-JOCHANNAN

> The Nile Valley has been carved by the passage of the Nile driving northward from Central Africa and Ethiopia over many thousands of years, and formed by a series of drainage systems finding their ways to the sea.
>
> The River Nile, is fed by three main tributaries: the parent stream, the White Nile, rising in lake Victoria, the smallest stream the Atbara, joining the river above the Fifth Cataract near Berber, and the Blue Nile joining Khartoum in Sudan, that gives the river its character.
>
> The Blue Nile rises in lake Tana in Ethiopia, though its head unnavigable as it flows waters. As it sweeps northwards it carries alluvial silt with it. Once passed the six cataracts, it flows into the plains of Egypt flooding the river banks. As it recedes, it leaves behind a rich belt of fertile silt which the ancient Egyptians called Kemet (the black land). As it continues northward, the torrent of the river slows and fans out to form the Delta. From Aswan the Nile flows between cliffs forming the boundaries of the valley. When it reaches Cairo, it is divided to flow north-east to Damietta and the sea, and north-west to Rosetta.
>
> Within this bounteous patch the twin rivers lie four large sheets of water, lakes Burollos, Idku, Mariout and Manzala. Only in 1971 was the water of the Nile partially tamed. The building of the High Dam in Aswan completely controls the river as it holds back the annual flood water. Consequently, it has helped to creat the largest man-made lake in the word: The High Dam Lake which has changed the fate and the future of Egypt.

Dr. Ben's Photo 54. Aswan. Nubian Museum. Information graphic about the Niles significance that determins the future of Egypt and Sudan.

FREDERICK MONDERSON

Archaeologists stumbled on several evidences indicating that common cultural features dominated the Nile Valley, north and south, during the Paleolithic Period. For example, the valley's inhabitants were fishermen and hunters of wild animals such as gazelles, antelopes, giraffes and elephants. Hunting tools and rock carvings refer to the daily activities of these inhabitants at the time. They also used to live in temporary communities near the river. Archaeologists found remains of these inhabitants' temporary communities in Afia, Khour Daoud, Amada, Wadi E-Sebou'o and Toshka.

About 11,000 years ago Nubians underwent new changes in their civilisation.

Antiquities unearthed in Napth, 45 km west of Abu Simbel, included homes and cemeteries, a clear indication referring to the fact that the Nubians established settled communities marked by the Neolithic Period.

However, Lower Nubia's cultural and traditional features were influenced by Upper Egypt's civilisation. Pottery vessels found in the Second Cataract area are similar to vessels common in Badari, Upper Egypt in 5000-4500 B.C. Moreover, Naqada's First and Second Culture, which flourished in Upper Egypt prior to the prehistory period, were common in several areas in Nubia such as E-Sebou, Aniba and Abu Simbel.

Dr. Ben's Photo 55. **Aswan**. Nubian Museum. Graphic indicates significance of Nubia and early culture along the upper reaches of the Nile River.

CELEBRATING DR. BEN-JOCHANNAN

After a successful career in archaeology, Margaret Murray in *The Splendor that was Egypt* (1949) (1957: 232-33) offered an experienced view: "The founding of a temple was a religious ceremony, performed by the Pharaoh in person assisted by the Goddess Seshat, who was probably represented by the Queen. Each of them held an end of the measuring-cord and marked on the ground the dimensions of the temple. After the measurements had been traced out a sand-bed was made, and on this rough stone blocks were laid to form the foundations. At each corner of the building, and wherever an internal wall touched the outside wall, foundation deposits were placed under the blocks. These deposits consisted of models of all the tools and implements used in the building of the temple, modes of offerings, and scarabs or plaques bearing the name of the royal founder. Even when a temple has been completely destroyed and the foundation blocks removed, it is possible to recover the plan and the name of the founder by means of the foundation deposits. The foundation blocks were scored with lines on the upper surface, which had been smoothed, and on these lines the walls were built. As the walls rose in height earth ramps were built against them, which dragged the stones on rollers. Pillars were built in the same way with ramps. This method of raising blocks of stone to the desired level is as early as the pyramids. It is uncertain whether a temple was built from a plan drawn out by the architect before beginning the work; if so all such plans have perished. If not, then one is confronted with the fact that the architects of those early days were capable of planning a temple or pyramid completely, including the lengths of ramps required, and carrying it through to completion without even a note."

Libraries were an important part of any temple, for scholars congregated in these religious institutions that were also considered "Colleges." Some temples had a well, Nilometer, granaries and dwellings for the temple staff. To help meet the needs of the daily rituals, gardens provided fresh flowers for the temple service and food for the staff. Granaries and storehouses were filled with staff-produce, tribute and taxes in kind looked-over by large contingents of scribes, overseers and managers in charge of administration. Significant industries or schools of arts and crafts were developed in these enclosures. Temples were frequently provided with allocations of prisoners-of-wars for work on its lands. They were also recipients of kingly and noble endowments for worship and mortuary cults, and must also have enjoyed tax-free status. While there were principally God or worship temples, Aldred (1980: 146) elucidates further regarding New Kingdom mortuary building practices: "The resources that had formerly been devoted to the building of the kings pyramid complexes now went into their mortuary temples, built along the desert margin of the western riverbank at Thebes, the birthplace of their founder Amosis. These were separated from their actual burial places, which from the reign of Tuthmosis I were hewn into the rocky walls of a wadi now known as the Valley of the Kings, about a mile to the west, beneath the dominating peak of a natural pyramid. The tombs themselves were decorated in painted relief, or with walls and ceiling paintings, of scenes from the sacred books that, under the influence of Heliopolis, now governed ideas on the royal destiny ...."

Besides representations of kings, figures of the Gods are commonly found. The age also saw a growth of ideas of divinities grouped into "Triads," consisting of a God, his consort and their child. Thus, the concept of the Holy Family with the child was first experienced on the Nile River.

The library was essential to every temple for the daily ritual, as well as aiding in the function as universities for training other priests, government bureaucrats, nobles and physicians. Hurry (1928) noted: "Every temple had a library. " In *Nile*

CELEBRATING DR. BEN-JOCHANNAN

Valley Civilizations (1985, 1986) Ivan Van Sertima informed: "One of the great temples of Luxor housed an elite faculty of priest-professors and at one time catered to an estimated 80,000 students at all grade levels. Temples were at teh center of religion, politics and education. The temple-university had a huge library and its faculty, called teachers of mysteries, were divided into five departments: astronomy and astrology; geography; geology; philosophy and theology; law and communication. "In addition," Shaw and Nicholson (1995: 285-86) add, the temple was also "considered to be an architectural metaphor both for the universe and for the process of creation itself. The floor gradually rose, passing through forests of plant-form columns and roofed by images of the constellations or the body of the sky-Goddess Nut, allowing the priests to ascend gradually from the outermost edge of the universe towards the sanctuary, which was a symbol of the inner core of creation, the Primeval mound on which the creator-God first brought the world into being."

Even further, White (1980: 50-51) believed: "The temple performed the same role in ancient Egypt as the cathedral in mediaeval Europe. It was the dual source of cultural inspiration and physical employment. As in mediaeval Europe, with the exception of the estates of the feudal barons almost the entire ownership of land and property was concentrated in the hands of the king with his chief priests. In theory, the king held the Black Land in trusteeship for his fellow Gods. His chief priests were therefore his principal tenants, although they gradually became more or less the unchallenged rulers of their own domains-in the way that the Abbot of Tintern or Rievaulx would carry out his ecclesiastic duties while superintending the agriculture, stock-breeding and building-work throughout his wide province. The main temples acted not only as the distributors of their own bounty, but of the royal bounty too. An entire population of civil servants, scribes, policemen, craftsmen, artisans, and artists was fed and clothed from the priestly granaries and storerooms. The chief priests collected taxes on behalf of the king and doled out rewards and necessities as they saw fit. They were thus the instruments and regulators of the state economy and wielded enormous power."

Thus, it is easier to speak about the ancient Kemet-Egyptian temple idea, rather than say what it really is, since it meant many things.

Understandably, one idea, "The Trinity," dominated the purpose, function and meaning of the temple. Principally, in his explanation of the "Trinity" Mariette-Bey states in the following statement: "Egyptian temples are always dedicated to three Gods. It is what Champollion calls the Triad. The first is the male principle, the second is the female principle, and the third is the offspring of the other two. But these three deities are blended into one. The father engenders himself in the womb of the mother and thus at once becomes his own father and his own son. Thereby are expressed the un-createdness and the eternity of the being who has had no beginning and shall have no end."

Dr. Ben's Photo 56. **Aswan**. Part of the beautiful Garden at Old Cataract Hotel.

CELEBRATING DR. BEN-JOCHANNAN

Dr. Ben's Books 5. Abu Simbel to Ghizeh: A Guide Book and Manual (1986, 1989). Notice the Author's autograph. Note, Dr. Ben's autograph of *Abu Simbel to Ghizeh* to Dr. Fred Monderson.

But who were these people, these early Africans resident in the Nile Valley in Northeast Africa? To answer this question, John Jackson (1970: 153), quoting Gerald Massey, author of *A Book of the Beginnings*, Vol. I, p. 4, wrote: "Egypt is often called Kam, the black land, and Kam does signify black, the name probably applied to the earliest inhabitants whose type is the Kam or Khem of the Hebrew writers."

Even more, Jackson (1970: 153-54) wrote: "It will be maintained in this book that the oldest mythology, religion, symbols, language had their birthplace in Africa, that the primitive race of Kam came thence, and the civilization in Egypt, emanated from that country and spread over the world. The most reasonable view on the evolutionary theory ... is that the black race is the most ancient, and that Africa is the primordial home." In addition, Jackson (1970: 154) continued: "The Hebrew Scriptures, among their other fragments of ancient lore, are very emphatic in deriving the line of Mizraim from Ham or Kam, the black type coupled with Kush, another form of the black. They give no countenance to the theory of Asiatic origin of Noah, Mizraim is the son of Ham, i.e., of Kam, the black race."

Now, to further understand the temple in ancient Kemet/Egypt, it can also be viewed within the context of the principle of sculptural decoration. On the temple walls, pictures are arranged symmetrically side by side. Several series of pictures are disposed in tiers one above the other and cover the walls of chambers from top to bottom. The role of the king is thus key as he "presents an offering (a table laden with victuals, flowers, fruits and emblems) and solicits a favor from the God. In his answer the God grants the gift that is prayed for." Thus, decoration of the temple consists of nothing more than an act of adoration from the king. As such, a temple can be both a primordial hill or the "exclusive personal monument of the king by whom it was founded or decorated." Reinforcing this view, foundation deposits and founders emblems, tools, food, and blood from sacrificial animals were deposited to ensure blessings to the temple.

At a later date, Anthony Browder in *African Contributions to Civilization* (1995: 120) displayed a superimposed figure of Rameses II on the Temple of Luxor and had this to say regarding the work of Schwaller de Lubicz who studied that temple with his wife and daughter Lucie, and "measured, recorded and drew every inch of the temple, including each stone, wall carving and statue." They produced *Le Temple de l'Homme (The Temple in Man) classic.* In this work, "Their combined research suggested that the temple was dedicated to the creation of man, and that the floor plan of the temple representative of the anatomical structure of man. Lucie Remy superimposed the skeletal framework of a statue of

CELEBRATING
DR. BEN-JOCHANNAN

Rameses II over the floor plan of the temple and discovered some interesting similarities. The open courtyard represents the legs; the hypostyle hall represents the thighs; the Peristyle court represents the abdomen and the inner temple represents the head. Within each segment of the temple, activities took place, which related to specific body functions. In the hall the king is generally shown in the pictures on one side and one or more divinities on the other."

"The worship consists of prayers, recited within the temple in the name of the king, and above all, of processions. In these processions which the king is supposed to head, are carried the insignia of the Gods, the coffers in which their statues are enclosed, and also the sacred barks which later are generally deposited in the temple, to be brought out on fete days. In the middle, concealed under a veil, stand the coffer within which lies the emblem, which no one must see. The processions are commonly held within the temple. They generally ascend the terraces and sometimes spread themselves inside the enclosure away from the prying eyes …. On rare occasions, the processions may be seen leaving the city and winding their way, either along the Nile or along a canal called the Sacred Canal, toward some other city more or less distant. Close to every temple is a lake. In all probability the lake played an important part in the procession and the sacred barks were deposited there, at least while the fete lasted."

These ancient Africans, therefore, were the genesis of their own genius who thought out the fundamental principles of religion as well as social and ethical practice and other dynamics of significance for salvation and development of their people. These "houses of life," that crafted its cosmological creation of the particular cult, grew from simple beginnings into huge and complex structures of stone particularly built and enhanced through captured imperial booty and endowments. As such then, the temple can be seen as a "royal proscenium, or ex voto that is a token of piety from the king who erected it in order to deserve the favor of the Gods. It is a kind of royal oratory and nothing more."

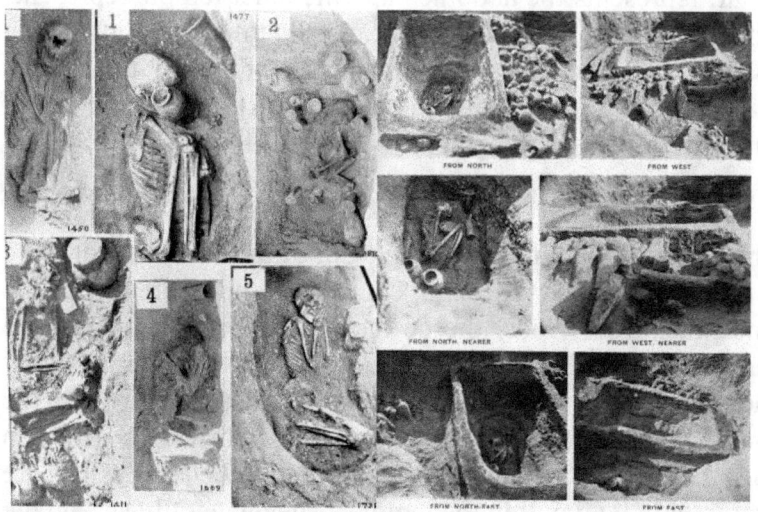

Dr. Ben's Illustration 19. Tarkhan. A burial with the body and "Goods of the Grave" viewed from different sides (left); and, Burials in various attitudes and with "Goods of the Grave" (right) in W.M.F. Petrie's *Tarkhan II* (1914)

Some two hundred years ago, in the aftermath of the American and French Revolutions, Napoleon invaded Egypt in "Carrying the war to the British." In the aftermath, the Rosetta Stone was discovered and with much effort this led to the decipherment of the ancient language by the Frenchman Champollion the Younger. His efforts gave birth to Egyptology and interest in the ancient culture. Within decades of that development, the discipline of archaeology significantly and systematically began the excavation and restoration of much of the ancient culture that also rescued existing temples and broadened our knowledge of their form

CELEBRATING
DR. BEN-JOCHANNAN

and function; erven recreating plans from bare outlines in the sand. Today, these excavated and restored edifices teach us much about the culture, structures, builders, functions, rituals, art and practical as well as the social and economic dynamics that prevailed therein.

Dr. Ben's Photo 57. Aswan. Pathway beside the Old Cataract and entrance to its beautiful Garden (left); and, front entrance to the Old Cataract Hotel.

As such, we now know the climate and geography was instrumental in dictating the types and nature of Egyptian temples. The landscape of Egypt is one of lines, vertical, horizontal or diagonal and thus columns and buildings within temple complexes were similarly utlay in vertical or horizontal, whose roofs were horizontal and pylons were sloping. There was little rain in Egypt, especially Upper Egypt, and hence the sky remained blue and this had something to do with the nature of its temple, mythology, religion and other forms of architecture. M.A. Murray's *Egyptian Temples* (London: Sampson Low, Marston and Co., Ltd., 1931: 1) explained, the climate impacted upon the psyche of the people and nature of building and other factors of the society. "It is a country of violent contrasts; the flat plain and

FREDERICK MONDERSON

vertical cliffs, the fertile fields and the dreary waste of desert, the brilliant sunshine and the dark shadows, the river which harbored edible fish and murderous crocodile; all these naturally had their effect on the mind of the Egyptian architect and showed themselves in the architecture."

We now know the temple consisted of four parts such as an outer court, an inner court, a vestibule and a shrine or sanctuary. In time however, the temple took on extra dimensions that were a result of the efforts of ruling families who vied with each other to please their God. In addition, support structures also played a role in temple life. Naturally, there were adjuncts to the temple within the enclosure wall such as the outside Avenue of Sphinxes linked by a canal from the Nile. Outside the same entrance gate, there might be another small temple or shrine, or even a or two. small obelisk

Essentially, there were two principal types of temples from the beginning of Egyptian history. One temple was dedicated to the God and another was dedicated to the king, though the latter, especially in the Old Kingdom was essentially associated with the mortuary cult. The God temple was always separate and was built in order that the God would be propitiated. The kings temple was designed to worship him when he died as then he became a God. If he lived long enough, he was worshipped when alive. Hence, the kings temple, in the earliest times was attached to his burial structure, as for example, in the pyramid complex. However, it in some cases it became a separate entity, certainly by the Middle and New Kingdoms times.

CELEBRATING
DR. BEN-JOCHANNAN

Dr. Ben's Photo 58. Aswan. Native Egyptian Guide Abdel Rady, "Shawki the Black," relaxes on way to the Temple of Isis.

Dr. Ben's Photo 59. Aswan. Nubian homes line the Nile (left); and, Visitors heading to the Temple of Isis (right).

1. Pre-dynastic Temples

These earliest God temples were made of perishable material and are only known from illustrations. In this respect, Murray states (1931: 2) regarding these early temples dedicated to a deity: "Of temples dedicated to a God none are in existence from the early periods, although the foundations of several are

FREDERICK MONDERSON

known; e.g., at Abydos there was a temple of Osiris in the Ist dynasty, at Hierakonpolis the temple of the sacred falcon was probably as early, at Bubastis the temple of the cat-Goddess is not later than the IVth dynasty, and the shrine of the crocodile-God in the Fayum had very primitive characters."

2. Old Kingdom Temples

The early temples dedicated to kings can be traced to the Old Kingdom and are a part of the burial apparatus. "As the primitive king or chief always had a better house than the common people, so the God who was superior to the king had a better house than the king; the original temple was then merely a finer hut than those used by human beings."

Thus, in this early period, temples were attached to pyramids and other royal burial places, and were intended for the worship of the dead king.

Dr. Ben's Temple Site Ticket 3. Philae Temple of Goddess Isis at Aswan.

As such, Petrie indicated: "At first the place of offerings was closely connected with the tomb, as shown by the large steles found at the tombs of the Ist dynasty; and such continue to be the case for the ordinary Egyptian in all times. But the place of offering to the kings was at the end of the IIIrd Dynasty...."

CELEBRATING DR. BEN-JOCHANNAN

3. Middle Kingdom Temples

Not much has survived of Middle Kingdom temples and those that are identified can only be done through plans of their faint outlines on the ground. The temple of Mentuhotep II was discovered in 1898 and excavated by Edouard Navile and H.R. Hall from 1903-1906. They determined, it is the oldest surviving temple at Thebes and the most complete of all Middle Kingdom temples. Hatshepsut's temple in the amphitheater was modeled on this structure, transitional from the Old to the New Kingdom building practice, during whose time it was still viable since her temple, instead of being in the center of the cirque is juxtaposed to Mentuhoteps and occupies more of the northern sector of the Deir el Bahari amphitheater. It is a wonderful structure and was richly decorated with a style that was very beautiful changing beliefs about the art of that period thought to be very archaic.

Dr. Ben's Papyrus 7. The complete Psychostasia where the deceased is introduced by Anubis (left) and stands before the "Scales of Justice" as Anubis adjusts the instrument with Am-Mit in his presence: Thoth records the findings; then Horus introduces the deceased to enthroned Osiris backed by Isis and Nephthys in his Shrine with a soaring hawk and the "four sons of Horus" on guard.

FREDERICK MONDERSON

4. New Kingdom Temples

With the expulsion of the Hyksos and triumph of Amon, or Amon-Ra, at the formation of the New Kingdom, temple building took on a new meaning, becoming more elaborate, complete, picturesque and built of more varied and durable stone. Begun in the Middle Kingdom, Karnak Temple, a principal God or worship temple, experienced its greatest development in the New Kingdom, though in its present form it took 2000 years to complete. Over this expansive period of "vegetative construction," all the elements and dynamics of an Egyptian temple came into play, particularly the ritual that remained essentiallyt intact as crafted in the beginning at Heliopolis under Ra worship influences.

The following are some features of the Egyptian temple such as at Karnak, at Thebes, in Upper Egypt. Indus Khamit Kush, author of *The Missing Pages of "His-Story"* writes in *What They Never Told You in History Class* (1983) quoting Desmond Stewart in *The Pyramids and Sphinx* pp. 61-62 regarding Karnak, "... the world's largest temple to the God, Amen-Re. The chief wonder of his temple was the Hypostyle Hall - a forest of 134 columns, some so massive that a hundred men could stand on their capitals, sixty-nine feet above the earth. But this vast hall was only the dominant feature, says Leonard Cottrell, of a building complex which would cover much of mid-Manhattan. Within the walls of the temple there would be room for St. Peters in Rome, the Milan Cathedral, and Notre Dame of Paris. The outer walls would comfortably enclose ten European cathedrals. The temple was constantly enlarged, embellished, and maintained from 2000 B.C. till the birth of Christ."

CELEBRATING
DR. BEN-JOCHANNAN

Dr. Ben's Photo 60. Aswan. Temple of Goddess Isis. The "Kiosk of Hadrian" as viewed from the Nile River.

Dr. Ben's Photo 61. Aswan. Temple of Goddess Isis. Walkway entrance to the Temple from the motor-launch that transports visitors.

Now, since the temple was built by the riverside, again, if we take Karnak as an example, the King would encounter the following when visiting:

1. Quay for greeting, ceremony and ritual.

2. Canal to move inland.

3. An "Avenue of Sphinxes" beyond the canal and while decorative, also provided philosophic and spiritual protective influences as one ascended to the entrance.

4. Obelisk and statues in front of the entrance as well as obelisks within the structure. Statues are of the monarch and some fortunate individual who distinguished himself in some exceptional way. Obelisks are monuments to the Sun God consisting of a pyramid on a high base. Sometimes they are decorated with gold or electrum on the apex, as those of Hatshepsut at Karnak, allowing them to be seen from great distances as reflected in sunlight.

5. Pylon – Wall enclosure. This is a gate. The number of entrances varies. Karnak had 4, Luxor 2, Edfu 1 and so on. The temple was also a refuge so that when the doors closed, it was difficult to get in. The idea was to protect the God and then the people inside its walls. On the Pylon were flagstaves that flew flags of the state, Nome and principal and subsidiary Gods worshipped within. Panes on the interior walls among other features depic the king being baptized before he could begin the daily ritual.

6. Courts – Oftentimes a Great Court possessed the following characteristics:

CELEBRATING DR. BEN-JOCHANNAN

a. An Altar used in outdoor ceremonies.

b. Sphinxes indicative of guardian forces sometimes with the head of a king or some animal, preferably a ram, as in the case at Karnak.

c. Seated and standing statues, generally of the king and deserving individuals.

d. Doors and supporting door posts, designed to give access and to inhibit the flow of people towards the inner reaches of the sacred space.

e. Jubilee Sed Heb Festival Court and Pavilion, in addition to the Great Court where the rejuvenation ceremony or festival was performed.

f. Chapels or Kiosks that are sometimes dedicated to the God or his Triad including the wife and child.

g. Columns or pillars are a decorative feature that also extends the reach, size or distance of the temple. It is considered a great honor to have ones name "written in the colonnade."

h. Portico to another Pylon – The Portico is simply a decorated entranceway to the pylon that some king wanted to add as an extension to an inner room. The Pylon, on the other hand, is a gateway of massive size that is sometimes decorated, but principallyseparates one section from the other as one ascends the inner realms of the temple. Karnak had 10 Pylons on two axes. The First Pylon at Karnak was undecorated because it was unfinished but the Second and especially the Third Pylon of Amenhotep III was decorated. Nonetheless, we should also ask, If the First Pylon and the Tenth Pylon are gates, should the east and north gates be considered Pylons as well and so numbered?

i. Hypostyle Hall of columns where the procession generally begins. It is often decorated with scenes of the ritual either depicting the king the divinity or receiving some blessing from the God; having his name written in the "Tree of Life" or some other boon. He naturally leads the procession of priests hoisting the Barque or he incenses the holy structure

j. Second Hypostyle Hall is a place where the procession also stops before proceeding further into the temple towards the sanctuary. Dendera is a good example.

k. Adjacent rooms for:

      a. Clothing

      b. Gold

      c. Vessels

      d. Liquid and solid offerings.

CELEBRATING DR. BEN-JOCHANNAN

e. Library with books of the ritual.

f. Subsidiary Gods represented in the illustration and in small temples on site.

g. Third Hypostyle Hall - Again, Dendera fits this description.

h. The Sanctuary where the God lives surrounded by corridors and doors for access and even stairways for roof access, up and down, where a Kiosk greets the God when he greets the sun in the morning.

i. On the outside a Sacred Lake, connected to the river via underground springs provide water for washing but also where the sacred boats are floated on festive occasions.

j. Quarters for priests, priestesses, stewards, scribes and singing women.

k. Schools for art and learning – calendars – measurement, etc.

l. Workshops producing cotton, dyes, statuary, woodwork, pottery, painting, basketry, matting, jewelry of gold and other precious stones, etc.

m. Gardens for pleasure, growing grape vines among other things as well as flowers for the daily temple ritual.

n. Nilometer also connected by underground springs but used for measuring the volume of the river that in turn determines levels of taxation.

o. Trees to provide shade and some fruit.

p. Chapels to other Gods

q. Decoration: Walls – Inside, Outside and some Ceilings, columns, pylons and enclosure wall with decorations in and outside.

r. The Sanctuary and rooms adjacent to the Sanctuary.

s. Kitchens and refractory for cooking and baking.

t. Wine Cellars for storage.

u. Granaries, store-houses for grain, oil, honey. Etc.

CELEBRATING DR. BEN-JOCHANNAN

    v. Treasury for hoarding the temples gold.

    w. Altar in the sanctuary or outdoors in the court.

    x. There could be a number of halls and minor courts leading to the Sanctuary. There is generally an area or court behind the Sanctuary.

    y. Calendar system for festivals, astronomy and Nile Watch to study the rivers behavior.

    z. The most important item in the temple, beside the Sanctuary is the axis line. In a temple such as Karnak, the axis runs east to west. Other temple axes, besides the east/west orientation is some variation of the north/south variation. Following the path of the sun, statues in proximity to the main axis face this center line. When there is ano ther axis, generally north to south, staues along that acis face the east/west axis not the north/south axis.

In addition, there may be residences for overseers, bakers and bakeries, boulevards, floors, pavement, gates, stelae, crypts and untold inscriptions and decorations. Naturally there were feasts and festivals celebrated therein and each followed a calendar pattern. Equally, there were barque stations for the ark of the deity, offering and oblation tables and furniture. Temples possessed ships, harbors, tributary territories, towns, magazines, slaves, cattle, geese, poultry, horses, vineyards, cultus utensils, as well as guards, archers, and even much more. The "Cachette Court" at Karnak, before the Seventh Pylon revealed thousands of states buried in water and discovered by the French Archaeologist Legrain in 1903, while doing clearance and repairs to the temple.

The mortuary temples at Thebes were temples dedicated to the king who upon his death became a God in his own right. Therefore, by building his temple he was oftentimes worshipped alive then dead and remembered. Unfortunately, many of these, for the major kings of the New Kingdom, were dismantled and used elsewhere after their death. However, Medinet Habu, built for Rameses III of the 20th Dynasty, is considered the "last major building project of the New Kingdom." This is so because no one came after to dismantle his temple. Processional Temples such as the "White Chapel," "Red Chapel" and several others, as well as kiosks as at Karnak, Luxor, etc., were resting places for the God while on the move. The "White Chapel" of Senusert I dates to the Middle Kingdom, 12th Dynasty and the "Red Chapel" of Hatshepsut to the 18th Dynasty, New Kingdom. Both of these are now repaired and on display in Karnak's Open Air Museum.

CELEBRATING DR. BEN-JOCHANNAN

Dr. Ben's Photo 62. Aswan. Temple of Goddess Isis. Dromos to the First Pylon showing another view of the Western Colonnade's 32 columns, each with a different capital and watermark showing the level reached by the Nile when the Temple was surmerged during the Inundation.

Dr. Ben's Photo 63. Aswan. Temple of Goddess Isis. Dromos to the First Pylon proper with 16 columns of the "First East Colonnade," to the right.

FREDERICK MONDERSON

Many Temples appear to have been oriented by the river; the main direction of the stream is to the north, but it naturally varies somewhat and runs occasionally east or west of north, the temples, therefore, also vary in their orientation. The rule, however, is that the temples lie parallel or at right angles to the river, e.g., Luxor and Karnak. The Astronomist Lockyer artgued in 1894, many temples were oriented toward some heavenly body or star.

In the temples of Thebes, which are almost entirely of the New Kingdom, the lighting of the hypostyle hall was by means of a clerestory. That is, a roofed hall with the central columns higher crating a clear-story, which, through the windows light entered the hall. Columns supported the nave of the hall. The temples were richly decorated on the inside and outside. On the outside the wars and struggle of the kings were depicted and on the inside the worship and ritual of the temples were depicted.

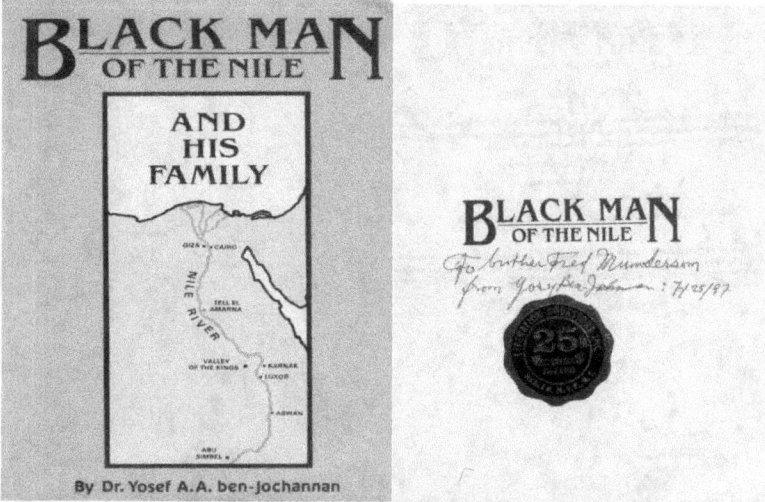

Dr. Ben's Books 6. Black Man of the Nile, (later) and His Family (1970, 1989). Note the Author's autograph to Dr. Fred Monderson.

CELEBRATING DR. BEN-JOCHANNAN

5. Graeco-Roman Temples

These were built by Nubian and Egyptian builders, working to Egyptian specifications dating to the earliest times and were supervised by Greeks and Roman overlords. Dendera, Edfu, Kom Ombo, Esneh, Philae, Kalabsha, were all built in Graeco-Roman times with new features, decorations and began to be inundated with illustrations depicting the ritual. Fortunately, these temples have helped preserve much of the cultural and religious history, giving evidence of the much earlier worship and practice.

E.A.E. Raymond's *The Mythical Origin of the Egyptian Temple* (1969) tells of the Edfu Documents on the History of the Egyptian Temple. Accordingly, on the walls of Egyptian temples of the Graeco-Roman period are inscribed "numerous ritual texts, among which occurs a series of texts that is found only in a very abbreviated form in certain of the Pharaonic temples." These sources are copies of much earlier material that go back to the earliest conception of the temple. "Those texts make it possible to reconstruct a reasonably complete history of the building of each temple concerned, a picture of the lay-out of the rooms and halls, and their ritual purpose and significance." Here we find the "Myth About the Domains and the Temple of the Falcon." This "myth is the contents of the first and second cosmogonical record and of a part of the fifth record which seems to have been originally included in the Sacred Book of the Early Primeval Age of Gods." The Edfu myth is the "unique source that discloses the Egyptian tradition concerning the origin of the sacred domains of the Falcon and the creation of his first temple."

FREDERICK MONDERSON

Another chapter of the *Mythical Origin of the Egyptian Temple* deals with the Myth about the Origin of the Temple of the Sun God.

"The 3rd, 4th and 5th Edfu cosmogonical records preserve a part of the myth described as the Coming of Re to his Mansion of *Ms-nht*. This myth concerns another period of the mythical age when the lands of the sacred domains were already in existence, and when the primeval houses of the Gods were found in places other than the original domain of the Falcon."

Smaller and more prolific in decoration, these late period temples added the Mammisi, or birth house, where the God was born. The decorations took on a different format as well during this new age in Egypt.

The Egyptian Temple, therefore, represented the philosophical, esoteric, cosmological and theogonic metaphysics of the cultural history of the Nile Valley experience. In that development the temple played a vital role in the development of science, building, trade, art, crafts, mathematics, mummification, astronomy, astrology and a whole lot more. The temple was the center of the intellectual lifeblood of the society and as such, it carried forth the growth and development of the culture with its insistence on religiosity and right behavior based on the philosophical and social axiom of *Ma'at*, viz., balance, order, goodness, truth, straightforwardness and respect and good judgment.

CELEBRATING DR. BEN-JOCHANNAN

Dr. Ben's Illustration20. Abydos. Inscriptions of Kings Ka, Narmer and Sam (left); and, the now famous 4 Bracelets on an arm from the Tomb of King Zer of the First Dynasty, left by early tomb robbers in W.M.F. Petrie's *The Royal Tombs of the Earliest Dynasties, Part II* (1901).

12. CELEBRATING DR. BEN" – Part I
By
Dr. Fred Monderson

When African people begin to count the stars in their heroic pantheon constellation, the large and small illumination emanating there from, Dr. Yosef Alfredo Antonio ben-Jochannan looms among the largest and most significant of these luminaries. While many of these "stars" manifest in politics, war, nationalism, religion, education and civil rights activism, etc., Dr. Ben, as he is affectionately called, excelled in intellectualism, praise of African womanhood, cultural conscious raising, unindingly challenged Westrn pillars of cultural genocidethe challenging of western pillars of cultural genocide depicted in the form of historical distortion, omission of meaningful historical contributions of Africans, blacks, and theresulting psychological damages to their heritage and futures such acts entail. Dr. Ben pioneered in recognition of the significance of indigenous naming of themselves, their cultural attainment and the geographical locations in which their genius originated all the fundamentals of civilization, such as religion, architecture, writing, art, medicine, agriculture, science, river travel and transportation of large stone and economics, among other forms of intellectual endeavors. He challenged, at great peril, financial and stigmatic, the onslaught of so-called "EGYPTOLOGISTS, AUTHORITIES ON AFRICA, SEMITICISTS, HAMITICISTS, WHITE LIBERAL HISTORIANS, AFRICANISTS," and the like of them. Yet, "NUBIANS" were, supposedly, the only indigenous Ethiopians (Blacks) the "NEGROPHOBES" conceded were "N-E-G-R-O-E-S" whatever this disgusting and nauseating term meant to the 16th or 17th century Portuguese RACISTS that invented it; a term which some of the worlds greatest "SEMITICISTS" and "CAUCASIANISTS" even breakdown to make the NUBIANS appear as "HAMITIC-TYPE CAUCASIANS, DARK-SKINNED CAUCASOIDS" and "NILOTIC HAMITES."

He frowned on the "SEMITIC NORTH AFRICA MYTH" and the equally ridiculous "CAUCASIAN NORTH AFRICA" which was "NEGRO-LESS." He severely criticized "EDUCATORS," "SCHOLARS," "AUTHORITIES ON AFRICA," characterizing them all as very sick minds! He was particularly incensed over "DARK SKINNED HAMNITIC EUROPEANS" and Seligman's *Races of Africa's* religious bigotry and Semitic racism as perpetuated by "AUTHORITIES," "LIBERAL HISTORIANS," "BLACK STUDIES PROFESSORS" who parrot racist and outmoded ideas of Africans, Africa and Egypt in the Nile Valley. Dr. Ben

CELEBRATING DR. BEN-JOCHANNAN

chose to "ignore the RACISTS actions and RELIGIOUS BIGOTRY of White and Black Jews, White and Black Christians, White or Black Muslims, in their bastardization and plagiarization of the history and heritage of my MOTHER-CONTINENT – Alkebu-lan." He spilled much ink on the Jewish Myth of Noahs curse of Black people!

In **The Black Man's North and East Africa** (1971) by Yosef A.A. ben-Jochannan and George Simmonds, originally published by Alkebu-lan and now re-printed by Black Classics Press, the Author's contend that there is much falsity and distortion in the manner in which the history of these regions is presented in the guise of "academic scholarship" by academicians, authorities and scholars, even men of the cloth as "Rabbi, Reverend, Minister, Priest, Iman." What is interesting about this ground breaking critique of the presentation of African history beginning in the 1940s but published in the 1970s, the Author's pull no punches but outline a scathing critique of academic falsity whose foundation is a complete distortion of the historical record whether preached particularly from the perspective of lay or religious history.

In this, *The Black Man's North and East Africa* is a wonderful *tour de force* challenge to western and American historical distortion and what the Author's call religious bigotry and racial prejudice. They take to task, the manner in which Egypt and Nile Valley culture in general is presented to represent the indigenous creators of that magnificent civilization in Ancient Africa. They present a very cogent argument to show ancient writers, and they show a whole slew of them, viz., Herodotus, Aeschylus, Strabo, Eratosthenes, Homer in the *Iliad* and *Odyssey*, Philostratus, Statius, Philo, Eusebius, Manetho, Josephus, Diodorus, Lucretius, Poenuhis, Agatharclude, and

FREDERICK MONDERSON

even the Church Fathers of Christianity, such as Tertullian, St. Cyprian, St. Augustine, among others, who never used the term Negro, Semite nor Hamite to describe the people of ancient Egypt, Nubia, Kush, the Nile Valley. Equally, the name the people themselves and the ancients called the land, Africa, is a late Roman nomenclature rather than the names of Olympia. Hesperia, Oceania, Corpyle, Ortygia. The Greeks and Romans called it Africa and Libya and the Ethiopians called Africa Alkebu-lan.

Dr. Ben's Photo 64. Aswan. Temple of Goddess Isis. View of the First Pylon and in the rear, First Pylon proper to the Temple of Isis.

CELEBRATING
DR. BEN-JOCHANNAN

Dr. Ben's Photo 65. Aswan. Temple of Goddess Isis. Beyond the First Pylon into the Goddess' Court, the Second East Colonnade with different column capitals, while further left, the inner face of the Goddess Temple's First Pylon.

Dr. Ben's Photo 66. Aswan. Temple of Goddess Isis. In the Godesses Court, the front of the Mammisi with its engaged columns with different capitals. Notice the protective uraei atop the entrance to the right. A similar one would have been at the opening to the left.

FREDERICK MONDERSON

In textual analysis, he states, "Xenophanes was the first to use physical characteristics as a point of racial identification of the Ethiopians rather than color of skin. Of this point, I cannot subscribe; for, what was it but PHYSICAL CHARACTERISTICS when Herodotus wrote ... the Colchians, Ethiopians and Egyptians have the most wooly-hair of all mankind." He continued that, "Herodotus wrote of the 'BLACK FLATTEN-NOSED ETHIOPIANS I MET...' etc. Even Strabo 17.1.2 and 17. 1.5 cites Eratosthenes works with regard to the Egyptians who fought against Cambyses and his Persian invaders of Merowe being BLACK (Ethiopian); this he wrote about c. 525 B.C.E. Further verification came from other Greeks who fought with the Ethiopians at the battle of Xerxes."

Dr. Ben argues further: "It is written that Aeschylus was the first of the Greeks to place the Ethiopian Kushites at a specific Geo-political boundary in Africa. This may have been very much true; but Ionian merchants and mercenaries who served in the army of Psammetichus I (otherwise known as "Psamtik" biblically), somewhere between the years 663-609 B.C.E., also described the Ethiopians they met in Africa, Egypt in particular, with respect to their geo-political setting." He is concerned, contemporary with the Egyptians, these writers never used such terms as "Negro, Hamitic, Semitic," etc., to describe these ancient Africans and the Author's show these are, and they criticize these, modern interpolations. In fact, the tone of the ancient commentators who used nothing but "Ethiopians" to describe the Africans, black people, contrasts remarkably well with the disparaging epithets moderns, fueled by racial hatred, distorted the evidence, omitted the facts and projected a description not found in the Egyptian, Greek or Roman lexicon. The racists invented disgusting terms as "Negro" not simply to disparage Africans and exclude them from Egypt, while misrepresenting even the religion the black man invented, claiming Judeo-Christian-Islamic origination

CELEBRATING
DR. BEN-JOCHANNAN

and underscoring white, Caucasian, blond hair, blue eyed, superiority in all forms of human creations, whether religious, scientific or social. For the most part, modern teaching casts ancient Egypt in a Graeco-Roman mold, using Roman terms describing even Pre-Roman developments in the Nile Valley.

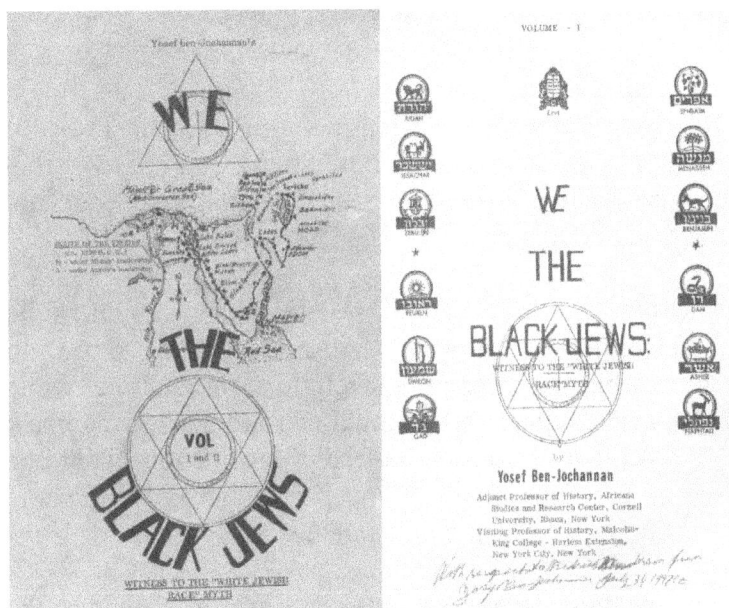

Dr. Ben's Books 7. We the Black Jews: Witness to the "White Jewish Race" Myth (1983). Notice the Author's autograph for Dr. Monderson.

This little book is a powerful resource for its identification of classical writers who commented on Egypt, Ethiopia and Ethiopians as well as the modern writers whose listed books are key to creating the foundation of falsity permeating current academic teaching, historical writing, newspaper reporting and museum representations of a "Negro-less" or "white only Egypt" that is far from the truth. In this, Dr. Ben takes to task a whole army of wrong doing "authorities on Africa" such as

FREDERICK MONDERSON

M.D.W. Jeffries; Elsy Leuzinger - *The Art of Africa*; Basil Davidson - *Africa in History*; Donald Weidner; Hayes of the Met; James H. Breasted; Alan Gardiner; Bovill - *The Golden Trade of the Moors*; C.P. Groves - *The Planting of Christianity in Africa*; even Frank Snowden's *Blacks in Antiquity*. Mentioning Waddell's *Manetho*, the traveler and commentator Leo Africanus, G.M. James' *Stolen Legacy*; James Frazier's *Golden Bough*; J.H. Lewis - *The Biology of the Negro* (Chicago, 1941); Poesner's *Dictionary of Egyptian Civilization*, Count Volney's *Ruins of Empire* and Baron Vivan Denon commentary and his painting a graphic image of the Sphinx before its facial disfigurement are issues Dr. Ben raised that scholars have had to contend with but not satisfactorily addressed.

Whether the proponents of a "white Egypt" are ignorant of the facts of history or knowingly misrepresent the record to proclaim white supremacy in religion and culture while waging psychological and spiritual warfare against the black race, fearful that if the truth be told, the white race would be viewed as covetous, harmful and perpetrators of a gigantic fraud is the line of argument he pursues.

Among the things Dr. Ben states, "Herodotus divided the Ethiopians into "MACROBIANS, ASMACHIANS" and "CAVE DWELLERS." As far as he was concerned, obviously, all the Ethiopians (Egyptians, Nubians, Carthaginians, Garamantes, Ghanians, Kushites, etc.), at least those he was aware of, were basically the same in physical characteristics (thick lips, broad noses, wooly hair) and color (black or "burnt skin"). At no instance in his writings did he relate to any of them being SEMETIC or HAMITIC, nor even CAUCASIAN. He was equally certain that many of the Ethiopians could be found in goodly numbers in parts all over the Eastern countries (Arabia Felix – the Arabian Peninsula, Persia, India, etc.).

CELEBRATING
DR. BEN-JOCHANNAN

The author writes, "Herodotus anthropological descriptions of the Ethiopians (so-called "NEGROES") were not only verified by Aeschylus, who also delineated Ethiopias geopolitical boundaries; he also wrote about the Ethiopians of Kush beliefs and mythology."

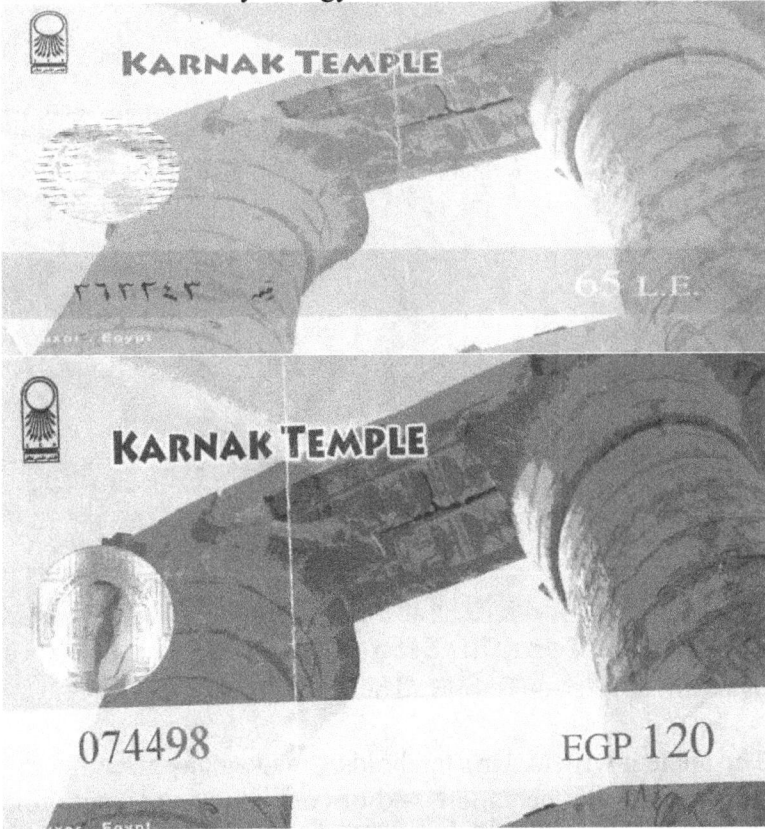

Dr. Ben's Temple Site Ticket 4. Karnak Temple, Home of God Amon (Amun, Amen, Amen-Ra, Amun-Ra, Amon-Ra). The Umbel capitals of the Processional Colonnade of the Hypostyle Hall (Then and Now).

FREDERICK MONDERSON

Dr. Ben's Temple Site Ticket 5. The Open-Air Museum at Karnak Temple (Thenand Now).

The ancient writers, Dr. Ben holds, "made many references to the Africans pigmentation, and of course made distinction in their remarks to the degree of BLACKNESS or variance of DARKNESS between different national groupings of Ethiopians ("Negroes" or "BLACKS") on the continent of Africa (Alkebu-lan). This factor was best observed by Philostratus in his description of "MEMNON" not being as "... BLACK AS OTHER ETHIOPIANS;" indicating that the

CELEBRATING
DR. BEN-JOCHANNAN

Greeks were quite observant of the variance in degree of BLACKNESS among the Ethiopians."

Dr. Ben's Illustration 21. Abydos. Ivories from the Tomb of King Zer-Ta (left); and, Tombs of Zet–Ath (1-4) and of Den-Setui (5-13) (right) in W.M.F. Petrie's *The Royal Tombs of the Earliest Dynasties, Part II* (1901).

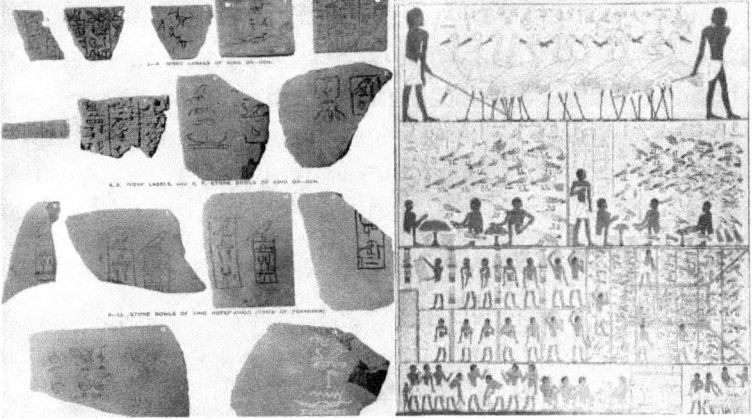

Dr. Ben's Illustration 22. Abydos. Tombs of Qa-Sen and Sekhemab-Perabsen in W.M.F. Petrie's *The Royal Tombs of the Earliest Dynasties, Part II* (1901) (left); and, men who tend to birds (right).

FREDERICK MONDERSON

As such, in Dr. Fred Mondersons **4th Annual Memorial Day Tribute to Dr. Ben**, June 3 and June 10, 2012, at True South Bookstore 492 Nostrand Ave, between Halsey and Hancock Streets 3:00 – 6:00 PM, the venerable and well-liked educator, Egyptologist, historian, Anthropologist, nationalist, etc., was praised for his *avante garde* championing of "Black is Beautiful," pioneering the wearing of the Dashiki when in the 1970s Blacks faced a cultural crisis he initiated his audacious effort to "take Egypt" to educate and enlighten African people of their heritage and the forces arrayed against them. He very early made it known how significant travel to Egypt really was and must continue in order to view the monuments where he often told such visitors, "Now that you have come to Egypt, seen what you have seen, what are you going to do with the knowledge!" Thanks to his efforts, conscious raising groups as the Association for the Study of Classical African Civilization (**ASCAC**) was born and today continue his identification. Let us not forget, Dr. Ben placed the Black woman on a high pedestal in praise and appreciation for her tremendous contribution as mother, spouse, nurturer and educator. Part II will be held Sunday June 10, 2012 at 3:00 PM. See you then!

Dr. Fred Monderson can be reached at fredsegypt.com@fredsegypt.com

In a final chapter entitled "Things done by Africa before Europe," Dr. Ben lists the following accomplishments on which he elaborates.

CELEBRATING DR. BEN-JOCHANNAN

"In this article the author will very briefly show some of the many Things the continent of Africa has given to the world before the coming of Europe into history. It is taken from the writers much more extensive work AFRICANS INFLUENCE ON EUROPEAN FEAR AND HISTORY," presently being edited for publication. The larger work shows the reasons why TRUE HISTORY has been suppressed and kept from the peoples of the world. Because of the old *myths and teachings* that AFRICA (Alkebu-lan) HAS NO HISTORY" this article is written from a point to that perspective. The reader in this context, can then see many reasons for the terrible fear of African History being taught *truthfully* in a white (European)-oriented society or setting."

"In order to control the numerous former chattel slaves, it was (from a white-European perspective) – AFRICA; and make him psychologically ashamed of himself and the color of his skin. Such controls make blacks think that they ought to be grateful and thankful to the whites for discovering" (a term Europeans love to use whenever they first find out that something, someone, or some places existed of which they knew nothing) them in "backward Africa" and taking them to "stolen lands" in what is commonly referred to in history and other disciplines as the "New World" (the Americas – both North and South, and the Caribbean Islands.)"

FREDERICK MONDERSON

13. CELEBRATING DR BEN – PART II

By Dr. Fred Monderson

Dr. Yosef ben-Jochannan's life has been one extraordinary experience of intellectual trail-blazing, daring cultural nationalism on a global scale, heavy in praise of African womanhood and in dynamic process author, lecturer, publisher, archaeologist, educator, historian and Egyptologist, among many others. Very few have done more extolling Africa in the forefront, lived as long and even many times challenged the angel of death, as the man lovingly called "Dr. Ben" by beloved fans and admirers worldwide. Ever wondered how Dr. Ben got his name? I made his acquaintance early in 1972 when a friend, Barney introduced me to this extraordinary individual through his classic *Africa: Mother of Western Civilization* at a time in the black consciousness movement when young people, even old people, were at a crossroad looking for leadership extolling nationalist sentiments, cultural patriotism, motifs, symbols, slogans representing positive role models. Since at first his name was puzzling to pronounce Barney and I began calling him "Ben Jo" in referring to his book *Mother*, and its message, imagery and bibliographic listing that exposed his readership to a new world of reference and referevt materials. After I enrolled at New York City Technical (then Community) College and met Curtis Dunmoodie, Curtis said we needed to show more respect and so we young students called him "Dr. Ben." By the time I moved to Hunter College in 1974 the name had stuck. So much so, when he came to sit in for Dr. Clarke in the Black and Puerto Rican Studies Department the fellow students began calling him Dr. Ben on a grander scale. It should be known, Dr. Ben was not well-liked at first, both by

CELEBRATING DR. BEN-JOCHANNAN

the general public and in academia, particularly among Black academics.

Having to defend his scholarship in challenge to western and American distortion, omission, plagiarization and religious, cultural and historical racial bigotry in genocidal behavior towards Africa and Africans as well as the uncomfortable position he put Black scholars in. Many dismissed him and infinitesimally critiqued his work claiming "Dr. Ben has no PhD!" Well established publishing houses refused to consider his works. As such, he initiated Self-Publishing of his books, producing small amounts that young students and others bought as encouragement to enable him to continue the work. As a young student at NYCTC, an episode of "Dr. Ben has no PhD" made me cry. I ran to the "A Train" from school on Jay Street, rode to 125th Street and onto Lenox Ave where his office was located on the second floor, opposite to Choc-Full-of-Nuts, and Professor Simmonds consoled me showing **Dr. Ben's Ph. D in Anthropology** displayed on the wall! Thus, Ibought many of his published books in First Edition that he subsequently autographed where the overleaf of the cover so indicates.

Dr. Ben's Photo 66a. Erik Monderson before the small temple of Isis at Deir el Shelwit.

Dr. Ben's Photo 67. Aswan. Temple of Goddess Isis. On the First Pylon, Nectanebo salutes Horus in Double Crown, while Isis, wearing horns and disk as Hathor, stands at the God's rear as if to say, "Ive got your back, Brother!"

Dr. Ben's Photo 68. Aswan. Temple of Goddess Isis. Engaged and elevated columns with different capitals on the Kiosk of Trajan.

CELEBRATING
DR. BEN-JOCHANNAN

Dr. Ben's Photo 68. Aswan. Temple of Goddess Isis. The majesty of Egyptian architecture that enables it to not only withstand the ravages of time and man but also to maintain its intrinsic value and unmatched beauty.

As an avid supporter of Dr. Ben I purchased every book he wrote in First Edition, traveled first with him to Egypt in the 1980s where he held the first and only "Panel Discussion" under the theme "What has coming to Egypt meant to you!" Subsequently he asked me, "Monderson, now that you have come to Egypt, seen what you have seen, what are you going to do with the knowledge?" Enthused by the subject of Egypt, motivated by the gifted scholar and in seeking advice as to the

FREDERICK MONDERSON

direction of my studies as a young student, Dr. Ben told me, "Monderson, there are fifty nations in Africa, choose one and specialize in it. Be a specialist not a generalist on Africa." Thus, while an african hsitorian, I chose Egypt for my specialization. Then he admonished further, "In doing research on Egypt, get the oldest material you can find and work from there." As a result of such master-taeacher woisdom, in 1990, at a dinner in Dr. Ben's honor hosted by Dr. Lewis at Mini-Sink in Harlem, and given the opportunity to speak before the Elders, I said: "Dr. Ben, as your vision becomes cloudy and youre looking for someone to pass the baton to, look for Monderson, for Ill be there!" Perhaps Elder wisdom prevailed, for on two occasions Dr. Ben recognized my work in letter form!

Dr. Ben's Photo 69. **Aswan**. Temple of Goddess Isis. A small chapel to Goddess Hathor that depict apes playing musical instruments, etc.

CELEBRATING DR. BEN-JOCHANNAN

In the co-authored *The Black Man's North and East Africa*, Dr. Ben and Professor George Simmonds, there is a final chapter entitled "Things done by Africa before Europe," Dr. Ben lists the following accomplishments on which he elaborates.

Before we begin todays Part two of this tribute, I wish to reflect on an aspect from the book, discussed in last weeks discussion. It goes as follows: "In this article the author will very briefly show some of the many Things [profound contributions] the continent of Africa has given to the world before the coming of Europe into history. It is taken from the writers much more extensive work AFRICANS INFLUENCE ON EUROPEAN FEAR AND HISTORY," presently being edited for publication. The larger work shows the reasons why TRUE HISTORY has been suppressed and kept from the peoples of the world. Because of the old *myths and teachings* that AFRICA (Alkebu-lan) HAS NO HISTORY" this article is written from a point to that perspective. The reader in this context, can then see many reasons for the terrible fear of African History being taught *truthfully* in a white (European)-oriented society or setting."

"In order to control the numerous former chattel slaves, it was (from a white-European perspective) – AFRICA; and make him psychologically ashamed of himself and the color of his skin. Such controls make blacks think that they ought to be grateful and thankful to the whites for discovering" (a term Europeans love to use whenever they first find out that something, someone, or some places existed of which they knew nothing) them in "backward Africa" and taking them to "stolen lands" in what is commonly referred to in history and other disciplines as the "New World" (the Americas – both North and South, and the Caribbean Islands.)" These were flushed out to make them mre understanbdable.

FREDERICK MONDERSON

THE BIRTH OF MAN OR MAN-LIKE CREATURES – man-like creatures, fossil man, pithecanthropus, erectus, sivanthropus, Zinjanthropus Boisie, Australopithecus, are the oldest forms of the human species dating millions of years old and only found in Africa.

THE STEP-PYRAMID – Created by Imhotep for Pharaoh Zoser of the Third Dynasty at Sakkara, the Step-Pyramid stands at the beginning of architectural history and attests to the ingenuity of ancient African science of building and operationalizing beaucratic and administrative organizations, that early in history.

THE TRUE PYRAMIDS – The best examples are those at Ghizeh in terms of size and preservation but they represent the highest form of organization of manpower, quarrying and transportation of stone, building to predetermined architectural planning, with accompanying logistics of medical treatment for injured workers, nearby housing for the workers, ordinances for their meals and the coordination of construction over great distances of a colossal nature.

THE PYRAMID TEXTS - Sayings and scriptures that are now ascribed to famous Hebrew prophets and other personages as Job, Jeremiah and King Solomon, had their origins in the Pyramid Texts.

THE COFFIN TEXTS – These grew out of the Old Kingdom Pyramid Texts in that now, during the Middle Kingdom, the religious words of inspiration that accompanied the dead were placed on the insides and outsides of coffins making such spiritual powers available to everyone who could afford it.

CELEBRATING DR. BEN-JOCHANNAN

THE BOOK OF THE DEAD – Represents a New Kingdom democratiaation of the afterlife in compilation of the Pyramid Texts with additional spells and incantations accompanied by colorful illustrations of the journey in the Afterlife and the obstacles encountered there.

THE WORLD'S EARLIEST NAVAL POWER – In a riverain country, the first thing one had to do was conquer the Nile. Even in the mythology the Gods traveled by boat and in the Pyramid Age boats were interred in the Pyramid Complex for the king to journey to meet the Gods. Found in 1954 and reconstructed, one is now housed at Ghizeh in the Boat Museum. The great military campaigns of initial unification, struggles against the Hyksos invaders, imperial forays into Asia and Ethiopian conquest all required mastery of the river, and important, descent from UYpper Egypt.

PLANNED PARENTHOOD – The Kahun Papyrus discovered by Flinders Petrie and dated to the 18th Dynasty discusses birth-control methods. This, like so many new features of pharaonic cultural practice have been attributed to the time of Queen Hatshepsut.

KINGS AND QUEENS IN EGYPT – Kings ruled Egypt in an orderly manner for more than three thousand years and they were often shown in surviving examples with their queens in a state of equality. Much of this is evident throughout the 3000 year period of dynastic rule. Queen Merneith of the Old Kingdom, Mentuhotep II's mother Queen Aam, Intef's mother Queen Achtothes, Queen Tetisheri of the 17th Dynasty and her daughter and grand-daughter Aahotep and Queen Aahmes-Nefertari, ancestress of the 18th Dynasty, Queen Hatshepsut and Queen Tiy, wife of Amenhotep III, and Queen Nefertari II wife of Rameses II were all beautiful and

FREDERICK MONDERSON

fabled ladies who stood beside their remarkable husbands in an equal status.

BUILDING OF THE GREAT SPHINX OF GIZEH – Current evidence seems to indicate Khafre, builder of the Second Pyramid at Ghizeh did repairs to the Sphinx c. 2500 B.C. and that it is probably as old as 10,000 tears based on water marks in the vicinity, as the scholar John Anthony West has held.

THE ONLY PERFECT GOVERNMENT RECORDED BY MAN – Rule by the Gods who handed down their legacy to their son the Pharaoh, but in time this dissipated.

THE ANKHS – Spiritual symbol of life often seen as an instrument of power accompanying the Gods, when the Gods imparted life to the pharaoh or when Gods baptized the king before his entering the temple to conduct the daily ritual.

SCOTTISH RITES – Secrets of the temple that migrated from Heliopolis and later the Grand Lodge at Luxor, built by Amenhotep and expanded by Rameses II. Those esoteric principles and practices migrated to the West through Greece and Rome then ultimately America.

TRADES: "SON LIKE FATHER" – Crafts and knowledge were handed down as family secrets.

THE EGYPTIAN ALPHABET – This is truly indigenous to the Nile Valley, evidence demonstrated in Upper Egypt. While Hans Winkler wants to attribute this writing to Mesopotamia, evidence of the flora, fauna and geographical features are native to Upper Egypt. Wallis Budge ultimately affirmed Egyptian was an African rather than

CELEBRATING
DR. BEN-JOCHANNAN

Asiatic language. The extraordinary Cheikh Anta Diop masterfully demonstrated its relationship to other African languages and cultural practices.

THE EARLIEST KNOWN PAINTING - Not cave man scrawl but actual painting comes from the Old Kingdom.

Dr. Ben's Photo 70. Aswan. Temple of Goddess Isis. The God Bes, protector of women at childbirth and acted aspurveyor of merriment, wine and song.

Dr. Ben's Photo 71. Aswan. Temple of Goddess Isis. In a nearby chapel, Pharaoh offers enthroned Goddess a baboon, emblematic of God Thoth, inventor of wisdom, mathematics, "legal eagle" of the Gods and companion of Osiris.

FREDERICK MONDERSON

Dr. Ben's Photo 72. Aswan. Temple of Goddess Isis. Above the winged Sundisk with protective uraei wearing red and white crowns, Hathor heads depict the Goddess with long hair, protected by uraei and sporting abacus of her temples entrance. Notice the faces defacement.

COLLECTION OF TAXES – The first government to levy taxes on their citizens so that the work of government could progress as well as to replenish the royal treasury. Taxes were in the form of produced food, cattle, labor or precious instruments whether from citizens or as conquered booty and tribute.

NAMING OF THE GODS – Ra, Osiris, Seth, Thoth, Amon-Ra, Montu, Khonsu, and many more who presided at the Judgment. There were national and local Gods.

CELEBRATING DR. BEN-JOCHANNAN

NAMING OF THE GODDESSES – Hathor, Isis, Mut, Ma'at, Selkis, Seshat, Neith, etc. These lady divinities were generally part of a triad of husband, wife and child, generally son.

MAKING OF THE OBELISKS – A single piece of stone quarried, transported, decorated and erected at a site hundreds of miles away from place of origin. Many were seized and dispatched to European and American cities. The Washington Monument is an obelisk but constructed of steel and cut-up stone, though not as creatively constructed as the Egyptian example or prototype.

DEVELOPMENT OF THE SCRIBES – Scribes were intellectuals of their day and all forms of recordings were the domain of these men of letters, whether letter writing, instruction, accompanying military expedition to record ordinances and events or simply as instructors who imparted knowledge.

CENTERS OF LEARNING – Heliopolis, Luxor, Abydos, Asuit, Sakkara. Generally, any place where temples were located were some form of center of learning with some being more important than others. Undoubtedly, a school was located at the Ramesseum.

DEVELOPMENT OF THE NEGATIVE CONFESSIONS – This moral and ethical imperative guided the society and its citizens behaviors, so much so, upon death at the "Judgment" or Psychostasia before the Assayers, the deceased confessed to the things he did not do. He also cited things he did to be positive in his favor.

FREDERICK MONDERSON

CREATION OF MANY RELIGIONS – Religion grew out of the need to explain local phenomena within the context of original thinking about this world and the next.

DEVELOPMENT OF BULLFIGHTING IN EGYPT – Bulls played an important part in the social as well as religious life of ancient Egypt and as part of sport entertainment and ritual sacrifice.

INTRODUCTION OF THE WORLD'S EARLIEST KNOWN SOLAR CALENDAR – Depending on which scholar one reads the calendar was invented in 4241 B.C. as stated by Breasted, while Petrie gives 5701 and Maulana Karenga 6200. Bauval and Brophy believe a calendar may have been invented possibly as early as 20,000 B.C. at Nabta Playa.

Adding to this, in the **Table of Contents** of his book, *What They **Never** Told You in History Class*, Indus Khamit Kush (1983) gives the following: Creators of the Human Race; Creators of Civilization; The First Gods (Deities) of Antiquity (Ancient Times); Creators of Religion; Creators of Christianity; The First Saviors of Mankind; The World's Earliest Messiahs; The Founding Fathers of the Church; Popes; The First Martyrs; Discoverers of Science; Creators of Mathematics; Astronomy; Aeronautics; Inventors of Steel; Discoverers of Medicine; Creators of the Alphabet; Originators of Paper; Creators of the First University; Creators of Architecture; Creators of Art; The First Ethiopians; The First Egyptians; The First Mesopotamians; The First East Indians; The First Chinese; The First Japanese and Indo-Chinese; The First Hebrews; The First Moors; The First Europeans; The First Greeks; The First Romans; The First Britons; The First Americans; Creators of Greek Philosophy;

CELEBRATING DR. BEN-JOCHANNAN

Royalty and Government; Black Emperors; Famous Black People (Past) and (Present); Conclusions.

In stating his philosophy of the Quintessential Nile Valley African Man Dr. Ben elucidates in *The African Called Rameses ("The Great") II and the African Origin of "Western Civilization"* as a lecture he delivered on April 29, 1989 for The Third Eye, Inc., in conjunction with the "Rameses (The Great) II Exhibition" held in Dallas, Texas. This profusely illustrated 100 page book contains 97 illustrations and as part of a Table of Contents or Citations he lists as follows: Illustrations, Glossary, Foreword by Dr. John H. Clarke, a Retrospection, All in Statistics, Greetings, Opening, Origins, Questions, Background, Direction, Family, Manhood, Leader, Symbol, Tragedy, Architecture, Myth, Image, Syncretism, Education, Literature, The Craft, Belief, Guardian, Justice, Conclusion, End Notes, Bibliography and Index. Therefore, given in a nutshell that he is "primarily a student and professor of Nile Valley and Great Lakes High-Culture of Africa with a major concentration on Ta-Meri," the Quintessential Nile Valley Black Man for Dr. Ben is embodied in Rameses II, "The great," who is a pharaoh, King, courageous leader, father, husband, conqueror, militarist, Imperial colonizer, architect, engineer and builder, patron of the arts and learning, peace maker, devotee of the Gods, whose history and heritage is greatly distorted as taught today in and outside of Egypt.

Insisting that the continent of Alkebu-lan or Africa be "the first and most important land of call whenever Africans and African-Americans decide to travel" he admonished "Lets always be prepared to meet the foe in full knowledge of Ta-Meris High Culture before we visit, remembering always that among the Nubian population the truest seeds of the ancient Nile Valley African stock are to be found today in the 20th Century of the Common Era."

Dr. Ben's Photo 73. Aswan. Temple of Goddess Isis. To the left, close-up of the Goddesses image with Uraei and temple Abacus while to the right, a lion sits at the ready to offer protection.

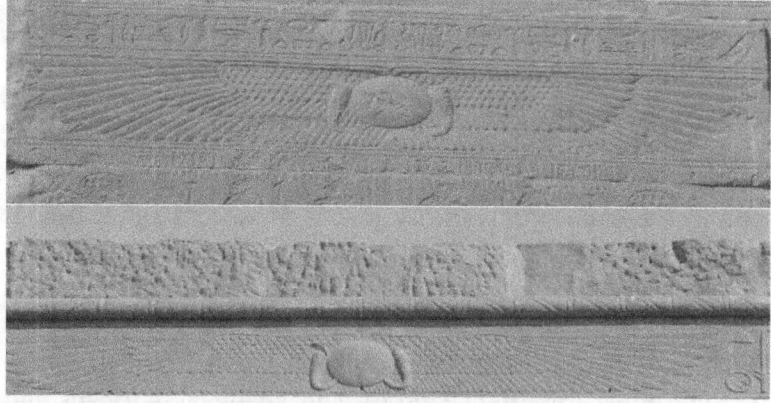

Dr. Ben's Photo 74. Aswan. Temple of Goddess Isis. Superimposed images of the Sun Disk with protective Uraei and extended wings on architraves of cornices.

CELEBRATING DR. BEN-JOCHANNAN

14. CULTURE AND SPIRITUALITY IN ANCIENT AFRICA
BY
DR. FRED MONDERSON

MAN KNOW THYSELF! Such was stated by Imhotep (2600 B.C.), "Philosopher of the Ages." He also said, "Eat, drink, be merry, for tomorrow we die!"

The Psalms teaches, "The fear of the lord is the beginning of wisdom" and Proverbs has pointed out, "Where there is no vision the people perish." Equally, Confucius stated, "I am not one who was born in the possession of knowledge, I am one who is fond of antiquity, and earnest in seeking it there."

The walls of the **Library of Congress** extolls: "Ignorance is the Curse of God, Knowledge the wings where we fly to heaven."

Prof. Diop has instructed: "The African historian who evades the problem of Egypt is neither modest nor objective nor unruffled; he is ignorant, cowardly and neurotic. Imagine, if you can, the uncomfortable position of a western historian writing of Europe without referring to Graeco-Latin antiquity and try to pass that as a scientific approach." Equally, Professor John H. Clarke laid down the law, "The final interpretation of African history is the responsibility of scholars of African descent." However, Gordon Parks has offered: "Steep yourself in black history, but dont stop there. I love Duke Ellington and Count Basie, but I also listen to Bach and Beethoven. Do not allow yourself to be trapped and snarled in limits set for you by someone else."

Dr. Ben's Photo 75. Aswan. Temple of Goddess Isis. The King makes a Presentation to enthroned Goddess Sekhmet, the wife of Ptah and mother of his son Nefertum, the Triad of Memphis.

Dr. Ben's Photo 76. Aswan. Temple of Goddess Isis. Pharaoh offers a Sphinx to enthroned Isis with Horus at her rear wearing the Double Crown.

CELEBRATING DR. BEN-JOCHANNAN

Now, when it comes to ownership of the reality of ancient Egypt, we must seek to understand what is at stake and only then will we realize spiritual warfare is an issue seriously waged Against Africa and Africans. A close examination of the academic and popular of Egypt, by some Western and American historians, despite their glossy or sanitized presentations they still reveal deep-seated spiritual and psychological African underpinnings that undergird the structural foundation of European culture and by extension that of America. The architects of the falsification of history through omission and distortion have "crossed the Rubicon" of cultural origination and cannot but deny Africas involvement in Egypt, otherwise admit the well-spring of their cultural and social, even psychological, even religious beings is African in origin and craftsmanship. Therefore, misrepresentation of Africas place in Egypts glory and equally universal history thus becomes necessary and not only reveals a soulless, calculating cultural manifestation but questions the integrity and honesty of learning based on deceptive writings and teachings. Remove the tropical blaze of Africas inventiveness and laid bare is a cold and covetous European mindset that projects a false reality of history. That is why the gift of Africas glory is misrepresented by such scholars and their followers, who, despite constantly revealing new and contradictory information, refuse to concede the errors of their insidious ways. Remember I said spiritual warfare is the issue and its shielded in a mental overcoat of obfuscation. Nevertheless, seeking to understand the ramifications of the involved dynamics, it is this writers contention; any scholar, after studying an issue for a generation or say 30 years, must come to some clearly defined conclusions of the subject, oftentimes requiring refutation or reversal of earlier falsified or misunderstood positions. Such an earnest appraisal by these European writers and historians will find honest persons themselves attacking the structural pillars that support their own cultural foundations because of the falsity of its construction that has also misled them.

Dr. Ben's Temple Site Ticket 6. The Temple of Luxor built by Amenhotep III, enlarged by Rameses II and earlier repaired by Tutankhamon, Horemhab and Seti I whose names also appear there (Then and now).

What does all this have to do with the topic Im presenting today? Everything, because when you deny a mans God relationship, his spiritual foundations, his cultural ethos, his moral, cultural, scientific and social creations, you deny the very existence of the man. You deny his very humanity! This has been done to the African, but thank God, courageous African scholars have struggled with and freed the shackles

CELEBRATING DR. BEN-JOCHANNAN

that have inhibited the African from seeing and enjoying the beauty of ancestral creations grounded in moral and spiritual foundations of truth, knowledge, wisdom and justice. Such efforts were aided by the realization and insistent practice of Ma'at. This phenomenal psychological and spiritual construct is the ethical and social elixir that is the source of all good, balance, and harmony in human relations! Robert Clarke aids an understanding of this code of spiritual and social conduct, in his statement: "The fourfold law was Gods, and not only did he create it, he lived by it. God ruled and was a righteous judge, and the law of man depended on and was founded on the word of God. God was good. His law was good, and He obeyed his own law. With God lay wisdom, truth and justice. This was the order of reality and the wrongdoer who transgressed against that order opposed God and the whole universe, material and spiritual." Therefore, to the Egyptians God was real and his creation *Ma'at* was real; hence this helped to bring about that "all life, matter, soul and spirit were part of the divine scheme." One of this writers teachers identified seven situations where *Ma'at* applies such as – Harmony, Order, Justice, Balance, Truth, Righteousness, and Reciprocity. This ethical principle, *Ma'at*, therefore, molded the behavior of Gods, kings and regular humans and should guide our teachings and actions today. However, that we be reminded, the opposite to *Ma'at* is *Isfet* - viz., evil, bad, disorder, disequilibrium, chaos. Thus, *Ma'at* seeks to limit the effect of this evil intent.

In his book, *Kemet and the African Worldview*, Maulana Karenga points to the *Book of Kheti* which says: "Follow in the footsteps of your ancestors, for the mind is trained through knowledge. Behold their words endure in books. Open them, and follow their wise counsel." (1986: 85) Again, in the Library of Congress we are reminded, "In books lies the soul of the whole past-times." Now, while there were some general

FREDERICK MONDERSON

books of Egyptian religiosity and knowledge such as the *Book of Gates*, the *Book of Am-Duat*, the *Book of Breathings*, the *Book of Caverns*, the *Book of the Heavenly Cow*, the *Book of Traversing Eternity*, the *Book of Two Ways* and the *Book of the Opening of the Mouth*, in his other work, *Selections from the Husia* Karenga explained his choices and that books structure as divided into seven sections. These outlined are: 1) *The Book of Knowing the Creations*; 2) *The Book of Prayers and Sacred Praises*; 3) *The Book of the Moral Narrative*; 4) *The Books of Wise Instruction*; 5) *The Books of Contemplation*; 6) *The Book of Declarations of Virtues*; and 7) *The Book of Rising Like Ra*. These ancient texts he determines are a "rich moral and spiritual legacy which ancient Africa gave humanity thru its daughter Kemet." We know these ideas developed in Ethiopia and descended the Nile to be preserved in Egypt! After all, credible scholars know *Africa before the white man* is not 1800 A.D., but even before 1800 B.C!

Dr. Ben's Books 8. Tutankhamon's African Roots haley, et.al., overlooked!? (1978). Notice the Author's autograph.

1. The *Book of Knowing the Creations*, Maulana Karenga explained, was not about "Creation" but "Creations" for the ancients viewed "Creation" on a daily basis. The rising of the sun was Creation renewed daily, after the long night of

CELEBRATING
DR. BEN-JOCHANNAN

threatened darkness. You call this breakfast but there was a deeper psychological and spiritual significance to this phenomenon as the ancients viewed it. He states: "The first creation was the first event at the first time. But creation is repeated each day in nature and in human history. In nature, sunrise and the new beginning it brings each day is a reflection of this. In human history, it is reflected in humanitys constant establishment and re-establishment of order and righteousness in the midst of chaos and evil in a role similar to that of Ras." He states further, in his unbounded beneficence, Ra declared he "created the four winds so that every person might breathe in his or her time and place," and made "the great flood for irrigation so that the humble might benefit from it like the great," and even further he "made every person like his or her fellow." This early in time, for Gods architects to structure his relations with humanity in such a manner is a hallmark for his creation and his creative process. In the divine-human relationship it places the African God on a higher plane and the spirit of the African man and woman somewhere near that top! Religion is therefore experiencing the sacred.

Dr. Ben's Photo 76a. Aswan. Temple of Goddess Isis. Erik Monderson stands before the Kiosk of Nectanebo on the Dromos to temple of the Goddess, Isis.

Dr. Ben's Photo 77. Aswan. Temple of Goddess Isis. View of Mammisi and Pylon from the Nile.

Dr. Ben's Photo 77a. Aswan. Temple of Goddess Isis. Pharaoh offers two sailing boats to Osiris enthroned beside Isis.

CELEBRATING DR. BEN-JOCHANNAN

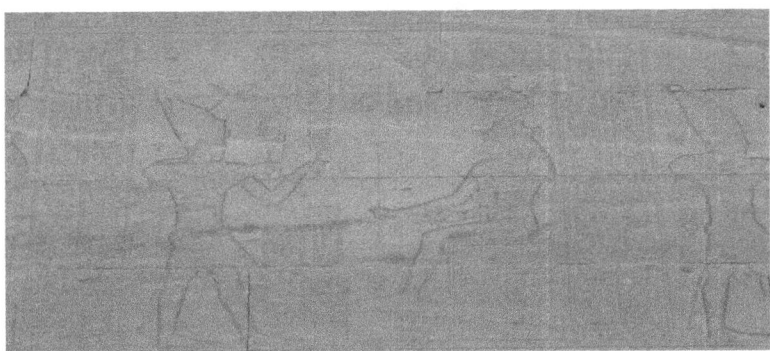

Dr. Ben's Photo 78. Aswan. Temple of Goddess Isis. Pharaoh offers two sistrums, emblems of Hathor, to enthroned Isis.

Dr. Ben's Photo 79. Aswan. Temple of Goddess Isis. The King offers a recumbent lion wearing horns and disk to enthroned Isis with Horus at her side wearing the Double Crown.

Im reminded; I was just back in New York from Haiti in April and went to listen to Brother Ron Daniels. He spoke about Bookman and the two sisters being the spiritual fire behind the

FREDERICK MONDERSON

Haitian Revolution. In the age when Britain and France fought over empire, America declared Independence and France sent Haitians to aid their fight at the Battle of Savannah. These Haitians soldiers were courageous and made the difference in that battle. On their return home as the Revolution unfolded, Bookman reminded a gathering of Haitians, "We have learned the ways of the white man." This meant they had learned how to fire the rifle with accuracy and how to load and fire the cannon. He said further, "We have seen the God of the white man and the people who preached the white man's religion. Our God is a just God. Our God will not let us fail. Let us march on to victory" knowing our God is good!

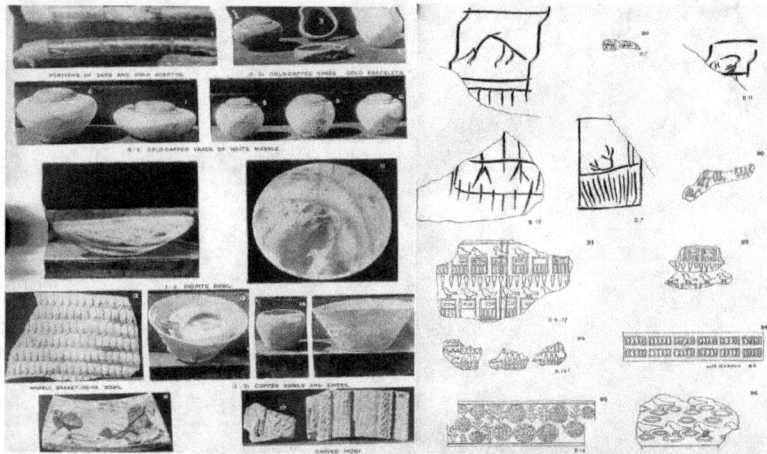

Dr. Ben's Illustration 27. Abydos Portions of scepter, bracelets, vases, bowls, all of sard and gold, white marble, diorite, copper and carved ivory from the Tomb of King Khasekhemui. (left); and, Sealings of Kings Ka and Narmer (right) in W.M.F. Petrie's *The Royal Tombs of the Earliest Dynasties, Part II* (1901).

CELEBRATING DR. BEN-JOCHANNAN

Dr. Ben's Illustration 28. Abydos. Tablets of King Aha-Mena. W.M.F. Petrie's *The Royal Tombs of the Earliest Dynasties, Part II* (1901) (left); and, men at work in a variety of attitudes.

In the constant conflict between **Ma'at** and **Isfet**, good and evil, the ancients lived the belief, "Justice is given to one who does what is loved and punishment to one who does what is hated," and "life is given to the peaceful and death is given to one who violates the law."

2. The *Book of Prayers and Sacred Praises* Karenga believes is "one of Africas most distinct and undeniable instructions and achievements in the spiritual and aesthetic realm – the praise poem."

In explaining this Dr. Karenga writes: "The praise-poem or the songs of praising and glorifying as they are called in the *Book of Coming Forth By Day* are acts of worship and offering, of Ra, a sharing in his strength and glory, his beneficence and beauty and in His creation and his active care of it." Equally, he points out and reminds us, "Though the servant be inclined to make mistakes, the Lord is inclined to be merciful"

3. The *Book of the Moral Narrative* – teaches humanity to not simply practice but also to cultivate Ma'at in others that they may do *Ma'at* themselves. Khun-Anup has been called the *Elegant Peasant*. Apparently he was done wrong and so appealed to a high official, the Vizier Rensi. His elegant flourishes impressed the Vizier thenthe King. Unexpectedly, he tells the Vizier, "Do not speak falsely for you are great; do not act lightly for you have weight; be not untrue for you are the balance and do not swerve, for you are the standard." We must seek to understand the significance and purpose of language used by these ancient Africans! Khun-Anup advises further, "Helmsman, do not let your ship go astray." Praising this powerful construct, Maulana Karenga reminds and teaches, "*Ma'at* is for eternity. It goes to the grave with those who do it. When they are buried and the earth envelops them, their name is not erased from the face of the earth." On the contrary, "they are remembered because of their goodness." Thus, *Ma'at* is diametrically opposed to Isfet or evil and its perpetrators as good hope evil would be gone too soon!

4. The *Book of Wise Instructions* main focus is on "*Ma'at* and the moral and spiritual obligation each person has in preserving and practicing it, in and for the community." Another example is given of Ptah-Hotep, a wise Old Kingdom philosopher who declared: "*Ma'at* is great, its value is lasting and it has remained unchanged and unequalled since the time of its Creator." These ancient Africans therefore strove for moral excellence in all they did, and the lesson for others is, act similarly "so no fault can be found in your character." Again, the Nobleman Kheti told his son Merikare, "Righteousness is fitting for a ruler." So again, one should "Think *Ma'at*, speak *Ma'at* and do *Ma'at* in secular and sacred situations."

CELEBRATING DR. BEN-JOCHANNAN

Dr. Ben's Photo 80. Aswan. Temple of Goddess Isis. Pharaoh prepares to incense Osiris enthroned beside Isis.

Dr. Ben's Photo 81. Aswan. Temple of Goddess Isis. Entrance to the "Kiosk of Trajan" with engaged columns, varied capitals, high abacus and winged sun-disk above.

FREDERICK MONDERSON

Dr. Ben's Photo 82. Aswan. Temple of Goddess Isis. Pharaoh, wearing the Red Crown, offers a plant to Osiris, Isis and their son Horus in Double Crown. Here we have the "Osiris Triad."

5. The *Book of Contemplation* – is a reflection of the state society had deteriorated into. Khakheper-Ra-Soneb, in criticizing his time noted, "Ma'at, righteousness and order, has been cast out and *Isfit*, evil and chaos, is in the Council Hall. The way of God is violated and His commandments are brushed aside. The land is in turmoil and there is mourning everywhere." Still, he counsels, be strong saying, "Another heart might bend or break, but a strong heart in the midst of difficulties is an ally to its owner."

CELEBRATING DR. BEN-JOCHANNAN

Dr. Ben's Illustration 29. W.M.F. Petrie's *The Royal Tombs of the Earliest Dynasties*, Part II (1901) Abydos. Tablets of Kings Narmer and Men.

6. The *Book of Declarations of Virtues* teaches as Karenga states, "Kemetic ethics and spirituality, like all African ethics and spirituality, have and stress a practical dimension. Righteousness is real only in personal and social practice." As Seba Ankhsheshonqi says, "There is no good deed except a good deed that is done for one who needs it. Ma'at, then, is a social as well as spiritual task for which the reward is an enjoyable and beautiful life in the community on earth and a spiritual life in the heavens as a living God." This is why mans life and total behavior should be structured in Ma'at so he can

stand confidently before his God when the final end comes and he is judged for his time on earth!

The ideal man was the *geru*, the self-mastered, that is, calm, silent, controlled, modest, wise, gently and socially active; and the *geru* Ma'at, was the truly self-mastered. The first was the self-mastered, the second a kind of master of the self-mastered. The opposite of the self-mastered is the unrestrained person – hot-mouthed, hot-tempered, aggressive, and generally infused with *isfit*, the opposite of Ma'at. The contrast of these two types is found in Amenemope who poses the unrestrained as "a tree grown in unfertile ground. Its leaves wither quickly and its unripe fruit falls to the ground. But the self-mastered man or woman sets himself or herself apart. He or she is like a tree grown in fertile ground. It grows green and doubles its yield of fruit."

Dr. Ben's Photo 83. **Aswa**. Temple of Goddess Isis. Priests in long flowing robes wearing sandals hoist high the Barque of Goddess Isis.

CELEBRATING DR. BEN-JOCHANNAN

Dr. Ben's Photo 84. Aswan. Temple of Goddess Isis. To the left, the King offers two vessels to the necklaced God wearing the Double Crown; while to the right, wearing the White Crown, he offers a sailing vessel and prepares to incense.

Dr. Ben's Photo 85. Aswan. Temple of Goddess Isis. Pharaoh in Double Crown, offers three feathers of Ma'at to Osiris with Isis wearing her crown with horns, disk and a throne and standing behind the God.

FREDERICK MONDERSON

Dr. Ben's Photo 86. Aswan. Temple of Goddess Isis. The King, in White Crown, pours a libation to Osiris backed by Isis who pats him on the back.

7. Regarding the *Books of Rising Like Ra* - Karenga simply says, "These books are singularly and together the oldest written record of the dawn of structured moral consciousness. They represent Africans leading the human rupture with the animal world and establishing not only an ethical standard of social behavior but posing the possibility of resurrection, ascension and transformation into a living God."

Without a doubt, therefore, Maulana Karenga has done an excellent job in his *Selections from the Husia*.

Notwithstanding, this writer affirms7, Africas art is older than man for man himself is art from Africa! Equally, African spirituality is nearly as old as man. An old ancient African/Egyptian belief holds "When the student is ready, the master will appear." In the unending millennia of mental

CELEBRATING DR. BEN-JOCHANNAN

preparation, as the metal was being prepared, the divine archetype finally descended from the heavens to impart spiritual guidance and consciousness to the African in a mutually beneficial covenant that spanned a geographical region that extended from the headwaters of the Nile throughout the Nile Valley region.

In *Signs and Symbols of Primordial Man*, Albert Churchward (1924) points to the Great Lakes region at the headwaters of the Nile as the place of the origin of the ancient Egyptian civilization. While James Baldwin reminds us, "Civilization lies first in the mind," Churchward points out, in the Nile Valley; this process was 300,000 years in the making! Let us not forget, its been purportedly argued, a New Kingdom Nobleman affirmed: "We came from the foothills of the Mountain of the Moon, at the headwaters of the Nile where the God Hapi dwells." This is the region of Mounts Ruwenzori and Kilimanjaro, East Africa. Now, the great Maspero says Hunefer was "Negroid but not Negro" but when, according to J.A. Rogers, the musical genius Beethovens biographers describe him they used words such as "swarthy," "Negroid," "Negro," etc. Now, could one be "Negroid" in reference in our own time but not "Negro" in another when both descriptions were contemporaries? Let us not forget, Professor John Henrik Clarke has instructed, "African history will not be complete until it is written by African historians," because the "People who preached racism colonized history" and "when Europe colonized the world, she colonized the worlds knowledge!"

Further, Dr. Cheikh Anta Diop advises we must connect Egypt to African history just as the West sees Greece and Rome as the foundation of their civilization. Another dimension to the problem now, most books on the subject of western civilization include a chapter on Egypt and no one is challenging this distortion. Thats what they think but

FREDERICK MONDERSON

Afrocentrists are vigorously and unalterably opposed and are working to correct distortions and include omissions relative to African history and culture.

That is probably what many think or even they think! But remember, Knowledge comes but wisdom lingers on! The Twa people actually started it all! They were the first to realize religion! By this I mean, not just spiritual and philosophical speculation but equally specializations that developed in the crafts to produce variety in pottery, smelting and patterns in gold work and other early technical industries.

Some adventurer, a "precursor to colonialism," who encountered these people during the Age of European Imperialism and extenson in Africa probably said: "Look at those little people, they look like pigs." The name stuck! So be careful of what you say. There is a belief even within Christianity that every word one utters or deed one does in this existence will be examined and the individual held accountable for your utterance and actions. Such a view is antedated by Egyptian teachings extolling *Ma'at* in thought and deed because every uttering is also recorded. Citizens may have heard of the concept of being weighed in the balance! This is all part of that experience. Thus, the Egyptian structured his life so he could stand confidently before his God in the Psychostasia or weighing of the heart in the balance! That is why the Africans great intellectuals, his priests, successors to the blacksmiths who became intermediaries with the Gods, crafted the 147 *Negative Confessions* or *Declarations of Sinlessness* or Innocence. These *Negative Confessions*, reduced to 42 affirm essentially, I didnt do this; but the *Positive Declarations* said I did this to aid the cause of humanity. Anyway, be careful of what you say because there are manifestations looking, listening and recording.

CELEBRATING DR. BEN-JOCHANNAN

Anyway, it was the Nilotic Negro from inner Africa who started us down the path of knowledge, utilizing mind and reason on the road to civilization and spirituality at a time when he did not even possess spoken language, but used signs and the dance. In this process, spirit and matter became manifest to his mind through reason. Thus, he had his first experience of the "One Great God" and expressed such in the "Zootype forms." Perhaps this is where he conceived of the concept of Personal and Collective Immortality as he expressed remembrance of the ancestors. Let us be clear, he did not worship animals and other creations of nature as Gods, but he realized there is a force of life, light, spirituality that "made the engine run!" This soul force is the God spirit manifesting in nature! So he developed his spirituality through the experiences of the Stellar Cult, the Solar Cult and later the Lunar Cult. This spiritualizing has continued through the Hebrew Cult and the Christian Cult. The Muslim Cult is equally a continuation of this line, though some choose to end it with the Christians. All this brings us to this date. Nevertheless, every step along this journey of expanding spiritual consciousness is an improvement, a refinement of what I call "Sweet Communion with Deity" all towards perfection of the human spirit. That is, a work in unending process; vreation renewed daly in thought nd deed and manifested reality. This is what Africa bequeathed and the world coveted. Albert Churchward has said: "Its all one and the same from the beginning, under different names." He did indicate this had been happening for some 300,000 years!

FREDERICK MONDERSON

Dr. Ben's Photo 87. Aswan. Temple of Goddess Isis. Standing before Horus in Double Crown and with a fellow Goddess wearing Queen Mother Crown with disk and feathers, Isis hold forth a scepter.

Simply put, therefore, in this evolving experience of divine drama, humanity was admonished, "You worship and ritualize me and I will bless and protect you; infusing a metaphysical potential to do and become anything! Now, while this contract initially held, after millennia of mental, moral, physical and spiritual blessings, the African began to backslide. Some scholars have argued it was his inability to field strong and vigorous rulers. Nevertheless, as such, his social, cultural, spiritual and intellectual foundations were affected; weakened, he became a victim of foreigners who attacked and

CELEBRATING DR. BEN-JOCHANNAN

destroyed his creations, appropriating and utilizing the good qualities for their benefit, even claiming initial origination. People of this hue, falsified the record, denying the Africans involvement in his own creation and consigning him to the lowest rung of human development. Wade Nobles in *Kemet and the African Worldview* calls this "white vested interest." However, and again, Professor John H. Clarke has held, "The people who preached racism, colonized history" and explained "When Europe colonized the world, it colonized the worlds knowledge," and Nobles states further: "This latter point is understood if one understands that the political control of knowledge is a necessary condition for white supremacy; and, that in this regard as Diop has pointed out, the common denominator characterizing the study of ancient Egypt by white Egyptologists has been their seemingly desperate pathological necessity and unrelentless attempt to refute ancient Africas blackness. Consequently, information regarding ancient Africa has been destroyed, distorted, falsified, suppressed and intentionally made unclear." I should add also stolen and this is not simply modern but ancient also. James in his *Stolen Legacy* pointed out how Aristotle appropriated much of the ancient knowledge attributing them to his own creation, while this was not so. He explained the volume of work Aristotle claims he wrote represents a period of 5000 years of accumulated knowledge through trial and error and experimentation, as opposed to some guy, within a decade, being able to write that many volumes of such profound thoughts.

FREDERICK MONDERSON

Dr. Ben's Illustration 30. The notion of a cow, Goddess of nourishment, is an integral part of the heavenly drama as she is tended by these divinities to influence earthly existence.

As regards this significant body of knowledge, the Guyanese George G.M. James *Stolen Legacy* (San Francisco, Calif.: Julian Richardson Associates, Publishers, 1954) (1976: 123-25) states, "The *Book of the Dead* which is actually the *Book of Coming Forth By Day*, identifies 9 inseparable parts of the soul." These are:

Dr. Ben's Photo 77a. Aswan. Temple of Goddess Isis. Erik Monderson stands beside the first column of the Western Colonnade with its 32 columns on the Dromos to the Temple's entrance.

CELEBRATING DR. BEN-JOCHANNAN

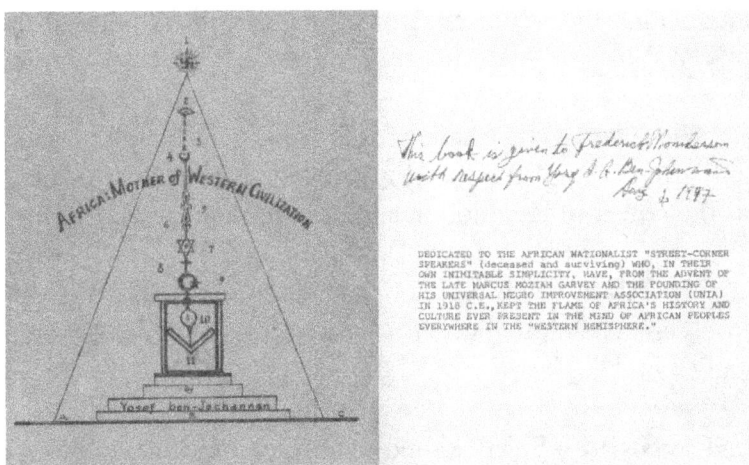

Dr. Ben's Books 9. AFRICA: MOTHER OF WESTERN CIVILIZATION (1971). Note the Autograph reads: This book is **given** to Frederick Monderson!

"1. The **Ka** – The abstract personality of the man to whom it belongs possessing the form and attributes of a man with power of locomotion, omnipresence and ability to receive nourishment like a man. It is equivalent to image.

2. The **Khat** – the concrete personality, the physical body, which is mortal.

3. The **Ba** – The Heart-soul, which dwells in the Ka and sometimes alongside it, in order to supply it with air and food. It has the power of metamorphosis and changes its form at will.

4. The **Ab** – The Heart, the animal life in man, and is rational, spiritual and ethical. It is associated with the Ba (heart-soul)

and in the Egyptian Judgment Drama it undergoes examination in the presence of Osiris, the great Judge of the Unseen World or "Afterlife.".

5. The **Khaibit** – Shadow. It is associated with Ba (heart-soul) from whom like the Ka, it receives its nourishment. It has the power of locomotion and omnipresence.

6. The **Khu** – Spiritual soul, which is immortal. It is also closely associated with the Ba (heart-soul), and is an Ethereal Being.

7. The **Sahu** – Spiritual body, in which the Khu or spiritual soul dwells. In it all the mental and spiritual attributes of the natural body are united to the new powers of its own nature.

8. The **Sekhem** – Power of the spiritual personification of the vital force in a man. Its dwelling place is in the heavens with spirits or Khus.

9. The **Ren** – the Name, or the essential attribute for the preservation of a Being. The Egyptian believed, "in the absence of a name, an individual ceased to exist."

Even further James continued, "The soul has nine parts, whose unity is so complete, that even the **Ren**, i.e., the **name**, is an essential attribute, since without it, it cannot exist."

"The **Ba** (or heart-soul), is connected with the **Ka**, **Khaibit**, and **Ab** (Abstract personality or Shadow and Animal life) - on the one hand, and also with **Khu** and **Sekhem** (spiritual Soul and spiritual personification of vital force), on the other hand, as the power of Nourishment.

CELEBRATING DR. BEN-JOCHANNAN

The **Sahu** is a spiritual body which is used both by **Khu** and **Sekhem**.

The **Khat**, i.e., physical body, is essential to the soul while manifesting itself upon the physical plane."

The soul has the additional following attributes:

Omnipresence – The ability to be everywhere at the same time.

Metamorphosis – A profound change in form from one stage to the next in the life history of an organism.

Locomotion – The act or power of moving from one place to another.

Nutritive – Serving to nourish; providing nourishment.

Mortality (in the case of the Khat) – The state or condition of being subject to death.

Immortality – Unending life.

Rationality – The state or condition of being rational.

Spirituality – The quality or fact of being spiritual.

Morality – Conforming to the rules of right conduct.

Ethereal – Heavenly or celestial.

FREDERICK MONDERSON

Shadowy – Resembling a shadow in faintness.

Hence, James concludes, "Aristotle obtained his doctrine of the soul from the Egyptian *Book of the Dead*, directly or indirectly."

But this thievery and misappropriation, omission, distortion, is being seriously challenged today!

Dr. Ben's Temple Site Ticket 7. Luxor.
Hatshpsut's Temple at Deir el Bahari (Then and Now).

Let us be clear, in the orchestrated sinister maneuver, concocted in the "Age of Hegel" and ossified as factual knowledge in the minds of his disciples who misled their own people, the universality of its contention is now proven false. Yet, misinformation reigns out of dishonesty and ignorance,

CELEBRATING DR. BEN-JOCHANNAN

Isfit. Hence, as we stand today, African people must trust their researchers who are laboring in the intellectual vineyards and have realized how pervasive the problem of falsification actually is.

In his *Life of Samuel Johnson*, Boswell tells us: "Knowledge is of two kinds. We know a subject ourselves, or we know where to find information upon it." Therefore, we must construct and employ a rigorous process of fact finding research and learning to search for and get to truth. Dr. Leonard James structured his teaching t create intellectual autonomy in the thinking of young people in which such problem-solving skills can address this problem.

As such then, and for this movement of reclamation we give thanks to the untiring research and writings of scholars of the caliber of Edward Blyden, born in St. Thomas in 1832 then in the 1850s, he went to live in West Africa and became steeped in African nationalism. There were ot hers as Samuel Lewis, James Johnson, John Mensah Sarbah, king Mutesa and others. Then theres W.E.B. DuBois who wrote *The Negro (1915)*, *Black Folks Then and Now (1903)*, and *The World and Africa* (1946). Let us not forget Marcus Garvey who gave us the Red, Black and Green in 1916 and insisted on reclamation of Africas glory. The noted "father of Black History" month celebrations, Carter G. Woodson wrote *The Negro Background Outlined (1926)* and *The Mis-Education of the Negro (1932)*, then *The Education of the Negro*. John G. Huggins and John Jackson penned *An Introduction to African Civilization (1970)* and John Jackson alone wrote *Man, God and Civilization (1974)*; Leo Hansberry, *Africa and Africans as Seen by Classical Writers* (1977) and *Pillars in Ethiopian History* (1974); J.A. Rogers, *Sex and Race (1952)* and *World's Great Men of Color (1946)*; and Chancellor Williams, *Destruction of African Civilization (1976)* are significant

FREDERICK MONDERSON

works that should be in any library. Yosef ben-Jochannan wrote *Africa: Mother of Western Civilization* (1970); *African Origins of the Major "Western" Religions* (1971) and *Black Man of the Nile and His Family (1972)*; Cheikh Anta Diops *African Origins of Civilization: Myth or Reality (1974)*, *The Cultural Unity of Black Africa* (1978) and *Civilization or Barbarism: An Authentic Anthropology*; Theophile Obenga's *Ancient Egypt and Black Africa* (1992) and *African Philosophy: The Pharaonic Period* – 2780-330 B.C. (2004); are all profound works of African research; while John Henrik Clarke's *Who's Betraying the African World Revolution* (2004) and his **Review** of Diop's *African Origins* (1974) represent an impressive collection. To this list we could add the works of Jacob Carruthers, Maulana Karenga, Molefi Asante, Dr. Leonard James, Asa Hillard, Charles Finch, Wade Nobles, Na'im Akbar, Anthony Browder, etc. However, let us not forget the outstanding contributions of Guyana's own Ivan Van Sertima, who very early, recognized "Mother Africa's" ancient influences in Asia, Europe, the Americas and particularly the Nile Valley.

Dr. Ben's Photo 88. Aswan. Temple of Goddess Isis. Standing before Horus in Double Crown and with a fellow Goddess wearing Queen Mother Crown with disk and feathers, Isis hold forth a scepter.

CELEBRATING DR. BEN-JOCHANNAN

Dr. Ben's Photo 89. Aswan. Temple of Goddess Isis. In a feathered crown, Pharaoh offers a symbol of longevity, the God Heh, endlessness of time, to Amon-Ra enthroned beside Isis in Double Crown as Mut.

As we evolve problem solving approaches to our condition, let us remember, Malcolm X has instructed "History is a good teacher," indicating examination of the past provides sufficient, substantive and significant evidence of cultural development and untold examples of peoples approaches to solving their problems. Professor John Henrik Clarke has reminded us: "History is the Clock that people use to tell their time of day; it is the compass they can use to find themselves on the map of Human Geography." He says further, "It is the role of history to tell a people where they have been. What they have been, where they are and what they are, but most importantly it is the role of history to tell a people where they still must go and what they still must be."

Now, as students of history we can gain much from historical examples that can benefit our situation as we theorize, strategize and implement workable plans of action to confront any situation but we must never shy away from values, form, motifs, symbols of our heritage, for herein lies our strengths. We must examine topics – cosmological – creation; epistemological – theory of knowledge; aesthetical – notions of beauty; metaphysics - science, etc.

As such, in our search for the origins of knowledge and with it understanding, this brings us to the heart and consciousness of Africa. However, contrary to Joseph Conrads highly publicized beliefs, Africa was not dark except in the deep recesses of the English mind, who not only slew the African, gorged on his carcass, in turn confiscated his physical, spiritual and intellectual wealth and denied his humanity and role as prime mover of the historical forces that shaped much of the Eastern and Western worlds knowledge, ideas and construct. *Ipso facto*, as we analyze this, let us not forget, Count Volney wrote around 1800, "The people we enslave today for their frizzy hair and sable skin, founded on the principles of science and technology that today govern the universe." Among these and simply as it may seem; the Register and Canon of Proportion were two of the most profound contributions Africans made to the development of culture in its various forms of artistic representation. The Register put order in representational art and the Canon of Proportion became the standard to represent the human form.

Moreover, and significantly, the view of physical and mental enslavement has not been universal for all time. What Martin Bernal called the "Modern Model" was able to replace the

CELEBRATING DR. BEN-JOCHANNAN

"Ancient Model" that recognized the opposite; evidence indicates not only did the ancient Africans innovate esoteric and spiritual consciousness, religion, governance, science and all branches of knowledge; nevertheless, despite all attempts to eradicate such evidence; more and more relevant data is being brought to the fore. But, in order to understand such, we must also know, proponents of the "Modern Model" came to dominate and shape the debate on perception and interpretation of who in fact the ancient Egyptians were, what is the proper role of Africans and Africa, viz-a-viz, Egypt and to whom should their legacy be attributed.

While ancient Egypt is the foundation of this address, developments and contributions of other areas of Africa and the Diaspora should come in for attention, time permitting.

Nonetheless, let me propose a manageable calculus to view the millennia of dynastic Egypt. First, we have the Prehistoric, then the following periods: Archaic, Old Kingdom, Middle Kingdom, New Kingdom, Later Period, Persians and Assyrians, Greeks and Romans.

The Prehistoric Period in Kemet/Tawi/Egypt/Kingdom of the Two Lands, is vast but for the most part, it has been limited to a manageable time period, some say, for convenience. That is, so it can be contemporary with Southwest Asian, Mesopotamian, and Sumerian origins. As science teaches, the earliest forms of man first emerged in Africa, South, Central and East! Still, here is a contradiction, because while foreign cultures had emerged by this "late date," Africa's cultural emergence had been reckoned in thousands of years prior. Nonetheless, the historic or Dynastic Period generally begins with Narmers unification of the two lands at c. 3100 B.C. according to the "Short Chronology." Therefore, any events and time before this is considered prehistoric or predynastic.

FREDERICK MONDERSON

Actually, the predynastic period is generally confined to the trilogy of cultures of the Badarian, Amratian and Gerzean or Naqada I and II, extending over a period of 1000 years from 4241 B.C. to approximately 3100 B.C. This too is wrong and should be pushed further back in Prehistory.

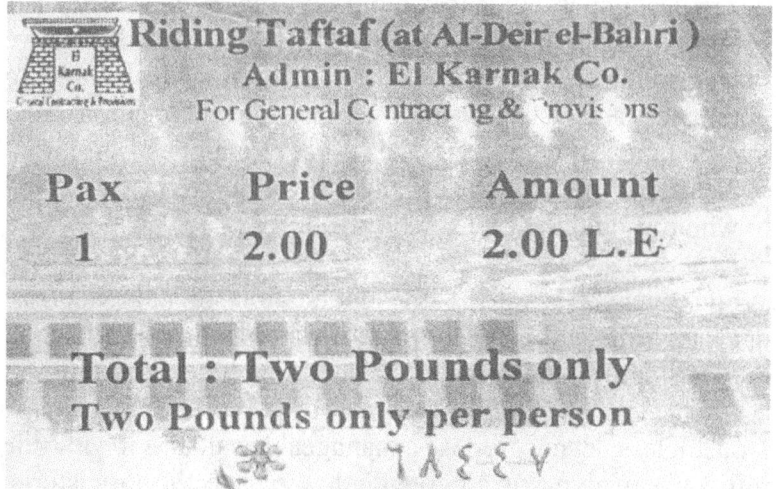

Dr. Ben's Temple Site Ticket 8. The Taftaf vehicle used to move visitors from the ticket entrance to the Tomb site at a cost of two Egyptian pounds. This is because buses and cars are no longer allowed near the monuments, given their exhaust pollute and degrade the ancient treasures.

Now, 4241 B.C. is considered the first fixed date in history when the Egyptians introduced their Calendar based on their observations of behavior of the star Sirius and flow of thre Nile for the Inundation. However, some scholars such as Petrie believe this date should be moved back an additional 1460 years to 5701 B.C. while Maulana Karenga believes it should be more properly c. 6200 B.C. or thereabouts

I draw your attention to a cycle of time measurement called the "Great Precession" dated to some 26,000 years. Some scholars have argued, to have one precession means they

CELEBRATING DR. BEN-JOCHANNAN

probably had to measure it against a second, maybe, a third. This means, 26,000; 52,000; or possibly 78,000 years of African star gazing and time measurement. Charles Finch proposed an additional precission which would extend this construct to some 104,000 years. Such a lengthy time period engaging in study of astronomy bodes well for the development of science and mathematics. You should also know there was a lot going on in this period that they dont want you to know about! We know of the existence of sophisticated stone technology in East Africa dated at more than 250,000 years; Katanga stone harpoons, according to Charles Finch's *The Star of Deep Beginnings*, date to 70,000-90,000 years; the South African iron-ore mine is dated to 43,000 Before Present; the Ishango bone fragment with mathematical markings is dated to 25,000 years ago. There is evidence of agriculture along the banks of the Nile that date to 18,000-16,500 B.P.; Catch basins in the Upper Nile show evidence of early agricultural practice and grinding stones to process wheat grown there and dated between 12,000-11,000 B.C. a indicated in the magazine **Science**; Albert Churchward's *Signs and Symbols of Primordial Man* states the ancient writers Eusebius and Syncellus, in their *Chronicles* tell of an **old tablet** called the "Old Chronicle" containing "30 dynasties in 113 descents, during a period of 36,500 years."

To reinforce some of this, let me use a quote from my latest book "The Holy Land" to gives one an indication of activity going on in Africa that seekers of truth and knowledge may not be familiar with.

Bernard Fages *History of West Africa* included interesting insights into the early history of this region. He showed fragments of coal were found at Nok, Nigeria sites that dated "greater than 39,000 years." Whether such sites were continuously occupied is uncertain. What is certain, by inference, is that many thousands of years ago, the entire continent seemed inhabited and producing art and social utilities, though much of it has not survived. To underscore such, Freeman-Granville (1976: 6) gives the following dates for other occupational sites in North Africa, Hawa Fata c. 38,750 to 2,910 B.C.; Malewa Gorge 31,000 B.C.; for Matjes in Southern Africa he gives dates at Pomongwe 33,570-19,700 B.C.; Florisbad c. 39,000 to 17,000 B.C., and Mufo in the Congo at c. 12,500 B.C. A recent article in *The New York Times* of October 2014, discusses red pigments in a bucket with brush, discovered at a "paint factory" in South Africa dated to some 107, 000 years and that there were other similar sites dated to 150,000 years. Conjecture would let us believe these early Africans had thought out some of the fundamental human questions regarding nature, science and spirituality. If they did, then their art may have shown it. However, not much has survived. However, not much as survived the Leakeys "catalogue" of hundreds of canvases in East Africa depicting African "Bushman" art using the "predominant red." Again, Freeman-Granville (1976: 4) calls attention to sites at Kanyatsi along the Upper Nile, having relationship to Olduvai, and Yayo in Chad. At Ain Hamech, Algeria; at the Atlas Mountains near Casablanca and at Makapan, Sterkfontein and Taung in South Africa, all dated approximately c. 1,800,000 B.C. After 500,000 B.C. many sites were in early occupation. Lochad in Zimbabwe, Broken Hill and Victoria Falls in Zambia, Ismailia and Kalambo Falls, Kharga Oasis in Kemet, Khodaine, Tachengitin, Algeria and Sidi Zin in Tunisia round out Early Stone Age culture in Africa.

CELEBRATING DR. BEN-JOCHANNAN

Dr. Ben's Photo 90. Aswan. Temple of Goddess Isis. The Kiosk of Trajan with its magnificent columns and their wonderful capitals, viewed from the land entrance.

Dr. Ben's Photo 91. Aswan. Temple of Goddess Isis. Thoth and Horus baptize the Pharaoh before he officiates at the Temple worship.

FREDERICK MONDERSON

The Later Stone Age boasted sites of occupation as follows and given by Freeman-Granville (1976: 6) who notes: "Kalambo Falls, 41,000-7,500 B.C.; Fashi, near Chad, at 19,350-9,750 B.C.; El Daba on the Libyan Mediterranean coast at 38,750-2910 B.C." For sure, as indicated, the illustrious African historical and cultural heritage has had ample time to experiment and create foundations for art and other forms of human philosophical, religious and spiritual progress.

All this, therefore, represent the period of early and ancient African prepared psychological, cultural and moral development in the relationship of spiritual consciousness between God and man. Thenceforth, while inner Africa bequeathed teh consciousness to crete conventions of human wisdom, Egypt and the Nile Valley cultivated, refined and preserved such profound knowledge and moral axioms as its religiosity expanded in praise of God that encouraged development in the cultural units of music, governance, language, medical know-how, art and architecture and mineral smelting for jewelry and domestic, agricultural and military implements.

In *An Order Outside Time* (2005: 9) Robert Clarke, in commentary regarding astronomy, states: "The standard constellations were representations of forces that were spirit in nature, of the Gods themselves. Though, the stars were not the actual Gods." We know of the four principal Gods of Egypt – such as Ra worshipped at Heliopolis; Ptah at Memphis; Amon at Thebes; and Osiris at Abydos. In this religious configuration, Ra particularly was associated with the sun. In fact, his worshippers were called "sun worshippers," but the Egyptians did not believe the sun was God. It was the magical, mystical, mythical force behind the sun that moved it; that was the God-essence that could not be seen, but reflected in the

CELEBRATING DR. BEN-JOCHANNAN

physical sun. This was like a sort of "power behind the throne" spirituality and that unseen force manifested as Amun and in the Middle Kingdom fusion with Ra as Amun-Ra, finding greater fruition in the New Kingdom as the visible and invisible that personified the sun disk symbol.

Today, as Africans struggle to combat the falsity of Egypt as generally presented, they are informed Egyptians had many Gods so they shy away. We need to understand Egyptian religious culture was monotheistic in its totality. Their theologians created harmony in their pantheon of Gods adhering to the monotheistic principle manifesting in a divine hierarchy. Todays religion, while subscribing to monotheism, ascribe "those Egyptian Gods" to be saints and significant others in their configuration.

Notwithstanding, there are certain easily identifiable markers that still confuse African peoples attention and inhibit inquiry and understanding of the subject matter. They begin rightly so by drawing attention to the face, wherein some of the hardest, most in-durable stone statues have their noses broken because this is the most prominent and readily discernible evidence of the Negro nature, mold, and heritage of the Nile Valley culture of ancient Africa. Some have argued, in the mummification process the brain was removed through the nose, so therefore... Well, the justification breaks down because there are mummies whose noses have not been broken or destroyed in any manner. So why break the nose of the statue and not that of the mummy, though this is the preferred prognostication. We must remember, for a law or rule to be applied effectively it must be universal in its application. Take for example Rameses II, who, because of his long reign of 67 years left statues all over the ancient land. His mummys nose was not broken. There were many statues of this king, perhaps depending on the artist and material used. The nose of the statue in the Memphis Museum is not broken nor the classic one in the Louvre. He built temples all over the land. The statues at the rear of the temple of Karnak, at the eastern gate, because of the prominence of this location, have had their faces disfigured, so too are those of his namesake Rameses III whose temple sits in the forecourt of Karnak. However, the statues of Abu Simbel are not disfigured nor the surviving one at Sebesi temple in Nubia.

Diop says the falsifiers of is tory could not hide nor erase the Sphinxs Negro face! While this is important, the problem with this situation is that African people seldom get beyond the nose to understand the archaeological, anthropological, artistic and scientific as well as linguistic evidence. Then theres the biometric, anthropometry and architectural data that together give a more comprehensive understanding of the subject. Then they must become familiar with arguments for origins that though false, are so ingrained in the human consciousness, they are acceptable as fact. We must debunk the movie *Ten Commandments* that was filmed in the desert in Arizona.

Dr. Ben's Illustration31. The "Great Cow" that suckles the monarch and Society to bring good fortune. "Hathor the Nubian" is also similarly shown as a cow-Goddess. This image, however, is of a bull! The Kings is considered, "The Bull of his Mother!"

CELEBRATING DR. BEN-JOCHANNAN

Architecture is the most profound and visible subject of human creations. Dr. ben-Jochannan has particularly instructed his students regarding what to look for upon entering a temple. The layout of the temple, its axial line "orientation towards some heavenly body," employment of the colonnade as a feature of nature as at creation and an honor for deserving officials, decoration of the outer wall where the king is shown combating forces of evil and destruction and the inside wall where the ritual is depicted and shows the king praising his God, conducting the ritual, even enengraving the names and associated images of king, queen and nobles, even erecting statues and stela, all add to the beauty and purposeful plan using the sacred space. The placement and orientation of statues of deserving individuals, the sacred lake that supports the notion of cleanliness next to Godliness, providing for the lustration of the God where he is awoken, washed, perfumed, dressed, fed, entertained, then returned to his place of rest until the next ritualistic meal time, or, when in a procession for some stately festival; all contributed to a sense of joviality, and joyfulness of being alive, worshipping and ritualizing their God, living according to the laws of the creator, preparing a tomb as place of final repose after the judgment and resurrection, were all part of the dynamic of heavenly spirituality, reliogiosity and culture in ancient Africa.

The Gods had instructed the priests as to the types of earthly house to build for their worship and protection. Thus, in this development religious or sacred architecture influenced other structural types whether domestic, civic or military as dictated by geographic conditions influencing layout. In turn, the architecture influenced art, stone transportation and the development of science. Temples became the hub for all types of activities as well as universities that trained practitioners of the medical and dental crafts, furtherance of science, competing schools of art and even trade. All people, but certainly African people, need to know this, but they also need to be familiar with the arguments to be able to demolish them. Therefore, the builder or architect had to be spiritually, psychically exact to achieve perfection in the final created project.

European scholars and *ipso facto* their people claim the ancient Egyptians were Indo-Europeans Caucasians and even Mediterranean types but all their arguments are "straw men." Diop's *The African Origins of Civilization* refutes the more significant ones. Two of these principal arguments are based on migration and linguistic connections. Later but still, Flinders Petrie, an early architect of migration influencing regional development, proposed the "New Race" theory that has largely been discredited because of its foreign imposed racial implications. The "New Race" theory held; a people migrated from South-west Asia bringing nothing but a superior mental faculty and a white skin! These invaders, we are led to believe, conquered a "low people" who inhabited the valley and contributed to the great cultural development but several points of their entry were debated. Let all persons in search of truth recognize all of what was stated previously! Their position is the same as the "Hamitic Hypothesis," now discredited that held, "A5ny evidence of a high culture found in Africa was brought there by people of a white morphology." How arrogant a proposition!

For entry into Egypt, firstwas proposed the Isthmus of Suez. This was changed to the Wady Hammamat region around Ethiopia, and moving across the desert, arriving at the Nile near Koptos and sailing downstream. Maspero proposed Europeans crossed the Mediterranean to North Africa and later entered the Nile Valley from the West! Lets all be familiar with arguments that the culture ascended the Nile! This is all confusing! Consistent with the view, Alexander Moret

CELEBRATING
DR. BEN-JOCHANNAN

proposed, "By whom was the South influenced if not by the North?" To this, Dr. Diop responded, "If so, why are the important monuments and sites located in Upper Egypt and not Lower Egypt."

Examining the place of origin of these early supposed "foreign" Egyptians and that these invaders were "agricultural folk" and "boat people," it does not follow that agricultural are migrant. Let us also not forget they supposedly arrived sometime during the Old Kingdom, left no evidence of Egyptian cultural manifestation in their place of origin but built the pyramids and erected the Negro Sphinx as guardian of the Necropolis. Conversely and starting in Nubia, Dr. ben-Jochannan traced the development of the pyramid concept through the silk pyramid, the natural, step and finally the true Pyramid at Ghizeh. Equally, Chancellor Williams, in the **Frontispiece** to *Destruction of Black Civilization* states regarding these migrants place of origin: "The traveler said to the old man, what happened to the people of Sumer, I hear they were black?" The old man replied, "They lost their history and died." We must never lose our history! Diop has instructed, "We must live and die on the battlefield of African historical reconstruction!" The old Asyriologists Rawlinson and Mortimer Wheeler, among others, have confirmed the Sumerians were black being part of the early migration out of Africa. Yet, invading peoples from that region arrived, white, and upon reaching the Nile, sailed northward. How silly!

Competent scholars, ancient and modern, have always argued, rightly so, the culture of ancient Egypt began in the south, as far as the headwaters of the Nile and sailed downstream. We know Narmer the Theban mobilized his armada and sailed north to conquer and unite the two kingdoms around 3150 B.C. The size of his army, furnished by a flourishing Southern

Kingdom, possessing an established system of writing, with highly developed mathematics numbering in the millions, as well as mastery of the Nile and art motifs, enjoying religion established and practiced, one has to wonder about the superior mentality of the migrating or wandering Bedouins who left their place of origin. Imagine these people arrived and began reinventing Narmers wheel! Lets face it, only people in search of a better life or outcasts leave their place of origin to migrate! Add to this, absence of any evidence of Nile Valley inventions and so, "You do the math!"

Dr. Ben's Photo 92. The Aswan Area. Temple of Goddess Isis. Osiris, Isis and Horus in Double Crown sit enthroned. All three wear necklaces.

CELEBRATING
DR. BEN-JOCHANNAN

Dr. Ben's Photo 93. The Aswan Area. Temple of Goddess Isis. Enthroned Nephthys, Isis sister, strikes a majestic pose grasping her scepter and ankh and wearing the Queen Mother crown surmounted by horns, disk and her symbol.

Wallis Budge identified "Hathor as Nubian." She is shown prominently on the **Narmer Slate Palette** as an established deity. The earliest wooden statues of God Min were painted black and today reside in a back room of the Ashmolean Museum, Oxford, England. In the Luxor Museum, the image of Amon-Min is that of a God painted

FREDERICK MONDERSON

Black who not "so painted for the funerary ceremony" as in the claim made for Tutankhamon's sentinels and the discovered seated statue of Mentuhotep II whom W. Stephenson Smith in *The Art and Architecture of Ancient Egypt* (1958, 1959), saying he had "black flesh." In the "Geography of the Gods," Ptah, "God of Artisans" who constructed the heavens and was grandfather of many of the younger deities was a bald-headed dwarf akin to the little people of Central Africa, "Twa" but mistakenly called "Pygmy." This place was called the "Land of the Gods." Osiris the "Great Black" came from Central Africa, his wife Isis represented the Black Madonna. Their son Horus and his namesake, the Elder Horus, were blacksmiths or metal workers who "went north to Egypt" possessing a power to be intermediary between God and man! Amun, God of the Empire, was "so black, he was blue!"

Need I say more!

Language is another trait used by those arguing for the Caucasian Southwest Asian origin of the Egyptians. But the argument has been made by 19th Century scholars that any similarities found in the language is miniscule and due to borrowing which probably occurred from exchanges in early trade. Notwithstanding, while Diop and Arnett have all identified the prototypal symbolism and rudimentary forms of hieroglyphics in the highlands to the south of Egypt, Henry Winkler attributes some of the earliest rock drawings to people from Mesopotamia. Nevertheless, Stephenson Smith has written the earliest Nile Valley drawings are to be found in the upper reaches of the river, which he dates to c. 7500 b.C. That is, much of the flora and fauna as well as geographical elements that comprised the corpus of the hieroglyphic language are native primarily to the Upper Egyptian/Central African, geographic region.

CELEBRATING DR. BEN-JOCHANNAN

No Egyptologist has studied Africa to determine its connection to Egypt more so than E.A. Wallis Budge, Keeper of Egyptian and Assyrian Antiquities at the British Museum. While at first he agreed with colleagues that Egyptian was an Indo-European language, later he broke ranks, reversed his earlier pronouncements and affirmed, rather than being Indo-European, the language was purely African in character. He came to the conclusion as he constructed his two-volume **Hieroglyphic Dictionary** in 1920.

Therefore, whatever the line of argument for or origin of the ancient Egyptians, whether migration, language, race, blue eye color, etc., its purely speculative at best, non-existent at worst. Circumstantial at best, a scribe was discovered with blue eyes and is now displayed prominently at the Louvre Museum in Paris. The argument has been made, "Well, you see, the Egyptians had blue eyes!" However, we know the Egyptians used inlaid eyes on their statues with whatever available material. Its like the young people who today use contact lens of all colors as fashion.

Let me say finally, because I need to rest my case!

Culture and spirituality in ancient Africa, the Nile Valley and Egypt in particular, has been indigenously long in development, an exceedingly original origination, a knowledgeable utility in its ramifications and purposefully uplifting to its creators and practitioners. Because God first appeared to the African, admonishing "keep my commandments" he has not only flourished in mental faculty but, despite adversity, has imparted tremendous soul force that has saved humanity. African peoples economic, political and cultural motifs must remain African; otherwise they are moved off their strengths. There must be critical thinking but not destruction and self-hatred. African people need to emphasize and stress tradition, culture, art, literature, history, politics and sociology. Therefore, People come back to African culture and spirituality, come back, for here is your destiny and salvation. In my new book entitled *The Holy Land* this writer quotes the Afrocentrist Molefi Asante, "To remain African is not to be primitive, backward or heathen but to be correct, positive, sane and intelligent. We must see ourselves as the masters of our own destiny."

Dr. Ben's Photo 94. The Aswan Area. Temple of Goddess Isis. While Isis nurses the baby Horus backed by a sister Goddess, "Khnum makes man on his Potters Wheel," as Thoth writes at his rear.

CELEBRATING
DR. BEN-JOCHANNAN

15. SPIRITUALITY IN ANCIENT EGYPTIAN TEMPLES BY DR. FRED MONDERSON

Recently I was reading an article written by G.W. Wainwright entitled "The Origin of Amun" published in the *American Journal of Archaeology* in 1931. While he developed the argument that Amun came to Karnak from Hermopolis in the Middle Kingdom, he posited the view that Min, Amuns alter ego, the God with the prominent creative organ and balancing not holding his flagellum, came from Mesopotamia in South-West Asia. There are a number of problems in this position.

A current argument holds, the ancient Egyptians were Caucasians who came from SWA, crossed the Arabian Desert and entered Africa by way of the Horn; traversing the Wady Hammamat they arrived on the Nile at Koptos, in Upper Egypt. From there they sailed down the Nile! Dates for this migration vary; but principally its given as in the Old Kingdom. Wainwright also contends that Min came from Mesopotamia specifically. James H. Breasted, fr all his "faults," argued any Mesopotamian or South-West Asia origin or anteriority over Egypt is "not worth a credible response!" If we concede that the Egyptians were Caucasian whites and we also acknowledge that they came from SWA, we still have a problem with this contention.

The English archaeologist Flinders Petrie, the "father of Egyptian Archaeology" found large wooden pre-dynastic statues of Min at Koptos that were painted black and are today housed in the Ashmolean Museum, Oxford, England, though

FREDERICK MONDERSON

not on prominent display! Like the "Long Chronology" adapted into the "Short Chronology" to make it contemporary with Mesopotamian developments, the Min statues have been re-dated to the Old Kingdom to appear contemporary with Mesopotamians arrival in Egypt. The first thing we ask ourselves, Why would white, Caucasians be worshipping a black God; even painting their God Black? Why were these statues painted black in Egypt? Were they painted black in Mesopotamia where these peoples cultural nucleus is to be found? Were any such or other statues found there painted same? Were any statues from Mesopotamia ever painted black? If perchance any statues were discovered painted black in Mesopotamia, were they painted black for a funerary ceremony or were they representative of the color of the people? Now, the "spin" on, first, Tutankhamon is that the sentinel statues were painted black for the funeral ceremony. A female Guide in the Cairo Museum in 2005 told this writer, "My teacher at the American University in Cairo told me Mentuhoteps statue in the Museum was painted black for the funeral ceremony." The Heb Sed festival is about life, rejuvination and not about death! When painted Black, Min appeared alive in Hatshepsut's apartments beside the Sanctuary at Karnak; so too in Thutmose IIIs image in the Luxor Museum; then again, he appears in "black-face" in Rameses IIs Abu Simbel temple; and further, he appears black, enthroned in Isis temple at Deir el Medina. Naturally, these are some examples of what has survived time and man. However, the understanding is that there were two statues in the Heb Sed Festival. That is, the one discovered wearing the White Crown while the other, the Red Crown. The above scenario breaks down the "painted Black for the funeral ceremony" argument. Fact is, wooden statues are the only material painted and represent people not the funeral ceremony, particularly since Min, a God, was not dead!

CELEBRATING DR. BEN-JOCHANNAN

Given again, we know, in Chancellor William's *Destruction of Black Civilization*, as the **Frontispiece** Caption states: The traveler said to the old man, "What happened to the people of Sumer, I heard they were black?" The old man replied, "They lost their history and died." Equally, Dr. Diop has argued that European and American scholars destroy evidence, omit information and distort the fact on Egypt, even making existing data confusing, atributing much to "Syria and Syrians" (Ha. Ha) in their desire to exclude Africans from the wonderful civilization of ancient Egypt, second oldest daughter of "Mother Africa;" that is, after Ethiopia.

The well-known elder and master teacher Dr. Yosef ben-Jochannan has taught this writer and scholar principally three things, listed as follows: "Monderson," he said, "There are fifty countries in Africa, choose one and specialize in it. Become a specialist not a generalist;" and though my first Masters degree from Hunter College of CUNY was as an African Historian with a Thesis on the *Cameroons: A Strategic Prize of German Imperialism* (Unpublished), I chose to specialize in Egyptian studies. To this I have devoted a great deal to research, books and travel to the Holy Land.

Dr. Ben's Photo 94a. Aswan. Temple of Goddess Isis. Facing the Kiosk of Nectanebo. Notice the graded steps that lifts the structure's floor to a higher level.

FREDERICK MONDERSON

Dr. Ben's Photo 95. Aswan. Temple of Goddess Isis. Thoth stands to the rear of Khnum (left) "making man on his Potters Wheel" as two Goddesses back him and the King offers a pectoral.

Dr. Ben's Photo 96. Aswan. Temple of Goddess Isis. With Thoth at his rear, Amen-Ra offers ankh or "life" to Isis nursing her son Horus as enthroned Nephthys wearing the Red Crown backs up her sister.

CELEBRATING DR. BEN-JOCHANNAN

Dr. Ben's Photo 97. The Aswan Area. Temple of Goddess Isis. Enthroned Amon-Ra sits with Thoth and other members of a "divine power team" stand at his rear.

After buying and reading his books in first edition in the early 1970s, when I first traveled with Dr. Ben in the 1980s, he issued his dictum, "Now that you have come to Egypt, seen what you have seen and secured the knowledge, what are you going to do with it?" Therefore, "Publish or Perish!" In response, I have written more than 1000 articles for the Black Press in New York and authored some 30 books on Egypt and African-America, not to mention particularly books and articles on Sonny Carson, Michael Jackson, O.J. Simpson, Mike Tyson, Dr. Ben-Jochannan, Barack Obama and written articles on Dr. John H. Clarke, Dr. ben-Jochannan, Dick

FREDERICK MONDERSON

Gregory, A. Philip Randolph, Dr. Leonard Jeffries, Marcus Garvey and having been to Egypt in excess of 20 times. Hence, as a scholar I speak for myself. Third and most important, "when doing research on Egypt and Africa" the good brother and friend instructed, "Get the oldest material you can find and work from there!"

Dr. Ben's Illustration 32. Abydos. Tombs of Perabsen and Khasekhemui (right); and, Tombs of Mena, Zer and Den (right) in W.M.F. Petrie's *The Royal Tombs of the Earliest Dynasties, Part II* (1901).

Now, in an interesting article entitled "Egyptian Mummy" among Antiquarian and Philosophical Studies in *The Gentleman's Magazine* of October 1820, pp. 349-350, in describing a mummy donated by Mr. Joshua Heywood to the Hunterian Museum at Glasgow, the writer states: "The body, shrouded in from fifty to sixty folds of coarse pale brick-red colored linen, is deposited in a strong wooden coffin, fashioned so as to bear a rude resemblance to the human shape. At the upper extremity is carved a face, the features of which (as in the case with all Egyptian sculpture) are very much of

CELEBRATING DR. BEN-JOCHANNAN

the Negro cast." We know the Egyptians loved the color red because they associated it with the sun, a solar and special phenomenon. They considered themselves special! Dr. Cheikh Anta Diop said the Egyptians painted themselves red to be distinguished from other Africans. Even Dr. Ben has often said, "The Egyptians painted themselves red with the Henna plant. Even young brides, particularly Nubians, were painted red with henna as they do today. " Going back to the most ancient African "Bushman Art" and even art among the "Tassili Frescoes" red was the favorite color; again like gold, it was considered to be of a divine nature! In her investigations of "Bushman Art" in East and Southern Africa, speaks of the "Predominant red," these painters used. Thus, we ask, "Are all of these red colored Africans Egyptias?" Let us also remember, the "paint factory" discovered in South Africa and dated by *The New York Times* in 2014 at 107,000 years, indicate red paint in a pot with brush, as the predominant color.

The article continued, "Though the features were very much collapsed, the face was nowhere divested of skin. The skin itself was of a chestnut-brown color. The brow was well shaped, though, if any way defective, narrow; and to some it may be interesting to learn, the organ of music was prominent. The nose, though slightly compressed, retained enough of its original shape to be recognized as Roman." Might I also add; the original color of the mummy of Rameses II when first unwrapped was similarly brown splashed with black! Dr. Van Sertima recounted Cheikh Anta Diops observations that the mummy of Rameses II was exposed to so much radiation in Paris when it was being repaired, it turned yellow. So, if in the future you are told the mummy is yellow understand how it got so.

FREDERICK MONDERSON

Even further, the gentleman of the article wrote, "One circumstance must have struck all who had an opportunity of seeing the above interesting examination; namely, *the dissimilarity of the features to what we are taught to believe were those of the inhabitants of Egypt* [This writers emphasis], at the remote period at which the custom of embalming existed in that country. A moments reflection will suffice to convince us that this circumstance can in no way throw discredit on the antiquity of the genuine character of the mummy."

The writer goes on to say, "Mr. Millar, portrait painter in Glasgow, is at present finishing a likeness in oil of the face and surrounding parts. As they appeared immediately after they were exposed; and was completely successful in the accuracy of the likeness before the exposure to the air had converted the face from a brown to a sable hue, which it did in the short period of three hours."

The above is quoted because, in contrast, John David Wortham in *The Genesis of British Egyptology: 1549-1906* (University of Oklahoma Press, Norman, Oklahoma, 1971: 93) has written: "Great progress was made during the nineteenth century in the study of Egyptian mummification. Augustus Bozzi Granville, a physician and a student of Coptic, undertook the earliest nineteenth-century dissection of a mummy at his London home in 1825. From his detailed dissection he correctly concluded that the ancient Egyptians were Caucasians. He also succeeded in clearing up many erroneous ideas about the embalming process. Among other things, he proved the correctness of Herodotus assertion that the ancient Egyptians had, when preparing a cadaver for burial, extracted the pituitary through the nostrils." We can confidently assume Herodotus never visited a mummy factory but was told this by priests, which Wortham believes. However, Herodotus' description that "The Colchians, Egyptians and Ethiopians have broad noses, thick lips and are

CELEBRATING DR. BEN-JOCHANNAN

burnt of skin" was an observed fact that Wortham and other writers dismiss! Now, I ask the reader "you do the math!" If Egyptians as late as the time of the Romans, after 30 B.C., could have "brown skin," particularly after admixture with Hyksos, Persians, Assyrians, Greeks and Romans themselves, since these soldiers do not carry their women when on expedition but mix with the local females, how then can we still believe they were "Caucasians with white skin?" Let us not forget, and in counter to this Dr. John Henrik Clarke has reminded us, "The people who preached racism colonized history" and that "When Europe colonized the world, she colonized the world's Knowledge!" In that case, "African history must be written by African scholars and researchers!"

Now, the purpose of this essay. The Egyptian temple has been a sacred place and a bastion of spirituality from its inception at the "first occasion" when the "God arose" from the waters of chaos and his aura created the protective space the temple came to represent. Of this first act, Gaston Maspero has written "the temple is molded on the principle of the Egyptian conception of the universe" and as such, its constructed and regulated on the same principles as the heavens. The only difference, the temple is in close proximity to humans, as opposed to the distant realm, and the human function and responsibility is to guard the portals and administer to the resident deity in hopes he or she would bring good fortune to the domain and society in general. However, the Egyptian temple was unlike any other religious structure, whether Jewish Synagogue, Christian Cathedral or Muslim Mosque, because people never came there to worship. Nevertheless, the creation, guarding and maintaining of these sacred spaces were very similar to that of the Egyptian temple in order that the business of divine ritual and worship would be conducted.

FREDERICK MONDERSON

Dr. Ben's Photo 98. Aswan. Temple of Goddess Isis. Another view of the Kiosk of Trajan as visitors either sit in the shade or move to the river entrance for the better view.

Dr. Ben's Photo 99. Aswan. Temple of Goddess Isis. The dynamic duo, Isis and Nephthys, in all their majestic splendor.

CELEBRATING DR. BEN-JOCHANNAN

Dr. Ben's Photo 100. The Aswan Area. Temple of Goddess Isis. At the temples rear, a view of the Mausoleum of Aga Khan in the distance across the river.

In respect to this experience, Byron E. Shafer in *Temples of Ancient Egypt* (1998: 2) has supplied an interesting description of cosmological forces at work when he says: "Temples and rituals were loci for the creative interplay of sacred space and sacred time. Sacred space is a place of clarification (a focusing lens) where men and Gods are held to be transparent to one another and a point of communication, the paradoxical point of passage from one mode of being to another. In sacred space one is oriented to the cosmos and immersed in primordial order; there one experiences truth and renews life. Over time, such space appears unchanged and unchanging, stable enough to endure without growing old or losing any of its parts." That is why so much respect is paid religious institutions where they stand in the sacred place.

FREDERICK MONDERSON

Even further, Shafer (1998: 2) continued: "What has been said of sacred place can, for the most part, be said of sacred time as well. It is a moment, or season, or cycle of such clarification and communication, orientation and immersion, experience and renewal. Time, however, is not so stable a dimension of order as space. Egyptians experienced time as a spiral of patterned repetitions, a coil of countless rebirths. The purest moment of sacred time was the first, the moment of creation, when the existent and its order emerged from the nonexistent and its aspect of disorder. Subsequently, time, as a component of order, proved vulnerable to chaos. So, for example, the intervals between sunrise and sunset came to change from day to day and season to season, and the beginning of each new 365-day year came to rotate slowly backward relative to the seasons and the helical rising of the star Sirius. Because of orders ongoing vulnerability to chaos, Egyptians needed to conceive of creation not as a single past event but as a series of first times, of sacred regenerative moments recurring regularly within the sacred space of temples through the media of rituals and architecture." Thus, according to Egyptian beliefs, because evil and demonic persons and forces existed, to combat such required priests be kept busy protecting their sacred space in unending ritual and prayer so the Gods safety can be assured, the wonder of his thoughts and actions manifest, and he maintain harmony or *Ma'at* in the universe keeping it in balance.

All this notwithstanding, while there is a religious, theosophical or spiritual aspect to the temple, the institutions survivability equally depended on an economic incentive and a security component that supported the sustainability of the sacred space and place. While early theorists have postulated the view priests were the earliest architects, in their other worldly connection with the divine who instructed them psychically as to the dimensions and arrangement of the

CELEBRATING DR. BEN-JOCHANNAN

principal features of the sacred space; temples were generally gifts of monarchs who actually built them. Having done so, they next created economic endowments to sustain their creation as an obligation to their father, being sons of the God in the divine lineage with its attendant obligations, responsibilities and benefits. However, having been endowed with the structure and "seed money," the caretakers of the temple sought to economically increase their largess by initiating a number of strategies such as the manufacture of crafts and creation of building and decorative skills that beautified their residence but also became trade commodities. Agricultural produce were grown to feed residents and surplus food exported in trade. Gardens produced flowers that were an essential part of the daily ritual of lustration of the God. All this involved an untold number of individuals working in harmony depending on the size of the temple and the prominence of the God relative to the age in which he or she was worshipped. Their specialists studied, predicted and followed up in aftermath of the Nile Rivers inundation with its impact on the farming community and control of water in a dry land through the maintenance of canals, dams, dykes and embankments. They were also excellent astronomers who long studied the clear Egyptian sky, mapped the heavens and regulated their calendar.

FREDERICK MONDERSON

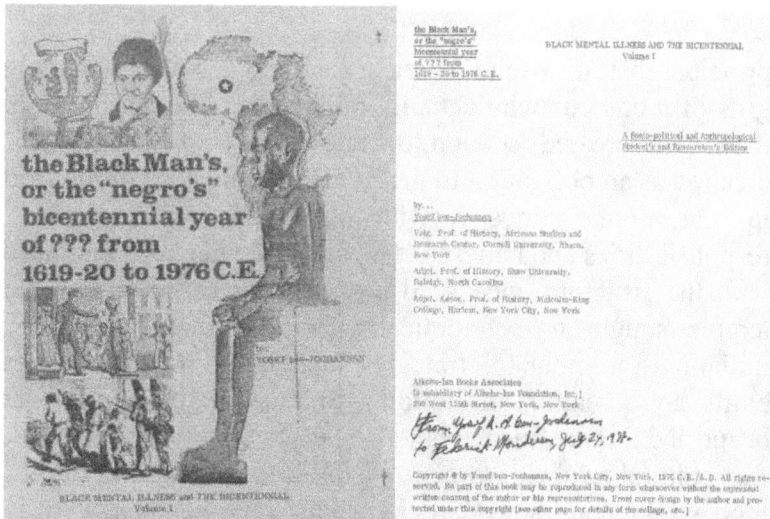

Dr. Ben's Book 10. **The Black Man's or the "negro's" Bicentennial year of ??? from 1619-20 to 1976 C.E. : Black Mental Illness and The Bicentennial Volume 1** (1976). Note the Author's autograph to Frederick Monderson.

In addition, the temples became schools that trained members of the government bureaucracy, produced medical and dental professionals, catered to mortuary needs of high and low and became literary help-centers for the majority of the population who were illiterate and needed documents such as letters, contracts, wills, etc. Even more important, as the God and priests conspired to instill an imperialist mentality in vigorous warrior pharaohs, who went forth to conquer, significant portions of their captured spoils in economic wealth and human captives were donated to the temple as endowments for the deity who had brought good fortune to the imperial efforts of these kings.

CELEBRATING DR. BEN-JOCHANNAN

This increased bounty enabled the Gods domain to be significantly beautified and expanded, so much so, the Middle Kingdom and New Kingdom capital temple at Karnak, home of the Empire God Amun (Amon, Amen, Amun-Ra), experienced 2000 years of "vegetative growth" as untold numbers of pharaohs vied with each other to reward the good fortune the God granted them. In all this, the priests, who formed a confederated body called the Priesthood, came to wield significant power and influence, becoming king makers and king breakers themselves. They became so powerful by the Late Period priests represented themselves in art on a footing equal to that of the pharaoh, previously an unthinkable development. In all this, weak pharaohs trembled at the prospect of the priests material and growing political power and influence coupled with their presumed spiritual power gained through being divine intermediaries with the God.

While the strong kings manipulated the priests through endowments, buildings projects and the threat of their military prowess, their weak counterparts stood in awe of the priests because, though they claimed to be Gods on earth, the priests as true God intermediaries knew these kings weaknesses while the kings themselves were unsure how much the priests knew or how much power and influence they could wield with the supreme God. This growing power of the Priesthood manifested and by the 22nd Dynasty priests challenged the established order and declared themselves kings beginning with the High Priest Herihor. Such an action of *Pontifex Maximus* (King and High Priest) began a long journey of the ultimate demise of Egyptian culture along with its inherent power and divine inspiration gained in adherence to the principles of theological and cosmological beliefs and religious practice guided by the principles of *Ma'at*. Nevertheless, as time passed and though the nation declined in its material and military power, its religious beliefs and spirituality remained a potent force even though conquerors came, destroyed much and even tried to inculcate and emulate what Egyptians had been doing for the three thousand years of pharaonic rule. Still, thousands of years later, this spirituality is still evident in any visit to a temple. That is, providing ones mind and body is in the right place to experience this spiritual and metaphysical phenomenon.

Dr. Ben's Photo 101. Aswan. Nubians at the waterside bid farewell to their "Nubian-American" brothers and sisters who visited their village.

Dr. Ben's Photo 102. Aswan. Close-up of young Nubians with an elder who really appreciated the visit of "their Nubian-American" brothers and sisters.

CELEBRATING
DR. BEN-JOCHANNAN

Dr. Ben's Photo 103. Aswan. Dr. Fred Monderson aboard a motor launch returning from a visit to a Nubian village.

The religious dogma and spiritual potency is encapsulated in the temple orientation and alignment. The architecture thus created in the sacred space is a fascinating subject that challenges the imagination, excites the intellect and titillates the art appreciation sensitivities. The well-known Dr. Yosef ben-Jochannan has always emphasized the principal architectural features of the temple and instructed his students to visit the Hypostyle Hall at Karnak five or six times, so as to comprehend what the magnificent hall stands for, as a "forest at creation." Equally too, Mann in his work *Sacred Architecture* (1993: 14) has supplied a splendid and penetrating view in describing several ways in which the symbolic or the spiritual is expressed through sacred architecture manifesting in sacred space. These are: "First, sacred architecture reflects the structure of the cosmos. Before there were buildings, humanity worshipped the stars and planets, the four elements, the earth, and its animals and plants, as Gods. In our progression from caves to modern buildings, the symbolism of this early integration with the cosmos has been central, and still activates the deepest essence within us, the core of our psyche. Initially, sacred monuments were associated with a particular God, Goddess, or the natural or supernatural powers they represented. They were aligned by or with the stars or planets in the sky, which represented the God or Goddess. They were also geographically oriented and located in places significant to the Gods. Some monuments were used by priests or priestesses as observatories to measure the movements of the planets or heavenly bodies they worshipped, while others were sited in accordance with planetary motions. Most megalithic monuments echoed some or all of these functions in their siting, design and function."

"Second, sacred monuments were organized using primary geometric shapes and proportions, described by number symbolism. Mathematical mysticism or sacred geometry is a profound part of sacred architecture, and its often mentioned in relation to the Egyptians and Pythagoreans. Pythagoras created a humanistic philosophy which utilized mathematical harmony and proportion as primary tools in daily life, including art, architecture, music, morality and history. He believed that the order inherent in numbers, a number symbolism, creates specific effects on the observer, both psychologically and spiritually. The discovery of the innate meaning of numbers is therefore a primary creative legacy of sacred architecture. The exploration of the numbers and proportions of the sacred brings a higher understanding to architecture."

"Third, the sacred lives in buildings or monuments in which the structure and decoration follow clear and basic patterns derived from the ancient conception of the four elements,

CELEBRATING DR. BEN-JOCHANNAN

earth, water, air, and fire, the forms of nature and from living energies and the geometries derived from them. Proportion systems amplifying natural rhythms and patterns bring a natural and organic energy and spirituality to sacred architecture – the building contains an elemental as well as a human quality evoking the spiritual."

As a result, Mann (1993: 106-07) concludes: "The creation of sacred buildings echoes the creation of the universe, and both seek to follow similar mathematical laws. Therefore, the Golden Section (phi) is found to govern the growth of plants and animals, and is also the primary proportion found in sacred buildings and monuments. In their use of numbers as a symbolic language, the Egyptians predated and influenced Pythagoras and Plato. The Egyptians communicated symbolic astrological and astronomical concepts beyond the actual form of the buildings. Similarly, their hieroglyphical language used symbols instead of mere signs. A sign has a limited meaning, while a symbol evokes correspondences and widens understanding. The Egyptians used their mythology to further understanding because it was more than simple history. Their Gods came from the stars, beginning wisdom, understanding and power. Their myths were cosmic myths, describing planetary movements, and brought the mathematic reality of the stars to humanity."

Equally, we need to look at the layout of the temple because of its significance that in many ways mirrors the design of the home of a noble or king. When the king visited the temple for a festival, to dedicate some new part of the temple, participate in temple ritual or offer some tribute, there is a particular protocol he participates in. The geography of the landscape and the Nile River played a significant role in not only the architecture but every aspect of the society whether in science, art, philosophy, religion, theosophy or economics. As such, it was also the principal highway of travel and on a visit to the temple the king arrived by boat at a pier to greeting of priests and other dignitaries. There was a principal and secondary entrance to the temple. The temples principal entrance was generally approached through a canal and he then entered an Avenue of Sphinxes that brought him to the First Pylon gateway where flag-staves flew flags of the resident God, temple, city and nation. Sometimes other Gods were also resident and their banners or flags were also flown. Here he was introduced to the three principal parts of the temple.

Comparatively, just as the private home is considered to have three principal parts, the temple also did. The roadway brings the visitor to the home where a fence, yard and walkway introduces him or her to the entrance door. This is comparable to the Avenue of Sphinxes that brings the visitor to the Egyptian Pylon and entrance into the Great Court that is often decorated with columns and colonnades, altars, statues, trees, even shrines and sometimes a pond or pool of water, that is, in addition to the Sacred Lake. In this area, images of lions and baboons are also placed strategically to greet the rising sun. Importantly, to have ones "name written in the colonnade" is a significant honor. The second part of the home is the living room where guests are entertained that sometimes even doubles as a dining room. The Hypostyle Hall is the second part of the temple described as a "forest as at creation" where a number of ceremonies in procession were performed and only certain individuals were allowed therein. The third part of the home is the bedroom area where no visitors are allowed and only the master and his family are permitted. Behind the Hypostyle Hall lies the "Holy of Holies" where the God resides and only the High Priest or King is permitted in this most sacred spot. In the room where the God dwells in complete darkness, a door shuts him off from all external activities and forces.

CELEBRATING DR. BEN-JOCHANNAN

When the King or High Priest visits the temple to meet his God, after he had been baptized or purified, the seal to the door is broken and the Gods sanctum is disturbed to awake him to have his "toilet" performed. At this time the Sanctuary is incensed and he is then given a bath; anointed with sweet smelling unguents and perfumes; he is dressed and his jewels and insignia put on; and then administered his meal. Then his chamber is incensed and prayers said and the ritual performed. Finally his chamber door is closed and locked. This ritual is generally done three times per day. In that environment and to be clean or pure, the priest must wash three times per day. After this encounter the door is locked until the next visit whether to bathe, feed or praise the deity. Therefore, while the Open Court is filled with sunshine, the "Holy of Holies" is maintained in complete darkness. We should be reminded Dr. ben-Jochannan has advised, visitors should not enter the "Holy of Holies," the "Sanctuary," for in ancient times only the pharaoh or high priest would enter this select space of the God! To do otherwise is a violation of the sacredness of this environment and should not be permitted.

Ancillary to the Sanctuary were adjacent rooms housing liquid and solid offerings, a library for the temple ritual, vestments of the God and the High Priest and such things as incense and other utilities used in the ritual. Other Gods associated with the temple are also housed nearby. There are open and closed sanctuaries depending on the nature of the temple. For example, the Temple of Karnak aligned east to west, has an open sanctuary that allows the sun to shine into the "Holy of Holies" upon rising and also a second opening to receive the suns rays being cast as it sets at days end. The temples of Luxor, Deir el Bahari, Ramesseum and Medinet Habu have closed sanctuaries. There is oftentimes a chapel on the roof where the statue of the God is often taken to greet his counterpart, the Sun God, and to bask in the power of his rays.

FREDERICK MONDERSON

Dr. Ben's Photo 104. Kom Ombo Double Temple to Haroeis and Sobek. The majestic upper reaches of the double entrance of engaged screened columns, varied column capitals, the decorated architrave topped by double disks with uraei and outstretched wings on the cornice.

Dr. Ben's Photo 104. Kom Ombo Double Temple to Haroeis and Sobek. Image of a Bull and Heifer, perhaps the latter, a form of Hathor.

CELEBRATING DR. BEN-JOCHANNAN

Dr. Ben's Photo 105. Kom Ombo Double Temple to Haroeis and Sobek. Double portal to Kom Ombo Temple showing Sobeks entrance to the right and Haroeis, the elder Horus, to the left.

Dr. Ben's Photo 104. Kom Ombo Double Temple to Haroeis and Sobek. Mother giving birth in the traditional stance.

FREDERICK MONDERSON

Dr. Ben's Photo 106. Kom Ombo Double Temple to Haroeis and Sobek. Another view of the previous image but featuring the left side of the entrance, that of Haroeis. Notice the double winged disks above on the cornice, the different capitals and uraei front left and iner rear.

Dr. Ben's Photo 107. Kom Ombo Double Temple to Haroeis and Sobek. Classic side view of the columns juxtaposed and providing the entranceway to the inner reaches of the Temple. The color changes depending on time of day photos are taken.

CELEBRATING DR. BEN-JOCHANNAN

Dr. Ben's Photo 104. Kom Ombo Double Temple to Haroeis and Sobek. Elder Horus Hareoris and Sobek, the Crocodile.

The principal axis line is very important and often aligned with the journey of the sun from east to west. In this respect, statues along the principal line face towards the axis. When there is a secondary north-south axis, again as in the case of Karnak, the statues do not face this secondary axis but stand parallel with it while yet facing the principal axis.

An significant feature of the temple layout is as one ascends into the deep recesses from the profane to the sacred environment, the floor rises and the roof lowers. This allows the "Holy of Holies" to rest on the highest point in the sacred space mirroring the rise of the God from the waters of chaos at creation. A Sacred Lake is an essential part of the temple where where water is provided priests wash themselves, again, sometimes three times per day, before administering to the God. These ancient Africans lived the notion, "Cleanliness is next to Godliness." On certain festival or feast days, the Ark or boats of the Gods are allowed to sail on the Sacred Lake. There is generally a Nilometer nearby where the rivers behavior is studied. Naturally, there are residences nearby within the enclosure for the Gods servants to be housed. A nearby garden provided flowers that adorn the sanctuary and other pivotal places in the temple. There may be other temples in the temple! Interesting, that while incense with its spiritual and esoteric potentialities was burned in the temple ritual as part of worshipping the God, it was never burned on an altar. An incense burner was generally placed in a nearby corner and once lit, the incense was placed within. Many illustrations depict the pharaoh about to incense the God but he holds the incenser in his hand. On the inner walls, individual frames of art illustration depict various parts of the ritual from start to finish. Interesting, the earliest incense burner had been found at Qustol in Nubia, centuries before Unification after which this important instrument appeared in Egypt!

The decoration of temples was significant for a number of reasons. On the outer face of the enclosure wall or pylon, the pharaoh is shown battling Egypts enemies, natural and spiritual; while on the inside he is shown in ritual offering to his God. There were principally three types of temples, the

CELEBRATING DR. BEN-JOCHANNAN

worship temple, the mortuary temple and the processional temple. The worship temple was dedicated to the deity of worship. The mortuary temple was dedicated to the king, who, upon his death, became a God. The processional temple was a shrine utilized by the God when away from the Sanctuary and priests needed to rest the Ark on way to some distant destination. Naturally there were chapels, kiosks, and even portable shrines but these played a less significant role.

In the Old Kingdom the mortuary and worship feature was a part of the same structure. By the Middle and then the New Kingdom, the mortuary and worship temples were separated. Only worship temples have survived from the Graeco-Roman period. While in the Old Kingdom temples were scantily decorated this increased during the New Kingdom being more beautifully illustrated. However, by the Graeco-Roman Period the temples were profoundly illustrated, so much so, this enabled the transmission of ancient ritual and building practices long lost through the ravages of time and man.

So here we are! The temple meant many things to the ancient Africans of Egypt but we need a different approach in seeking to understand what they did in the time in which they lived. Remember, everything they did was original because they had not one to imitate. Because these ancient Africans feared their God and wanting to stand confidently in his presence in the afterlife judgment, they structured their lives in strict adherence to the 42 Principles of *Ma'at*, often called the Negative Confession. Why 42? Its hard to tell. We know there were 42 Books of the God Thoth that encompassed every form of knowledge. There was a great Company of 42 Gods in the Judgment and the famed Temple of Seti I at Abydos had 42 steps in its ascent to the entrance.

FREDERICK MONDERSON

Dr. Ben's Photo 108. Kom Ombo Double Temple to Haroeis and Sobek. Side view of the entrance Hypostyle Hall deecorted columns, each with a different capital below abacus and architrave.

Dr. Ben's Photo 109. Kom Ombo Double Temple to Haroeis and Sobek. Out hunting with the Royal Lion who devours the crocodile on a wall enclosing the magnificent columns with their different capitals.

CELEBRATING DR. BEN-JOCHANNAN

Dr. Ben's Photo 110. Kom Ombo Double Temple to Haroeis and Sobek. From the Court, beyond the screened wall with uraei and viewing the magnificent columns against a clear, blue sky. Notice the uraei and winged disks above the frame.

Dr. Ben has pointed out there were 147 of these of which the 42 were extracted and so too were the **Ten Commandments**. The Negative Confessions or "Declaration of Innocence" simply affirmed "I did not do such and such." There were also Positive Confessions, things the Egyptian proudly boasted he did. These principles undergirded their spirituality, shaped their ethical beliefs and practices and laid down rules of scientific and social principles that still govern our lives today. Thus, whether religion, ethics, science, architecture, art, mathematics, theosophy, and theogamy, all these were gifts of Africa and Africans as a legacy to the human family and must be considered within the philosophical construct of the fatherhood of God and the brotherhood of man.

May I add, the antithesis to **Ma'at** was **Isfit**. As **Ma'at** represented goodness, order, balance, reciprocity; **Isfit** represented evil, disorder and all the forces of wrongdoing. The King constantly did **Ma'at** to combat the spiritual and moral threat **Isfit** represented for the individual and the state. In the contest of the drama of the Psychostasia where the individual made his **Declaration of Innocence** he extolled the good he did in the **Negative Confessions** and denied committing actions associated with **Isfit** views and practices.

Dr. Ben's Photo 111. Kom Ombo Double Temple to Haroeis and Sobek. Close-up of the decorated architrave crowned by decorated protective disk with wings and protected by uraei. Notice the Son of Ra cartouche.

CELEBRATING DR. BEN-JOCHANNAN

16. "MYSTICAL NATURE OF AFRICAN SPIRITUALITY"
By
Dr. Fred Monderson

Recently, on New Year's Day, I was in San Juan de La Maguanas in the Dominican Republic, and visited a nearby Batey for the annual religious ceremony. I observed the people in procession and noticed that many of the aged icons they carried depicted white faces, but it soon dawned on me, it was not the white faces these people worshipped. These were simply available symbols of the spirit and spirituality, these people, black as they were, worshipped as handed down by their ancestors, who worshipped in similar fashion. This made me remember something Ivan Van Sertima once said.

In a *tour de force* lecture on the "African Origins of Egyptian Civilization," the renowned author covered most bases as he demonstrated how the Africans contributed greatly to Egyptian civilization and with significant later world history; as this view is similarly and particularly articulated by Cheikh Anta Diop in *The African Origin of Civilization: Myth or Reality*. Dr. Van Sertima elaborated on the significance of archaeologist Bruce Williams discovery of the "Worlds Earliest Monarchy found at Qustol in Nubia," as published in *The New York Times* of March 1, 1979 and later again in his *Journal of African Civilizations*. The symbols discovered at Qustol in the royal tombs, viz., an incense burner, with depictions of a palace façade with the Horus falcon; enthroned monarch wearing white crown; a Nile Boat sailing, etc., predated pharaonic Egypt by almost 2 centuries and by 10 prehistoric kings. Interesting, but Emile Amelineau mentioned 16 pre-Narmer kings from his work at Abydos. Given Amelineau commented on Petries find of a town at Abydos dated at 14,000 years, such a discovery supports the acceptance of "Amelineaus kings." Equally, this also supports the idea of Abydos being the place of the Archaic Periods kings being buried there for, as they followed Narmers burial; perhaps, he also followed those king preceeding him.

While Diops work was articulated some two decades before these revelations, they reinforced the fundamentals of what he argued. Diop, in proposing the "Two Cradle Theory" of matrilineal as opposed to patrilineal descent in Egypt, offered what others nicknamed "Sun" and "Ice" dispositions. The Mercer Cook's translation of *The African Origin of Civilization: Myth or Reality* (1974) highlights Immanuel Wallerstein's critique of Diop's work explaining: "The Aryans have developed patriarchal systems characterized by the suppression of women and a propensity for war. Also associated with such societies are materialist religion, sin and guilt, xenophobia, the tragic drama, the city-state, individualism, and pessimism. Southerners, on the other hand, are matriarchal. The women are free and the people peaceful; there is a Dionysian approach to life, religious idealism, and no concept of sin. With a matriarchal society comes xenophilia, the tale as a literary form, the territorial state, social collectivism, and optimism." To support his contention, Diop cited language and totemism then postulated the view in summary that while the "branches of the tree" in his argument could use some "pruning," the roots and the trunk are firm in the role of Black Africans in Egypt.

CELEBRATING DR. BEN-JOCHANNAN

Dr. Ben's Photo 112. Kom Ombo Double Temple to Haroeis and Sobek. One of two cornices depicting the protective disk with wings and protected by uraei. Notice the two ladies image as protective of the King of Upper and Lower Egypt.

Dr. Ben's Photo 113. Kom Ombo Double Temple to Haroeis and Sobek. Columns in the Double Temple's Peristyle Court with screened walls.

FREDERICK MONDERSON

Dr. Ben's Photo 114. Kom Ombo Double Temple to Haroeis and Sobek. Another view of the left side decorated columns before the entrance.

However, the important thing on which Van Sertima elaborated was, by using the revelations at Qustol, the notion of omission and by extension distortion was a hallmark of Western scholarship on Egypt and Africa in general. In this he explained, how in the construction of the Aswan High Dam, temples of Nubia were threatened by the impending "Lake Nasser" created by the stored water. **UNESCO** appealed to nations with a history of, and experience in, Nile Valley excavation. Such nations as Britain, France, Germany, Italy, the United States of America and so on, responded to engage in the rescue of many Nubian temples.

Regarding Qustol, the American archaeological team led by Keith Seele, author with Steindorff of *When Egypt Ruled the East* under the auspices of the University of Chicago, made the famous discovery in 1962; yet, the team packed the find

CELEBRATING DR. BEN-JOCHANNAN

away in the basement of the University without making known its significance. Such a revelation would have greatly undermined the projection and preaching of white supremacy scholarship in attributing Egypt to non-Africans: first Caucasians, then a "brown-Mediterranean race." This argument is no longer tenable in view of continuing archaeological and other scientific challenges to the edifice of historical misinterpretation. Seele died and probably thought that he would carry the finds
significance to his grave.

While Bruce Williams discovery is an early release of this significant information, only heaven knows what other hidden secrets lie in the basements of institutions such as the British Museum, the Louvre, Metropolitan Museum of Art in Manhattan and in such cities as Brooklyn, Chicago, Philadelphia, Turin and even in the Cairo and Luxor Museums.

Seeles omission is not unique. For, when we think of the great Egyptologists Maspero, Breasted, Howard Carter, Flinders Petrie and his wife Hilda, Griffith, Erman, Weigall, Mayberry, Mahaffy, T.E. Peet, Reisner, Hall, Lepsius, Naville, Hayes, Wilson, etc., etc., who visited the Cairo Museum even after the 11th Dynasty monarch Mentuhotep was discovered in a tomb in 1898 that was cleared between 1903-1906, none correctly noticed or noted the statue's complexion. It was not until 1959 that W. Stephenson Smith observed and wrote in *The Art and Architecture of Ancient Egypt* that Mentuhotep had "black flesh." Imagine, half a century of omission and the untold number of books written but their information withheld! We should also note J.H. Breasted in his *Ancient Times* published in 1916 writes of the Egyptians as "tall, brown skin men" and later changed this to write of the "Great white race." Some have argued, Nelson Rockefeller donated significantly to the University and Museum's "Chicago House Museum" in Luxor to begin and continue epigraphic work in Luxor, Egypt. So, beyond heaven, who knows what else is hidden, omitted, misrepresented, distorted, destroyed and purposely lost. Even "doctored" in Museum basements!

The anti-Afrocentrists, Lefkowitz, et al.; based on these and other omissions and distortions falsely argue the Egyptians were Caucasians! Students of history, in search of truth must challenge and refute, by evidence, these white supremacist interpretations. The fact that none of these scholars, despite the mounting evidence, has gone back to revise any of their previous positions attest not only to their ideological intransigence but to their professional dishonesty and superciliousness.

As a good example, John David Wortham, makes the same argument, for in *The Genesis of British Egyptology: 1549-1906*, University of Oklahoma Press at Norman, (1971: 93) he boldly asserted: "Great progress was made during the nineteenth century in the study of Egyptian mummification. Augustus Bozzi Granville, a physician and a student of Coptic, undertook the earliest nineteenth-century dissection of a mummy at his London home in 1825. From his detailed dissection he correctly concluded that the ancient Egyptians were Caucasians. He also succeeded in clearing up many erroneous ideas about the embalming process. Among the things, he proved the correctness of Herodotus assertion that the ancient Egyptians had, when preparing a cadaver for burial, extracted the pituitary through the nostrils." How about his giving Herodotus credit for describing the mummification process but discounting his eyewitness account that the "Egyptians had broad noses, thick lips and were burnt of skin." It is clear Herodotus observed some things and others were told him. He probably never observed the embalming process and thhus was told him. However, he did observe the ethnicity

CELEBRATING
DR. BEN-JOCHANNAN

of the people among whom he lived and traveled for his researches. Such a view would certainly question Wortham's interpretation.

Dr. Ben's Photo 115. Kom Ombo Double Temple to Haroeis and Sobek. The King, in different attitudes, makes presentations to different deities on different columns.

Dr. Ben's Photo 116. Kom Ombo Double Temple to Haroeis and Sobek. Another pair of decorated columns featuring the King making presentations to the temples deities.

FREDERICK MONDERSON

Dr. Ben's Photo 117. Kom Ombo Double Temple to Haroeis and Sobek. Thoth and Horus baptize the King with ankhs before his entrance into the Temple to perform the daily ritual.

Therefore, when these scholars argue that the Egyptians were Caucasians, from their firmly planted flag in quicksand, we have to question who knows the truth and dismiss all forms of porous arguments. And, like Zahi Hawass' contention that Tutankhamon is the only certainly identified monarch "because we find him in a sealed tomb;" that is, including the now identified Hatshepsut; the others need to be vetted to finally determine their true identity. Thus, systematic and concerted analysis of all reports, writings, presentations and displays on ancient Egypt must be subject to meticulous scrutiny as the work of Tutankhamon and Hatshepsut were subjected to.

Nevertheless, and regarding Van Sertima's now famous 1986 lecture in explaining the atom and its sub-particles, he touched upon the nature of the universe saying that there was something very mystical, even magical, about it that even the most profound scholars find it more and more interesting and moe complex as they delve even deeper into its mysteries.

CELEBRATING DR. BEN-JOCHANNAN

What we see, those African peoples from Haiti and Dominican Republic demonstrating in their worship, then, has a deeper intrinsic psychic and spiritual significance. Consider these are the traditions handed down by their contemporary forebears seeking to express their religious spirituality, restricted as they were under the horrible institution of slavery. Thus, we see a heritage now continued as esoterically charged exercises with deep spiritual and cultural underpinings manifesting profound meanings in these modern times.

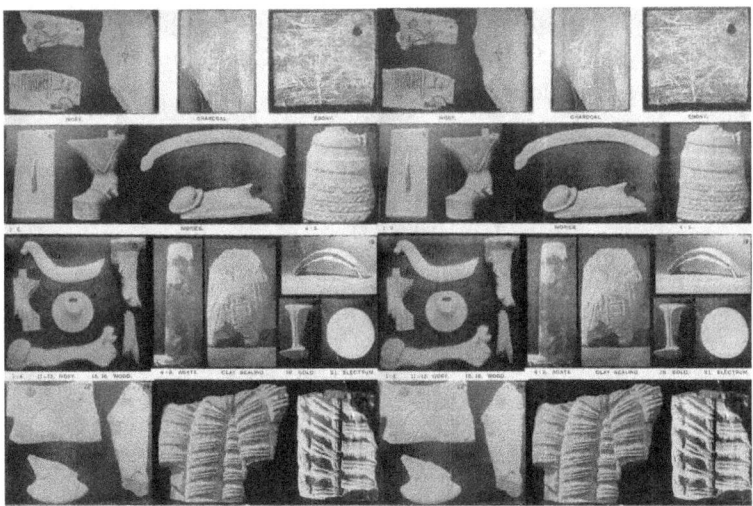

Dr. Ben's Illustration 33. Abydos. Ivories, Charcoal, Ebony, Wood, Clay Sealings, Agate, Electrum, Marble, Brown Schist, etc., from the Tomb of King Zer-Ta (left) and, Stone Bowls, Sealings from the Tombs of Merpaba, Qa and Perabsen (right) in W.M.F. Petrie's *The Royal Tombs of the Earliest Dynasties*, Part II Extra Plates (1901).

It should be remembered, in the subterfuge of "putting on ole Massa" to inflate his ego, one of the devices used by enslaved Africans to sustain them through those horrendous and perilous days of their historical experience as chattel slaves was the practice of Christianity. When they had nothing in that time of despair, these Africans had that new world Christian tradition fused to their traditional faiths which brought them through. And, even this, the slave master and his descendants tried to stamp out. Hence, the African descendants created a metamorphosis of religious and cultural expression whose foundation was undergirded by this spirituality and spiritualism practiced in Africa for millennia upon millennia.

There is ample historical evidence to support the African origins of Christianity. Among many others, Godfrey Higgins in *Anaclypsis* (1836) tells, many of the ancient religious personalities of Judeao-Christianity were black.

Indeed, the antecedents or proto-spiritual essence of Christianity manifested itself along the banks of the Nile, thousands of years prior to the conversions of Europeans. We know, for example, that the foremost Gods such as Ra, Min, Amon, Osiris, Ptah, Hathor, Isis and others, were Black!. How then the Caucasian originators of Egyptian civilization could have created and then worshiped black Gods?

Dr. Ben's Photo 104. Kom Ombo Double Temple to Haroeis and Sobek. Mother nursing a young child.

CELEBRATING DR. BEN-JOCHANNAN

Dr. Ben's Photo 118. Kom Ombo Double Temple to Haroeis and Sobek. Winged Sun-Disk with uraei highlight this illustrated board showcasing left to right Hieroglyphic writing.

It is refreshing to recall, in 1989, Dr. ben-Jochannan, the famed African authority on Egyptology, while in Egypt, convened "The Panel Discussion," a unique and never to be forgotten or repeated experience. The Panelists included a Philadelphia Christian Minister and a young California Sister. Amidst the discussions of "What has coming to Egypt meant to you," the Sister said to the Minister: "Rev. McNair, now that you have seen all that you have seen in Egypt, how can you still preach the same thing to your congregation?" To this dare, Rev. McNair responded: "I cannot teach my people there is no God, I can only show them where God comes from." In fact, this respected Christian minister recognized God was manifested amidst those most ancient Africans millennia upon millennia ago. Perennially re-establishing that connection in sweet communion with deity is what African people seem to experience and relish; in that spiritual, psychic and metaphysical connection, worldwide, no matter what the conditions, they joyfully relish in the heritage. Those who derogate, based on the perceived outer manifestation of those Africans in their annual ecstatic and spiritual bliss, are simply uninformed and archaic in belief. The mystical significance of these ceremonies is too deep for the ignorant and insensitive to comprehend. For, African people, worldwide, constantly return to the regenerative wellspring of their deep spiritual integrity, autonomy and psycho-cultural continuity in recognition of the omnipotence and omniscience of the all-powerful divine nature of the fatherhood of God pervading the brotherhood of man.

Dr. Ben's Photo 118a. Three-time Karate Black Belt, Luis Casado, is fascinated with the early evidence of Martial Arts in a Beni Hasan Tomb.

CELEBRATING DR. BEN-JOCHANNAN

17. MOUNTAIN VIEW OF AFRICAN SPIRITUALITY BY DR. FRED MONDERSON

A closer look at a religious festivity this past Christmas day in Dominican Republic revealed a deeper meaning to the ceremony being performed by participants. A visible image of adoration in the particular ceremony was Mary, Joseph and the bambino. While the coloration of the images was standard for Spanish and Latin America, beyond the race factor there was a deeper meaning to what the people saw, felt and expressed. The careful observer may see the deep religiosity encapsulated in the mysticism of African spiritualism unfolding in the religious experience. That is to say, the participants had moved beyond the mundane view of the racial outer covering of the objects of their veneration to the philosophical and theological, esoteric and mystical underpinnings in their genuine and heartfelt expression of spirituality praising the divinities and their significance without. Surprisingly, this was done in proximity to the mountain range straddling the border of Haiti and the Dominican Republic.

Mountain ranges have featured significantly in religious and other movements and ideas that have impacted cultures and civilizations significantly. In time perspective, as to the origins of the ancient Egyptians, a popular view is they came from "the foothills of the mountains of the moon where the God Hapi dwells." This increasingly contradicts the now disredited view, the "white Egyptian rulers" are stated to have migrated

FREDERICK MONDERSON

from the Caucasus mountains; the Zagros mountains; and even inhabitants at Picu Manchu in South America show connections to early religious and societal settings.

Dr. Ben's Photo 119. Kom Ombo Double Temple to Haroeis and Sobek. Offering a vessel and applying incense pebbles before Haroeis (Horus).

Herodotus, the "father of history," in his *Histories* tells of Pharaoh Necho of the 7th Century B.C., who sent sailors to circumnavigate Africa. When they reached the vicinity of the Cameroons in West Africa, from the seas they observed volcanic activity on Mount Cameroons. Thinking deity was in residence, they termed the place "Chariots of Fire." Lest we forget, according to biblical lore, Moses, "schooled in all the

CELEBRATING
DR. BEN-JOCHANNAN

wisdom of the Egyptians" received the 10 Commandments from Jehovah on Mount Sinai. Such beliefs associate God and his manifestations with the sky and in the minds eye of ancient man, any elevated location, whether natural or man-made was associated with divinity worship. Even the old saying, "faith could move mountains" seems to imply a divine intervening connection to make such a phenomenon possible.

These examples help to show a philosophic, spiritual, theological and esoteric connection between divinity on those elevated surfaces and human religious practices. Important, however, religious admonition had been so profound from the beginning, it indelibly implanted in the consciousness of mankind the need and desire to worship and ritualize the Gods for the emotional, spiritual and even material salvation associated with attendant religious practice.

Dr. Ben's Photo 120. Kom Ombo Double Temple to Haroeis and Sobek. Horus, Shu and Sekhmet, the Lion Goddess.

Dr. Ben's Photo 121. Kom Ombo Double Temple to Haroeis and Sobek. Double presentation to Horus in Double Crown while Isis as Hathor stands behind the God.

Dr. Ben's Photo 122. Kom Ombo Double Temple to Haroeis and Sobek. In White Crown with feathers, Pharaoh offers a magnificent golden girdle to the two sisters, Isis and Nephthys. Notice the Hathor head on the Girdle.

CELEBRATING DR. BEN-JOCHANNAN

Nevertheless, no one knows for sure when the omnipotence of almighty revealed its comprehensibility within the consciousness of man providing appropriate instructions on the nature and dynamics of residence and ritual. Inherent in these instructions, then, were also guidelines for protection and sustenance of the deity so as to effectuate its mission of saving the world and humanity in perpetuity. To establish and effectuate the evolved guidelines a professional class, priests, emerged "knowing" the desires and objectives of which deity mysteriously imparted to followers.

Inasmuch as its always helpful in order to measure and understand the present and future, looking at the past provides practicable examples of the human journey from then to now and the standards of moral and ethical behavior designed to better the human spirit.

It is a credible argument that God first appeared to African man inhabiting the equatorial belt to instruct and impart the psychological and philosophical benefits of sweet communion with deity. Our ancestors along the Nile and its safe to say were first recipients of the comprehensibility of the esoteric nature of this divine interaction. Having received this Godly largesse, their experts soon systematized and refined it, while establishing parameters for the practice of worship and ritualizing the deity as outlined in the inspirational admonitions. Thus, as the deity imparted cosmological manifestations of their earthly descent to interact with man, the divine intermediaries conveyed the ritualistic guidelines, requirements and benefits to be gained in faithful execution of protection, provision and praise of the deity.

The notion of the "Geography of the Gods" in Africa, the Nile Valley and Egypt is an interesting one. Contrary to 19th and 20th Century imperialist propaganda that the ancient Egyptians were "white," we know the principal Egyptian Gods were Black! Let us remember, Ra, the foremost of the Egyptian deities, after he had created the first pair of lesser Gods, Shu and Tefnut, air and moisture, created the "people of Nubia." Ptah, the creator God who was responsible for all physical features of the universe was a "baldheaded pygmy." Osiris originated in Central Africa, manifesting as an aspect of the Nile River God Hapi whose source of origin is the headwaters of the river and the highlands of Ethiopia. Lest we forget, some ar guments place the God Hapi at the foothills of the mountains of the moon. Hapis (Osiris) son Horus went north with his "blacksmith" companion. Isis as Hathor is of Sudani origin. Now, if the kingdom of Osiris, "Gods land," was in Central Africa, then his chief minister Thoth, "The Onian," had to have been African and resident in this part of Africa to effectuate his duties. Anubis, the God of the dead could not have been an expatriate working for Osiris, and thus, he too had to have been native African. The prototype of Amon, Amon-Ra, his alter ego, Min of Koptos, whose two black colossal statues discovered by W.M.F. Petrie, now reside at the Ashmolean Museum in Oxford, England. Let us not forget Amon-Mins image in the Luxor Museum.

Now, if one continues to insist the Egyptians were "white" as does Wortham, despite O'Connor's affirmation to the contrary, and these are both white scholars, then I affirm these white Egyptians worshipped black Gods who created black people before their white counterparts. Thus we argue the absurd conclusion, as did Cheikh Anta Diop, that "black people are basically white" who first emerged in the Equatorial belt of Africa. **Absurdity, ad infinitum!**

Nonetheless, these ancient Africans of the Nile Valley were steadfast in practicing their religiosity particularly from elevated locationsand this was actually a process that developed over millennia, constantly refining its philosophical

CELEBRATING
DR. BEN-JOCHANNAN

tenets and becoming more ingrained in the consciousness of its adherents.

Dr. Ben's Photo 123. Kom Ombo Double Temple to Haroeis and Sobek. Close-up view of the Sobek side of the Temple's Sanctuary.

Dr. Ben's Photo 124. Kom Ombo Double Temple to Haroeis and Sobek. Close-up of the Haroeis (Horus) side of the Temple's Sanctuary.

FREDERICK MONDERSON

Dr. Ben's Photo 125. Kom Ombo Double Temple to Haroeis and Sobek. From the rear, view of the Haroeis (Horus) side of the Temple's Sanctuary.

18. BLACK GENESIS I BY DR. FRED MONDERSON

BLACK GENESIS: The Prehistoric Origins of Ancient Egypt is not for the faint of heart for it strikes at and shatters the racially charged and falsely propagated theory that the ancient Egyptians were Caucasian migrants from South West Asia who entered Egypt from different and conflicting points because upon close scrutiny each point of entry betrays the "straw man" nature of the argument since it was designed to falsely portray Caucasian supremacy in a scheme offering no logic and despite overwhelming evidence to the contrary of that stated position.

CELEBRATING DR. BEN-JOCHANNAN

The Author's, Robert Bauval and Thomas Brophy apply state of the art scientific investigatory techniques to trace the prehistoric origins of the ancient Egyptians emanating from the Saharan region, far in the west of Southern Egypt at a time when the desert area was indundated in terrential rains and teeming with vegetation that supported a zoological horde of wildlife including cattle. This time was contemporary with freezing temperatures in the Caucasian region when the astronomical, architectural and artistic accomplishments of the desert dwellers could not have been duplicated in the South-West Asia environment.

It is interesting how, when the architectural structure of Zimbabwe was first discovered by westerners, it was "Expertly" determined "Shipwrecked Chinese" or even "Phoenician sailors" found themselves in the heart of Southern Africa and built these architectural marvels. In the same way, origins of the Egyptians were ascribed to the Caucus region in South West Asia but the point of the entrance into Africa became a question of contention in the 19th Century because emerging new information made each theory obsolete. First, the Isthmus of Suez was thought as the point of entry, thence an ascent of the Nile River to the southern capital that emerged as the center of most prominence of the culture from the Middle Kingdom onward.

FREDERICK MONDERSON

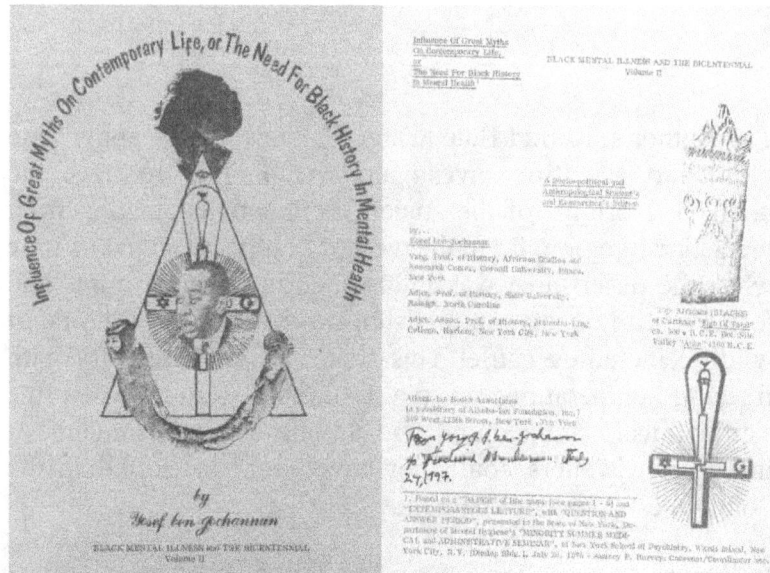

Dr. Ben's Book 11. Influence of Great Myths of Contemporary Life, or The Need for Black History in Mental Health: Black Mental Health and the Bicentennial Volume II (1976). Note the Author's autograph for Dr. Fred Monderson.

Another argument held, "for some unknown reason," a migrating group left South West Asia, following a path during the Old Kingdom that brought them to the Horn of Africa, entering Egypt from the Red Sea, traversing the Wady Hammamat and arriving at the Nile in the region of Koptos. Once there, they sailed down the Nile conquering the indigenous peoples, who, incidentally had already built the foundations of a cultural civilization unheard of in the place of origin of these wanderers. The significance of this contact is that though these individuals did not bring the units of culture then manifesting in the Nile Valley, they brought a "superior mental attitude" that "gave an added impetus" to the civilization they found. Unfortunately, this "superior" mentality never created the rudiments of any comparative

CELEBRATING DR. BEN-JOCHANNAN

civilization in their place of origin. Sir Gaston Maspero of "Negroid not Negro" fame, proposed people from the Sahara region migrated to the Nile Valley when that region had begun to desiccate. Unfortunately, he claimed these were Caucasians who had crossed over from Southern Europe and inhabited North Africa. Then they migrated into the Nile Valley. Notwithstanding, however, argument for a North-African entry into the Valley of the Nile differs from an entry from the Sahara.

Dr. Ben's Photo 126. Kom Ombo Double Temple to Haroeis and Sobek. Hathor wears horns and a disk above the "Queen Mother Crown" vulture headdress.

FREDERICK MONDERSON

Dr. Ben's Photo 127. Kom Ombo Double Temple to Haroeis and Sobek. Horus wears the Double Crown with uraeus on the brow. Notice his necklace.

We all know researchers have a tendency to construct a theory and then set out to find data that supports such, irrespective of how off base it may be. Nevertheless, all arguments for a "Caucasian," "European," "Semitic," "South-West Asian" origin of the Egyptians is based on speculation whether through language borrowings or scant, if any at all, substantive information in support, more likely smoke and mirrors.

The notion of a cow, Goddess of nourishment, is an integral part of the drama in the heavens as she is tended by these

CELEBRATING
DR. BEN-JOCHANNAN

divinities. The question this raises is simply this – How dissimilar is this idea from that articulated by Brophy and Bauval in *Black Genesis* that the people of *Nabta Playa* were earliest astronomers who practiced "cow c ulture" and initiated the idea of the "Cow Goddess" or great mother who nourished mankind as they were pastoralists who actually the precursors to the pharaohs!

For example, the Louvre Scribe, purportedly from the Old Kingdom, resides in a prominent position in that French Institution. One of its more prominent features is that it has blue eyes! As such, gullible yet ill-informed particularly European visitors buy into the theory, "See, the ancient Egyptians had blue eyes." No one entertains the fact, ancient Egyptians utilized inlaid eyes of whatever color in their statuary. Another example is that of Wortham in *The Genesis of British Egyptology* wherein he states, Augustus Bozzi Granville conducted an autopsy on a mummy in his London home in 1825 and correctly concluded the Egyptians were Caucasians. Both examples go from a specific to the general, using deductive rather than inductive logic, a sort of "one sparrow so its summer" syndrome. Nonetheless, all arguments for an alien origin of the Egyptians nust the pivotal nature of Upper Egypt though circuitously seek to inculcate this region into their scheme but to no avail.

It is interesting how the obstinacy of white racial intellectual arrogance can perpetuate, and, in defiance of credible evidence, cling to outdated and outmoded positions on the origins of the culture of ancient Egypt and the role of Africa and Africans in that ancient African culture. Many people have commented on the statement by Zahi Hawass as he oversaw the **Supreme Council of Antiquities** in its never ending work to rescue, recover and revitalize the culture of ancient Egypt. He was quoted as saying the ancient Egyptians were not White, Black, Africans. They certainly were not Arabs though Arabs claim ancient Egypt as their ancestral culture! We do know, however, the Arabs were a long line of invaders who conquered Egypt but generally added little to the culture complex that developed there. In fact, in their marauding through any territory, conquerors are too busy destroying rather than preserving and when they do settle down for the long haul, their efforts at preservation fall short having destroyed much. Still, it is interesting to read what Dr. Hawass has to say about Robert Bauval and Thomas Brophy's *Black Genesis*: *The Prehistoric Origins of Ancient Egypt* (Vermont: Bear and Company, 2011) that not only provides evidence for the foundation of Egypt but also shatters much of the myths of a Caucasian Egypt.

Montesquieu, the French *philosophe*, admonished persons act, think, write" as if their behavior can become a universal law." Universal laws are unalterable! Much of the conclusions about the ancient Egyptians, particularly of the 19th and 20th Centuries interpretations have now been proven not to be universal laws, but more like orchestrated falsities. For instance, Europeans on exploration love to name places and things and the proliferation of British heroes names in geographical features of Canada is a remarkable example of this. Nevertheless, as Europeans began ascending the Nile, they began naming landmarks and other features. Using the "king and queen metaphor" they named the large room in the Pyramid of Khufu, the "king's chamber" and the next sized one, the "queen's chamber." At Amarna this was also repeated, only to find out the large room was in fact the queens not the kings chamber! Equally too, at Aswan the cataract encountered there was described as the first and the sixth at the rivers source in Central Africa. Whereas, the river flowed south to north, the first cataract should be where the sixth is stated to be and the sixth is where the first has been identified

CELEBRATING
DR. BEN-JOCHANNAN

in this scheme of reckoning. These disparities have not been corrected.

Dr. Ben's Photo 128. Kom Ombo Double Temple to Haroeis and Sobek. A King wears horns, disk, feathers and with uraei with disks.

FREDERICK MONDERSON

Dr. Ben's Photo 129. Kom Ombo Double Temple to Haroeis and Sobek. God Shu wears his feather with uraeus on his brow. Thus, if the Nomes are counted South to North, why not so for the Cataracts. Simple. The Egyptians counted the Nomes but moderns counted the Cataracts.

One incontrovertible fact no naming could tamper with is the situation of the Nomes. The first Nome began at Elephantine Island in the Aswan vicinity and the 22 Nomes of the South stretched all the way towards the apex of the Delta. The 20 Nomes of the North began at Memphis and is numbered out

CELEBRATING DR. BEN-JOCHANNAN

towards the Mediterranean Sea. How the significance of the first Nome this far towards inner Africa has escaped so many is a surprise among the many caveats that point to the "Black Genesis" of ancient Egypt!

Dr. Ben's Illustration 34. Abydos. Steles Around the Tomb of Zer-Ta (left); and, Granite Floor, Chamber and Wall of the Tomb of Den (right) in W.M.F. Petrie's *The Royal Tombs of the Earliest Dynasties*, Part II, Extra Plates (1901).

While Bauval and Brophy mention Cheikh Anta Diops work, one of the recommendations the old master has insisted upon is group research or partnerships to which these scholars so wonderfully excel in this fascinating new book. The back cover description mentions, "uncovering compelling new evidence Egyptologist Robert Bauval and astrophysicist Thomas Brophy present the anthropological, climatological, archaeological, geological and genetic research supporting this highly debated theory of the Black African origin of Egyptian civilization."

This book should be read by as wide an audience as possible.

FREDERICK MONDERSON

19. BLACK GENESIS II

Robert Bauval and Thomas Brophys *Black Genesis: The Prehistoric Origins of Ancient Egypt* is a thought provoking and methodologically laid out, treatise that uses state of the art scientific techniques investigating contemporary and new data that convincingly traces the beginnings and routes of Black People from the Sahara region who migrated to Southern Egypt armed with a surprisingly sophisticated astronomical knowledge that ultimately laid the foundation for science and other practices upon which pharaonic Egypt later built.

Showing that these Blacks were the progenitors of ancient Egyptian culture, they came with a scientific sophistication developed over several millennia associated with early stargazing of the clear skies of the western desert of Upper Egypt. Nabta Plays is a place the monsoon rains of that time had made fertile for several months of the year in which the occupants were able to raise a cattle culture, making them early pastoralists. This may have formed the basis for the myths of Hathor, the cow Goddess, generally ascribed to being of Sudanese origin.

The significance of *Black Genesis* rests in its systematic examination of the calendar through use of astroarchaeological data that bring to life the later prehistoric years of the last **Precession** of some 26,000 years, a time of early scientific innovations that make these years very real. The archaeoastronomical sleuthing of the Author's vividly highlight the tangible features of their creations, viz., stone

CELEBRATING
DR. BEN-JOCHANNAN

carvings, placement and astronomical orientation of stones, creation of a calendar, together with cave paintings depicting red persons even though the people were black! Added to this is the significance of the monsoon rains and development of agriculture and pastoral culture that influenced religious beliefs. Equally, location of principal sites that encouraged early desert movement to extensively traverse a hostile environment that, in the latter years, rapidly desiccated and forced these original inhabitants to migrate to the Nile arriving in the Aswan, Elephantine region. Here they brought their extensive and long developed early scientific knowledge and techniques then providing a profound impetus to pharaonic civilization clearly leaving evidence of its connection to these early desert dwelling Africans.

However, unlike Caucasian migrants who "for sme unknown reason, left their place of origin" and brought nothing but "a superior mental attitude," really the arrogance of a white skin; on the other hand, Nabta Playa Africans brought their creations, viz., the calendar, religion, cow-Goddess, mapping of the heavens, cow culture, agriculture evidence, connection with Egypt, Cartouche, etc., and left evidence of their place of origin and possibly migration route. More important, their leaving their original home was due to dessication of the area which is a more substantive reason and not simply "for some unknown reason" which is an indefensible proposition.

FREDERICK MONDERSON

Dr. Ben's Photo 130. **Kom Ombo Double Temple to Haroeis and Sobek.** Pharaoh wears the Double 'White resting on Red' Crown, neclace and a beard.

Dr. Ben's Photo 131. **Kom Ombo Double Temple to Haroeis and Sobek.** Often considered Cleopatra who wears a crown of horns and disk surmounting the Queen Mother Crown, the beauty sports a necklace and has her right breast exposed.

CELEBRATING
DR. BEN-JOCHANNAN

The book also recounts early pharaonic efforts at connecting with these desert dwellers at Nabta Playa, the "Land of Yam," reaching out to them as if recognizing their ancestral heritage as precursors to their own cultural manifestation. At least one Old Kingdom cartouche was found in the region.

1. The desert dwellers, in heading east, first entered the Nile in the Aswan vicinity and their traveling knowledge seems to have manifested in a temple of Satet at Elephantine where astronomy, magic and religion may have percolated to create the powerful generator that set in motion significant features of Egyptian culture.

A number of happenings of significance can be associated with these peoples arrivals anywhere between 3500 B.C.E. and the start of dynastic rule.

First, Bruce Williams discovery from Qustol in Nubia, proximate to Upper Egypt, where pharaonic symbols of enthroned pharaoh, white crown, Nile boats, palace serekh facade, incense burner, cattle etc., were associate with such paraphernalia emerging in Southern Egypt some two centuries later.

The Great Mother as a cow that suckles the monarch and Society to bring good fortune, resulted from "cow culture." . Hathor the "Nubian" is also shown as a cow-Goddess and this may be related to the black Africans of Nabta Playa who initiated the "Cow Goddess" worship and thus were considered the precursors to the Pharaohs.

Second and tremendously significant, the First Egyptian Nome encompasses the Elephantine vicinity and since we generally associate one or first with beginnings, it is conceivable this is the point of origination, from whence, following the river, Egyptian civilization developed as the culture evolved.

Let us not forget, in the spurious claims of the origin of the ancient Egyptians, migration was considered a significant factor by Flinders Petrie author of the theory. However, as the Delta entry into Africa turned out to be a "straw man," the "Horn of Africa" was offered as a viable alternative in which these wanderers crossed over to the Nile through the Wady Hammamat arriving at the Nile in the vicinity of Koptos, home of God Min, who despite efforts to link him to Mesopotamia, origin of these migrants, Min has been determined to be Black and linked to Black Africans. So, if these people could arrive at Upper Egypt, the key to Egypt, and sail down the Nile, why cant the original inhabitants with their demonstrated scientific and social underpinnings not do same?

Third, despite what may be said about antecedents in the north, Narmer, from the south, Thebes, was able to muster a significant military force that sailed north, defeated that region and began the process of unification at a time when, as the slate palettes and early Abydos burials indicate the culture was just coming into credible vogue. Notwithstanding, social theorizing and administrative practicalities were sufficiently "advanced," Narmer was able to lay the social, administrative, political, military, scientific and religious parameters that served as pillars of the society for the three thousand years duration of dynastic rule. To have had the wherewithal to institute such developments means they had to have existed prior to Narmers expedition.

CELEBRATING DR. BEN-JOCHANNAN

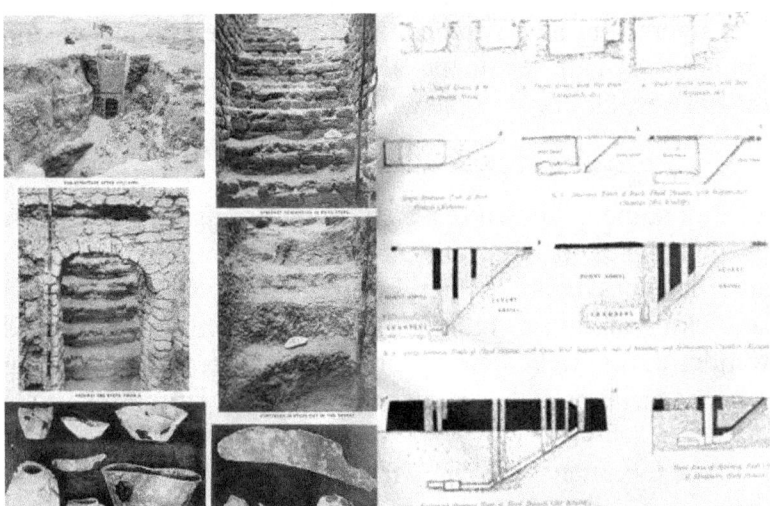

Dr. Ben's Illustration 35. Reqaqnah. Stairway Tomb R 40. IIIrd Dynasty Architectural Features showing Sub-structure after collapse; Stairway descending in Brick Steps; Archway and Steps; Continued Steps cut in the Desert, etc. (left); and, Reqaqnah and Bet Khallaf. Evolution of Stairway Tombs – Sections in John Garstang's *Tombs of The Third Egyptian Dynasty* at Reqaqnah and Bet Khallaf (1904).

Fourth, Bauval and Brophy have connected prehistoric scientific observation with dynastic architectural developments that locate or contribute to both the Step Pyramid at Sakkara and the "True Pyramids" at Gizeh with astronomical happenings as the dynamics of the heavens unfolded and the Egyptians not only observed, built structures but also formulated cosmic myths that regulated their society through inter-connected religious practices.

The Author's have shown an astral relationship to the calendar and how this social register has had the most significant impact on the totality of Egyptian culture, cultivated from a profound and long standing observation of the heavens.

It is interesting how persons of questionable knowledge and intent have made statements about Egyptian culture that lead the masses, far afield in the wrong or opposite direction. Case in point!

a. For some unknown reason a group of migrants left SWA following the sun and, well, ended up in Egypt. This myth was articulated as tangible fact. After all that Narmer and his southern administrators had accomplished, what could wandering migrants coming out of the desert actually bring except "racial prejudice in a supreme mental attitude?"

b. The Egyptian Gods came from the skies; they myths came from the skies. This misunderstood pronouncement has engaged the creativity of Hollywood to produce "Battle star Galactica," the "Fifth Element," associated mummy movies; and even indulged the creativity of the falsity of Van Deniken and his "Chariot of the Gods" syndrome. Of course, let us not forget Charleston Heston and Cecil deMille's epic *Ten Commandments* shown thousands upon thousands of times ingraining a false reality in the minds of the world's peoples.

Fifth, *Black Genesis* connects panels of the Step Pyramid built by Imhotep with the Sothic Cycle of 1461 or 1459 years showing knowledge of the shifting nature of this solar phenomenon. Everyone is familiar with the attributes of Imhotep as priest, astronomer, administrator, physician and poet. He has been called the worlds first multi-genius and a "Poet of the Ages" for his now famous admonition, "Eat, drink and be merry, for tomorrow you die!"

It is a well-known fact, knowledge and skill in ancient Egypt was generally a family trait, closely guarded and handed

CELEBRATING DR. BEN-JOCHANNAN

down, secretly from generation to generation. We know Imhotep descended from a long line of architects whose heritage may reach back to Narmers age. As *Black Genesis* connects the Step Pyramid, its panels with Imhotep's architectural and astronomy skills at a time not too distant from the emergence of the desert people with their architectural and astronomy observational accomplishments, these Author's have articulated a powerful thesis that flies in the face of the innumerable falsities about ancient Egypt by 19th, 20th and 21st Century writers. As the Egyptian archaeology science struggled to be born under its architect Flinders Petrie, many significant discoveries were made. However, the problem with the age was the interpretation of the data in the "mad dash climate to discover and rapidly publish" at a time when no African stood at the bar of discussion to critique. Lacking serious critical scrutiny, egotistical gents prognosticated at great length to an audience yearning to be influenced by these experts who ossified the false interpretation of ancient Egypt in impressionable minds.

Dr. Ben's Photo 132. Kom Ombo Double Temple to Haroeis and Sobek. Sobek, "Lord of Ombos," in all his majesty.

Dr. Ben's Photo 133. Kom Ombo Double Temple to Haroeis and Sobek. Hathor wears horns and disk surmounting the Queen Mother Crown.

Dr. Ben's Photo 134. Kom Ombo Double Temple to Haroeis and Sobek. Wearing horns with four feathers above disk and uraei with disks as well as two necklaces, Pharaoh presents a baboon or ape, emblem of Thoth, God of science and knowledge.

CELEBRATING DR. BEN-JOCHANNAN

One of the arguments for the origin of the Egyptians has been that they were a "boat people." So we are to believe, either these mythical migrants of SWA dragged their boats across the unknown desert passage or upon arrival in Africa, Egypt, on the Nile, made boats on which they descended the river. To accept such, we must disregard the existence or incapacity of the Nile dwellers of Central Africa, Nubia, and Upper Egypt, particularly from the Aswan are on the Nile as being incapable of being "boast people" even though they "live on the river!" Let us not forget the Qustol find has shown evidence of a Nile boat with the other accoutrements. Notwithstanding, the Nile River folks who accompanied Narmers armada that descended the Nile give no indication other than long standing mastery of the river and this capability has been continuous as late as Piankhy and the 25th Dynasty Ethiopians descent and ascent of the Nile, clearly indicates river navigation and mastery.

Dr. Ben's Photo 135. Kom Ombo Double Temple to Haroeis and Sobek. Standing beneath her symbolic crown, Nephthys extends an ankh.

FREDERICK MONDERSON

In the evolution of Egyptian boat culture, particularly as sketched in Baines and Malek's *Cultural Atlas of Egypt*, boat building developed from age to age as greater mastery of the craft and river was demonstrated. We know in the earliest times the sun God sailed across the sky in a solar barge and this certainly connects this myth with the earliest stargazers since religious beliefs and practices go back millennia before dynastic rule and continued as a powerful force in many different aspects. In the Old Kingdom, pharaohs had boat pits dug and boats buried adjacent to their pyramids. Hence, boat culture pervaded every aspect of the culture even to this day.

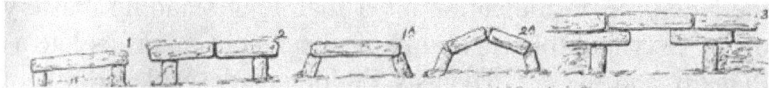

Dr. Ben's Illustration 36. John Garstang's *Tombs of The Third Egyptian Dynasty at Reqaqnah and Bet Khallaf* (1904) - Diagrams showing origins of "Simple Arch" and "Off-set Arch."

Another attribute of the ancient Egyptians is that they were a pastoral people for without a doubt cattle played a significant role in the cultural and religious practices. Bauval and Brophy have demonstrated the significance of "cow culture" among the desert dwelling Black people who left drawing of cows and were the genesis of the Egyptian genius. The Goddess Hathor of Sudani or Upper Egyptian origin played a tremendous role in Egyptian religion that permeated every aspect of the culture and the general belief is that Hathor, the cow Goddess, was a manifestation of every female deity in whichever pantheon.

CELEBRATING
DR. BEN-JOCHANNAN

Dr. Ben's Photo 136. Kom Ombo Double Temple to Haroeis and Sobek. In Red Crown, Pharaoh shakes a Hathor head rattle or sistrum.

Dr. Ben's Photo 137. Kom Ombo Double Temple to Haroeis and Sobek. In Double Crown, Pharaoh presents double "Eye of Horus."

FREDERICK MONDERSON

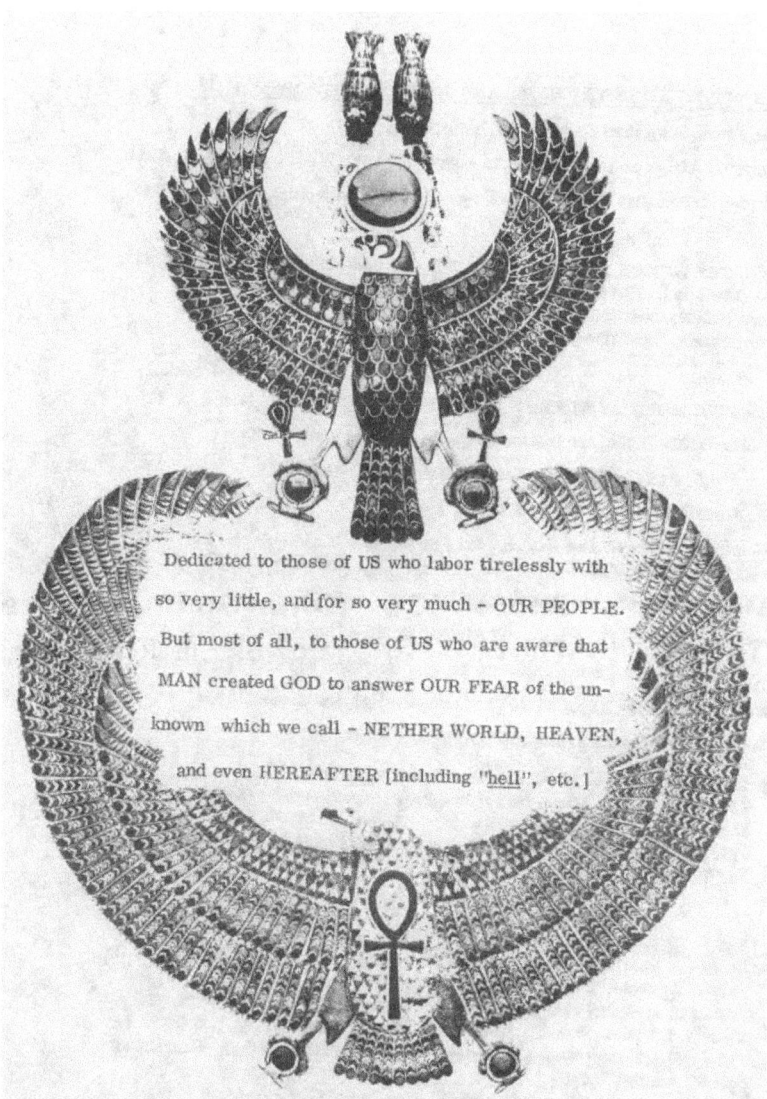

Dr. Ben's Dedication to "Laborers in the African vineyard" who give so much without thought of payment, **all for OUR PEOPLE!**

CELEBRATING DR. BEN-JOCHANNAN

20. HAITI: BY THE GRACE OF FAITH
By
Dr. Fred Monderson

Dr. Ben had a great love for the Haitian people and respect for their religion. He often discussed the fact the indigenous religion of **Voo Doo** was grossly maligned and this report is designed to add some clarity to the understanding that goes with the name and practice of an indigenous African religion practiced in the West.

Visiting an official with a colleague in Haiti recently, I was asked "How do you see Haiti?" The response, in part was "Haiti is a challenge but with potential and possibilities." That Haiti is challenged is no doubt but the potential is there. The Haitian people can solve most of their problems if they come together, work together, respect their country, then they could look confidently into the future.

Dr. Ben's Photo 138. Haiti. View from the air!

FREDERICK MONDERSON

While this visitor did not go very far outside of the capital Port au Prince, observations were striking. Sure there is a dust cloud that hovers within and over the capital but beyond the city the stark beauty of the country is manifest. Traveling along the coast road going north, the magnificent, clear blue skies with a few lazy clouds is a story book sight in which the possibilities of the great promise resides. But there is more to Haiti than meets the eye and this can be viewed principally from three perspectives, political, socio-economic and religious.

Dr. Ben's Photo 139. Haiti. Memorial to the Haitian Constitution of 1801, erected by President Bertrand Aristide honoring Toussaint L'Ouverture on March 29, 2002.

CELEBRATING DR. BEN-JOCHANNAN

Politically speaking, and not delving into the dynamics of the Haitian experience; yet, one gets the feeling leadership, young and experienced, is tired of the destructive behavior that characterized the past. There is a feeling, a sense of a new start, a sort of renewal with a vision to thrust the nation forward. This means, all Haitians, at home and abroad, young and old must come together to solve the nations problems. Recognizably, it is hard to change established social behaviors and naturally, entrenched social and economic interests may ultimately create obstacles on the road ahead. Thus, they must be cultivated into the new Haiti realities but equally must be prepared to share in the sacrifices all will be required to make. However, one truism of this reality is, the entrenched socio-economic elements or class have consistently demonstrated a lack of interest in the public good and this must change.

Dr. Ben's Photo 140. Haiti. Religious conviction and faith carries Haiti forward.

FREDERICK MONDERSON

Dr. Ben's Photo 141. Haiti. Expressions of religiosity in Haiti is unsurpassed and matches such practices anywhere in the world.

Dr. Ben's Photo 142. Haiti. Pastoral leadership anchors the faith of the people of Haiti indicating their future is a blessed one, full of promise and with devotion and commitment will bear fruit as symbol of a credible Black Republic and its people.

CELEBRATING DR. BEN-JOCHANNAN

Dr. Ben's Photo 143. Haiti. The partnership for success is unmistakable for, as Dr. Ben has so often pointed out, women were at the forefront of the Haitian Revolution.

Dr. Ben's Photo 144. Haiti. Pastoral leadership of the highest order has always been instrumental for progress of African people worldwide.

FREDERICK MONDERSON

Dr. Ben's Photo 145. Haiti. The consecrating power of the many infuses greater spiritual essence into the one to bring home and deliver quintessential service towards fellow man that equally instills confidence in people near and far.

Dr. Ben's Photo 146. Haiti. This image announces to the world, what Dr. Ben has always taught, that Black men are, have been, and will always be men of substance, integrity and moral and spiritual fiber that can be emulated by all people, wherever.

CELEBRATING
DR. BEN-JOCHANNAN

Dr. Ben's Photo 147. Haiti. Tap Tap, oftentimes colorful mode of public transportation. American Snoop Dogg is the featured celebrity for "69."

Dr. Ben's Photo 147a. Erik Monderson strolling in the Plaza at Edfu Temple to God Horus in 2018.

FREDERICK MONDERSON

Dr. Ben's Photo 148. Shawki Abdel Rady and his brothers on the staff at **Sonesta Hotel**, Luxor.

Dr. Ben's Photo 149. Temple of Edfu to God Horus. Chariots line-up in an orderly manner in the newly reconstructed Plaza entrancing the temple.

CELEBRATING DR. BEN-JOCHANNAN

Dr. Ben's Photo 150. Temple of Edfu to God Horus. The "Sphinx of Edfu," a Roman interpolation, has been moved from within the Temple's gates to this new position in the Plaza.

Religiously speaking, with a peculiar history of religious practice, Haiti presents a sort of distinct circumstance making it different from most societies and in this very complex. That is to say, the religious dynamic is not simply complicated but perhaps as difficult as the political situation even though it has not been as deadly or openly hostile or competitive. To understand this one has to look at the four religious forces shaping the Haitian mind through traditional experience, socio-economic realities and the promise of the future, particularly in view of recent history within the last decade or two. More importantly, having had a recent earthquake with the threat of a tsunami and contemporary seismological evidence predicting a second set of such circumstances people are jittery and people have come to lean more heavily on the pillars of religious, psychological and moral support.

The first of these realities is the Catholic religion with two active branches of its practitioners. That is, the high church, the Cathedral branch, under control from Rome which preaches the traditional belief as practiced over the last two thousand years with the promise those things will remain stable for the next two thousand years. Surprisingly, this is in conflict with the community church, the small parish institution faced with practiced socio-economic realities and thus espouses a liberation theology that is in opposition to the promise from Rome. Here the local parish priest faces the difficult task of reconciling religious theory and social practice.

The third element in the equation is the multi-denominational reformed church itself in discord because of the differing realities of their origin in efforts to do Gods work. The Protestant Baptists, Wesleyan, Methodist, Pentecostals, can offer carrots in a time of austerity. Owing to the political and economic missionary power or muscle these groups bring to bear on any situation is significant since many are financed by foreign money. An old saying holds; money can buy power and influence that can influence any equation in a given situation. Thus, the above are all in competition with the local, traditional, ancestor worship, animistic practices of Voo Doo. All of the above, notwithstanding, in Haitian society, Voo Doo transcends class, socio-economic position or religious practices. Naturally, a tremendous misunderstanding about Voo Doo has developed and this has generated a great deal of negative propaganda against the practice.

The reality is, the **Voo Doo** priest is a multi-functional personality much unlike the practitioners of the three previous groups. That is, besides being a priest, he is a family counselor,

CELEBRATING
DR. BEN-JOCHANNAN

psychiatrist and medicine man. Without a doubt medicine is expensive. So much so, 25-30 percent of Haitian society can afford traditional western medicine, most of which is imported. The pills, syringes, books, solutions, bandages, complex machinery and the staffing and administration is expensive even if it is effective. Besides his many functions, the Voo Doo priest is an herbalist. He has studied nature and learned his craft through traditional practice and though some prescriptions may work and some dont and some cure and some kill, people seem to remember grandmother or aunty used this when she had that and it probably worked. Additionally, however, the Voo Doo priest not only knows which herbs to prescribe, he prays over the prescription which seems to give it a psychological seal of approval. Even more important, the Voo Doo priest supplies more affordable medicine that must people can afford and when the wealthy have paid the cost of western medicine with not sufficient results, superstitions aside, they seek out the **Voo Doo** priest for herbal advice.

Beyond these complex realities, even more mundane factors interplay, adding to the mix of what constitutes the totality of Haiti and the Haitians. First, Haitian people are very industrious and possess the capabilities of making something out of nothing. Everywhere you go in Haiti people are involved in business opportunities, either making, creating or selling something. As necessity is the mother of invention, and given the lack of economic abundance, entrepreneurs constantly try to make a buck, turn it over and make two more.

FREDERICK MONDERSON

Dr. Ben's Illustration 37. Hierakonpolis. Both sides of the **Narmer Palette** showing the King as a **Conqueror** at **Unification** in J.E. Quibell's Hierakonpolis II (1898).

Dr. Ben's Photo 150. Temple of Edfu to God Horus. Presenting three feathers on platter to Horus and Hathor.

CELEBRATING
DR. BEN-JOCHANNAN

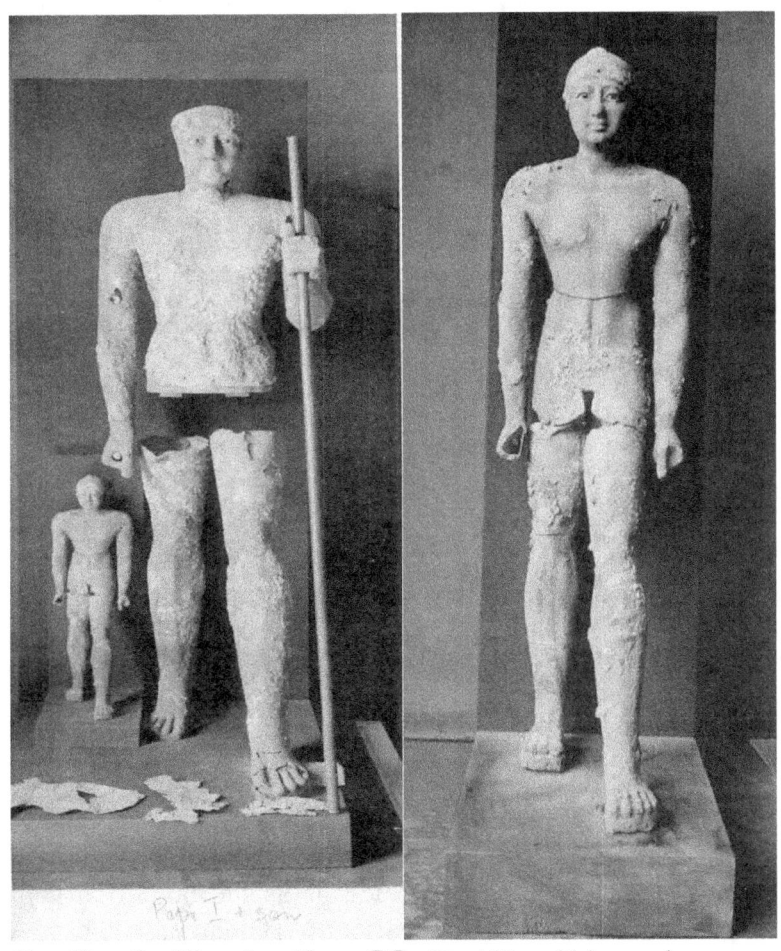

Dr. Ben's Illustration 38. Pepi II and his son in copper were found at the Temple at Kierakonpolis; Close-up of his son. J.E. Quibell's *Hierakonpolis II* (1898).

FREDERICK MONDERSON

Dr. Ben's Illustration 39. Broken facial features of seated statue thought to be Khasekhmuwi and Golden Hawk Head with Plumes of Amon-Ra. J.E. Quibell's *Hierakonpolis II* (1898).

Even in the aftermath of the earthquake damages, the book trade, cultural creations such as art and music, song and dance, led the recovery of the psychic-self as the body and soul suffered the torture of the devastation. Haitian people have a passion for education and elevation of their young. Like or unlike many other cultures, school uniforms instill a sense of pride and purpose in the young. Everyone seems to understand the benefits of education and that it empowers those hardy enough to struggle to attain its promise.

CELEBRATING DR. BEN-JOCHANNAN

When the earthquake devastated the country nearly a dozen hospitals in Port Au Prince alone suffered serious damage. Rather than await the arrival of foreign medical assistance, institutions as the University of the Haitian Academys medical school deployed student doctors whose baptism under fire aided the helpless while challenging the young medical personnel to experience trauma first hand and they gloriously rose to the occasion. That experience raised the standard of medical practice but unintentionally the disaster bred a unifying spirit as good Samaritans had a field day among the unfortunate situations. That self-help cooperation manifesting unity is a quintessential factor that can contribute tremendously in helping solve some of Haitis problems.

The greatest asset at the disposal of the Haitian people is their faith, their religious faith. Underlying the problems as stated above is the competition for the soul of the Haitian people, for they possess reservoirs of faith that God hears their prayers, talks to them and promises them salvation.

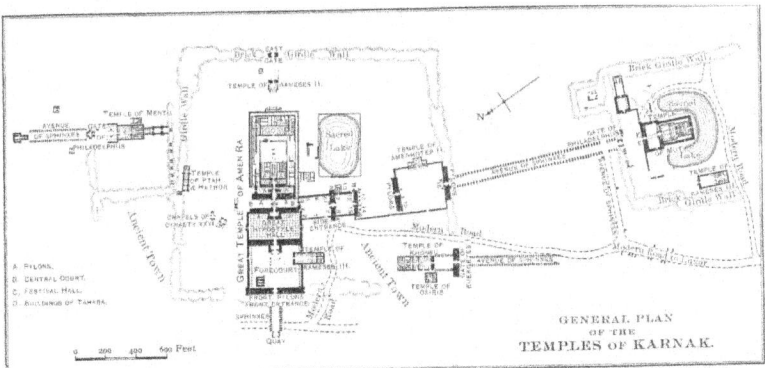

Dr. Ben's Plan 10. General Plan of the Temples of Karnak.

21. HAITI: EYEWITNESS TO DISASTER
By Dr. Fred Monderson

Dr. Ben's Photo 151. Haiti. The National Catholic Cathedral is totally destroyed and whatever part still stands will have to be demolished.

Flying into Toussaint LOuverture International Airport in Port Au Prince, Haiti, in light of recent events, I did not know what to expect. Much was reported in the news, but being here to see for ones self is an entirely different situation. The airport was damaged in the earthquake that had been so catastrophic to that beautiful country. A new entrance into Immigration and Customs enabled arriving passengers to enter with the slightest difficulty through this important portal. The customary commotion greeted us at the gate as we awaited the

CELEBRATING DR. BEN-JOCHANNAN

arrival of our host, Dr. Marie-Pologne Jacques Rene, Chancellor of the University of the Haitian Academy with its medical school and hospital at **Petit Goave**. Thenceforward, we ventured to transit the historic city of Port Au Prince. On way to our domicile at the Haitian Academy, 13 miles outside of the city, much of what we read about greeted us, with the promise to return the next day to get a first-hand view of devastation of the city. chauffeur me in the city but also visit and point out institutions and residences hardest hit by the calamity. The earthquake devastation had affected practically every facet of the societys fabric, viz., education, medicine, religion, art, culture, literacy, food, transportation, even fuel resources.

The tragedy aside, Haiti is fortunate to have untold numbers of missionaries visiting the stricken land who create torrential outpouring of prayers to help heal the nation. However, beyond prayers, material support and rebuilding is taking place to help alleviate the inconvenience, discomfort, and emotional strain and psychological trauma so many are constantly exposed to. Non-Governmental Organizations (**NGOs**) and Missionary Organizations as well as churches, are in Haiti enmasse helping in a multitude of situations encompassing the organization and distribution of food, clothing, shelter, education, medical care, etc.

FREDERICK MONDERSON

Dr. Ben's Photo 152. Temple of Edfu to God Horus. The Temple's majestic Propylon, two halves of the Pylon, depicts the illustration in duplicate and boasts two statuette images of the God, Amon, left: and Ra, right; though the one to the left of the gate is better preserved.

Dr. Ben's Photo 153. Temple of Edfu to God Horus. Better preserved close-up image of God Horus wearing the Double Crown as he is often depicted in illustration.

CELEBRATING DR. BEN-JOCHANNAN

Dr. Ben's Photo 154. Temple of Edfu to God Horus. Horus as a falcon wearing the Double Crown with Hathor and the King at his rear.

I had the privilege of visiting **Food for the Poor**, whose buildings were partly damaged. I was surprised to see the workers wearing a blue shirt uniform with flag insignias of the United States, Jamaica, Haiti and Guyana, all juxtaposed. However, though their building was damaged they were able to continue to distribute food and other supplies to needy persons in a variety of areas.

Beyond the untold numbers dead, injured and those suffering from emotional trauma, the earthquake damaged Haiti in key sectors of the society and culture. Some have argued the rise of Haiti will rely significantly on 4 key areas of social progress, viz., education – schools; religion – churches; physical – medical; and culture – the arts. Naturally, jobs will play an important role in any form of recovery! However, and first and foremost, our equivalent of the Minister of Education reported some 4,000 schools were destroyed. The Education Department building was completely destroyed and with it the records of so many. There was also loss of life in this structure. A phone company donated a large tent allowing the Ministry to refit and conduct what level of business it could muster in the short term, while the general building is being rebuilt. This catastrophe has had an immeasurable impact on education particularly for the young. In addition, because of the displacement and people being housed in tents, school is in recess perhaps for the summer with intent to re-open in September. Still, a few schools are functioning, but the numerous kids one would see on a school day in their uniforms is solely lacking.

The University of the Haitian Academy, while outside of Port Au Prince area was also badly damaged but, as some have argued, "God was on their side!" All their school buildings were cracked, forcing cancellation of classes but yet allowing the institution to conduct whatever classes in the open air of the campus, which so happens to be spacious.

The role of schools in past, present and future development of Haiti calls into question response to the destruction of these structures as well as the future of the Haitian Academy. For example, in Port Au Prince, Trinity School was destroyed completely and is being rebuilt rapidly. They are building in wood. A prevalent view is its better to build in wood, which means, in the event of a similar disaster, all you have to do is remove the nails and reuse the wood. With concrete, all becomes useless rubble. As such, one of the things the Haitian Academy is making an appeal for persons to donate money to purchase wood to rebuilt classrooms because of the need for

CELEBRATING DR. BEN-JOCHANNAN

children to return to school. They indicate the need for a long tent to serve as a school. A big tent costs US$38,000.00, as an example. Its interesting, the people who are doing any form of work, such as removing debris in post-earthquake Haiti, are calling for money in dollars.

Dr. Ben's Papyrus 8. Hathor holds the hands of Queen Nefertari as Goddess *Ma'at* extends her wings before enthroned Hathor with Horus in Double Crown accompanied by two ladies.

The National School of Science was leveled. There is nothing there behind the fence. St. Martin Boys High School was destroyed and is being rebuilt. Sisters of Mary School was flattened with loss of many Nuns lives, as well as 200 flutes in their Music School. Its been reported the Sisters bodies were never recovered but were scooped up with the rubble and disposed. Sacred Heart College was completely demolished. Also, St. Louis de Gonzales High School was demolished and the area is now a tent city. The three stories of the Methodist School was flattened. With the loss of so many schools in the Port Au Prince and surrounding area, the still functional Haitian Academy is one of a few schools of substance able to absorb some of the students who need to further their education.

FREDERICK MONDERSON

Who was not killed in the earthquake was badly wounded and hospitals were especially hard hit, hampering their care. Some 8 hospitals were destroyed or badly damaged in Port Au Prince alone that this reporter was able to observe and photograph. **The Haitian Academy** is a New York State accredited educational institution from first to twelfth grade. It also boasts a Medical School and a Hospital. While the earthquake destroyed much of the buildings of the conventional school, the Medical School also suffered with many students not being able to finish especially their fourth year of medical college. Nevertheless, there is a Hospital attached to the institution. It is the only hospital in the area, some 13 miles outside of Port Au Prince, Petite Guave.

Their Mission Statement is somewhat akin to New York Citys Health and Hospital Corporations which means they take all comers, 24X7. They do deliveries, Caesarian Sections, pediatric cases, some asthma, abdominal, accident cases, clinics and small surgeries. The state of medical care before the earthquake had been very problematic and now with the collapse of so many such institutions, the situation is chaotic. Dr. Duval, the one physician on staff said: "Im always here!" He expressed the need for an ambulance, as they use peoples cars to being patients to the hospital. He added, "Even the police bring their patients to us because they know we take care of all." The day I arrived, April 9th, incidentally my birthday, he treated 40 patients. Classrooms have been converted to patients' rooms.

CELEBRATING DR. BEN-JOCHANNAN

Dr. Ben's Illustrations 40. View of excavations of 1912-13, seen from North-western corner of the First Pyramid, looking West-North-West (left); and, view of the Royal Cemetery from the Second Pyramid, looking North (right) in *Annals du Service Des Antiquites de L'Egypte* (1913) Ghizeh Plateau.

FREDERICK MONDERSON

Dr. Ben's Illustrations 41. Ghizeh Plateau. View of Royal Cemetery from First Pyramid, looking West-North-Wes in *Annals du Service Des Antiquites de L'Egypte* (1913).

Saint Francis de Sales hospital was destroyed. So too the Hospital François D'Haiti, damaged but is one of few hospitals surviving. General Hospital was damaged, though its still functioning. Some of the Obstetrics and Gynecology Hospital is still standing, though it is not operating. St. Charles Hospital was destroyed. Thankfully, the Hospital of Peace got no damage and is functional.

Beyond these two critical concerns, religion is an important area that was tested. The National Cathedral is destroyed totally. The church at Trinity school was destroyed and now they are operating in makeshift surroundings. Several churches were destroyed, particularly larger ones with a historic significance.

Around the question of religion, two important ingredients are apparent. The people of Haiti are profoundly religious! One of the first things I observed after leaving Toussaint L'Ouverture Airport was a vendor selling a stack of bibles. Practically everyone goes to church. There is constant prayer going on. Even more important, following the disaster, untold numbers of missionaries have descended on the island and have constantly engaged in prayer vigils, services and perennial

CELEBRATING
DR. BEN-JOCHANNAN

praises of giving God the glory. They are giving support to the belief in the power of prayer in religious brotherhood.

Culture is another area that will light a torch to show the way and help the nation to heal. Booksellers are playing a crucial role in the renaissance and rise of Haiti by providing literature for the minds of those who will craft the New Haiti. Literacy and education have always been the hallmark of Haitian intellectual development. Some artists have returned to the street to ply their wares of painting and sculpture.

Dr. Ben's Photo 155. Temple of Edfu to God Horus. Gods and animals. On top, Isis sits atop a shrine holding a feather of Ma'at while an owl and vulture precede her; and below, Horus wearing disk with uraeus, squats before a hawk as a baboon of Thoth, the head of Anubis atop a Standard and dog of his emblem look into the future!

All this notwithstanding, there is a sense of cooperation and civility that has returned despite the dire circumstances. I saw no violence in the street; mendicants are few and far between, though some are very persistent. The food distribution network has alleviated that pressing need so lines are more orderly. Nevertheless, the juxtapositioning of people in confined tents in the heart of the city is cause for concern about epidemics. Some say women advocates were killed in the earthquake and this has exposed their constituents to the proclivities of rapists, exploiters and those who encourage prostitution.

Dr. Ben's Photo 156. Temple of Edfu to God Horus. Horus wears the Double Crown, faces Goddess Nekhbet and is backed by a Horus hawk wearing disk.

A serious study has to be done on the prevalence of asthma on Port Au Prince residents. Constant clearing of debris is a cause for concern. Many workers have no mask and are breathing the dust, fumes and odor. Some of the collapsed buildings that have not been cleared; word is, if people were under there, theyre still there! Nevertheless, despite the crowding from tent city and challenges posed, there is laughter in the street, relative calm and no sign of violence. There is some music on the street but not sufficient. There was much excitement over a football (soccer) game between Real Madrid and another team. Children were playing soccer in fields in the city. The United Nations is there doing its thing like everyone else, trying to help a sister nation devastated by what some would call "an act of God!"

CELEBRATING DR. BEN-JOCHANNAN

Dr. Ben's Photo 157. Temple of Edfu to God Horus. Horus wears the Double Crown, faces Goddess Nekhbet and is backed by a Horus hawk wearing disk.

22. AFRICA: "MOTHER OF WESTERN CIVILIZATION"
By
Dr. Fred Monderson

Africa: Mother of Western Civilization is Dr. Yosef A.A. ben-Jochannan's **magnum opus** in his Trilogy that includes *African Origins of the "Major" Western Religions* and *Black Man of the Nile and His Family*. This work, in fact these three, established him as thinker and historian that early projected a positive attitude regarding African contributions to civilization, whose concept ultimately migrated to Europe through the Graeco-Roman experience of the Mediterranean culture cluster. Equally, he presented a number of theories and positions promulgated by western writers who, in the majority, projected a negative perception of Africa, its culture, history and people. Years ago, this writer heard the late and distinguished Dr. John Henry Clarke declare, "People buy Dr. Ben-Jochannan's trilogy (books) but do not read them." As if to say, these are profound critical and constructive analyses on Egypt, Africa and Europe/Western scholarship and should be given the serious consideration they deserve because much that the author discusses are still relevant today. That is, the criticisms still being leveled against Africas dynamics and the positive revelations Dr. ben-Jochannan emphasized.

Africa: *Mother of Western Civilization* (New York: Alkebu-Lan Book Associates, 1970) (First Edition and signed by the author) is a massive 717 page reservoir of, at that time, new information supported by extensively copious references that upholds the Author's devastating analytic dissection of, first, western writers pejorative depiction of the whole African experience. In refutation, the author painstakingly develops his arguments to show not only that Africans originated the fundamental tenets and practices that advanced the social and scientific development of humanity, that Europe has tried to covet as originating in the West.

Dr. Ben's Photo 158. Temple of Edfu to God Horus. The Horus hawk faces a feather atop outstretched wings.

CELEBRATING DR. BEN-JOCHANNAN

While the book is "Dedicated to the African nationalist Street-Corner Speakers (deceased and surviving) who, in their own inimitable simplicity, have, from the advent of the late Marcus Moziah Garvey and the founding of the Universal Negro Improvement Association (UNIA) in 1918 C.E., kept the flame of Africa's history and culture ever present in the mind of African peoples everywhere in the Western Hemisphere."

The **Table of Contents** Reads: Prelude; The Nile Valley and Great Lakes; Preface; Introduction; Illustrations; The Dawn of Civilization, and the Value of a Name; (1) Prehistoric Homo Sapiens or Ancient African Man; (11) Who Were/Are the Africans of Ancient Alkebu-Lan (Africa); (111) Historic Quotations and Comments About, and of, the Africans; People Who Made Middle Nile Valley History Yesterday and Today; Racism, Historians and Ethiopians; The Return of Kemet, Zimbabwe, and Nubia to the Continent of Alkebu-Lan; Nubia – "Mother of Kemet" – Gateway to the North; (IV) Predynastic and Dynastic Kemet, Nubia and Kush; The Egyptian Dynasties and Comments by High-Priest Manetho; Notes on Egyptology; (V) African Origin of "Greek Philosophy;" Arguments and Answers Relative to the African Origins of "Greek Philosophy;" Who Were the Indigenous Africans of Kemet (Egypt); (VI) Reflections on Ancient Kemet (Sais or Egypt) (VII) Chronology of Egyptian Rule Over Kush and Nubia; "Cleopatras Needle": A Stolen African Treasure in America; (VIII) The Rise and Fall of the Africans of Khart Haddas (Carthage); The Black Man of Antiquity; What "Black is Beautiful" is Not Ready to Hear; Judaism, the "Black Jew" Or "Israelite: Roots of Biblical Anti-Negroism," etc.: A Cause for Black "anti-Semitism;" A Lecture on the Beginnings of the Christian Church in North and East Africa; The Africans Right to be Wrong is Sacred; Conclusion; Maps,

FREDERICK MONDERSON

Acknowledgements; Front Cover Design Description; Author's Statement on African (Black) History and Culture.

Africa: Mother of Western Civilization is a unique analytic examination of Africa, its contribution to the intellectual and cultural development of human progress and western scholarships attempts to claim such while negating the Africans role in this phenomenon. In this, the significance of Dr. ben-Jochannan's contribution is manifold, in that, he drew attention to a number of problems European and American scholars have posed in their studies of Africa in general and Egypt and the Nile Valley in particular and their wrongfully seeking to displace Africans from Africa, replacing them with varieties of light skinned and dark skinned Caucasian peoples with emphasis on the superiority of the Caucasian race.

The good doctor points out on page xv of "Mother" that "this work is not intended to purposely attack any person or institution, religious or secular, vindictively; but, only to cite and correct the erroneous myths about the inferiority and primitiveness of the indigenous African peoples and their descendants who are today, in the late 20th century, still being maligned by the archaic terms – Negroes, Bantus, Pygmies, Hottentots, Bushmen, and the likes of the same misnomers, none of which the Africans created." In addition, he supplies an outstanding bibliography for independent examination of these sources and for research purposes. He is of the view, one need to "Get the oldest information available and work from there."

Even more important, Dr. ben-Jochannan pioneered the insistence of indigenous African names regarding the various cultures and he frowned upon the use of such disgusting names as those previously mentioned as well as Negroes, Negroids, Nilotes, Semites, Hamites, etc.

CELEBRATING
DR. BEN-JOCHANNAN

Dr. Ben's Photo 159. Temple of Edfu to God Horus. Wearing the Double Crown, Pharaoh makes a presentation and Horus assumes the "traveling stance."

Dr. Ben's Photo 160. Temple of Edfu to God Horus. Empty-handed King and again, with one hand empty, before Horfus in Double Crown.

FREDERICK MONDERSON

Dr. Ben's Photo 161. Temple of Edfu to God Horus. Simply grasping an ankh and sporting a tail; defaced Horus in Double Crown image.

Dr. Ben's Photo 162. Temple of Edfu to God Horus. Horus alone (left); and, Horus with Hathor, both of the latter have been defaced.

CELEBRATING DR. BEN-JOCHANNAN

He was critical of Napoleon Bonaparte, the French Emperor, whom he explained did not come to Egypt as a tourist but as conqueror and as such he held the culture in contempt. He insisted, "Too many modern educators try to change the whole meaning of ancient history." As an example, he compares the work of two important Frenchmen Baron Denon who was in Egypt with Napoleon and the renowned Egyptologist Gaston Maspero. Denon, who drew the face of the Sphinx of Ghizeh with its nose intact and reported, from his observations, Napoleon's soldiers blew off the nose with their canon fire. Maspero, on the other hand, writing a century after Denon, wrote the Mamelukes, who ruled Egypt, actually blew the Sphinxs nose off.

Frowning on the disrespects Western writers hold towards Africa and Africans, Dr. ben-Jochannan takes to task Black Studies and African Studies Departments that parrot "racist stereotypes regarding Africa and its cultural history." Some of the things he pointed out were: "An Egyptian and a South African are classified as being of two separate races; whereas a Greek and a Swede are both of the same Caucasian races." He does emphasize the difference between reciting facts and the interpretation of the data. While insisting on the "Africans right to be wrong," he frowns upon the "new left" distracting African Americans with the "rhetoric of instant revolution."

FREDERICK MONDERSON

23. Third Annual Memorial Day Tribute to Dr. Ben-Jochannan

Dr. Ben's Illustration 67. Flyer designating the Third Annual Memorial Day Tribute to Dr. Ben, June 5 and 12, 2011.

Contrary to most books on Egypt which seems to erect a wall at Egypt's southern border, Dr. Ben offers a more comprehensive inclusion that connects Egypt with much of Africa far into the south, even beyond the headwaters of the Nile. He admonished that "as people are criticized for being anti-Semite, Blacks must be critical of any anti-Black, anti-Negroism spewed by race haters."

CELEBRATING DR. BEN-JOCHANNAN

24. AFRICAN ORIGINS OF THE "MAJOR" WESTERN RELIGIONS"
By
Dr. Fred Monderson

AFRICAN ORIGINS OF THE "MAJOR" WESTERN RELIGIONS (New York: Alkebu-Lan Books, 1970) is a masterfully presented analytic discussion highlighting the role Africa and its sons and daughters played in the development and propagation in modern religions beliefs and practice. Dr. Yosef ben-Jochannan, in his own inimitable fashion, reveals a great body of information that demolished religious stereotypes stigmatizing Africa and its people as he includes significant accomplishments generally absent in the sanitized portrayal of religion and who was responsible for these achievements.

Dr. ben-Jochannan, an anthropologist, historian, Egyptologist and black-African nationalist is an educator confronted by exclusion and omission of constructive African contributions to the development of religious consciousness. Because, many, particularly modern, writers, engage in a pejorative depiction of African religious expressions, Dr. Ben takes them to task by analyzing their statements, contrasting them with more constructive commentary in order to challenge those distortions, then paint Africa in its proper light.

In this exercise, *African Origins* is dedicated to: "The innocently recent born and those yet-to-be-born African and African American infants who must one day take their place in mankind's world as the inheritors of the religions their forebears created – hoping that they may become the forces of change to bring this work to its equilibrium once more."

The author begins with a poem translated by Sir Richard F. Burton entitled **The Kasidah of Haji Abu el-Yezdi** which reads:

> "All faith is false, all faith is true
> Truth is the shattered mirrors strewn
> In myriad bits, while each believes
> His little bit the whole to own."

The **Table of Contents** reads: Preface; Introduction; Shango: A source of African religion; St. Augustine: African influence on Christianity; Moses: African influence on Judaism; Bilal: African influence on Islam; King, Mohammed, Divine, Matthews, and Garvey: Religions New Dimensions; Conclusion; Notes and Bibliography.

A symbolic glossary explains the imagery of the **Cover Illustration** where the author explains the compendium of nine symbols that conceptually reflects the totality of the Author's message. These include: Ra: God – Sun God of the Nile – Sunburst; Symbol of the first principles of religion- Coffin Text – Pyramid with All-Seeing Eye; God: Damballah Ovedo, Voodoo – West African Rooster; Key of Life of the Mysteries – Grand Lodge of Luxor – Ankh, Nile Valley Cross; God: Jesus Christ – Christianity – Westernized Version; God: Traditional African Religions – Cross – Nile Valley and Central Africa; God: Yahweh – Hebrewism (Judaism) – Star of David; God: AlLah – Islam – Crescent of Tigris and Euphrates.

CELEBRATING DR. BEN-JOCHANNAN

Dr. Ben's Illustration 42. Ghizeh Plateau. Extreme northwestern corner of Mycerinus quarry, looking North-West in *Annals du Service Des Antiquites de L'Egypte* (1913).

25. BLACK MAN OF THE NILE AND HIS FAMILY
By
Dr. Fred Monderson

BLACK MAN OF THE NILE AND HIS FAMILY (New York: Alkebu-Lan Books, (1971) 1981 is the second volume in Dr. Yosef A.A. ben-Jochannan's **trilogy**, and in many ways can be considered a history of Egypt though its more an analytic dissection of the Nile Valley experience. In many ways, this work defines the author, his thinking and the respectful influence he had come to exert as a concerned and knowledgeable truly indigenous African authority, struggling against the farcical portrayal of ancient Egypt and its relationship with the Nile Valley states and people.

This book is dedicated, writes the author: "To my daughter Colette Denise [Makeda] and son Kwame Edwin, both of whom represent the future African peoples everywhere; Also, to Miss Laurie Heard who passed on to an untimely death in 1969 C.E. at age 24, after having won the Pulitzer Prize with others for her story on the Detroit Riot of 1968. She was an inspiration to young black womanhood everywhere."

The **Table of Contents** reads: Illustrations (727); A Special Glossary; Preface to the First Edition; Foreword of First Edition; Special Tribute: To The Mothers of African/Black Families – Past, Present, Future; Preview of the Third Edition; Chapter I: Who Were/Are the Africans; Chapter II: Prehistoric African Homosapiens; Chapter III: Historic Quotations and Comments About The Africans; Chapter IV: Another Look At Nubia, Meroe, Egypt, Ethiopia, Paunit, Etc.; Chapter V: Reflections Of The Ancient Egyptians: A Brief Chronology Of The Ancient Indigenous African and His Family of the Nile Valley; Chapter VI: A Pictorial Review of The Ancient Africans Of Egypt and Other Nile Valley High Cultures/"Civilizations;" Chapter VII: The Africans of Khart-Haddas/Carthage [Its Founding, and Its Destruction]; A Chronological Outline and Data; Chapter VIII: African Origins of "Greek Philosophy" [The Myth]; Chapter IX: Mother of the Gods of Man/Woman; Chapter X: Questions and Answers About Africa; Conclusion: Orthodox and Liberal African History and Historians; Poem: "Mother African Cries of Pain" by Lloyd [boney] Thomas; General Notes; Added Bibliography; Personal Index.

CELEBRATING DR. BEN-JOCHANNAN

Dr. Ben's Illustration 43. Ghizeh Plateau.
Looking South-South-West – Place of the slab stela in *Annals du Service Des Antiquites de L'Egypte* (1913)

In the Preface, adopted from the First Edition, the author writes: "In this volume facts of African history which have been for so long purposely withheld from the public shall be revealed and carefully explained. Africa [Alkebu-lan] will be seen from the eyes which are different to the Henry Morton Stanley and Dr. David Livingstons drama; the salvation through Jesus Christ view-point; the Tarzan and Jane atmosphere; the Great White Father paternalism; and last, but not least, it will not include the lazy Africans who did nothing in Africa before slavery, and developed nothing or created nothing historically propaganda angle of the Christian missionaries. These age-old stereotyped racist conceptions about the Africans shall not appear in this book."

He talks about deliberate suppression and distortion of true African history.

FREDERICK MONDERSON

"This work is also an attempt to create in the young African, African-American [Black person], and all other youthful people, a sense of pride in his or her great African heritage. For Heritage is that something which all other people are reminded of daily. And since this work is being produced in the United States of America, it is specifically directed to those who have criminally demasculinized, denuded, and otherwise debased the Africans of their cultural, economic, political, scientific, spiritual, and all other forms of their heritage and human decency. Religion and the European and European-American colonialists, for over the past three to four-hundred years, shall be shown to be two of the basic causes of Africas downfall. Of course there is no attempt to dismiss from guild those African (Blacks) who contributed in the past, and in the present, to the criminal conspiracy of genocide against their African brothers and sisters for their own selfish economic gains."

Dr. Ben's Photo 163. Temple of Edfu to God Horus. The battle is on in the search for Seth with Horus, in the boat to the right, wearing the Double Crown and accompanied by Thoth and Ra-Horakhty in his shrine.

CELEBRATING
DR. BEN-JOCHANNAN

Dr. Ben's Photo 164. Temple of Edfu to God Horus. More boats in the search with Horus in Double Crown accompanied by Ra-Horakty in his shrine.

Dr. Ben's Photo 165. Temple of Edfu to God Horus. Still more boats in the hunt but these images are defaced, perhaps by Christian zealots. Seth seems to be captured disguised as a Hippopotamus below.

FREDERICK MONDERSON

Dr. Ben's Photo 166. Temple of Edfu to God Horus. Soldiers in the hunt, but all defaced.

Dr. Ben's Photo 167. Temple of Edfu to God Horus. With Isis in the lead boat in full-sail, Horus in Double Crown captures Seth disguised as a Hippopotamus below.

CELEBRATING DR. BEN-JOCHANNAN

Dr. Ben's Photo 168. Temple of Edfu to God Horus. With his lawyer Thoth at his rear, Horus, in Double Crown, greets Hathor on shore as his image captures the Hippopotamus.

Still another objective of this work is its presentation of pertinent data needed in the African peoples re-identification with their great ancestral heritage. For the Black peoples have maintained that: If the European Jews can fight for an arid piece of desert; the Irish for a small Emerald island; the British for a barren island of misery; Protestant Anglo-Saxon American for their stolen "Indian empire; why should the Black man [the African, African-Caribbean, and African-American] not fight for the richest piece of real estate on the planet earth – His original Homeland – Mother Africa [Alkebu-Lan]?"

He must persevere, though the struggle seems at times insurmountable. For it is in the doing of the impossible which made the Blacks and Africa great for hundreds of centuries and it is only by the recapturing and recreation of new values by the Black man will he free his mind, then his body, and lastly – his power. The Black man must, therefore, return to his temples in Ethiopia and Egypt and read his age-old reminders, which emphatically states to him and the world these prophetic words "**Man Know Thyself!**"

FREDERICK MONDERSON

The Black man [indigenous African and his descendants] must once more write about himself, his cultures, and his continent Alkebu-lan [Africa, Ethiopia, Libya, Etc.]. For no one cares about anothers history to the point where he can feel the emotional values of the inheritors. Moreover, when a mans history is written by his masters religion or economic philosophy, such history is always distorted to suit the Master-Slave relationship, which is the only possible result from such an enforced union. Such paternalism does not have to be vindictive. The mere fact of the relationships existence forces one to feel, in fact, superior to the other. And if the history of such a union is of very long duration, much of the research in the ancient heritage of the captured show they begin to accept their status of inferiority. They then allow themselves to be renamed accordingly. With their new Name, a new psychology naturally develops, and with the new mind, a new docility ... This was done to the Negro."

Dr. Ben's Illustration 44. Signet crown featuring the Goddess Nekhbet with her talons holding Shen Rings (left); and, outstretched wings of the Vulture Goddess Nekhbet with her hands or Talons also full with Shen Rings.

The major desired accomplishment this volume seeks to achieve is to provide an anthropological research in the ancient heritage of the Africans and their descendants over the world. This is to be, for the first time, in a manner and writing which persons of average ability and understanding can digest. For this reason the parenthesis or bracket is generously used

CELEBRATING
DR. BEN-JOCHANNAN

throughout this volume. Equally, certain words have been repetitiously used by intent; so are a number of statements and questionable phrases which one erroneously uses under the belief that their authenticity [correctness] is sacred and have been used sanctioned by God. Of course God is dependent upon ones own religious beliefs! If God is Hebrew [misnomered Jew], He is according to the Holy Torah; if Christian, He is according to the Christian Holy Bible [all versions]; and if Muslim [or Moslem], He is according to the Holy Koran. All of the three mentioned religious interpretations of a God or Gods are accepted in America or Europe by either group; at least to some extent. But if he God [or Gods] be Ra, Krishna, Damballah Cuedo [of West Africa], or any other than the three acceptable to the so-called Western or Modern man, then such a God [or Gods] is relegated to obscenity and paganism. Yet, in this society it is fashionable to say: America was founded on the basic belief of freedom of worship. Such freedom of worship is always with a proviso. That is, providing ones God is the Christians Jesus Christ, Hebrews Jehovah [Yvh], and maybe the Muslims/Moslems Allah."

Dr. Ben's Photo 168a. Erik Monderson beside the two images of Horus at the temple of Edfu in 2018.

FREDERICK MONDERSON

26. RELEVANCE OF EGYPTOLGICAL STUDIES TODAY
By
DR. FRED MONDERSON

A LECTURE IN HONOR OF PROF. JOYCELYN LONCKE (GUYANA). IF WE DO NOT HONOR OUR BEST AND BRIGHTEST THEN WHAT ARE WE TO ASCRIBE FOR.

Egyptological study of the ancient Nile Valley civilization of Northeast Africa is the most profound academic subject in the world today for it contains not just the foundation of, but elements of all contemporary disciplines. However, but like so many disciplines or even countries, it is in a state of constructive disarray. Why? Perhaps it is because of leadership in the discipline and that modern European and American scholars did the reclamation or recovery through archaeological exploration and employing anthropological analysis, they shaped the interpretation of the subject without critical commentary or scrutiny from Africans. This was a period in the 19th and early 20th Century in which Africans were being colonized and had slowly emerged from the ghastly experience of "naked imperialism" followed by "enlightened imperialism," then colonialism. These Africans were too "busy getting a meal" or "getting the shilling" to be involved in critical commentary on Egyptian writings being published in Europe and America. The same can be said for the Black-American, but with some exception such as in the mid-19th Century work of Martin Delaney. However, in the Caribbean it was a bit different. People like Prince Hall the Mason had shown some interest in the subject as well as

CELEBRATING DR. BEN-JOCHANNAN

Bishop Adjai Crowther. The Pan-African nationalist Marcus Garvey met Duse Mohammed, an Egyptian in London, who convinced him of Egypts black roots. Even more, there were people crying in the wilderness; yet, all forms of critical dissent was crushed because it challenged the pillars and foundation of a system falsely represented.

This view is best represented by Maulana Karenga in *Ma'at: The Moral Ideal in Ancient Egypt* (2006: 16) where he states: "A Central Diopian (1981a, 9-10) contention is that enduring attempts to deny the African character of ancient Egypt and recent claims that the racial or ethnic identity of the ancient Egyptians is irrelevant (Yurco 1989), although it is relevant for the rest of Africa and the world, are both products of an ideological scholarship which grew out of an age of imperialist expansion and the resultant need for a justificatory ideology. This, he states, led to a concerted effort to discredit dominated peoples through the manipulation of science and the falsification of human history, a falsification which in Africas case involved depriving it of its most important classical civilization. The thrust seemed to have been one of taking Africans out of Africa, and then Africa out of human history. Such a project and view reaffirmed Hegels and others Eurocentric claims that Africa was a non-historical continent and aided in justifying centuries of oppression and denial of African history and humanity (Mudimbe 1988; Amin 1989)."

People often wonder about the essential elements of the subject but more than a hundred years ago, the Englishman W.M. Flinders Petrie, the "father of Egyptian archaeology," defined Egyptology as "the study of" a combination of "language, geography and history." In this respect, a good example of the significance of ancient Egypt called Kemet by the ancients, is given by W.J. Perry in *The Growth of Civilization* (1924, 1938) as he quotes G. Elliot Smith in the

FREDERICK MONDERSON

second edition of Smith's *The Ancient Egyptians* (1911), who noted: "The Egyptians did a great deal more than merely invent agriculture and devise the earliest statecraft and religion. Not only did they devise methods of working wood and stone and the art of architecture, they seem also to have been inventors of linen and of the craft of weaving, of the use of gold and copper, and the making of metal tools and implements. They were the first people to measure the year and to devise a calendar, and later on to substitute for the rough calculation based upon the date of the annual Nile flood the exact measurement based upon the observation of the suns movement. They also invented shipbuilding and constructed the first sea-going ships. In a thousand and one of the details of our common civilization the originality of Egyptian civilization is revealed. The art of shaving, the use of wigs, the wearing of hats, the invention of the kilt and of the sandal and subsequently of a variety of other articles of dress, many of our musical instruments, chairs and beds, cushions, jewelry and jewel-cases, lamps — these are merely a few of the items picked at random out of our ancient heritage from the Nile Valley." However, when Smith speaks of "our ancient heritage" he is not simply referring to Africans or humanity in general, but Europeans and Americans take this to mean Caucasians. Importantly, the Afrocentrist Molefi Asante has pointed out there are no white people in Europe, only English, Irish, French, Spanish, German, Poles, and so on. Thus, this and more is why we must be involved in this study but more particularly because this is the legacy of the African ancestors! It is essentially then, our foundation, our roots!

Even more significant, I say to you today, the privilege of standing before you and delivering this lecture is actually a lifelong quest. You see, my brother, Stephen Peter Monderson was a mason who laid some of the earliest stone foundation in constructing this august institution. As a youngster I vowed, "If my brother could build this University, one day I will

CELEBRATING DR. BEN-JOCHANNAN

lecture here." Ive been gone for some 44 years but as you probably know its even more than that. However, I wish to put all at ease; I am not in search of a position!

So, therefore, the fundamental lesson we can learn from these ancient Africans from Pharaoh to fellaheen is the insistence on and practice of good governance divinely inspired with significant consequences for the practitioner in this and the next world. That is, leaders are always expected to be held accountable!

First, if we begin with the language of Hieroglyphics. Despite what early Egyptologists preached, Hieroglyphics is actually an African language for we find the rudiments of the language, much of its flora, fauna, geographical features, etc., native to Southern or Upper Egypt. Notwithstanding, while we may find some foreign words in the language it is been deduced these may be due to borrowings derived from trade and other cultural contacts. Nevertheless, in its evolution, scholars have identified eight forms of the Egyptian Language. These were:

1. Predynastic markings that helped define the beginnings of dynastic rule.

2. The Pyramid Texts were discovered by Gaston Maspero in pyramids of kings of the V and VI Dynasties. The texts are, however, certainly much older than the time of the Vth Dynasty and they remained unchanged until discovery.

3. Texts of the Old Empire, mostly inscriptions.

4. Texts of the Middle Empire – These subdivide into two classes in which the language is quite different; (a) The

inscriptions which have a peculiarly heavy and often unintelligible style; and (b) the language of some few papyri, which differs grammatically and linguistically from the inscription. Still, Middle Egyptian is generally the language upon which most scholarship is based.

5. Language of the Transition period, between the Middle and New Kingdoms.

6. The New Egyptian Language of the New Kingdom.

7. The Period of Decline – In this period the language rapidly deteriorates.

8. Demotic (From about the VIIth Century Before Christ) the language had reached its lowest ebb, the grammar is much the same as in Coptic; the difficulties are entirely paleographic in nature.

Dr. Ben's Photo 169. Temple of Edfu to God Horus. Horus greets the Queen, King and others of their retinue.

CELEBRATING DR. BEN-JOCHANNAN

Second, we could speak of geography of humans and geography of the Gods. If we begin with the latter, again, contrary to what the racists have taught, theres a great deal of reference to "Gods land" in Central Africa. The Twa people or "pygmies" of Central Africa were thought to know how to "dance the dance of the Gods." Anyone who knew how to dance the "Dance of the Gods" held a special place in the Egyptian society, especially during the Old Kingdom! Thus, this dance was important and many pharaohs are represented as dancing a ritual dance in praise of their God and in the Heb Sed rejuvenation festival we see this also taking place.

We know Ptah, "God of the Artisans" who constructed the heavens was a bald-headed pygmy. We also know the pygmies came from the "Land of Punt!" Since they were the people of Gods land, Did they originate the philosophy of the "People of Punt?" Ra, the supreme God, after he had created the world, "first created the people of Nubia." So we ask, if these Africans were Caucasians why did their principal God first create the Black people of Nubia. His female counterpart the cow-Goddess Hathor was of Sudani origin. Osiris was of Central African origin and his son Horus, the "blacksmith went north with his followers" the *shemsha hor* who settled in Egypt. As evidence seems to indicate, a *Papyrus* purportedly stated regarding origins of the Egyptians, "We came from the foothills of the mountains of the Moon at the headwaters of the Nile, where the God Hapi dwells." Hapi, the God of the Nile, is also a name of Osiris who is also always shown wearing the White Crown of Upper Egypt. Amon, the Sun God was fused with Ra as Amon-Ra, and he loved to travel to Nubia. His alter ego God Min, often pictured as a Black God, was native to Koptos in Upper Egypt, generally associated with Negroes of Egypt and Nubia. In the earliest times every local region had their God who became incorporated in the great pantheon of Gods of the most significant eras.

FREDERICK MONDERSON

Nevertheless, they all expected the king to practice *Ma'at* and cultivate equality principal in foundation of his responsibility to rule justly.

On the other hand, human geography can be represented in the work of reclamation done in the 19th and 20th Century of our era where scholars traveled up and down the country excavating sites and publishing their reports in book form, as reports to antiquarian societies, in museums journals, in university excavation reports, and in other exhibits. Their reports were full of pertinent data that for the most part, many of the students of this university should seek to access. I hope some of my work donated today will help to fill this void.

A great deal of original research was published under the auspices of **The British School of Archaeology in Egypt** and **The Egyptian Research Account** – Adjuncts of the **Egypt Exploration Fund** with the intent of exploration and publication they rapidly produced many works on excavation of various sites. The enormous volume of work produced by the Egyptian Exploration Fund included *Ballas, The Ramesseum, El Kab, Hierakonpolis I and II, El Arabah, Mahasna, Temple of the Kings, The Osireion, Saqqara Mastabas I, Hyksos and Israelite Cities, Gizeh* and *Rifeh, Athribis and Memphis I, Qurneh and the Palace of Apries* (*Memphis II*). All persons interested in truth regarding Egyptian knowledge must know of the existence of these important sources. Even more, *Meydum and Memphis III, Historical Studies, The Labyrinth and Gerzeh, Portfolio of Hawara Portraits, Tarkhan and Memphis V, Heliopolis I and Kafr Ammar, Riqqeh and Memphis VI, Tarkhan II, Lahun I: The Treasure and Harageh*. We must also include *Scarabs and Cylinders, Tools and Weapons, Prehistoric Egypt, Lahun II: The Pyramid, Sedment I, Sedment II, The Gospel of St. John, Coptic MS., Tomb of the Courtiers and Oxyrchynchus,*

CELEBRATING DR. BEN-JOCHANNAN

Buttons and Design Scarabs, Ancient Weights and Measures, Glass Stamps and Weights, Gurob, Objects of Daily Use, Gerar, Qua and Badari I, Badarian Civilization, Bahrein and Hemamieh, Beth-Pelet I, Corpus of Palestinian Pottery, Qua and Badari III, Antaeopolis (Qua), Beth-Pelet II, Ancient Gaza I, Ancient Gaza II, Ancient Gaza III and Ancient Gaza IV.

Foreign scholars assisted by the Egyptian Antiquities Department conducted the thorough **Archaeological Survey of Egypt** – This became another British vehicle for archaeological excavation, mapping, drawing, creating line drawings, and publication of books and reports relative to Egyptian studies, also under the auspices of **The Egypt Exploration Fund**. Their publications, edited by F. LL. Griffith include *Beni Hasan I, Beni Hasan II, El Bersheh I, El Bersheh II, Beni Hasan III, Hieroglyphics from the Collections of the Egypt Exploration Fund, Beni Hasan IV, The Mastaba of Ptah-Hotep and Akhethetep at Saqqareh, The Rock Tombs of Sheikh Said, The Rock Tombs of Deir el Gebrawi I, The Rock Tombs of Deir el Gebrawi II, The Rock Tombs of el Amarna I, The Rock Tombs of el Amarna II, The Rock Tombs of el Amarna III, The Rock Tombs of el Amarna IV, The Rock Tombs of el Amarna V, The Rock Tombs of el Amarna VI, The Island of Meroe, Meroitic Inscriptions, Five Theban Tombs, The Rock Tombs of Meir I, The Rock Tombs of Meir II,* and *The Rock Tombs of Meir III.*

Another arm of the Fund included the **Graeco-Roman Branch** dealing with papyrus, which published: *The Oxyrhynchus Papyri I, The Oxyrhynchus Papyri II, The Oxyrhynchus Papyri III, The Oxyrhynchus Papyri IV, The*

FREDERICK MONDERSON

Oxyrhynchus Papyri V, *The Oxyrhynchus Papyri VI*, *The Oxyrhynchus Papyri VII*, *The Oxyrhynchus Papyri VIII*, *The Oxyrhynchus Papyri IX*, *The Oxyrhynchus Papyri X*, and *The Oxyrhynchus Papyri XI*. In addition, there were also yearly summaries of **Archaeological Reports** Edited by F. Ll. Griffith and presented to the Egypt Exploration Fund, as well as listings in the **Journal of Egyptian Archaeology**, *Sayings of Jesus* and *Fragment of a Lost Gospel*, *Fragment of an Uncanonical Gospel* by B.P. Grenfell and A.S. Hunt and *The Theban Tomb Series* Vol. I, by Nina de G. Davies and Alan H. Gardiner. Adding to this, Flinders Petrie founded the Journal **Ancient Egypt** in 1914, which aided in publication of his and other scholars works on Egypt. The *Journal of Egyptian Archaeology* began at this time. So too was the **American Journal of Archaeology** *begun* in 1898, the British Archaeological Journal **MAN** and the **Journal of the Anthropological Institute** as well as **Reports** published as part of the **British Association for the Advancement of Science** contribution. The Metropolitan Museum of Art began its *Journal* in 1905 and through this organ chronicled the Museums acquisition of its extensive Egyptian collection. There were private individuals, who, out of curiosity and adventure plied the Nile River visiting various sites and filing reports to various organs in their countries. These reports served as early descriptions of sites with potential for later exploration and excavation. After Britain colonized Egypt, particularly after the Berlin Congress partition of Africa in 1884-85, concessions were generously doled out to British, French, German, Swiss and American excavators, many working for museums, private collections, and antiquities societies who augmented their holdings through choice selection in "pick of the crop" opportunities offered at the various archaeological digs.

CELEBRATING DR. BEN-JOCHANNAN

Notwithstanding, and importantly, from the start of the 19th Century antiquities hunters had been seizing artifacts for sale to national museums and private collections in Britain, France, Italy, Germany, Belgium, etc. This plunder was so pervasive; in his book Brian Fagan called it *The Rape of the Nile*! As a comparative example of foreign collections, I give you; in 1881 the "Deir el Bahari Cache" revealed untold wealth and the mummies of the great pharaohs of the New Kingdom. A published report indicated, only now with this significant "find" would the Egyptian Museum at Bulaq, in Cairo, be equated with the museum in Turin, Italy. Of course, there was another find of mummies discovered in the Tomb of Amenhotep II in 1898 which further augmented the Egyptian Museums collection striving for world class standards comparable to such as the British, Louvre and Berlin Museums.

Again, by the end of the 19th Century, Oxford and Cambridge Universities sent out a number of "fast-guns" who assisted unfolding archaeological excavations breaking ground across the Egyptian landscape discovering, chronicling and cataloging the ancient knowledge. Many of these were attached to the **Egypt Exploration Fund** founded by Amelia Edwards. Into the new 20th Century, as sites across the Egyptian landscape became exhausted, interest was turned to explore and initiate the **Archaeological Survey of Nubia**. So, in assessment, the **Egyptian Exploration Fund**, the **British School of Archaeology in Egypt**, **Egyptian Research Account** and the **Graeco-Roman Branch** that collected and published papyrus, within a fifty year period from 1880-1930, the Fund and its appendages published nearly 100 volumes of Egyptian archaeological evidence. There were also numerous Reports from the field. This has been called the period of "the ancient records of the ancient records." Add to these again another 100 or so journals and magazines as well as a thousand newspapers managing untold reservoirs of new information; they all catered to an insatiable readership as part of the "Penny Press" generation. Sadly, however,tis readership purporting to prove the Egyptian was caucasian who originated in Suth-West africa. Thus, we should not forget, George Foucart admitted, "The early Egyptologists made mistakes," but Dr. Leonard James explained, "The mistakes were purposeful." Much of this revelation and interpretation remained unchallenged as it permeated European and American cultural ethos and mindset solidifying beliefs of the superiority of Caucasians in creating Egyptian culture, a view many held from birth to grave. That is not to say excavators did not fperform an extraordinary job of recovering the ancient knowledge. The problem is, however, as Malcolm X used to say, "They know how to put it." So, in the mad rush to publish, there was much omission and distortion.

Dr. Ben's Photo 170. Temple of Edfu to God Horus. Isis as Hathor wearing the horns and disk atop the Queen Mother Crown, while having her exposed breast.

CELEBRATING DR. BEN-JOCHANNAN

Dr. Ben's Photo 171. Temple of Edfu to God Horus. Who could countenance defacing the face of such a beautiful woman.

Dr. Ben's Photo 172. Temple of Edfu to God Horus. Horus and Thoth baptise the King before he enters the Temple to perform the daily ritual.

Dr. Ben's Photo 173. Temple of Edfu to God Horus. Sister Goddesses in White Crown (left) and Red Crown (right) lay hands on the King in Double Crown.

CELEBRATING DR. BEN-JOCHANNAN

Dr. Ben's Photo 174. Temple of Edfu to God Horus. Hathor, wearing horns and disk, sits enthroned among other defaced Gods.

Dr. Ben's Photo 175. Temple of Edfu to God Horus. Again, defaced divinities in horns and disk and Double Crown.

FREDERICK MONDERSON

For example, a statue of the 11th dynasty pharaoh Mentuhotep II was discovered in 1898 in his temple at Deir el Bahari that was excavated from 1903-1906. He is shown wearing the Red Crown of Lower Egypt and his skin is painted black. The assumption is there was another statue wearing the White Crown of Upper Egypt. However, it was not until 1959 that William Stephenson Smith in *The Art and Architecture of Ancient Egypt* reported Mentuhotep had "black flesh." All the great archaeologists and Egyptologists visited the museum and saw the statue but it took more than fifty years to comment on his ethnicity. Does it mean the hundreds of books published on the subject from Mentuhoteps discovery to Smith were suspect? Weve got to critically read modern books that are tremendously sanitized for as stated above, many insist the ethnicity of the ancient Egyptians is unimportant. Nevertheless, in this vein, the unstated assumption is that they were Caucasian not African.

Equally, a current view by Wortham in the *History of British Egyptology* 1580-1906 holds an Englishman Augustus Granville dissected a mummy in London in 1825 and proved the Egyptians were Caucasians! We dont fully know what age the mummy was from. This writer encountered an article in *Gentleman's Magazine* of 1820, five years earlier where the writer donated a mummy to the Hunterian Museum. He noted, as the mummy was being unwrapped its skin was of a brown color and within 3 to 4 hour period it turned black owing to exposure to wind, sunlight, etc. However, he did say the mummy was from the Roman age in Egypt and that he had an artist paint a portrait capturing the brown color of the mummy before its color changed. If as late as the Roman Period, despite invasions by the Hyksos, Persian, Assyrians, Greeks and Romans the skin color had not changed one has to wonder about any comparisons of these ancients with modern ethnics. Let me also add, the American Egyptologist J.H. breasted began his 1916 *Ancient Times* speaking of "then, brown skin"

CELEBRATING DR. BEN-JOCHANNAN

Egyptians. Its said his benefactors gave money to launch the Chicago Universitys Oriental Institute and in the 1935 reissue of *Ancient Times* (1916), he began discussing the "great white race." Further, the mummy of "Rameses the great," was described as "brown with black splotches." Ivan Van Sertima stated Cheikh Anta Diop observed so much radiation was used on Rameses when his mummy was repaired in Paris, the mummy actually turned yellow!

Evidence has shown much destruction of monuments and pertinent data linking Africans role in Egypt. Again, though the occasional writer found problems with the reporting, preponderance of interpretation credits Caucasians with being the originators of this African culture. This is what we much continue to challenge!

That the ancient Egyptians were Caucasians, I must remind you is a false interpretation! If we read this new book *Black Genesis* (2011) by Bauval and Brophy they argue the Black people of Nabta Playa, a region to the west of Upper Egypt, were the originators of Egyptian civilization. These Black African people were the earliest astronomers, scientists, mapping the heavens, creating a calendar, farming, painting and were also pastoralists who practiced cattle or "cow culture" and traveled extensively across the desert they navigated by star-gazing or positioning. Their knowledge, accumulated between 20,000 and 3500 B.C., the Author's argue, provided the wherewithal of the origins of pharaonic civilization. In *Genesis of the Pharaohs* (2003), Toby Wilkinson argued, "Civilization began in the desert then moved to the Nile Valley."

FREDERICK MONDERSON

Dr. Ben's Illustration 45. The Gods, Osiris flanked by Horus and Hathor (left) and, Dish with illustrated fish.

Dr. Ben's Illustration 46. Neclace Pectoral depicting Amon (left) and Osiris (right).

CELEBRATING DR. BEN-JOCHANNAN

From time immemorial scholars have commented on Ancient Egypt beginning with Hecataeus of Abdera who actually coined the phrase often attributed to Herodotus that "Egypt is the gift of the Nile!" Later, Herodotus of Halicarnassus visited Egypt in 450 B.C. He wrote *The Histories*, devoting Book II *Euterpe* to Egypt. Credited with making the earliest anthropological studies, he observed and wrote, "The Ethiopians, Colchians and Egyptians have thick lips, broad noses, wooly hair and are burnt of skin." The Greek-Egyptian priest Manetho of Sebennytus had access to all the accumulated priestly wisdom and he wrote a *History of Egypt* that has only survived in fragments through commentary of other writers. Diodorus Siculus visited Egypt and wrote about its people and culture; so too did Josephus, Strabo and Pliny, all ancient writers. However, Horapollo made the first attempt to decipher the language. In the Middle Ages men like Athanasius Kircher applied themselves to the task, but they met with little success. Though Theodosius closed the temples after 352 A.D., the latest dated hieroglyphs were carved at the temple of Isis at Philae in 394 A.D. Some have even argued there were Egyptian priests living underground who knew how to read Hieroglyphics and were pressured to reveal secrets of the ancient writings as late as 1750. This may be pure speculation, and we must be careful of such, since Chmpollions success came 72 years later.

Following the French Revolution and rise of Napoleon Bonaparte who invaded Egypt with scholars attached to his army, the Rosetta Stone was discovered in August of 1799. This was a decree of Ptolemy Epiphanes V inscribed on a block of black basalt written in Greek, Hieroglyphic, and Demotic. Its now in the British Museum and the Egyptians have only a replica! Thomas Young, an English mathematician and Francois Champollion, a French savant and linguist set out to decipher the languages of the stone.

FREDERICK MONDERSON

Champollion was successful in 1822. He then set out to decipher as many inscriptions as he could. So much so, within 10 years by 1832 he was dead from exhaustion but he left a tremendous legacy. Interesting, in 1922 a hundred years after Champollions decipherment, King Tuts tomb was discovered intact. Zahi Hawass of the Supreme Antiquites Council has called for scientific treatment to identify all, particularly royal mummies. Since only Tutankhamon's mummy was discovered in his sealed tomb, he wa the only one rightfully identified. Following that insistence, Queen Hatshepsut's mummy has since been identified through a missing teeth. Now she has joined that exclusive club.

Richard Lepsius, the celebrated German scholar led the Prussian expedition through Egypt and Ethiopia from 1842-1845. Fred Gladstone Bratton in *A History of Egyptian Archaeology* (1968) reported: "Lepsius shipped 15,000 artifacts to Berlin" and thus its Museum to accumulate one of the finest Egyptian collection in the world. Chabas, a French scholar translated and published many papyri. Mariette Bey built up the Museum of Boulak. Gaston Maspero was undoubtedly one of the greatest French Egyptologists of his age. He wrote extensively on the subject because he had ready access to all the knowledge as Director of Antiquities. He described the Nobleman Mahepra as "Negroid" but not "Negro." On the other hand, the musical genius Beethovens biographers described him as "black," "Negroid," "Negro," "swarthy." Have you noticed any inconsistencies in the two descriptions? Wallis Budge as Keeper of Egyptian and Assyrian Antiquities at the British Museum wrote extensively on Egypt and did tremendous research on its African roots. W.M. Flinders Petrie, the "father of Egyptian Archaeology" spent fifty years in Egyptology. He compiled an impressive bibliography of some 1200 publications of books, articles, reviews, etc., The French **Encyclopedist of Science** George Sarton had even more. I used these two to motivate my

CELEBRATING
DR. BEN-JOCHANNAN

quest and now I have surpassed 1000 pieces of published works.

Dr. Ben's Photo 176. More of the terrain in the vicinity of Hatshepsut's Temple at Deir el Bahari.

The unique thing about ancient Egypt, their's was an ordered society that valued tradition by establishing rules for governance, social conduct and moral and ethical practice because the pharaoh was held accountable by his fellow Gods. In this respect, there are three areas in which the ancient Egyptian culture can serve the interests of modern man, particularly the African, to become more Godlike and in tune with nature, inasmuch as *Ma'at* as fundamental to social and political conduct would dictate. That is, within the realm of governance, modern man can grow tremendously from an outstanding of the literary legacy and the moral precepts they teach of the practice of doing good as opposed to doing evil deeds. The most important outcome of this admonition of the practice of doing good is not so as to be the recipient of future good deeds in return or to store up good deeds for a future judgment in this life or the next. The most important reason for doing a good deed is that the person for whom one does a good deed in turn does a good deed based on that good deed as *Ma'at* dictates. The whole idea is that everybody practices good so that the world become overwhelmed with goodness and we all grow in the process.

In his book **Ma'at**, Maulana Karenga provides the essential meaning of this ideal stating "*Ma'at is rightness in the spiritual and moral sense in three realms: the Divine, the natural and the social. In its expansive sense, Ma'at is an interrelated order of rightness which requires and is the result of right relations and with right behavior towards the Divine, nature and other humans.* As moral thought and practice *Ma'at is a way of rightness* defined especially by the practice of the seven Cardinal Virtues of truth, justice, propriety, harmony, balance, reciprocity and order. Finally, as a foundation and framework for the moral ideal and its practice, *Ma'at is the constantly achieved condition of and requirement for the ideal world, society and person*, i.e., the Ma'atian world, the Ma'atian society, and the Ma'atian person."

Thus, in the realm of governance, while the pharaoh was head of the government, it was through his administrative officials that his thoughts were made tangible. Jacob Carruthers in *Essays in Ancient Egyptian Studies* (1984: 93), while stating that "Ma'at is the foundation for official conduct," describes

CELEBRATING DR. BEN-JOCHANNAN

the structure of the national government of ancient Egypt which the ancients called Kemet. Here, he states: "The organization of the National government seemed to include the office of *Niswt* (the head of state), a National Council of Advisors (the Legislature), a Prime Minister, a Minister of the Treasury, a Keeper of the Seal (Minister of State Affairs), Commanders of Expeditions (including army and navy) and regional and colonial governors (in the later period). These cabinet level officials were assisted by a host of overseers and petty officials who were promoted according to achievement. Judicial functions were evidently carried out by the governmental officials acting as judges sometimes in consultation with the national Council." In many cases, judges were admonished, for example: "If your brothers case came before you, he lost!" That is, you have to lean in the opposite direction so as not to appear partial. Carruthers says further of a 5th Dynasty Prime Minister Ptah-Hotep who established the philosophy of governance for officialdom: "If you become a leader commanding plans of the many, seek out every excellent occasion; let not your governance be wrong, Ma'at is great and enduring in effect; it has not been confounded since the time of *Wosir*, in the end Ma'at endures, a man may say it is my fathers property."

The 12th Dynasty pharaoh Usertesen or Senwosret told a high official: "It is your advice that brings about every work that I desire to happen; you are superintendent of it, the one who will act according to what is in my heart. Skill demands vigilance; it is to him who is free of laziness, that it comes. All work demands insight. The one who is effective is he who applies himself ... command the workers to act in accordance with what has been destined for you."

In this divine dispensation, the King was the Son of God. In fact, he was a God himself on earth and when he died he was expected to fly to heaven to mingle with his fellow Gods. There he was judged based on his actions as a ruler. On earth, he was "a minor God!" After being declared "True of Voice;" "Justified," he became a full-fledged divinity. In reflection, the kings principal responsibility was to bring about Ma'at in every way possible. That is, the society should be balanced in every respect! Again, as Maulana Karenga, in *The Book of Coming Forth by Day*: *The Ethics of the Declaration of Innocence* (1990: 97) states, "one is cultivated to do good by instruction in the seven cardinal virtues of Ma'at: truth, justice, propriety, harmony, balance, reciprocity and order. These are cardinal in that all of these categories can be and are translated in the sacred text as Ma'at. Thus, to speak truth, do justice, act properly, live in harmony, be balanced, practice reciprocity and recognize and respect the personal – social, divine and natural order are all [attributes] of Ma'at. The thrust to cultivate the Ma'atian character is to create a self-enriching process in which the Ma'atian person and Ma'atian society, in a dynamic reciprocity, reinforce and sustain each other and foster each others expansiveness."

In addition to his striving for *Ma'at* to keep balance and order in the society, a principal function of the King was to protect the God who resided in an earthly home, a temple. This protection meant he had to build his God a house, a temple of imperishable material, that is of stone and to outfit it with the wherewithal for its survival. Thus, from within an enclosure wall, a functioning priesthood not simply orchestrated the daily ritual but also practiced economic survivability in use of industrial workers who made objects for trade, built ships to carry their produce, possessed extensive tracks of land to provide food for the God and his servants; grew flowers for the daily ritual and trade of surplus food as part of their produce. The temple ultimately expanded its repertoire to include architectural constructions because sometimes more than one King built a temple and there was need for kiosks,

CELEBRATING
DR. BEN-JOCHANNAN

chapels, statues, doors, obelisks, columns, etc., as kingly donations or endowments. In need of stone, they quarried the material sometimes from great distances which required flat bottomed boats to transport the stone to site of erection. As an ancillary, stone finishing and artistic decoration were added.

Dr. Ben's Illustration 47. The King being baptized by Ra-Horakhty (left) and Amon (right) in the Boat of the Gods.

Dr. Ben's Photo 187. Hatshepsut's Temple at Deir el Bahari. Middle and Upper Terrace Colonnade and Upper Court before the Sanctuary.

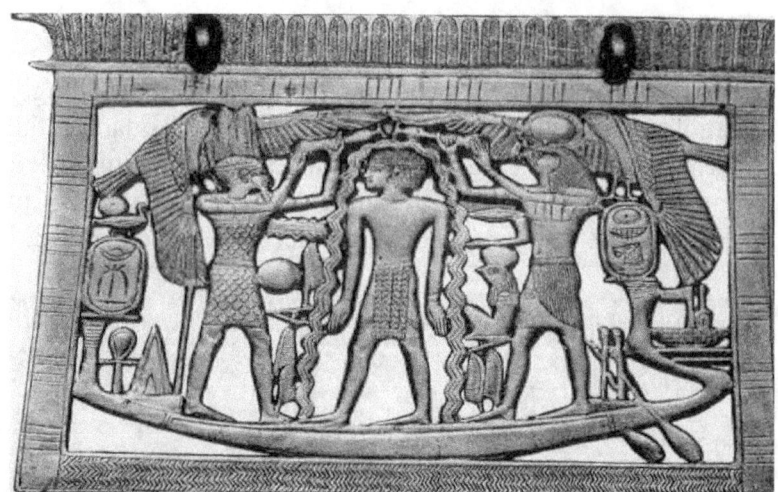

Dr. Ben's Illustration 48. The King being baptized by Amon (left) and Ra-Horakhty (right) as they sail in the "Boat of the Gods."

Dr. Ben's Illustration 49. Pectoral. Double image of the King smiting a kneeling enemy beneath outstretched wings of the Vulture Goddess Nekhbet and two Cartouches as Ankhs with arms hold standards (left); and beneath outstretched wings of Goddess Nekhbet, double images of the King wearing an apron as he raises the mace to strike a kneeling enemy beneath Cartouches and with Ankhs with hands holding Standards. Look closely, they are not the same. To the left the vulture loooks right and to the right the vulture looks left.

CELEBRATING DR. BEN-JOCHANNAN

Some temples such as Luxor became Universities that taught a higher Liberal education in such subjects, as S.E. Frost in *History of Education* in The Barrons Educational series Inc., (1947: 9) has indicated, including "writing, geography, cosmography, astronomy, chronology, sculpture, painting, ritual dancing, theory of music, law, medicine, morals, arithmetic, mensuration, hydrostatics, and architecture. Education for professional careers emphasized practice rather than theory. Secrets of each profession were handed down within a family and transmitted through apprenticeship. The area of professional training included medicine, the priesthood, the military, architecture and skill of the scribe."

All this notwithstanding, the principal function of the pharaoh having established Ma'at in the society, was to conduct the ritual to placate the God who in turn would bring good fortune, balance and order to the society. The God did this through the ethereal substance of his being, *Ma'at*, again meaning justice, order, balance, right, the good, righteousness; and this was the opposite of *Isfit*, disorder, chaos, evil, etc.

Social conduct was passed down in the form of **Instructions**, whether the King instructed his son or some high official instructed his son, or the society at large. There were also **Lamentations** that decried the poor state the nation had succumbed to especially during the First Intermediate Period. In addition, prizing tradition they looked to their earliest learnings that were transmitted in book form. Much of this was copied by schoolboys and transmitted down through the ages.

In his *Selections from the Husia: Sacred Wisdom of Ancient Egypt* (1984) Maulana Karenga provided a listing of the Books that have had a profound impact on Egyptians down through the dynastic period and Karenga hopes it will help edify and uplift the modern African in America and elsewhere in the Diaspora. He lists:

The Book of Knowing the Creations – Ra, the Lord of All, has said, "I am the one who came into being as Kheper, He who comes into being and brings into being. When I came into being, being itself came into being. All being came into being after I came into being. Many were the beings that came forth from the commands of my mouth …."

I did Four Good Deeds on the threshold of the horizon.

I created the four winds so that every person might breathe in his or her time and place.

I created the great flood for irrigation so that the humble might benefit from it like the great.

I made every person like his and her fellow; and I did not command them to do evil. It was their own hearts and minds that caused them to disobey that which I commanded.

I made the hearts of men and women so that they would not forget the day of death, so that sacred offerings might be made to the divine powers of the districts.

He said further, "I am **Kheper**, the Bringer into Being. In the morning; **Ra**, the Most High and Glorious at noon; and **Atum**, the Complete One in the evening."

The Book of Prayers and Sacred Praises – NebRa says: "Though the servant be inclined to make

CELEBRATING DR. BEN-JOCHANNAN

mistakes, the Lord is inclined to be merciful. The Lord of Thebes does not spend a whole day in anger. He is angry for but a moment and none of it remains behind. The wind turns for us in His mercy and Amen-Ra comes back upon the breeze. May your spirit be always kind, may you always forgive. And may what has once been turned away not come back to us."

The Book of the Moral Narrative – that is, **The Book of Khun-Anup**. Here Karenga speaks of the central character, "a peasant or farmer who is unjustly treated and appeals for relief, justice and righteousness from the High Steward, Rensi, who handled such matters. Rensi is impressed with Khun-Anups literary eloquence and reports it to the pharaoh who is also impressed. He makes nine petitions and says to the high official Rensi: "Let me raise up your name in this land as the embodiment of every good law. You are a leader without greed, a great man free of baseness, one who destroys falsehood and brings righteousness into being, one who comes at the voice of the caller."

Dr. Ben's Photo 177. Hatshepsut's Temple at Deir el Bahari. View of the Ramesseum and vegetation beyond, from the highlands of Deir el Bahari.

FREDERICK MONDERSON

Dr. Ben's Photo 178. Hatshepsut's Temple at Deir el Bahari. The "Red House" built for Edouardo Naville when he cleared Deir el Bahari temple in the 1890s.

Dr. Ben's Photo 179. Hatshepsut's Temple at Deir el Bahari. From the highlands affording the "Birds Eye View," the new staging area for buses to avoid pulluting the monument with their exhaust fumes.

CELEBRATING DR. BEN-JOCHANNAN

"Do not speak falsely for you are great. Do not act lightly for you have weight; be not untrue for you are the balance and do not swerve for you are the standard. You are on the level with the balance." "Be patient that you may learn righteousness and restrain your anger for the good of one who enters humbly. No one hastily achieves excellence and one who is impatient is not leaned on." "Helmsman, do not let your ship go astray. Life-giver, do not let the people die." "One who lessens falsehood encourages truth. One who supports good diminishes evil – even as satisfaction comes and ends hunger and clothing removes nakedness; even as the sky becomes calm after a storm and warms all who are cold; even as fire cooks that which is raw and water quenches thirst." "Those who prey on others achieve no real success. Their success is, in truth, a loss."

The Books of Wise Instruction

The Book of Ptah-Hotep – The great man says: "Be not arrogant because of your knowledge. Take counsel with the ignorant as well as with the wise. For the limits of knowledge in any field have never been set and no one has ever reached them. Wisdom is rarer than emeralds, and yet it is found among the women who gather at the grindstones." "If you are a leader and command many, strive for excellence in all you do so that no fault can be found in your character. For Ma'at – the way of Truth, Justice and Righteousness – is great; its value is lasting and it has remained unequalled and unchanged since the time of its creator." "Do not terrorize people for if you do, God will punish you accordingly." "The plans of men and women do not always come to pass, for in the end it is the will of God which prevails." "Established are those whose standard is righteousness, who walk according to its ways. They shall surely prosper thereby, but the greedy will not have even a grave." "If you are a powerful person, gain respect through knowledge and gentleness of speech and conduct." "The character of a righteous person is an honor to him or her and a thing of value which is long remembered."

The Book of Kagemni – "Let your name go for, then, while you yourself, are silent and you will be recognized and respected."

The Book of Kheti says - "Be skilled in speech so that you will succeed. The tongue of a man is his sword and effective speech is stronger than all fighting. None can overcome the skillful. A wise person is a school for the nobles and those who are aware of his knowledge do not attack him. No evil takes place when he is near. Truth comes to him in its essential form, shaped in the sayings of the ancestors." "Follow in the footsteps of your ancestors, for the mind is trained through knowledge. Behold, their words endure in books. Open and read them and follow their wise counsel. For one who is taught becomes skilled. Do not be evil for kindness is good. Make the memory of you last through love of you."

The Book of Ani – "Do not go in and out of the court of justice so that your name may not be soiled." "Walk each day in the way of righteousness and you will reach the place to which you are going."

The Book of Amenemope – "Beware of robbing the poor and oppressing the weak and helpless. Raise not your hand against the aged nor address the elderly with improper speech. Let not yourself be sent on an evil mission nor stand in the company of those who have performed it. Rage not against those who injure you, nor on your account answer

CELEBRATING
DR. BEN-JOCHANNAN

them." "Let us steer a righteous course so that we may carry the wicked across without becoming like them." "Do not argue with the contentious nor provoke them with words." "Now, the unrestrained man or woman in the temple is like a tree grown in unfertile ground. Its leaves wither quickly and its unripe fruit falls to the earth. It reaches its end in the lumber yard or it is floated far from its place. And its burial cloth becomes a flame of fire. But the self-mastered man or woman sets himself or herself apart. [Their tree] grows green and doubles its yield of fruit. It has its place in the eyes of its owner. Its fruit is sweet, its shade is pleasant and its end is reached in the garden." "Better is bread with a happy heart than riches with worry."

Dr. Ben's Illustration 50. Pectoral. With Nekhbet hovering overhead with wings outstretchend and holdig shenrings supporting a cartouche, the king as two sphinxes tramples enemies (left); and, a necklace bearing the name of Senusert II showing double Horus hawks wearing the Double Crown and standing on a Nebeet or Gold Necklace and backed by Uraei swinging from disks and sporting ankhs.

FREDERICK MONDERSON

The Book of Ankhsheshonqi - Oh, what great wisdom the ancients possessed! For example, the *Book of Ankhsheshonqi* teaches "Service is righteous action towards and for God, humans and by extension, nature which in some meaningful and moral way returns a reciprocal benefit."

Again, Ankhsheshonqi cautions, "The only real good deed is the one done for one who needs it." Perhaps in the American culture that proponent of ancient African deep thought foresaw and foretold of the conflict of the one and the ninety-nine percent. Within this same prophetic construct can be placed the "Millionaires Tax Cut" for those who do not need it; and to this we may add the Health Care Reform Act that benefits the fifty million Americans who need its protection. Can we thrown in the Lilly Ledbetter Act for women certainly need to earn the same as men if they do the same work?

Nevertheless, Ankhsheshonqi admonishes as Maulana Karenga has pointed out, "One should not be disappointed for not being recognized or thanked by everyone for whom one does good." Antedating the wisdom of the *Book of Ecclesiastes* which urges, as we all sometimes do, "Cast your bread upon the waters and after many days it will return to you;" yet, Ankhsheshonqi admonishes, "If you do good by a hundred persons and just one of them acknowledges it, no part of it is lost." His optimism is reflected in the law of reciprocity in that, "Do a good deed and throw it in the water and when the water dries up, you will find it." Again, we see in the ancient Egyptian/African reservoir of deep thought wisdom many paraphrased modern wise sayings such as "Its better to give than to receive." In Ankhsheshonqis original thought, "Sweeter is the water of one who has given than the wine of one who has received."

CELEBRATING
DR. BEN-JOCHANNAN

Dr. Ben's Photo 180. Hatshepsut's Temple at Deir el Bahari. A look at the Second Court and Second Ramp as well as the Enclosure Wall to the right view from the mountain.

Dr. Ben's Photo 181. Hatshepsut's Temple at Deir el Bahari. A better view of the First and Second Courts as well as the Upper Court, the First and Second Ramps, the true Northern Colonnade to the left, the Hathor Shrine to the lower right and the colonnade in the Upper Court.

FREDERICK MONDERSON

b

Dr. Ben's Photo 182. Hatshepsut's Temple at Deir el Bahari. The Middle Kingdom Temple of Mentuhotep II, the architectural form transitional from the Old to the New Kingdom supporting ramp, a high base and colonnades surrounding a small pyramid now in rubble.

The Book of Phebhor – "If a beam is longer than its right measure, the excess is cut off. If the wind blows beyond its right measure, it wrecks the ship. Those who apply the right measure in all good things are not blamed. The God of just measure has created a balance in order to establish right measure on earth. He placed the heart deep in the body for the

CELEBRATING DR. BEN-JOCHANNAN

right measure of its owner. Thus, if those who are learned are not balanced, their learning is of little use and a fool who knows not balance does not escape misfortune. Pride and arrogance are the destruction of their owner. But those who are gentle in character create their own fate."

The Books of Contemplation:

The Book of Khakheper-Ra-Soneb – "I meditate on what has happened, on the things which have come to pass throughout the land. Changes are taking place and it is not like last year. One year is more troublesome than the next. The land is in turmoil, and being destroyed. Ma'at, righteousness and order, has been cast out and Isfit, evil and chaos, is in the Council Hall. The way of God is violated and His commandments are brushed aside. The land is in turmoil and there is mourning everywhere."

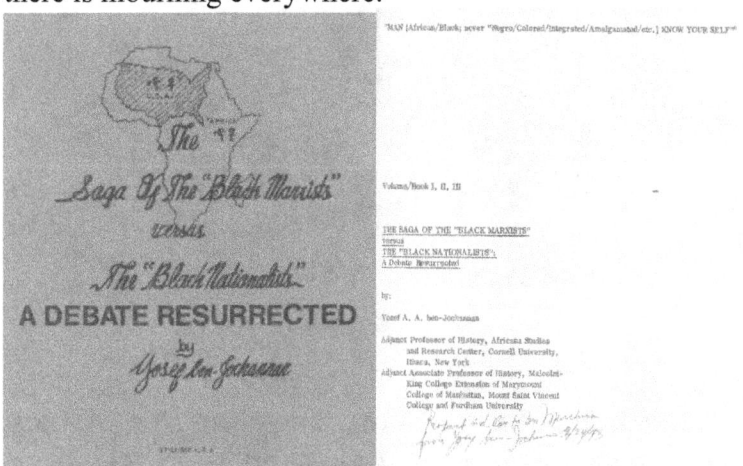

Dr. Ben's Books 12. The Saga of the "Black Marxists" versus the "Black Nationalists" A DEBATE RESURRECTED (1978). Note the Author's autograph for Dr. Fred Monderson.

FREDERICK MONDERSON

IF I HAD NO DEFINITE POLITICAL IDEOLOGY, I AM IN FACT EXISTING IN LIMBO. YET, ON THE OTHER HAND, IF MY POLITICAL IDEOLOGY ISOLATES ME FROM MY FELLOW AFRICANS TO THE POINT WHERE I BELIEVE THAT MINE AND GOD'S [anyone of the hundreds] ARE ONE; I AM IN FACT ALREADY A "LIVING DEAD". FOR "IGNORANCE IS CONTEMPTABLE, EVEN IN THE EYES OF GOD AND HIS GODDESS". Ra-Isis

Dr. Ben's Books 12. The Saga of the "Black Marxists" versus the "Black Nationalists" : A DEBATE RESURRECTED (1978).

CELEBRATING
DR. BEN-JOCHANNAN

> To whom am I addressing all of my remarks to follow in the text of these three Volumes: I, II and III?[0] Certainly, To Those Who Preached/Preach From Their "Street Corner Ladders" The Following Words: "AFRICA FOR THE AFRICANS, THOSE AT HOME AND THOSE ABROAD". They Were/Are The [so-called] "Irresponsible Blacks" Like Myself - Your Author. Thus Each Ai Every Word In These Volumes/Books Are...
>
> > DEDICATED to the unknown HEROES and HEROINES who, in their own way and form, preached/preach "The One And Only True African/Black Philosophy" at Marcus M. Garvey - Adam C. Powell, Jr - Malcolm "X" Square: Arthur Reed, Carlos Cooks, "Ras de Killer", Abdoul Soufee, James Thornhill, Jimmey Lawson, Elombe Brath, Eddie ["pork chop"] Davis, Sister Bessie Phillips, Lewis Michaeux, Sister Lucile, "Shorty", Charles ["27 X"] Kenyatta, Arnold Lewis, George E. Simmonds, Abdul Krim [Bro. Mayhew of the "Black Brotherhood"], and even myself - Yosef ben-Jochannan, along with countless others. Everyone of us, too many already dead, in the tradition of "The Great One" and/or "Man Of The People Of Our Motherland - Africa", Founder and President-General of the Universal Negro Improvement Association and African Communities League - MARCUS MOZIAH GARVEY.... These Were/Are The Stalwart Africans/Blacks Who Kept "African/Black Consciousness" Alive When Most Africans/Blacks In The [so-called] "Diaspora" Were/Are Still Ignorant Of Their/Our African Origin And Heritage: Cultures, Religions, History, etc. ad infinitum; all of which preceeded "The Creation Of Adam And Eve" by the ancient Hebrews no longer than ca. 3670 B.C.E./B.C. at best, but recorded in ca. 700 - 500 B.C.E./B.C. in their "Holy Scriptures" - otherwise called THE FIVE BOOKS OF MOSES, TORAH, PENTATEUCH, OLD TESTAMENT, COMESH, etc. - allegedly "Written By God's [Jehovah/Ywh] Holy Scribes"[20]....

Dr. Ben's Books 12. The Saga of the "Black Marxists" versus the "Black Nationalists" : A DEBATE RESURRECTED (1978).

The Book of Ipuwer - "Behold now, how greatly the people have changed. One who once did not sleep even on a box now owns a bed. Those who once owned robes are now in rags and those who once did not weave for themselves now own fine linen. Behold, those who once did not build boats, now own ships and the former owners just look at them, for they are no longer theirs. Those who once lacked shelter now

FREDERICK MONDERSON

have homes and those who had homes are in the blast of the storm. And those who knew nothing of God now make offerings to Him with the incense of others."

The Book of the Dialog with the Soul – "I spoke to my soul that I might answer what it said: To whom shall I speak today? Brothers and sisters are evil and friends today are not worth loving. Hearts are great with greed and everyone seizes his or her neighbors goods. Kindness has passed away and violence is imposed on everyone." "To whom shall I speak today? People willingly accept evil and goodness is cast to the ground everywhere. Those who should enrage people by their wrongdoing make them laugh at their evil deeds. People plunder and everyone seizes his or her neighbors goods."

The Book of Songs – Song of Pharaoh Antef – "Let your heart be happy then, and forget your day of departure. Follow the desire of your heart for as long as you live. Put myrrh on your head; and clad yourself in fine clothes. Enjoy the wondrous things fit for a God. Increase the number of things you enjoy and let not your heart become lax or lose its vigor. Follow the desires of your heart and do that which is good for you. Fulfill your needs on earth according to the commands of your heart til the day of mourning come for you. For the God of the departed hears not the mourning, and wailing saves no one from the grave. Celebrate, then, the days of rejoicing and do not tire of them. For lo, none may take their goods with them and none who depart ever come back again."

The Book of Declarations of Virtues – Djedkhonsefankh, Prophet of Amen-Ra says: "Hail to you who come after me, who shall live in times to come. I shall make you call me blessed for my destiny was great. Ra, as Khnum the Great Potter, fashioned me into one most able, an advisor of excellent counsel. He made my character superior

CELEBRATING
DR. BEN-JOCHANNAN

to others and guided my tongue to that which was excellent. I kept my mouth free from attacking those who attacked me. My patience turned my foes into friends and my enemies into allies. I controlled my mouth and was skilled in response, yet I did not submit to evil doing."

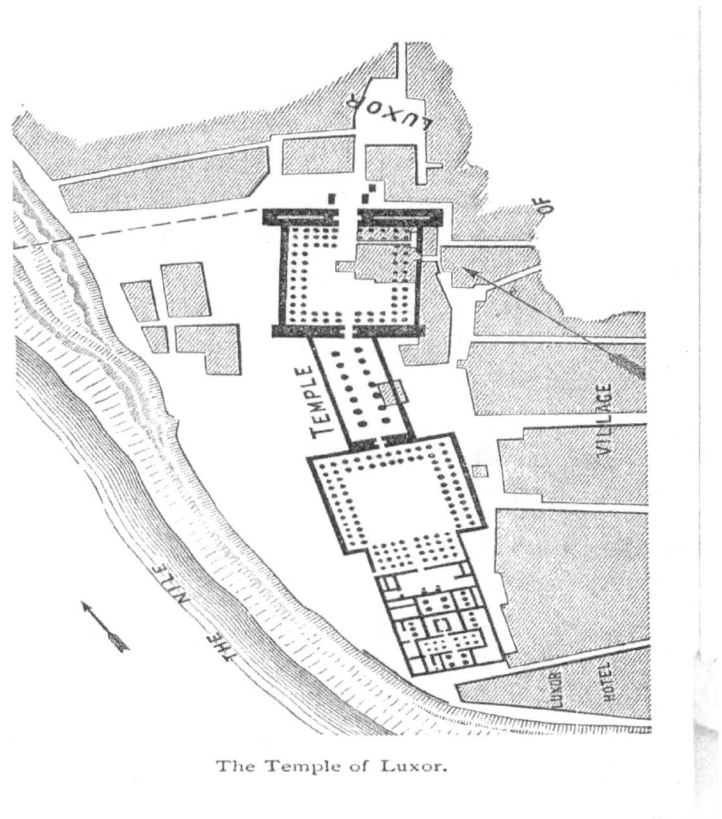

The Temple of Luxor.

Dr. Ben's Plan 12: The Temple of Luxor.

FREDERICK MONDERSON

The Books of Rising Like Ra

The Book of Coming Forth by Day – May I not be judged according to the mouth of the multitude. May my soul lift itself up before my heart, and be found to have been righteous on earth. May I come into your presence O Lord of Lords, May I reach the Hall of Righteousness. May I rise like a living God and give forth light like the divine powers that are in heaven. Let me proceed in peace to the West. May the Lords of the Sacred Land receive me and give me three-fold praise in peace. May they make a seat for me besides the Elders of the Council. May I ascend in the presence of the Beneficent One. And may I assume whatever form I want in whatever place my spirit wishes to be."

The Book of Vindication –

The Book of Rising and Transformation – "The Heavens declare: This royal vindicated one is my beloved son in whom I am well pleased …. My first born upon the throne of earth, and Ra has given him his heritage in the presence of the great Powers of heaven. All the powers of heaven rejoice saying how blessed is this vindicated one, for His Father is greatly pleased with him."

Thus, what this all teaches is that we can and must enmesh ourselves in the teachings of the ancient African, Egyptian culture and in process transform ourselves, our immediate circle and our society.

CELEBRATING
DR. BEN-JOCHANNAN

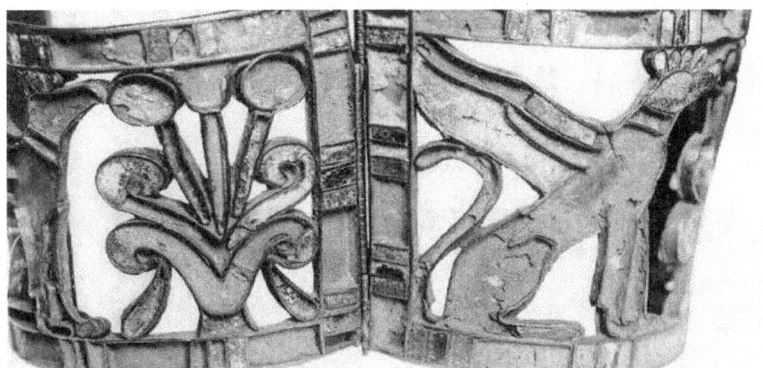

Dr. Ben's Illustration 67. Pectoral of a flower (left); and, Winged Lion (right).

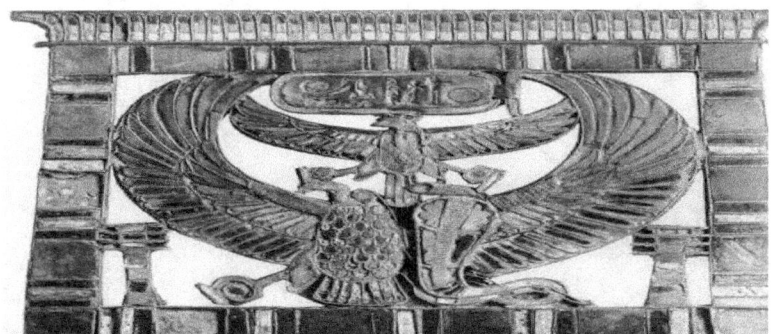

Dr. Ben's Illustration 68. Pectoral of winged *Nekhbet* and *Wadjit* Goddesses, surmounted by another winged Nekhbet holding Rhen Rings.

FREDERICK MONDERSON

27. DR. FRED MONDERSON – Presents The Fourth Memorial Day Tribute to Dr. Yosef ben-Jochannan

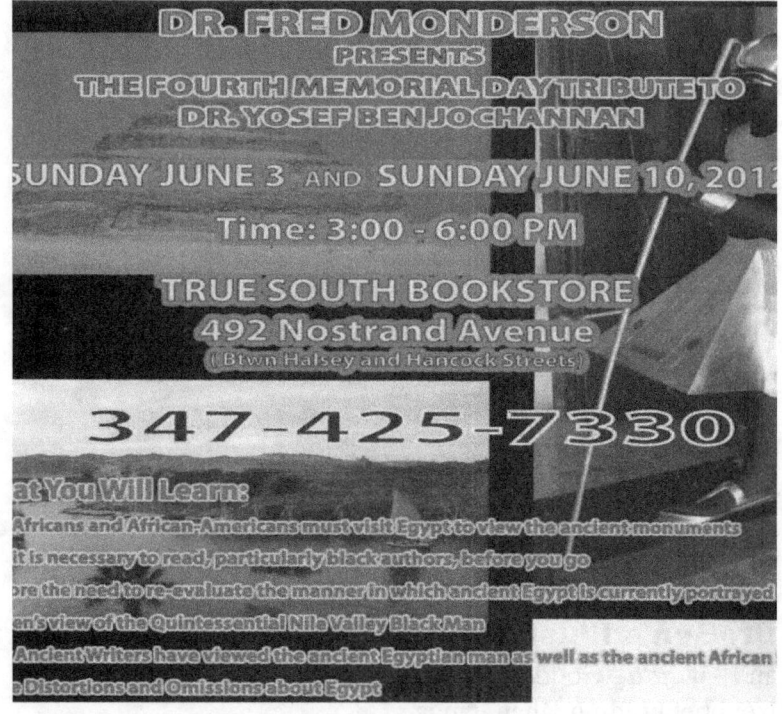

CELEBRATING DR. BEN-JOCHANNAN

Dr. Ben's Photo 182a. Erik Monderson stands before the Kiosk of Nectanebo at Isis's Temple at Philae, now on Agilka Island, in 2018.

28. ETERNAL, YET CHANGING EGYPT 2005
By
Dr. Fred Monderson

Dr. Jacob Carruthers ends his book *Mdw Ntr: Divine Speech* with a quote from the ancient Egyptian philosopher Ptah-Hotep: "The limits of art are never achieved; the skills of the artist are never perfected."

When I visited the Temple of Karnak recently, Brother Abdul, the Patriarch of that august complex was deeply moved and expressed the strongest sentiments of condolences to the Brothers and Sisters in the United States. He mentioned how

FREDERICK MONDERSON

he grieved tremendously for the losses of the "Nubian Brothers and Sisters" who were victimized by hurricane Katrina. Interestingly, in many places in Egypt, people of all walks of life were saddened by the devastation of the hurricane. Some, particularly Nubians, were outraged by the delayed official response to that devastated region and people, purportedly due to race, class and poverty. One thing is certain, many, many Egyptians have a great fondness for Americans and Nubians are equally enthused by "Nubian-Americans."

I have traveled to Egypt on many occasions and besides that first time this was the most memorable, and special of all my trips. Perhaps it was because I was traveling with my niece "Kash" and we had a wonderfully accommodating guide in the person of Hassan Elian. He was knowledgeable, kind, considerate and helpful and took us many places including a wedding in his village at Luxor. This was indeed a special trip, because on my previous trip I had a bad experience. Nevertheless, the wonderfully enlightening experience of this trip seems to have exorcised the bad taste of the last one with the insulting ignorance I was subjected to in 2003!

This time we flew from New York into Cairo, over-nighted and then onto Aswan and Abu Simbel. Informed that photography was no longer permitted in the Cairo Museum, this was also the case at Abu Simbel. Nonetheless, photography aside, the spectacular twin temples of Rameses II and his wife Queen Nefertari (the Nubian) at Abu Simbel that took 20 years to build, were always enjoyable, enlightening and a wonderful site to behold. Ludwig Burckhardt was the first European to view the magnificent structure in 1813 and four years later the "strongman Egyptologist" Belzoni, cleared the entrance and entered the temple in 1817.

CELEBRATING DR. BEN-JOCHANNAN

Dr. Ben's Photo 183. Hatshepsut's Temple at Deir el Bahari. Close-up of the end pillars of the Punt Colonnade beside the Hathor Shrine and the Retaining Wall separating Mentuhotep's Temple with its ruined Pyramid and column arrangement from that of the Queen.

Dr. Ben's Photo 187. Hatshepsut's Temple at Deir el Bahari. The Temple's three levels of colonnades and the opening below is entrance to Senmut's unthinkable tomb in the temple.

FREDERICK MONDERSON

Dr. Ben's Photo 184. Hatshepsut's Temple at Deir el Bahari. From the "Birds Eye View" the Second Court, Second Ramp, Middle Colonnade with the Punt Colonnade to the left and the "Birth Colonnade" to the right; the Upper Terrace with its hypostyle colonnade and remaining statues that stand before the Upper Court with its colonnade and Portico that entrance the Sanctuary. Mentuhotep's Temple is further on.

CELEBRATING
DR. BEN-JOCHANNAN

Dr. Ben's Photo 185. Hatshepsut's Temple at Deir el Bahari. Coming down the mountain, view of the First Ramp and the Lower Colonnade. Notice the platform of Mentuhotep's Temple approximates the height of the Middle Colonnade that entrances the Second Ramp with the Middle Colonnade partly visible, as visitors mill about.

The 4-seated colossus of the pharaoh with his wife beside him, at the temples entrance, Ra-Horakhty on the cornice beneath the uraei and 22 baboons, the prisoners on the base of the seated statues, and the other smaller statues as well as the illustrations on the outside, are not only inviting but a promise of the artistic beauty and wonderful scenery within. Besides Ra-Horakhty, Amon and Ptah as well as the deified Rameses

II, these are the Gods worshipped in this temple as seen seated in the Sanctuary.

Dr. Ben's Illustration 69. Winged Hawk wearing broken crown (left); and, image of golden plumed hawk found at Hierakonpolis (right), now in the Cairo Museum.

The vulture decoration of the ceiling and the 8 colossal Osiride standing statues in the Hypostyle Hall or Pronaos; Rameses attacking his enemies at the Battle of Kadesh; the king worshipping and ritualizing the Gods; his making offerings and being embraced by the divinities; are scenes well-preserved and beautifully done. The decorated columns of the king in different attitudes with the various Gods enthroned,

CELEBRATING DR. BEN-JOCHANNAN

along with side rooms depicting the king mainly in kneeling attitudes, making Presentations before the divinities, are all stunning sites to behold. Also, of interest is the blend of color in the various parts of the temple. As the visitor faces the Sanctuary, the four-seated Gods in Abu Simbel are (from right to left) Ra-Horakhty, the defied Rameses II, Amon and Ptah. Interestingly, this temple was built so the rays of the sun at rising would bathe the persons of Ra-Horakhty, Rameses and Amon on February 20 and October 20 of each year. Ptah was not to be touched by the sun's rays though he sat next to Amon. Some scholars say it's the 22nd of the months. Nevertheless, with all of modern technology, when the temple was moved to a higher elevation to avoid the river, this was never able to be duplicated. That is, the feat of the sun bathing the Gods on the appointed days was never duplicated as in olden days, despite modern technology.

The Temple of Nefertari, "possessor of charm, beauty and love," was dedicated to Hathor, Goddess of love. It is fronted by four standing statues of the king interspersed by two statues of the Queen and Hathor. The Hypostyle Hall or Pronaos has 6 pillars with beautiful Hathor Head Capitals. The decorations are pretty well preserved with good color in which the Goddess is shown in a papyrus thicket boat being presented with flowers by Rameses. Nefertari is shown embracing Rameses while Gods including Thoth and Ptah are on the pillars and walls.

Next is Isis Temple of Philae, now removed to Agilka Island. This is a classical Graeco-Roman temple complex representing much earlier worship of Osiris and his faithful sister and wife. The architecture is superb with pylons, colonnades, temples, Nilometers, kiosk, courts, and chapels, all rich in decoration. The Temple of Kalabsha to God

Mendulese, Rameses II's small Temple of Beit Wali and that of Gerf Hussein in the Aswan vicinity, are also masterpieces. The Old and New Cataract Hotels and the Oberoi are all beautiful hotels with wonderful gardens and service. The weather and climate of Aswan, the Nubian Museum, Kitchener's Garden, the High and Low Dams, Lotus Memorial, Unfinished Obelisk, Mausoleum of Aga Khan and Tombs of the Nobles, as well as shopping in the Aswan Sook (market) make this region a quite memorable and enjoyable city in Upper Egypt.

The five-day, four-night Nile Cruise from Aswan includes stops at Kom Ombo, Edfu and Esneh with passage through the Locks on way to Luxor, and is a pleasant, while exhilarating, experience. After leaving Aswan, we visited Kom Ombo, Edfu and Esneh before arriving at Luxor, all along the sail down the Nile was informative, enlightening and relaxing. The temples were delightful. The food on board daily was a sumptuous 3-meal buffet banquet designed to please the appetite, but also to add pounds to the waistline. Of course, the pool on board helped ease the heat; the masseur helped with the tension, the disco was entertaining and the cool Nile wind was most pleasant and enjoyable.

Dr. Ben's Photo 185a. Hatshepsut's Temple at Deir el Bahari. From the "Bird's Eye view," the Second Court, Second Ramp and Upper Court with remains of its Hypostyle Hall columns before the Sanctuary.

CELEBRATING DR. BEN-JOCHANNAN

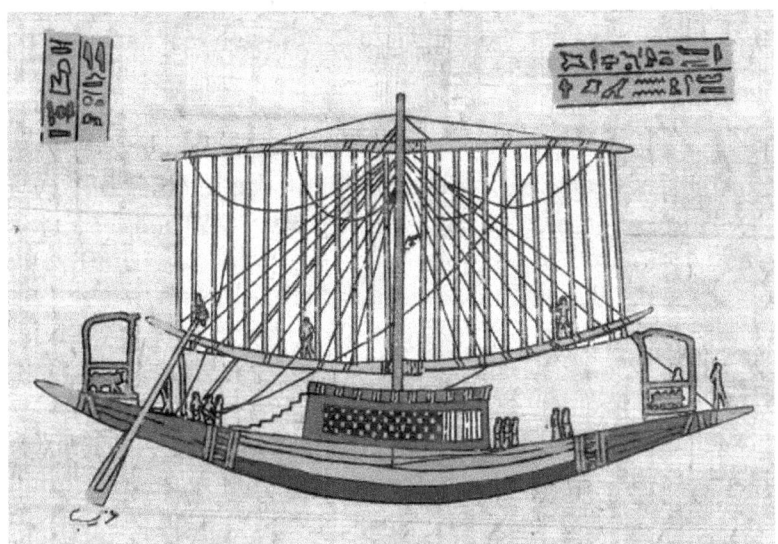

Dr. Ben's Papyrus 9. A boat on the Nile in full sail with lookout at the bow.

The first stop, Kom Ombo Temple, at the water's edge, was dedicated to two Gods, the Elder Horus, Haroeis, and the Crocodile God, Sobek. This twin temple had twin protective winged disks with uraei on the cornice above the entrances, and two aisles, two hypostyle halls, two sanctuaries, respective decorations, two corridors as well as two priesthoods in service to the two deities. Like so many other temples, much is destroyed but what remains is sufficiently enlightening. The reliefs are beautiful, being a mixture of sunk and raised; while the ceiling boasts painted illustrations of the protective vulture Goddess. There is one Nilometer. On the back wall along the outer corridor there are several colossal reliefs as well as one showing Isis in the birth chair, a table with medical instruments and a basin with water for the physician to wash his hands after any "operation." Other illustrations include a pair of ears for the priests to hear petitions of the faithful. In this temple like so many Graeco-Roman temples the art is a bit more liberal and a bit more of the Queens and Goddess anatomy are evident. There is a Nilometer just outside the enclosure wall of Kom Ombo.

The next stop on the Nile cruise was Edfu Temple of God Horus. This is the best preserved of all the temples of Egypt consisting of an intact Girdle or Enclosure Wall, a huge Pylon entrance, a three-sided roofed Peristyle Colonnade Court with statues of the falcon God at the entrance pylon and in the Great Court before the Hypostyle Hall. The temple proper includes an outer Hypostyle Hall or vestibule, an inner Hypostyle Hall, and two antechambers before the Sanctuary. All this is surrounded by an outer corridor, or "Corridor of Victory." There are adjacent rooms to the sanctuary for garments, liquid and solid offerings, incense, and books and implements concerned with the ritual of the temple.

Dr. Ben's Photo 186. Hatshepsut's Temple at Deir el Bahari. The author, Dr. Fred Monderson, in adoration of the majesty of Hatshepsut's Temple.

CELEBRATING
DR. BEN-JOCHANNAN

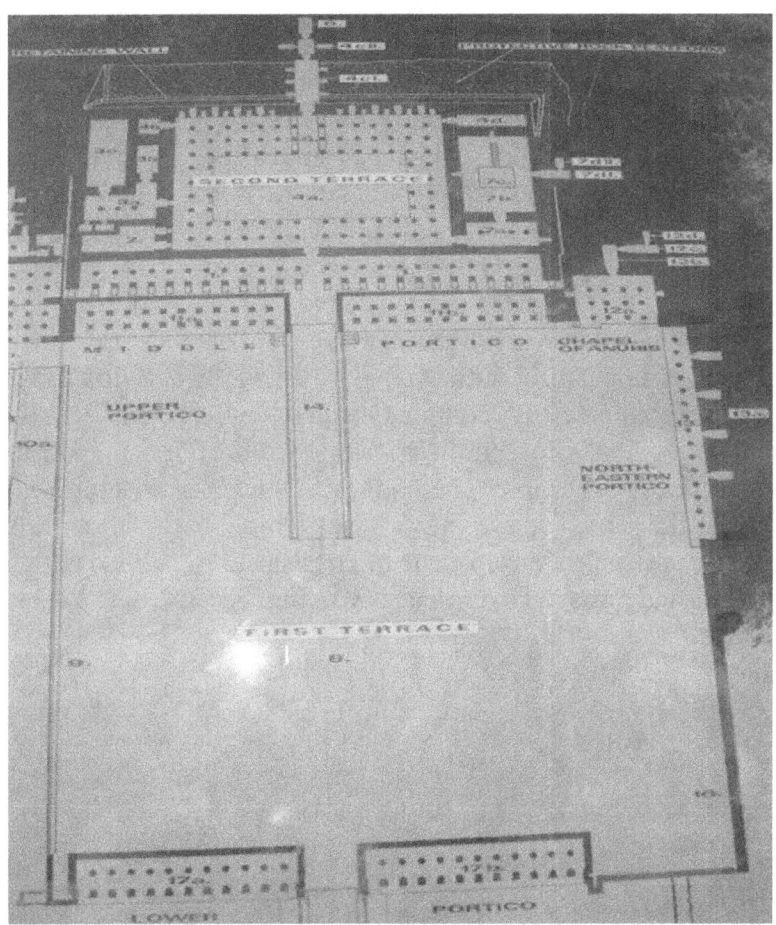

Dr. Ben's Photo 187. Hatshepsut's Temple at Deir el Bahari. Plan of the principal features of the Temple.

There is an inner passage round the temple called the "Corridor of Victory." One version of the Legend has it, after Seth killed his brother Osiris, and the Immaculate Conception as depicted at Abydos; Horus, now grown to manhood, engaged his uncle and his band of traitors in armed combat.

Battling him throughout the country, Horus finally captured and slew Seth at Edfu. There he built the temple designed as a guard against machinations of Seth's followers. The "Corridor of Victory" recounts much of the battle in illustration with other features in the life of the God. There is a Nilometer to the east along the "Corridor of Victory" in the Girdle Wall. There is also evidence that an old Nilometer existed to the southeast of the temple. That is beyond the Mammisi, which is now viewed at the front of the temple since the modern means of entrance has changed. In addition, Edfu shows evidence of columns below the present temple informing that the spot was sacred before Graeco-Roman times. However, given the battle was fought n mythological times, the sacred space and original temple may date to this early time. In fact, a cartouche of Hatshepsut was found in this temple and removed to the Cairo Museum because of its rarity.

Dr. Ben's Photo 187a. Hatshepsut's Temple at Deir el Bahari. Scenic view of clear blue sky against rugged desert and mountain terrain.

CELEBRATING DR. BEN-JOCHANNAN

Dr. Ben's Books 13. "Understanding the African Philosophical Concept Behind the Diagram of the Law of Opposites" (1975).

The significant change at Edfu is the carriage ride from the Nile Cruiser that does not bring visitors to the old entrance, through the village, one entered from the rear along the outer corridor. The present entrance is from a new and buildup area where the carriages park in an orderly fashion. Then visitors walk along a newly built pathway lined with shops or Bazaars and enter through the Mammisi.

FREDERICK MONDERSON

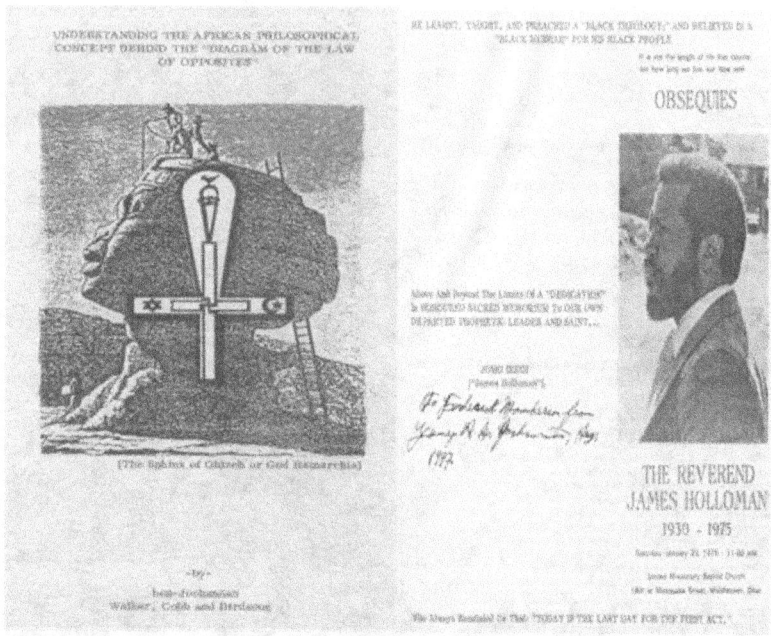

Dr. Ben's Books 13a. Understanding the African Philosophical Concept Behind the "Diagram of the Law of Opposites" (1975). Note the Author's autograph for Dr. Fred Monderson.

Esneh is a temple of which only the Hypostyle Hall has survived some 30 feet below the city; though it believed the "inner portions" may be buried beneath some 30 feet of earth. Dedicated to the God Khnum who made man on his potter's wheel; there are several unique features of this temple. The present temple replaces an older XVIIIth Dynasty structure with possible connections to even earlier times. There are 24 massive decorated columns comprised in 4 rows of 6in this hall, each with a different type of capital. The first row is joined by screen walls. The temple is profusely illustrated both in and outside with Ptolemaic pharaohs and Roman emperors depicted. Being that far below the street level, it is

CELEBRATING
DR. BEN-JOCHANNAN

beginning to suffer damage as the water-table-level has begun eroding the structure. There is talk of relocating the building so it may be better preserved.

A zodiac can be observed on the ceiling, though much of this is covered with black soot from the fires modern inhabitants living in the temple, during the last few hundred years before it was cleared. Another zodiac is found at Dendera temple of Hathor that we did not visit. Shortness of our trip precluded a visit to Abydos as well.

On a rear wall inside the hall, Isis sits on the birth chair; it's probably the only place, certainly the only one that has survived, depicting a baby in the embryonic sac. Nearby, Khnum is seen making man on his potter's wheel. Khnum is depicted in large size higher up on a rear wall. After the walk around Esneh temple, we retrace our steps; return to the boat and sail through the locks before our arrival at Luxor.

Dr. Ben's Papyrus 10. The Vulture Goddess Nekhbet extends her wings and fills her talons with scepters.

FREDERICK MONDERSON

Dr. Ben's Photo 188. Hatshepsut's Temple at Deir el Bahari. Bust of a surviving statue of the Queen on the Upper Terrace that depicts her beard and holding the instruments of power.

Dr. Ben's Photo 189. Hatshepsut's Temple at Deir el Bahari. Profile of a head from a destroyed statue.

CELEBRATING DR. BEN-JOCHANNAN

Dr. Ben's Photo 190. Hatshepsut's Temple at Deir el Bahari. Thutmose III, *Men-Kheper-Ra*, offers two vessels to Sokar, a Theban God of the Dead.

The Old Kingdom capital was Memphis and its funerary location was Sakkara and the Ghizeh Plateau. However, Luxor, ancient Waset – "the Scepter" or "The fighting province" while Thebes of the Greeks, became the national capital during the Middle and New Kingdoms. The east bank is considered the "land of the living" and the west bank, the "land of the dead." More appropriately, Simpkins (1992: 4) tells: "The west is the land of dreams and deep shadows, the resting place of those that are there." In this respect, the east bank contains worship temples while on the west bank there are mortuary temples, or temples to the dead kings who became Gods. However, this is not wholly exclusive. A few kings were worshipped in their mortuary temple while yet alive. As such then, deceased persons were buried across the river, where Kings were interred in the Valley of the Kings; Queens in the Valley of the Queens; Nobles in the Valley of the Nobles; and Artisans in the Valley of the Artisans. There were cemeteries for the poor in the desert at the edge of cultivation. Most of the artisans who built the structured tombs were confined and lived in the village of Deir el Medina because they knew the "secrets" of the mortuary structures. Equally too, on this west bank, nearly every New Kingdom pharaoh built a mortuary temple, his "Mansion of Millions of Years," in which he was worshipped as Osiris.

On the east bank of the river at Luxor, the worship temples of Karnak (*Ipit Isut*) and Luxor (*Southern Isut* or the "Gods harem") epitomized the majesty, the power and the glory of New Empire Egypt, where God Amon-Ra ruled supreme. Adjacent to Karnak, home of Amon, are temples of the Goddess Mut and Montu the war God. It took two thousand years to build Karnak as numerous pharaohs vied with each other to please the God Amon who dwelt therein. Together with his wife Mut and son Khonsu, they comprised the "Theban Triad." Karnak had a whole social and religious system of individuals who thrived within sphinxes, pylons, courts, chapels, kiosks, halls, doorways, processional way, colonnades, twin axis, porches, porticoes, temples, statues, obelisks, pillars, a sacred lake, as well as painted, sunk and raised relief decorations. Complementing this there were stewards, priests and priestesses, cooks, wine makers, gardeners, slaves, artisans, teachers, guards and a whole lot more. Dr. ben-Jochannan recommended that his students visit the Hypostyle Hall at Karnak at least six times to fully comprehend the magnificence of this structure. This writer has done such and more.

Regarding the Hypostyle Hall at Karnak Temple of God Amon, Baedeker's *Guide to Egypt* (1929: 284) makes known: "The breadth of this great hall is 338 ft., its depth 170 ft., its area 6000 sq. yards, an area spacious enough to accommodate the entire cathedral of Notre Dame at Paris. One hundred and thirty-four columns arranged in sixteen rows supported the

CELEBRATING DR. BEN-JOCHANNAN

roof, of which the two central rows are higher than the others and consist of lotus-columns with open capitals, while the other rows have clustered columns with closed capitals. The hall is divided into nave and aisles. The nave, itself divided into three aisles, is c. 79 ft. in height. The roof is supported by the two central rows of columns and one of the lower rows on each side, the deficiency in the height of the latter being met by placing square pillars above them. The spaces between these pillars were occupied with windows with stone lattice-work (one on the S. side is still almost perfect). The side-aisles are 33 ft. lower than the nave."

Baedeker continued to confirm: "The columns are not monolithic but are built up of semi-drums, 3 ½ ft. in height and 6 ½ ft. in diameter. The material is reddish-brown sandstone. Each of the twelve columns in the two central rows is 11¾ ft. in diameter and upwards of 33 ft. in circumference, i.e., as thick as Trajan's Column in Rome or the Vendome Column in Paris. It requires six men with outstretched arms to span one of these columns. Their height is 69 ft., that of the capitals 11 ft. The remaining hundred and twenty-two columns are each 42 ½ ft. in height and 27 ½ ft. in circumference."

We now turn to the Temple of Luxor, built to celebrate the Festival of Opet for which Amon left his Karnak abode to spend time there, sometimes for 24-days, with his wife Goddess Mut. Amenhotep III built the original temple but several pharaohs decorated, added or did restoration as well as injurious work to the temple. Tutankhamon decorated the colonnade, Horemheb and Seti I and Seti II did restoration work to it, Rameses II added the pylon, changed the axis, added a columned Peristyle Court with seated and standing statues and Alexander the Great redecorated the inner

Hypostyle Hall and rebuilt the Sanctuary of the main temple. Akhenaton erased the name of Amon where it could be found. Seti I replaced many of these.

The Temple of Luxor is therefore an outer Peristyle Court of Rameses II called the "Ramesseum front," beyond the Pylon, an inner pylon to the original temple, then the Processional Colonnade of 14 columns, unlike Karnak's 12 columns, and Court of Amenhotep III consisting of three colonnades of double rows of 11 columns on the north, east and west that fronts the Hypostyle Hall. The Hypostyle Hall and two inner chambers front the Sanctuary. Beyond the Sanctuary are a large hall with 12 columns and a central chamber of 4 columns with 2 smaller flanking chambers with 2 columns each.

The Opet Festival, depicted and decorated by Tutankhamon, flanks the walls alongside the 14 columns of the Processional Colonnade. On entering, the right side represents the procession coming from Karnak along the river and the left side represents the procession returning to Karnak from Luxor, by land. Visitors must first read from the southern end of the western half.

Next is the return flight to Cairo. There the hallmark of Egypt, the pyramids and sphinx are monumental and attractive. More importantly, the Cairo Museum is still an exciting place as ever for an entrance fee of 65 Egyptian pounds, and security is even more upgraded. Metal detectors greet the visitor, "pat downs" is the order and all cameras must be checked! There is no photography in the Cairo Museum of Egyptian Antiquities at this time. There are more security people in the museum, and cameras have been installed throughout. However, for an additional 75 Egyptian Pounds, a visitor can view the Egyptian mummies in a separate room. This too is new!

CELEBRATING
DR. BEN-JOCHANNAN

Dr. Ben's Photo 191. Hatshepsut's Temple at Deir el Bahari. Columns and Capitals of the Hathor Shrine with the Sanctuary door facing.

FREDERICK MONDERSON

Dr. Ben's Photo 192. Hatshepsut's Temple at Deir el Bahari. The Middle Terrace housing the "Birth Colonnade" and the Anubis Shrine with end columns of the true Northern Colonnade to the right and the Upper Platform or Terrace above.

Dr. Ben's Photo 193. Hatshepsut's Temple at Deir el Bahari. In the Upper Court, the Portico to the granite entrance to the Sanctuary with niches right and left for statues of the Queen.

There are over 120,000 pieces of antiquities in the Museum and 1 replica, the Rosetta Stone. The original Rosetta Stone

CELEBRATING
DR. BEN-JOCHANNAN

is in the British Museum in London. This precious artifact is the basis upon which Jean Francois Champollion was able to decipher the hieroglyphic language in 1822. Found by the French at a place called Rosetta in 1798, it is a tri-lingual inscription (Hieroglyphic, Demotic and Greek) recounting the pharaoh Ptolemy Epiphanes dealings with priests who praised him, in the three languages, for generous temple relations.

For the most part the average tour of the Cairo Museum takes two hours but there is so much to see, only the major pieces as Tutankhamon treasures, some papyrus and a few other pieces including statues and sphinxes are covered. There is a bookstore on the first floor. Thus, anyone with an interest in ancient Egypt must return to the Cairo Museum to broaden his or her understanding of the culture. The grounds are landscaped with greenery and statues and photography is permitted outside in the garden grounds. Now, since 2015 photography is again permitted in the Museum with a photography ticket in addition to the regular museum entrance ticket. In addition, for an extra 100 Egyptian pounds visitors can also view royal mummies in their cases.

Dr. Ben's Papyrus 10a. Psychostasia scene; a female with a perfume cone on her head greets Thoth as a baboon; and, with two goddesses at his rear, Osiris pours a libation before a female holding a rattle or sistrum.

FREDERICK MONDERSON

Dr. Ben's Illustration 70. Hawara. Canopics and Mace, XII Dynasty (left); and, Pectoral and Beads.

Throughout Egypt, the Tourist Police do an outstanding job of providing protection for tourists, whether it's at the Museums, at hotels, at temples and at tomb sites, on the streets and on lengthy trips they provide guarded convoys, all to ensure that no harm come to visitors. Hence, the police should be commended so people ought not to be afraid to travel to Egypt, for they will experience a remarkable collection of historically important sites and scenes that will remain imbedded in their memories forever. African-Americans must go to Egypt to see and experience the rich cultural heritage that awaits them, created by African ancestors. We must go to Egypt and "Let the monuments teach!"

What is memorable about this trip is the manner of respect and appreciation the Egyptians have for Americans, the love Nubians have for their "Nubian brothers and sisters" who come to visit, and the wonderfully enlightening transformation one experiences in the profoundly religious, spiritual, artistic, philosophic, cultural, historical, architectural and

CELEBRATING DR. BEN-JOCHANNAN

photographic adventure that's part of this pilgrimage to the "Holy Land," Egypt. The growth in outlook is noticeable when one considers the maxims of the great philosophers of Egypt, viz., Ptah-Hotep, Merikara, Due Khety, and the literary tradition of the *Pyramid Text, Coffin Text, Book of the Dead* or *Book of Coming Forth by Day*, as well as so many others seen in the tombs of the kings, the *Book of Gates, Book of the Am Duet*, and more. Then there are other wisdom works of literature as the *Book of Kuhn Anup, Book of Knowing the Appearance of Ra, Book of Maa-Kheer* and so on.

Dr. Ben's Photo 195. Art for sale at Hatshepsut's Temple.

All this is reinforced in the knowledge that from this early burst of Egyptian, African, creative expressions, religion, cosmology, cosmogony, theology, metaphysics, art, architecture, the colonnade, science, medicine, surgery, mathematics, stone construction, river transportation, geometry, astronomy, farming, astrology, as well as a thousand household, domestic, civic, military, political, religious and scientific and surgical implements were created in the cultural and geographical effluence generated from the "gift of the Nile."

Now you know why we must visit Egypt for a reinforcement of the intellectual foundation the ancient Egyptian Africans bequeathed to the world. In so doing we can and must set the young on the road to imbibe in this knowledge to embolden them, for the sometimes difficult, still challenging, journey they must experience in today's world. In this, they must know, good speech is preferred to babble; truth and justice to untruth or injustice (*Isfit*); good listening is a virtue; respect for elders is respect for self; to practice self-control and silence is wonderful; Ma'at is the essence of wisdom and prudence as well as balance, order and truth. The challenge to cultivate and apply intellectual autonomy is foundation to all this. Thus, practice of these ethical principles will cultivate good individuals who will become model citizens, and in turn will help improve the next generation, and in that, perhaps, knowledge and wealth will become a "divine gift."

Dr. Ben's Photo 193a. Karnak, Home of God Amon-Ra. On the Hypostyle's outer north wall, Seti I presents prisoners to the Theban Triad of enthroned Amon-Ra, Mut and their son Khonsu.

CELEBRATING
DR. BEN-JOCHANNAN

Dr. Ben's Photo 196. Karnak, Home of God Amon-Ra. General map of the outer Enclosure Wall encompassing the Northern, Central and Southern Groups of temples for Montu (left), Amon (center) and Mut (right).

Dr. Ben's Photo 197. Karnak, Home of God Amon-Ra. The new and extensively built-up Plaza with shops or "Bazaars" and the entrance further on.

FREDERICK MONDERSON

Dr. Ben's Photo 198. **Karnak, Home of God Amon-Ra**. Security apparatus before the First Pylon.

Dr. Ben's Photo 199. **Karnak, Home of God Amon-Ra**. Croix-Sphinxes or Sphinxes with Rams' heads of the raised platform entrancing the First Pylon.

CELEBRATING
DR. BEN-JOCHANNAN

Dr. Ben's Photo 200. Karnak, Home of God Amon-Ra. View of the Southern Colonnade with Sphinxes in the Great Court, and right, evidence of a remaining mound for scaling heights against the southern inner face of the First Pylon.

Dr. Ben's Photo 200a. Karnak, Home of God Amon-Ra. Dr. Fred Monderson with "Karnak Men."

FREDERICK MONDERSON

Dr. Ben's Photo 201. Karnak, Home of God Amon-Ra. Cherise Monderson-Maloney of Brooklyn, New York, stands in Karnak's Great Court ready to explore the Temple.

Perhaps it's best to end this with a quote from Dr. Carruthers (1995: 139) who says: "The Instructions of Ptah-Hotep contained a collection of maxims which instructed the youth in the correct values, attitudes, and modes of behavior suited

CELEBRATING DR. BEN-JOCHANNAN

for those who would become civil servants from the office of prime minister down. Indeed, in all probability, the future pharaohs also received this education alongside some of the children from various ranks including the poorest. Although the Meryukare text states that the Pharaoh is born wise [though the Ptah-Hotep text says no one is born wise] this is a trope signifying that the pharaohship is wise because of its inherent resources, its advisors and the records of officeholders. These students were taught what was expected of a good official. A good official was wise and knowledgeable about the country and the people. He was advised to listen and learn from people in all walks of life, especially the so-called uneducated. He understood that listening was the major source of acquiring knowledge and wisdom. Above all, he understood that Ma'at (Truth and Justice) was the foundation of all existence and that it must be adhered to in all actions."

Dr. Ben's Photo 201a. Erik Monderson at Al Fayal Garden, Aswan in 2018.

29. EGYPT 2008
By
Dr. Fred Monderson

Egypt today is a changing culture, yet, in some respects while change has come, some things remain the same. In the first instance, changes are due to the economic realities of the tourist industry and the dynamics of the "exchange rate" for foreign currency. Nevertheless, gone are the days when one could visit the monuments for cheap. Remember when it was 20 Egyptian pounds for the Valley of the Kings? Now it is 75 Egyptian Pounds. Remember when it was 20 Egyptian Pounds for the Cairo Museum? Now its 65 Pounds! And, those people who have waited until now to visit will pay the price, for, as Dr. ben-Jochannan has said: "You must visit the great Hypostyle Hall at Karnak Temple in Luxor six times before you begin to comprehend the significance and accomplishment of those ancient Africans."

Everywhere one goes, particularly a black man traveling alone, the question is always, where are you from? When the answer is New York, USA, the response is always: "Welcome, America, ah, America is Number One. In one of the temples I visited, to the same question and reply, one Egyptian said to me: "America! Welcome! We like Americans, we don't like Bush!" I could only reply, "Many Americans don't like Bush either." In the Cairo Museum an American woman talking to an official said: "It's getting so we don't want to say were Americans because George Bush is such a jackass. All he wants is war."

CELEBRATING DR. BEN-JOCHANNAN

Dr. Ben's Photo 202. **Karnak, Home of God Amon-Ra**. One standing of ten "Taharka Columns," though evidence seems to indicate perhaps twelve, with the entrance to the Temple of Rameses III of the 20th Dynasty between the statues left, and the Southern Colonnade with its sphinxes to the right.

FREDERICK MONDERSON

Dr. Ben's Photo 203. Karnak, Home of God Amon-Ra. Double statue of Rameses II and Amon-Ra at the entrance to the Hypostyle Hall.

CELEBRATING DR. BEN-JOCHANNAN

Dr. Ben's Photo 204. **Karnak, Home of God Amon-Ra**. An aisle among the Hypostyle Hall's columns with an illustrated wall to the rear of the northern wing decorated by Seti I.

FREDERICK MONDERSON

However, it's a different story with the Nubians and Black Egyptians. It's always: "Brother! Welcome Brother." "Master of Karnak Temple," Brother Abdul sends his deepest respect to the Nubian Brothers and Sisters in America. Hes getting up there in age, for those who are familiar with this amazing Brother, but hes supervising an enormous over-haul, development and beautification of Karnak. He may be retiring soon. Brother Shawki also sends his warmest regards to Dr. ben-Jochannan. The talk is always, how Dr. Ben helped so many people. He would drop 10 Pounds here, 25 Pounds there, and 50 Pounds here and there. He was especially helpful to the Daboud Nubian Village. In every hotel he used, the baggage handlers, kitchen and house-keeping staff, everyone got an envelope.

Naturally the security apparatus in the temples is ongoing to protect the antiquities and the tourists. Besides the north face of Rameses IIs "Girdle Wall" at Karnak an enormous wiring system is being installed to provide electric potential as the temple is being overhauled. Near the eastern gate a systematic archaeological dig is in progress. Elsewhere to the east and south of the Great Lake and along the southern Courts on the north/south axis, as well as the temples of Khonsu and Opet, archaeological digs and restoration work continue to make new revelations. Karnak is still as busy as a beehive with visitors from Europe and now China, Japan and Korea providing the much-needed foreign exchange. More important, however, is the enormous beautification taking place at the Plaza on the frontage of Karnak. The two "speakezies" selling film and other accessories north of the ticket booth have been upgraded with a few new bazaars added. Beyond or south of the new gated walkway to the temple, a security corridor separated the new esplanade being developed and beautified to put Karnak's entrance on a more professional and world class attractive standard. In two or

CELEBRATING DR. BEN-JOCHANNAN

three years it will be a site to behold. Luxor Temple still attracts its visitors and the best time to visit is still early afternoon when the sun throws back its reflection on the colonnades and other structures, particularly the "Girdle Wall" of Rameses II.

Across the river on the west bank where visitors get the customary 3 tombs in the Valley of the Kings, most visitors are familiar with the Eastern Valley housing its 65 tombs. However, a Western Valley has been opened up and the tombs of Aye, who succeeded Tutankhamon and the "magnificent" Amenhotep III, have been located. The former is now open to visitors while the latter is being prepared for opening within the next year. Naturally, there's no video in the Valley or other photography in tombs in the Valley of the Kings. Those earlier visitors who took photos years ago now appreciate those early opportunities.

Medinet Habu, Mortuary Temple of Rameses III retains its wonderfully beautiful colorful depictions recounting the reign of this, the last of the imperial warrior pharaohs of the New Kingdom.

People should not be afraid to take a trip to Egypt to view the antiquities. This cultural, historical, art and architectural as well as religious, spiritual and metaphysics particularly photographic adventure is well worth the initial outlay of about $3200.00 for 15 days. Today, at $3900.00 for 15 days, it's still a bargain. The Tourist Police go to extraordinary lengths to guarantee security of visitors. A case in point! I was part of a convoy to visit Abydos and Dendera. As I rode in a private car, the police were very excited and concerned, we have an American with us. Oftentimes they would say to my driver and guide, do you have the American? So, I say, go to Egypt like Dr. ben-Jochannan said, "Visit Egypt, visit

FREDERICK MONDERSON

Karnak Temples Hypostyle Hall six times," make the spiritual connection with the legacy of the ancient Africans along the banks of the Nile, who gave the word so much.

Dr. Ben's Illustration 71. Peoples contemporary with the Ancient Egyptians (1-2) *Annales des Antiquities De L'Egypt* (1910).

Dr. Ben's Illustration 72. Peoples contemporary with the Ancient Egyptians (3) *Annales des antiquities De L'Egypt* (1910).

Abydos Temple of Osiris built by Seti I has always been the highpoint of any trip to Egypt because it not only has the best colored illustrations in all the Nile Valley. It is the world's earliest site of pilgrimage boasting levels of 10 temples dating

CELEBRATING DR. BEN-JOCHANNAN

back 5000 years. It is also the foremost site of the Immaculate Conception. This phenomenon, involving the God Osiris and Goddess Isis is remarkable, for their union produced Horus or Heru, after Osiris unfortunate death at the hands of his evil brother Seth. Even more important, however, this unique temple has 2 courts, 2 hypostyle halls and 7 entrances for 7 shrines to 7 deities, Horus, Isis, Osiris, Amon-Ra, Ra-Horakhty, Ptah and the deified Seti I. Rameses II closed all but the middle of his father Seti's 7 entrances. The Abydos Tablet listing 76 kings from Menes to Seti is also located here intact or *in situ*.

Dr. Ben's Photo 205. Karnak, Home of God Amon-Ra. In Red Crown, Seti dances before Horus.

FREDERICK MONDERSON

The Osireion or "tomb of Osiris" is also located here at Abydos. It is the only Nile Valley structure or tomb completely surrounded by water and comprised of an underground passage leads into the desert. There are 5 convoys in and out of Luxor every day. So, the security, in arranging and administering as well as operationalizing the safety of visitors, have got it down to a science. They communicate with elements stationed along the route that halt traffic so the convoy could whiz past, real VIP style; it's a sight to behold and experience.

Dr. Ben's Photo 206. Karnak, Home of God Amon-Ra. Seti presents a platter to Amon-ra with Mut beside the God.

Well, the convoy to Edfu and Kom Ombo again enjoyed the same VIP treatment in the drive-thru. For those familiar, the

CELEBRATING DR. BEN-JOCHANNAN

new entrance at Edfu is from the south not the north, in a newly developed and orderly plaza. Here carriages, which bring the tourists from the Nile Cruisers, park to await their passengers return for the 12-minute trek back to the boats. I often wondered where the black people from America are. "Ever since Dr. Ben stopped coming" said Shawki, "I have not worked with any Black groups. My brother Farouk has had the same complaint. The few Black groups who come don't give us the jobs like Dr. Ben did!"

From the time I started going to Egypt with Dr. ben-Jochannan in the 1980s, he introduced us to Shawki and Farouk. These are the most authentic Black Egyptians, Nubians, who give a more correct view of the history of "our ancestors," so we should support them!

Edfu is a beautiful Graeco-Roman style temple, very well preserved with a magnificently illustrated Pylon entrance, a Peristyle Court with two hawks before the Pronaos or Hypostyle Hall just as outside the Pylon where two also stood. Only one of the former remains intact and visitors rush to take photographs in front of it. The "Sphinx of Edfu" is no longer beside the gate but has been moved to the newly renovated Plaza. Repairs continue in the "Corridor of Victory" where the struggle between Horus and Seth is vividly depicted with Isis and other deities assisting Horus, the avenger of his dead father, Osiris.

The Most unusual thing happened at Kom Ombo. After an hour at this temple, the convoy left for Aswan. Shawki said: "There is no need to go to Aswan with the convoy, let's wait until they return in 4 hours." So, I was alone in the temple to roam and get all the photos I wanted, uninterrupted. We then joined the convoy on its return and headed back to Luxor.

FREDERICK MONDERSON

In another visit. the Temple of Isis at Philae, now on Agilka Island, remains a beauty to behold, a joy to experience. It is also an art and architectural wonder compelling one to envision how its august nature could have withstood all the challenges of history and still retains its picturesqueness, with such stately majesty. The East Colonnade, with its 16 frontal columns and 1 on the southern end, and the Western Colonnade with its 32 columns on the dromos; the Kiosk of Nectanebo, the altar on the dromos, all before the decorated First Pylon with its two stone lion sentinels, mesmerizes the visitor. Visitors pass this portal into the Courtyard of the Temple of Isis proper, with a second East Colonnade of 10 columns facing the Mammisi opposite also with 7 columns in front and 7 in rear as viewed from the river. Then the visitor beholds the Second or First Pylon proper to the Temple of Isis.

Dr. Ben's Photo 207. Karnak, Home of God Amon-Ra. Mut introduces Seti I to Amon-Ra.

CELEBRATING DR. BEN-JOCHANNAN

Dr. Ben's Photo 208. Karnak, Home of God Amon-Ra. In Red Crown, Seti stands before Amon and Mut.

When the visitor considers the trauma this temple experienced down through the years, from the vicissitudes of nature and the Nile, invading forces, Christian and Muslim adherents and fanatics, modern plunderers and antiquities collectors and the dynamics of visitors' presence and proclivities, one has to laud the builders of antiquity whose mastery of the art of construction has deified time and all its challenges. One should never forget the floral beauty of the capitals of columns, each with a separate and distinct work of art that continues to amaze lovers of this genre of art and architecture.

The greatest architectural and artistic remains are located in Upper Egypt. Throughout most of dynastic rule there was always a distinction between the east and west bank of the

FREDERICK MONDERSON

Nile, as there was Upper and Lower Egypt. Some scholars refer to the East Bank as the land of the living and the West Bank as the land of the dead. Equally, of the two principal types of temples, worship or God temple and mortuary or king temple, some have argued the former belongs to the East Bank while the latter belongs to the West Bank.

Of course, this is not always true. For example, moving from south to north, Abu Simbel, a worship temple is on the west bank. Philae, on the other hand, is in the Nile. However, Esneh and Edfu, worship temples are on the west bank. The Valley of the Kings, Queens, Nobles and Artisans are on the West Bank as they are associated with mortuary practice and place of final rest. Equally, during the New Kingdom, practically every king built his or her mortuary temple on the West Bank, on the Plain of Thebes. Seti I of the 19th Dynasty built his mortuary temple at Kurneh and another at Abydos, dedicated to Osiris and six other deities including him. Both temples are on the west bank.

On the other hand, Dendera, while a worship temple to Goddess Hathor is on the west bank, and the temples of Kom Ombo, Luxor and Karnak, all worship temples, are on the east bank. Also, the temple of Montu, the war God and that of Mut, wife of Amon is on the east bank adjoining Karnak. There is a worship temple to Hathor near Deir el Medina on the west bank at Thebes, while some scholars have argued Seti Is Hypostyle Hall is a mortuary temple or "mansion of Millions of years" in the Karnak worship complex.

Finally, the Cairo Museum of Egyptian Antiquities has made many changes. Naturally, security is very tight at the entrance even in the once Tarik Square Plaza, that is now converted. Visitors have to check your camera as no photographs are permitted inside. Since 2015, however, this has changed and for an additional fee photography in the Museum is permitted.

CELEBRATING
DR. BEN-JOCHANNAN

There are cameras throughout the museum for security reasons. There is the same rush to view Tutankhamon's treasuries. Some pieces of his display are on loan. The cost to view the Royal Mummies is up from 75 to 100 Egyptian Pounds.

Two unusual things happened while I visited the Museum. It rained that day while I waited to enter. In all my years in Egypt I never saw rain both in Upper or Lower Egypt. Second, in the hall of Tutankhamon, they were removing his mask from its case to put it in another case and I had the privilege to see this and some golden necklaces in their natural state outside of their cases.

Dr. Ben's Photo 209. Karnak, Home of God Amon-Ra. Native Guide in the Temple gives Thumbs-up (left); and, Nefertari beneath Rameses in the Court as visitors prepare to exit the Court.

FREDERICK MONDERSON

Dr. Ben's Photo 210. Karnak, Home of God Amon-Ra. View of the ruins of the Hypostyle Halls Processional Colonnade and evidence of the Clerestory that lets light into the Hall.

Dr. Ben's Photo 211. Karnak, Home of God Amon-Ra. The *Wadjyt* area before the Sixth Pylon enclosing the Sanctuary in open area ahead.

CELEBRATING DR. BEN-JOCHANNAN

Dr. Ben's Photo 212. Karnak, Home of God Amon-Ra. From the Middle Kingdom Court looking through the Sanctuary and pass the two Obelisks and the ruins of the Hypostyle Hall, as visitor ambles by.

The chariots, vases, coffins, statues, sphinxes, etc., are still there, catching dust yet attract an enormous numerous of visitors. Unfortunately, there are few or no noticeably Nubian or Black guides in the museum so the visitors, when it comes to issues of ethnicity, are given incorrect information that, in a way reinforces prejudices. Maspero's famous description of Maherpra, the 18th Dynasty nobleman, as being "Negroid but not Negro," I equated with being "Caucasoid but not Caucasian," is still in that part of the museum that is not generally visited. There is no place card that gives an accurate description of the 11th Dynasty Theban King Mentuhoteps statue, which W. Stephenson in the *Art and Architecture of Ancient Egypt* described as having "black flesh." This gives many of the young Egyptian Guides the opportunity to give European tourists inaccurate information about this important Middle Kingdom monarch who united the two lands. Importantly, however, while wood is painted, stone is never painted, though Mentuhoteps statue is colored black. This is purposeful, it is not the color of the stone, and thus cannot be dismissed as being painted for the funeral ceremony.

All in all, Egypt is as warm, entertaining, enlightening and educational as any culture on earth. The tombs, temples, art and photographic opportunities give the visitor a rush and a spiritual and philosophic as well as cultural and historic awakening that's well worth the trip. Read the books and visit Egypt to get a real grasp of the intellectual, scientific, art and architectural even medical foundations early Africans established in the Valley of the Nile. This will go a long way to enlighten our people about this proud African heritage and legacy.

Dr. Ben's Photo 213. Karnak, Home of God Amon-Ra. From across the Sacred Lake, the two Obelisks and ruins of the Hypostyle Hall, with the "Coca Cola Temple" behind the bushes.

CELEBRATING DR. BEN-JOCHANNAN

30. EGYPT 2010
By
Dr. Fred Monderson

As the dig continue and the monuments continue to tell their remarkable story, modern Egypt is undergoing tremendously rapid changes of beautifying the landscape while imposing more and more restrictions on the increasing number of visitors who come to behold the ancient treasures while spending their money. Still, in a society that takes great pride in and benefits tremendously from its wonderful history, there is a hospitality the Egyptians extends that beckons the visitor return to the Nile River country for the museums, pyramids, temples, tombs, food, shopping, balloon rides, horse-drawn carriage experience and ancient and modern architecture as well as the warm reception that goes along with it.

The dollar is holding at 5.68 Egyptian pounds (2019 it was 1800), tipping is still the rule and it behooves the tourist to haggle, haggle, haggle; negotiate, negotiate, negotiate; bargain, bargain and more bargain for everything from taxi or horse-drawn buggy rides to purchasing cartouches, gold, silver, books, clothing, etc., Nile River excursions, you name it.

The Egyptian authorities have long realized the value of their ancient history to modern antiquarian lovers and are doing whatever it takes to extend the welcome mat and to beautify the esplanade of the monuments to protect these treasures and enhance the ambiance which in turn encourages more visits and greater foreign exchange benefits to the nation.

FREDERICK MONDERSON

On a whirlwind 10-day tour, this writer visited 10 Egyptian temples with the exception of Abu Simbel and Kom Ombo, previously visited. At mighty Karnak the entrance reconstruction is complete though the digging within continues. Earlier visitors Oldsters who are familiar with the old entrance layout to Karnak will be surprised to know the old shops are gone and the entire area, from the street to the pylon is a reconstructed plaza square with a park-like atmosphere where the gate and entrance is some 1500 meters removed. The customary metal detectors and the numerous antiquities police officers ensure safety on the grounds and also help protect the monuments. Such security precautions are designed to assure visitors who may be fearful of coming; but the show of security force quickly allays such fears and people feel relaxed not simply at Karnak but at all sites on the circuit.

Dr. Ben's Photo 213a. Erik Monderson at Aswan with the old Oberoi Hotel in the background across the Nile.

CELEBRATING
DR. BEN-JOCHANNAN

Dr. Ben's Photo 214. Karnak, Home of God Amon-Ra. Middle and New Kingdom statues on the North/South axis before the Seventh Pylon.

FREDERICK MONDERSON

Dr. Ben's Photo 215. Karnak, Home of God Amon-Ra. Brother Abdul, "Master of Karnak," has been in the temple for 50-years.

The venerable Brother Abdul is no longer in charge at Karnak due to health concerns. Still, he sends his greetings and well-wishes to the "Nubian brothers and sisters" in America. More important, however, in exasperation he complained "I'm angry Nubian brothers and sisters do not come to Egypt as in

CELEBRATING DR. BEN-JOCHANNAN

the days of Dr. Ben." Further, he implored, "Dr. Fred, you should become the next Dr. Ben and bring our people to view our ancient heritage. Too many may be going to other places that teach them nothing about their ancestral culture. And those that do come need to use the Nubian guides." All I could say, I'll deliver your concerns.

Karnak is still as beautiful as ever from the walk through the sphinxes entrancing the Pylon and Great Court with Seti's Kiosk to the left, the northern and southern colonnades with their sphinxes, the mud ramp inside the southern half of the Pylon, two altars, a sphinx of Tutankhamon, Taharka's Kiosk, two standing statues of Rameses II and the perpendicular temple of Rameses III, all giving access to Rameses I and Horemheb's Second Pylon that entrances the Hypostyle Hall.

This magnificent building consisting of 134 columns, 122 in two wings separated by 12 larger, and the largest columns in any building worldwide, that comprises the Processional Colonnade. While opinions vary at to its beauty, profusely illustrated with the temple rituals, it represents a "papyrus thicket at creation" when the God arose from the waters and created the world. It also reflects the caliber of architect who could plan and execute a work with such boldness and immensity that not only has it defied time in its duration of existence, but it also staggers the imagination with the architecture itself and the decoration.

Pylons Three, Four, Five and Six were built by Amenhotep III and Thutmose I and III and encompass the Courts housing Thutmose Is and Hatshepsut's single standing obelisks with statues, decorated walls, and colonnades all stand before the Sanctuary where Dr. Ben has forbidden his students to enter.

FREDERICK MONDERSON

Beyond the Sanctuary, the Middle Kingdom Court esplanades the *Akh Menou*, festival temple of Thutmose III.

The "Girdle Wall" of Rameses II is still breathtaking in its fabulously illustrated depiction of the king before the Gods in a multitude of attitudes. The "Coca Cola Temple" still serves the thirsty visitor beside the Sacred Lake, while the Sacred Scarab has been moved some 50 feet to the west near the Eastern Wall of the "Cachette Court." A distinct addition to the temple, pictographic and textual signs stand illustrating specific monuments on the temple plan in English, French and Arabic languages, the Open-Air Museum, Courts along the north-south axis with their Pylons continue to exhibit their wonderful architecture, illustrated depiction and broken statues and stones. Work continues on the restoration of the temple of Khonsu. The Temples of Mut and Montu remain closed to visitors. Still, the ruins of some 22 temples in the Northern, Central and Southern Groups remain a rich, rewarding and enjoyable experience to behold. "Sound and Light" Show, as regular feature at all popular temples as Karnak, Luxor, Philae and even the pyramids, is evening entertainment.

The Western entrance to the Temple of Luxor is now closed and visitors enter from the East beside the Mosque of Abu-Haggag. The area in front of the Pylon is undergoing extensive rehabilitation and the Avenue of Sphinxes on the "Sphinx Road" there has been beautified. Even more important, work has commenced on mapping, excavating, repairing and replacing the Sphinxes of the buried Avenue of Sphinxes linking Luxor with Karnak. Naturally, all the immediate houses and businesses along this route have been cleared. Therefore, the mud-brick Sphinx Road, a major thoroughfare is not only congested but passage is terribly uncomfortable, much to the consternation of visitors and locals alike. Restoration of the walls of the Processional Colonnade at

CELEBRATING DR. BEN-JOCHANNAN

Luxor Temple depicting the procession for the Opet Festival from Karnak to Luxor and back continues to illustratively beautify this area. The "Free Open-Air Museum" to the east of the Temple of Luxor displays more than 50,000 pieces of broken stone recovered from the temple.

The temple of Deir el Bahari has instituted an interactive video of the Discovery Channel's expose on the recent research identifying the mummy of Queen Hatshepsut. In addition, old photographs line the walls depicting the work of clearance of the temple as well as a new plan of the temple imitating limestone of which the temple was built that guides use as a teaching tool for their groups before entering the temple. The two Ramps; First and Second Courts; Lower, Middle and Upper Colonnades; and the True Northern Colonnade; the Fishes and Birds and the Obelisk Colonnades; the Punt and Birth Colonnades; the Anubis and Hathor Shrines, all with good color; Upper Terrace and Upper Court, still exhibit their wonderful architectural features, beautiful artistic depiction and ancient color while the magnetic attraction to the Sanctuary door still evokes the wonder exuded when the temple was in use that in combination makes this temple the beautiful and magnificent work of art that it is.

Medinet Habu is still just as beautiful while the Ramesseum is undergoing extensive renovation, nearly complete that not only highlights the architectural features of the temple proper with its statues, columns, Hypostyle Halls and arched rear area, but has substantially reconstructed the magazine storage area, priests' quarters, kitchens, school and there's much more to see.

Cameras are now permitted in the Valley of the Kings for a fee though no more climbing the mountain under threat of arrest. Yes, that is correct! Years ago, you could take pictures in the tombs, then without flash; then no photos were permitted in tombs, only outside the tombs. At one time no photos were permitted in the Valley but, now, cameras are permitted, since 2015.

Naturally, the price for all sites has risen. For example, the prices now in Egyptian pounds are as follows: Karnak 65; Open-Air Museum 25; Luxor 50; Ramesseum 30; Medinet Habu 30; Valley of the Kings 75; Philae 50; Dendera 35; Deir el Bahari 30; Egyptian Museum in Cairo 60; Royal Mummies in the Museum 100; Sakkara's Imhotep Museum 60; Sakkara New Tombs 30; Olwet Abdel Qurna 25; Memphis (Mit Rahinah) 35; Photography at Archaeological Sites (Use of a stand) 20 pounds at each site; Riding the Taftaf at Deir el Bahari and the Valley of the Kings 2 pounds. If you rent a private taxi to any site and they wait for you, there is a 5-pound parking charge, not to the taxi but to the government, for which you get a ticket. Add this to the expected tips everywhere. If a man such as move a chair for you, he holds out his hand to shake yours, but in fact is expecting a tip.

Dr. Ben's Photo 216. **Karnak, Home of God Amon-Ra**. Front elevation of the *Akh Menou*, Festival Temple of Thutmose III.

CELEBRATING
DR. BEN-JOCHANNAN

Dr. Ben's Photo 216a. Erik Monderson at Kitchener Garden in 2018.

Dr. Ben's Photo 217. Karnak, Home of God Amon-Ra. Temple of Rameses II to the east of the *Akh Menou*, Festival Temple of Thutmose III.

FREDERICK MONDERSON

Dr. Ben's Photo 218. Karnak, Home of God Amon-Ra. A surviving statue from Rameses IIs Temple to the east of the *Akh Menou*. Notice the features and how they have been defaced by time and man.

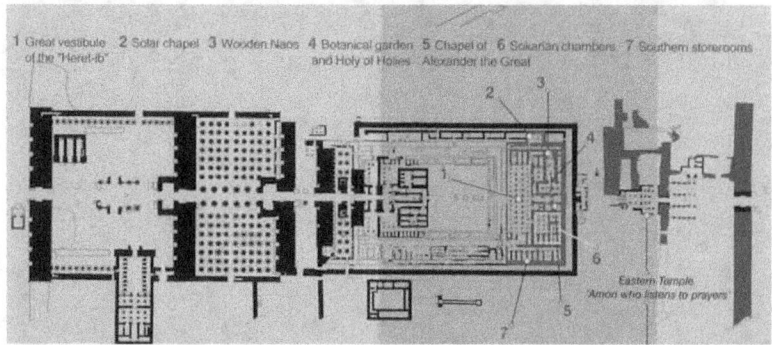

Dr. Ben's Photo 219. Karnak, Home of God Amon-Ra. Plan of the Temple with structures of Rameses II and Taharka beyond the *Akh Menou*. Strange, no one counts the back gate as a pylon!

CELEBRATING DR. BEN-JOCHANNAN

Edfu Temples entrance has been changed and reconstructed with the passageway strategically placed between bazaars. Here merchants display their attractive and inviting merchandise as they pester you with the chant of cheap prices where instead the goods are overpriced. Once pass this merchant gauntlet, the magnificent intact entrance pylon welcomes all to come see its ancient treasures.

The great Peristyle Court with its 32 roofed columns, the Pronaos or Hypostyle Hall with 18 massive columns of which are screened, the Second Hypostyle Hall with its 12 smaller columns, two vestibules before the Sanctuary and 14 rooms for vestments, liquid and solid offerings connected with the temple ritual extends this site back to the most ancient times, though the present temple was built between 237 B.C. and 17 B.C. The temple has a library at its entrance.

In the myth of the Revenge of Osiris, after Horus had defeated Seth, he and the "Followers of Horus" built this temple on the spot where the slaying took place. The temple was built and rebuilt from that time onward. There is a spot in the temple where, protruding from the ground are a set of columns which testify to the degree of which the most ancient site has built up and been built on so that the present temple literally sits on top of the columns of the earlier temple.

The "Corridor of Victory" vividly depicts the struggle and final capture of Seth disguised as a hippopotamus. Incidentally, Edfu is the only site in Egypt that boasts two Nilometers for measuring the volume of the river; one inside the temple and an old one to the south of the temple itself. The plan of the temple, the resident God and pharaoh and Goddess Seshat breaking ground are also shown.

FREDERICK MONDERSON

The river voyage to Philae Temple of Goddess Isis (Now on Agilka Island) is one of the most exhilarating experiences as the temple seems to literally rise out of the Nile in the approach, beginning a photographic bonanza. The rear of the Birth House is a photographer's treasury. Upon landing, the stairs, Kiosk of Nectanebo with its beautifully illustrated depictions and Hathor heads; the Forecourt lined by an Eastern Colonnade of 16 and 1 at the side columns and a Western Colonnade of 32 columns, both roofed, esplanade the temples of Arsnuphis, Mendulese and Imhotep. At the end of this court steps rise to entrance the massive decorated pylon before which stand 2 stone lions. Passing through the Pylon gateway, the visitor enters the Court proper of the Temple of Isis.

Here the front of the columned Birth House on the west and the Second Eastern Colonnade on the east display columns with capitals of varied styles. In Isis temple, three Hypostyle Halls stand before the Sanctuary. Very well decorated, this temple was also host to St. Stephen Church after Emperor Justinian closed the temple. Evidence of earlier occupation of this site is dated to an altar and relief blocks of Taharka of the 25th Dynasty; while Psamtik II built the Kiosk and a temple of Amasis of the 26th Dynasty attest to the holiness of the site before Ptolemaic times. Prior to this the Island of Elephantine was the site of occupation in this region and may have sported such a temple taking it back to the beginning of dynastic times. Nevertheless, in the Temple of Isis, the last of the hieroglyphics (A.D. 394) and latest Demotic writing (A.D. 452) can be found. There is a small temple or Kiosk to Hathor to the east with a small Courtyard in which the God Bes is shown playing a tambourine, an ape plays a stringed instrument and Pharaoh offers a necklace to the Goddess.

A little further east, the magnificent "Kiosk of Trajan" is a beautiful and monumental testimony to Egyptian building techniques though it was erected during foreign, Roman rule.

CELEBRATING DR. BEN-JOCHANNAN

Each of its 16 columns has a distinctly different capital, here and the Eastern and Western Colonnades flanking the entrance. This feature is also evident at Edfu and Dendera where each column in the Peristyle Court and the Outer Hypostyle Hall has a different capital.

Seti Is 19th Dynasty temple to Osiris at Abydos has been described as possessing the most beautiful illustrations, that is surviving; in the entire Valley of the Nile. Its famed 42 steps lead to a First Pylon and First Court, now destroyed; then a Second Pylon and Second Court, also destroyed. An illustrated Pillared entrance leads through 7 doorways, all but one now closed. A First Colonnaded Hall leads to a Second Colonnaded Hall that give rise to an elevated Platform before the Chapels of the seven divinities, viz., Horus, Isis, Osiris, Ra-Horakhty, Amon, Ptah and the deified Seti I, worshipped in this temple.

While popular belief holds the temple was dedicated to Osiris, it is in fact built as a memorial monument to Seti's predecessor kings of the earliest dynasties buried in the desert at Abydos. The axis points in this direction so when the king faces the resident divinities, he was also facing his ancestor kings. This temple hosts *in situ* the *Abydos Tablet* of which 76 ancestor kings are listed from Menes to Rameses I and Seti is the final one. There are 5 blank cartouches of "kings who have transgressed against the state." These are those associated with the Amarna Heresy including Akhenaton, Smenkhare, Tutankhamon and Aye. Hatshepsut's name is also included because she chose to rule as King, wore a beard, dressed as a man, built a tomb in the Valley of the Kings and built Deir el Bahari temple, larger than her ancestor, Mentuhotep II of the 11th Dynasty. She, however, was not associated with the later "Amarna Revolution." In the passage leading out to the Osireion, Rameses is shown teaching young Merenptah how to lasso the bull.

FREDERICK MONDERSON

The Pyramids are still fixtures on the Giza horizon, while Sakkara boasts the testament of Imhotep's Step Pyramid for Pharaoh Zoser of the 3rd Dynasty, beginning the colonnade concept and initiating the glorious history of Egyptian architecture. Three new tombs were recently discovered at Sakkara; the tomb of the two brothers Niankhnuun and Khnumhotep; Irukaptah; and the Mastaba tomb of Nefer and Kahay. There is a separate charge of 30 Egyptian pounds to view these tombs. All in all, while there are changes, it's all for the betterment and sustainability of the monuments and their history. Meanwhile, many persons invite American Nubian brothers and sisters come home to the culture of the ancestors built in Egypt, Northeast Africa.

Dr. Ben's Photo 220. Karnak, Home of God Amon-Ra. From the Great Court looking west towards the south-half of the Entrance Pylon gate with end columns of the southern colonnade (left). That last column shows how these columns were erected in square slabs then pounded round and the remains of an earth mound that enabled workers to scale the heights.

CELEBRATING DR. BEN-JOCHANNAN

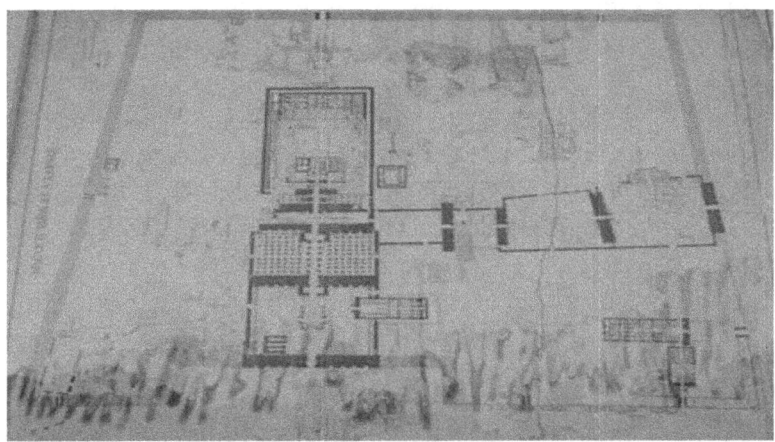

Dr. Ben's Photo 221. Karnak, Home of God Amon-Ra. Plan of the Temple within the Enclosure Wall showing Pylons 7-10, etc., on the north/south axis to the right; while the first six can be seen on the east/west axis.

31. Who Were the Ancient Egyptians?
By
Dr. Fred Monderson

I. Introduction

The "great researcher" Danny Kaye in his monumental and groundbreaking work *The King's New Clothes* eloquently articulated and identified that the king was not wearing anything, as he paraded before the people. He was embarrassingly naked! Equally, Baron de Montesquieu, author of the *Spirit of the Laws*, has argued, among other things, that man should act as if your actions, and in this case, writings, can become a universal law. Now, when we examine some early writings on Egypt by what we can easily call pseudo-scientific writers, in view of historical revelations and perpetuation of seeming falsity, their work certainly emerges as questionable and pejorative at best. At worst, it appears somewhat dishonest, vindictive and mean-spirited, some say racist! Reinforcing such a belief, Georges Foucart, a French Egyptologists at the beginning of the 20th century, stated, "The early Egyptologists made mistakes, to which Dr. Leonard James responded, "Those mistakes were purposeful." Thus, this falsity became ingrained and much of it persists to this day. So much so, Prof. John H. Clarke, in his **Introduction** to Anthony Browder's *Nile Valley Contributions to Civilization* (1992: 9) puts it best in the statement: "Except for Egypt, African people have been programmed out of the respectable commentary of history. Europeans have claimed the non-African creation of Egypt in order to downgrade the position of African people in world history. They have laid the foundation of what they called Western civilization on a structure that the Western mind did not create. In doing so, they have used no logic!"

That being so, let us not forget, modern interpretation of the culture of ancient Egypt/Kemet is oriented as Europeans ascended the Nile from north to south as opposed to the flow of the river and culture from South to north and therein lies the conundrum; some say misinterpretation, some say racist, view of ancient Egypt and its relationship with Africa or should we say, Africa's relationship with Egypt, the second daughter after Ethiopia.

As an example, we know the Tigris-Euphrates Rivers flowed from north to south. The comparative view would be to argue civilization ascended the river by an invading force. This is the type of argument being presented in the European conception of culture ascending the Nile River.

CELEBRATING
DR. BEN-JOCHANNAN

Conversely, because of its relation to the Nile, at its headwaters, the ancients believed the Ethiopians influenced Egypt evidenced in the cultural flow of the Nile. The Ethiopians, in fact, argued they colonized Egypt, and so this supports the view the people of the Nile were the same, being only shades of difference in color. Culturally, in support of such a view, many modern scholars not only read the ancients but also saw the resemblance and depicted such in their works. Khamit Indus Kush in his book, *The Missing Pages of "His-Story"* (1993: 42) quotes several people affirming the connection between Egypt and Ethiopia. First, Basil Davidson in "The Ancient World and Africa, Who's Roots?" (*Race and Class*, XXIX, Autumn 1987, No. 2, p. 2) wrote: "The ancient Egyptians were black (in any variant you may prefer) - or, as I myself think, it more useful to say, were African, is a belief which has been in Europe since about 1830."

Dr. Ben's Photo 221a. Carmen Monderson and Shawki Abdel Rady, Native Egyptian Guide, at Abu Simbel in 2017.

FREDERICK MONDERSON

Dr. Ben's Illustration 74. Priests in Procession at the Temple of Dendera.

The American Egyptologist George Gliddon in *Ancient Egypt: The New World* (1843: 59) pointed out: "The advocates of the African origin of the Egyptians cling to the superior antiquity of the pyramids of Meroe as a proof of the origin of civilization in Ethiopia, and its consequent descent into Egypt." Again, according to Kush, Professor Rosellini: "Accepts and continues the doctrine, of the descent of civilization from

CELEBRATING DR. BEN-JOCHANNAN

Ethiopia and the African origin of the Egyptians." Prof. Naumann equally believed: "We will first deal with the Ethiopians, as they are the nearest neighbors of the Egyptians, and further because it is historically affirmed that the latter originally migrated from Ethiopia. Indeed, the music of the Ethiopians offers strong internal evidence in support of the assertion." In *Prehistoric Nations* (New York: 1898, p. 276), John D. Baldwin wrote: "Diodorus Siculus adds to his statement that the laws, customs, religious observances, and letters of the ancient Egyptians closely resemble those of the Ethiopians, the colony still observing the customs of their ancestors." And on and on!

Bruce Williams of the University of Chicago discovered, from the remains of Qustol, in Nubia, evidence of Pharaonic regalia, viz., white crown, sailing boat, enthroned king, scepter and flail, incense burner, palace facade, etc., two hundred years before such appear as pharaonic iconography in Egypt. Dr. Clarke previously had said the Tasians, Badarians, the people from Merimde and Badari, all prehistoric Egyptians, were Negroes. In fact, he said, the Egyptian civilization was "rehearsed in Ethiopia before it made its debut on the stage in Egypt." Again, Prof. Moret's bold assertion, "By whom was the South influenced if not by the North?" To which Dr. Diop responded, "If so, why are the important sites and monuments in the South and not the North?"

Dr. Ben's Photo 222. Luxor Temple of Amenhotep III and Rameses II. One of two surviving obelisks, two seated statues and one of four standing statues and a fallen head before the decorated Entrance Pylon.

Dr. Ben's Photo 223. Luxor Temple of Amenhotep III and Rameses II. View of the Entrance Pylon from the West with the one standing and two seated statues and the remaining obelisk.

CELEBRATING DR. BEN-JOCHANNAN

Dr. Ben's Photo 223a. Façade of Luxor Temple with statues restored in their original position as of 2019.

The reason for the great hunger for Egypt is best explained in a quote from W.J. Perry in his *The Growth of Civilization*, Penguin Books (1924) (1937: 48-49) where he quotes G. Elliot Smith in *The Ancient Egyptians* (1911) stating: "The Egyptians did a great deal more than merely invent agriculture and devise the earliest statecraft and religion. Not only did they devise the methods of working wood and stone and the art of architecture, they seem also to have been the inventors of linen and of the craft of weaving, of the use of gold and copper, and the making of metal tools and implements. They were the first people to measure the year and to devise a calendar, and later on to substitute for the rough calculation based upon the date the observation of the sun's movements. They also invented shipbuilding and constructed the first sea-going ships. In a thousand and one of the details of our common civilization the originality of Egyptian civilization is revealed. The art of shaving, the use of wigs, the wearing of hats, the invention of the kilt and of the sandal and subsequently of a variety of other articles of dress, many of our musical instruments, chairs and beds, cushions, jewelry and jewel-cases, lamps – these are merely a few of the items picked at random out of our ancient heritage from the Nile valley."

Interestingly, however, when he uses the term "our" he means Europeans, not all of humanity or Africans. This, then, is what is at stake; the cultural bonanza and inherent falsity in the manner in which it is represented and so, must be corrected!

In the aftermath of the Slave Trade and Slavery, the western world could not admit at the back of their civilizations of Greece and Rome, such were the creations of the people they were enslaving. In fact, this is what Count Volney affirmed in his *Ruins of Empires* (1792), p. 16.

Nonetheless, commenting on the significance of ancient Egyptian contribution to civilization, Margaret Murray in *The Splendor that Was Egypt*, New York: Hawthorn Books, Inc., (1949) (1969: xvi) has written the following reinforcing the view previously expressed and attributed to G. Elliot Smith: "For every student of our modern civilization Egypt is the great storehouse from which to obtain information, for within the narrow limits of that country are preserved the origins of most (perhaps all) of our knowledge. In Egypt are found the first beginnings of material culture – building, agriculture, horticulture, clothing (even cooking as an art); the beginnings of the sciences – physics, astronomy, medicine, engineering; the beginning of the imponderables – law, government, and religion. In every aspect of life Egypt has influenced Europe, and though the centuries may have modified the custom or idea, the origin is clearly visible. Centuries before Ptolemy

CELEBRATING
DR. BEN-JOCHANNAN

Philadelphus founded his great temple of the Muses at Alexandria, Egypt was to the Greeks the embodiment of all wisdom and knowledge. In their generous enthusiasm the Greeks continually recorded that opinion; and by their writings they passed on to later generations that wisdom of the Egyptians which they had learnt orally from the learned men of the Nile Valley."

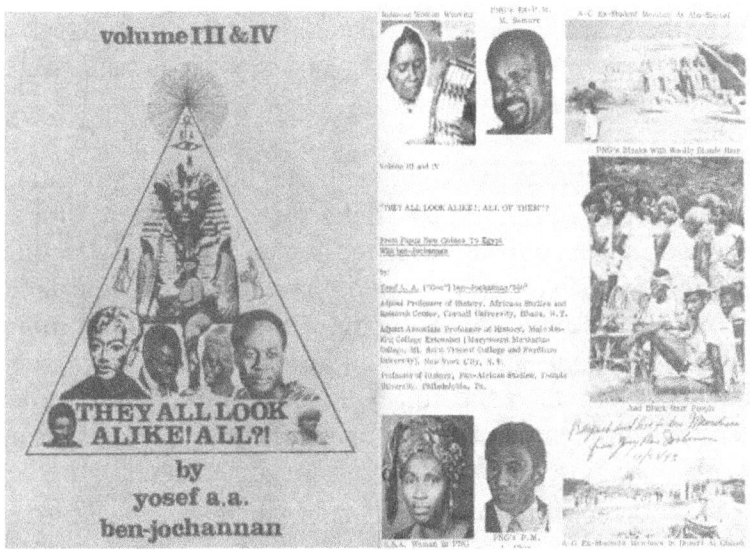

Dr. Ben's Books 14. THEY ALL LOOK ALIKE! ALL?! (1980). Notice the Author's autograph to Dr. Fred Monderson.

Further, in her explanation, Murray (1969: xvii) revealed: "Egypt was the supreme power in the Mediterranean area during the whole of the Bronze Age and a great part of the Iron Age; and as our present culture is directly due to the Mediterranean civilization of the Bronze Age, it follows that it has its roots in ancient Egypt. It is to Egypt that we owe our division of time; the twelve months and three hundred and sixty-five days of the year; the twelve hours of the day and the twelve hours of the night are due to the work of the Egyptian astronomers. The earliest clocks, the clepsydra, were the invention of Egyptian physicists. The earliest known intelligible writing is the Egyptian, so also are the earliest recorded historical events. It is due to the passion of the Egyptians for making records that so much has been preserved of their history and their literature, of their religious beliefs and their religious ritual. This passion for writing made them invent the first actual writing materials – pens, ink, paper – materials which could be packed in a small compass, were light to carry, and easy to use."

Murray (1969: xvii) continued, highlighting Egyptian contributions even more, by contrasting this earliest culture with subsequent civilizations in the human drama and pointing out how Egyptian accomplishments have left them in the dark. She wrote: "The splendor of Egypt was not a mere mushroom growth lasting but a few hundred years. Where Greece and Rome can count their supremacy by the century, Egypt counts hers by the millennium, and the remains of that splendor can even now eclipse the remains of any other country in the world. According to the Greeks there were **Seven Wonders of the World**; these were the *Pyramids of Egypt*; the *Hanging Gardens of Babylon*; the S*tatue of Zeus at Olympia*; the *Temple of Diana at Ephesus*; the Tomb of Mausoleum; the *Colossus of Rhodes*; and the *Lighthouse of Alexandria*. Of all these great and splendid works, what remains to the present day? Babylon and its gardens are a heap of rubble, as ruined as a bombed city; the statue of Zeus was destroyed long ago; the Temple of Diana is utterly demolished, leaving only a few foundations; fragments of the Mausoleum are preserved in museums where they are a source of interest to experts only; the Colossus of Rhodes survives only in legend, so completely has it disappeared; the

CELEBRATING DR. BEN-JOCHANNAN

Lighthouse of Alexandria has perished almost without a trace. Of the Seven Wonders the Pyramids of Egypt alone remain almost intact, they still tower above the desert sands, dominating the scene, defying the destroying hand of Time and the still more destructive hand of Man. They line the western shore of the Nile for more than a hundred miles, and are the most stupendous and impressive as they are the most ancient of all the great buildings of the world."

Equally too, Lester Brooks in *Great Civilizations of Ancient Africa* (1971: 28) confirms: "From the cemeteries dating back before 3200 B.C., anthropologists have identified remains they label Europoids (indicating those of Cro-Magnon types), 'Negroid' and some Asian types, with the Europoids predominating in the north and the Negroids predominating in the south. As one expert puts it, the races were fused on the banks of the Nile well before Pharaonic civilization came into being. These people were black by the operating definition of skin color as well as by the general physical characteristics they had then." Even further, Brooks (1971: 28-29) continued: "The Greeks were surprised twenty-five hundred years ago to discover that the Egyptians were the darkest-skinned peoples of the so-called Near East. Typically, they were - and are today – not homogeneous. Their skin color ranges from red-black to yellow. Their hair is black and wavy, curly or wooly; their eyes are bright and black; their bodies are lean and muscular, generally tending to tallness. Egyptian noses usually are large and straight, but frequently aquiline; their jaws generally tend to thrust forward with fleshy lips, often curled back. We can say without the slightest hesitation that the ancient Egyptians would have been considered Negroes by American standards, and until the passage of the Civil Rights Act of 1964 not one of the Egyptian Pharaohs could have bought a cup of coffee in a white drug store in the southern states of the U.S.A."

FREDERICK MONDERSON

Dr. Ben's Photo 224. Luxor Temple of Amenhotep III and Rameses II. The Kiosk of Hatshepsut usurped by Thutmose III and later Rameses II behind the "Great Pylon" in the "Ramessean Front" with the pinnacle of the Obelisk standing in the rear.

Dr. Ben's Photo 225. Luxor Temple of Amenhotep III and Rameses II. Close-up double images on the architrave of Hatshepsut's Kiosk, (front) a falcon and bull stand before enthroned Amon-Ra while (rear) the King dances before enthroned Amon-Ra.

CELEBRATING DR. BEN-JOCHANNAN

In his "Argument for A Negro Origin" in *African Origin of Civilization: Myth or Reality*, Cheikh Anta Diop (1974: 134-155) cites "Totemism," "Circumcision," "Kingship," "Cosmogony," "Social Organization," "Matriarchy," "Kingship of the Meroitic Sudan and Egypt," "Cradles of Civilization Located in the Heart of Negro Lands," and "Languages," as evidence for his position. His "two-cradle theory" for "and sun environments" and their influences, and patriarchy as opposed to matriarchy, viz., Europeans in the North and Africans in the South, were very convincing. Brooks (1971: 29) on the other hand, sheds more-light on this cultural situation: "What African elements can be discovered in the extremely sophisticated civilization of Egypt? Among others, the complicated religious beliefs wherein tribalism, animism and taboos had extraordinary force – with special rites for the major activities such as planting, harvesting, fishing, hunting and war, in addition to the *rites du passage* – birth, marriage, death." Further he points out: "We think of African witch doctors with fantastic, colorful costumes. Look again at a formal portrait of a Pharaoh. Note that, he wears an enormous headdress. From his double crown sprout the head of a vulture and the fire-spitting flamed head of a female hooded cobra, supposedly capable of consuming rebels in flames. The pharaoh was the son of the falcon-God, and was considered a falcon himself, endowed with magical powers and an all-seeing eye. From his waist hangs an animal tail; on his shaven chin he wears a false beard, which is, itself, considered a God. In his hand he carries a scepter with the head of the God Seth atop it – recognizable in the curious curved snout, long, straight ears and almond-shaped eyes."

Adding even more to this fanfare, Brooks demonstrates further: "In processions, banners are carried before the king. These banners bear the symbols of the many powerful brother

FREDERICK MONDERSON

Gods who have blessed him and whose aid is his to command." Of course, he also wears arm bands, a necklace, rings, a girdle or apron with Uraeus, sandals and carries a dagger, a flail, and either a mace or bow and arrows, with which to slay his enemies, who as a God and superhuman on the battlefield could slay hundreds of enemies at a stroke all by himself. His eyes scrutinize the depths of every being. Nothing is impossible for him: Everything which he ordains comes about."

In this respect then, the answer to the question of "Who were the ancient Egyptians?" while it should not have done so, it still has baffled, confused, contradicted and often been obfuscated by modern scholars, viz., historians, journalists, archaeologists, anthropologists, and every other form of commentator particularly those who use the film and video medium as well as persons involved in printing, dissemination and distribution of information relative to Egypt. All this has left many scholars, students, and average citizens in a state of confusion. Quite frankly, these latter have been misinformed intentionally, unintentionally and because of the falsity fed the previous generations upon whose "facts" they have come to rely. Truthfully, and upon close examination, generation after generation of scholars and lay people, have been misinformed regarding the origin of the ancient Egyptians. Much of this has been intentional and when it has not been so it has been due to ignorance, but more profound in museums and other exhibits aided by lighting and "doctoring." Some of this is traceable to Wilhelm Hegel and other German scholars, who held, for much of the 19th Century that Africa was outside the realm of history, and by extension the Egyptians were an Asiatic people in the "Middle East" being part of the "Fertile Crescent."

CELEBRATING DR. BEN-JOCHANNAN

Dr. Ben's Photo 226. Luxor Temple of Amenhotep III and Rameses II. Statues seem to be coming out from between the columns wearing different head dresses while a seated statue to the right wears the White Crown extant in the "Ramessean Front."

Dr. Ben's Photo 227. Luxor Temple of Amenhotep III and Rameses II. Close-up of the striding statues seemingly coming out from between the columns in the "Ramessean Front."

FREDERICK MONDERSON

Dr. Ben's Photo 228. Luxor Temple of Amenhotep III and Rameses II. A fat cow with priests in procession to the Temple of Luxor. Notice "the Nubian lady coming out of the cows head," at top left.

Still more significant, it is understandable this position was enunciated during the greatest humiliation, degradation and inhumanity perpetuated against Africans that is at the height of the slave trade, slavery, the emergence of the abolition movement to outlaw the slave trade, and in aftermath of the American, French and Haitian revolutions and the discovery of the Rosetta Stone. Millennia prior to that period most people believed the Egyptians were Africans and Black! In this "Dark age of Africa" perpetuated by Europeans and European-Americans equally stole Egypt and grossly misrepresented it. However, in unfolding world history and after the discovery of the Rosetta Stone in 1799, Champollion, DeSacy, and Young became involved in the process of linguistic development decipherment of the hieroglyphic script, which the ancient Egyptians had named *Medu Netcher*. Of these, Champollion was the most successful deciphering Hieroglyphics in 1822. This discovery of the Code of Hieroglyphics gave birth to the discipline of Egyptology and an effervescence of societies was founded fueling an

CELEBRATING
DR. BEN-JOCHANNAN

antiquarian movement. His brother Champollion-Figeac, as Dr. Diop has demonstrated, has falsified the older antiquarian pioneers' intent, based on his studious observations matching others much as Herodotus observations about the ancient Egyptians, has conveniently been ignored. Contemporary with Champollion's observations and work, the mad dash for antiquities resulted in what Brian Fagan later dubbed "The Rape of the Nile."

Now, when it comes to the ancient Egyptians there is an unbridgeable chasm, because most European and European-American people believe the ancient Egyptians were white, as they chose to see themselves so portrayed. However, and equally, most blacks with any sense of historical understanding believe the ancient Egyptians were black and there is much evidence to support, a la Diop! Nevertheless, a lot of ink has been spilled on the color of these early Egyptian Africans. This is particularly so of the "red color" of the Egyptians. Let me say at this point, I don't have all the answers! However, what I do know, while we have heard of "red white men," "black white men," and "white white men," one thing is certain, the ancient Egyptians were not white! David O'Connor, a Curator at the Philadelphia Museum has confirmed such to this author back in 1992, "The Egyptians were not white!" That is not to say others have not also done so! The point is, if this "mainstream white scholar" could say the "Egyptians were not white!" then the issue should have been put to rest long ago, but it is not! Then who the hell is John David Wortham to claim Egyptians were Caucasians? Let us not forget, if there were any painted evidence of white Egyptians, it would have been magnified many times. However, while the ancient Egyptians were painted red, they were also painted black; and even Osiris was painted green but Egyptians were never painted white!

FREDERICK MONDERSON

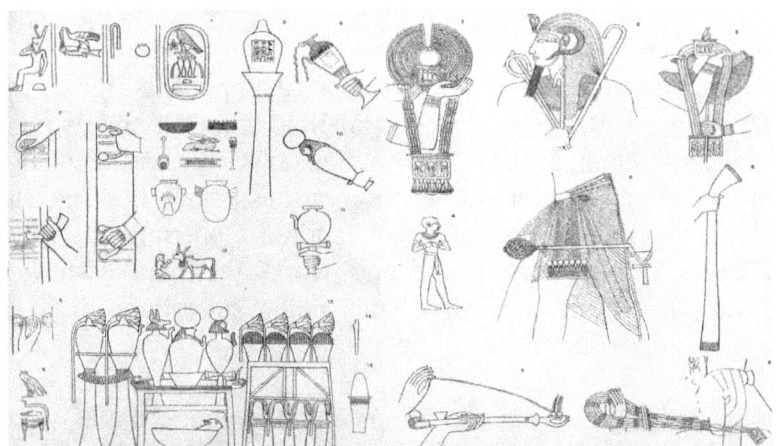

Dr. Ben's Illustration75. Abydos. Temple of the Kings. Selected Vases (left); and, Kings clothing, etc. (right) in A. St. G. Caulfield's *The Temple of the Kings at Abydos* (Seti I) (1902).

From the time of the Stone Age, man has had a penchant for red as his favorite color and this led us to believe the Egyptian, followed in this vein, and painting of himself the color red is simply to culturally demonstrate love for this color. Gay Robbins has informed, the Egyptian believed red and even gold had a solar connection and as a people who believed they were divinely chosen they used red to depict themselves. They, however, also used black to depict themselves, (Mentuhotep, Thutmose I, Aahmes-Nefertari, Tutankhamon, among survivals) though they never used white for such a depiction! Cheikh Anta Diop said the Egyptians painted themselves red to distinguish themselves from other Africans since they considered themselves special.

In September 2005, a young female guide in the Cairo Museum, in referring to the statue of Mentuhotep II found in his Middle Kingdom temple at Deir el Bahari, told this writer: "He was painted black for the funerary ceremony." Obviously, she did not know, and is probably being taught to

CELEBRATING DR. BEN-JOCHANNAN

falsely propagate such by saying My Professor told me this at the American University in Cairo! For though found in 1898 and his temple cleared between 1903-1906, untold commentators wrote and spoke on Egypt without ever mentioning Mentuhotep II, until in 1959, he was described by E. Stephenson Smith in *The Art and Architecture of Ancient Egypt* as having "black flesh!" The guide even told this researcher she never saw Osiris, God of the Dead, painted black! So, I searched him out in the Museum and found numerous examples, not just of Osiris but other kings as well. We must also remember; these wooden models are what have survived the destructive elements of time and man! They are also the only materials generally painted!

In the Cairo Museum, Number J 95,655 Osiris in White Crown is painted green. However, in JE 36,465 Osiris is painted black; JE, 95,645 Osiris is black; J, 26,228 Osiris is black; J, 35,669 Osiris is black; papyrus B 24 Osiris is black. This is a lengthy papyrus depicting a winged snake with 4 feet; as 4 Goddesses ride 4 uraei with double heads. Then 7 Goddesses ride a lengthy snake crossing a river chasm while 6 Goddesses pull the snakes tongue as it stands behind a line of 6 Goddesses and 6 Gods led by Khepre towards the deceased with his back towards Nephthys and Isis standing behind enthroned black Osiris who greets the deceased who in turn offers a plant.

In Room 12 is housed funerary furnishing from royal tombs.

Statue No. 2374 – made of wood, Osiris is painted black.
Statue No. 2372 – made of wood, Osiris is painted black.

In this room, Case GL contains 9 large Afro wigs. These were discovered in the "Deir el Bahari Cache" in 1881.

FREDERICK MONDERSON

Wooden statues Numbers 3827, 3836, 3834, 3832, 3824, are all painted black. The wooden duck Number 3838 and a wooden panther No. 3840 and wooden panther No. 3842 are all painted black. In front and outside Room 12 large wooden statues 3834a and 3834b are painted black.

In room No. 22, 9 wooden statues, painted black, are placed above Case J.

4 wooden statues are above Case I
4 wooden statues above Case O
4 wooden statues above Case P
7 wooden statues above Case R
7 wooden statues above Case T

Dr. Ben's Photo 229. Luxor Temple of Amenhotep III and Rameses II. From the west, columns of the Peristyle colonnade of the "Ramessean Front," the First Pylon, Obelisk and minaret of the Mosque of Abu al-Haggag with the northernmost tip of the Processional Colonnade to the right.

That is 38 in all as recounted here and there's probably more. Many may very well be displaced in the New Museum being built. Still, imagine being a "Guide" in the Museum and "never seen Osiris or other images painted Black!"

CELEBRATING
DR. BEN-JOCHANNAN

Dr. Ben's Photo 230. Luxor Temple of Amenhotep III and Rameses II. The majestic 14 columns of the Processional Colonnade.

Dr. Ben's Photo 231. Luxor Temple of Amenhotep III and Rameses II. From the North-West, a parade of colonnades in the "Ramessean Front," then Processional Colonnade and Court of Amenhotep III.

FREDERICK MONDERSON

These are all painted black. Still, who knows what is in the basement. We must remember the place cards for much in the Museum was done by Gaston Maspero. He, incidentally, in the 19th Century, described Hunefer, whose papyrus indicated the origin of the Egyptians, as "Negroid but not Negro." He probably did not even use capitals. However, contemporary with such a description, the biographers of the musical genius Beethoven described him as "black," "swarthy," "Negroid," "Negro," etc. Thus, I ask readers "You to do the math!"

Conversely, Dr. Yosef ben-Jochannan said the Egyptians were painted "red" because they were dead. Even further, that the Henna plant is used to paint particularly young brides red, as part of a cultural ceremony. Evidence elsewhere indicated the Egyptians "killed red people" even though they painted themselves red and, again, this may simply be a cultural expression. Now, in the Tomb of Rekhmara, the Vizier, the numerous individuals are all painted red. As a reminder, Cheikh Anta Diop says the Egyptians painted themselves red to distinguished from other African blacks. All this notwithstanding, there are pictorial "survivals" of Egyptians and Gods painted black, viz., Amon, Min, Thutmose I, Tutankhamon, Ahmose-Nefertari, wife and sister of Ahmose and their brother Kamose whose mother Aahotep and her father Sekenenra Tao must have been black to have produced their "coal black Ethiopian" daughter. Let's face it, in *Red Land, Black Land*, red represented barrenness of the desert; and blackness represented fertility of the cultivable land. Yet, the Gods often say they give pharaoh "The Black Land!" Obenga and others hold this is actually the black peoples land which also includes the "Red Land," unless this designation has another meaning. After all, the Gods cannot give the king one part of his domain comprised of 4 percent while withholding 96 percent comprised of desert! Again, the desert is red. The painted figures are red. Thus, red does not represent life nor resurrection. Brugsch-Bey held, "The Egyptian was

CELEBRATING
DR. BEN-JOCHANNAN

painted red for illumination in the dark passage to the Judgment." Osiris was Black so he represented resurrection and eternal life! In fact, Osiris was called "the Great Black!" Again, Theophile Obenga has reminded all Kemet or the "black land" referred to the people not the land itself.

Rameses IIs wife Nefertari was Nubian. Yet she is painted red in her tomb in the Valley of the Queens. In December 2005, someone called this writer to look at a program on the History Channel entitled *Black Pharaohs* about the 25th Dynasty where these Blacks are represented as painted Black! who were Nubian and black. In a fleeting glance the camera showed an image of Tanutemon, one of these Black pharaohs and lo and behold, this ruler was painted red in the tomb! Let us not forget also, images in the tomb of the nobles at Aswan also show these southernmost Egyptians, where Nubia interacts significantly with Egypt and who were essentially black, also painted red. What does all this mean? It means the Egyptians were African not European or Asiatic, black not white and Egypt was and is still located in Africa not the Middle East or Asia. Now what is the evidence for all of this?

Thus, this presentation will focus on a chronological approach showing how principally eyewitnesses portrayed the ancient Africans of the Nile Valley, Egypt; first, and as interest intensified in modern times, how Egypt was viewed particularly in the 19th and 20th Centuries. One thing is certain as European writers, historians and antiquarians first encountered Egypt they "colored" their reports to appease an emerging reading public in Europe. With time, African scholars did significant research unearthing the distortions, omissions, and misrepresentations and revealed what they had found. Despite profound scholarship by Blacks, European writers and their American cohorts have found it difficult to accept the revealed facts or have refused to deal with the issue, sidestepping it. Those Europeans who bucked the trend and wrote otherwise of the distortion, were ostracized.

For example, much confusion has been created as European scholars, not finding any evidence of "White Egyptians" have emphasized "Red Egyptians" as being "Red Egyptian White men." Let me give this example and pose a question before we begin. Murnane (1983: 231) in discussing the Sanctuary area of the Temple of Karnak where the God Amon-Ra dwelt, wrote: "The walls are covered with scenes illustrating the episodes of the offering rite with Amun appearing in his usual anthropomorphic guise and also in the ithyphallic form he shares with Min, the God of fertility." Further, another writer Cadogan in *Cairo, Luxor, Aswan* (2002: 212) adds: "On the north side of the sanctuary, where there was much rebuilding, a wall erected by Hatshepsut was found concealed behind a later wall of Thutmosis III, thus preserving the original freshness of the coloring. The wall has now been removed to a nearby room, and shows Amon, his flesh painted red and with one foot in front of the other, and also Amon in the guise of the ithyphallic Min, a harvest God, often amalgamated with Amon, his flesh painted black." Let us remember, while Amon is here represented with "his flesh painted red," in the back room at Deir el Medina, he is shown enthroned and his skin is painted black. He is also painted blue here and at Karnak beside the *Akh Menou!*

CELEBRATING DR. BEN-JOCHANNAN

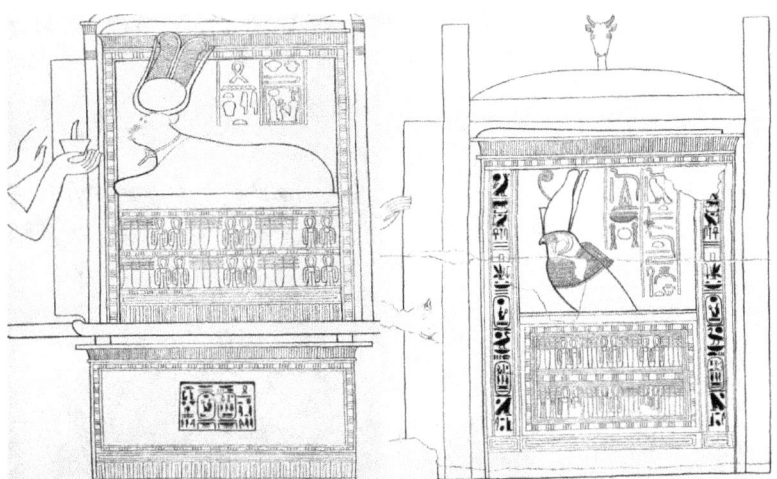

Dr. Ben's Illustration 76. Abydos. Temple of the Kings. Seti offers a plant to kneeling Hathor (left); and, Back Hall: Shrine of the Mummied Hawk (left) in A. St. G. Caulfield's *The Temple of the Kings at Abydos* (Seti I) (1902).

Dr. Ben's Photo 231a. Luxor Temple of Amenhotep III and Rameses II. From the west, the Processional Colonnade and first columns of the Court of Amenhotep III's colonnade.

FREDERICK MONDERSON

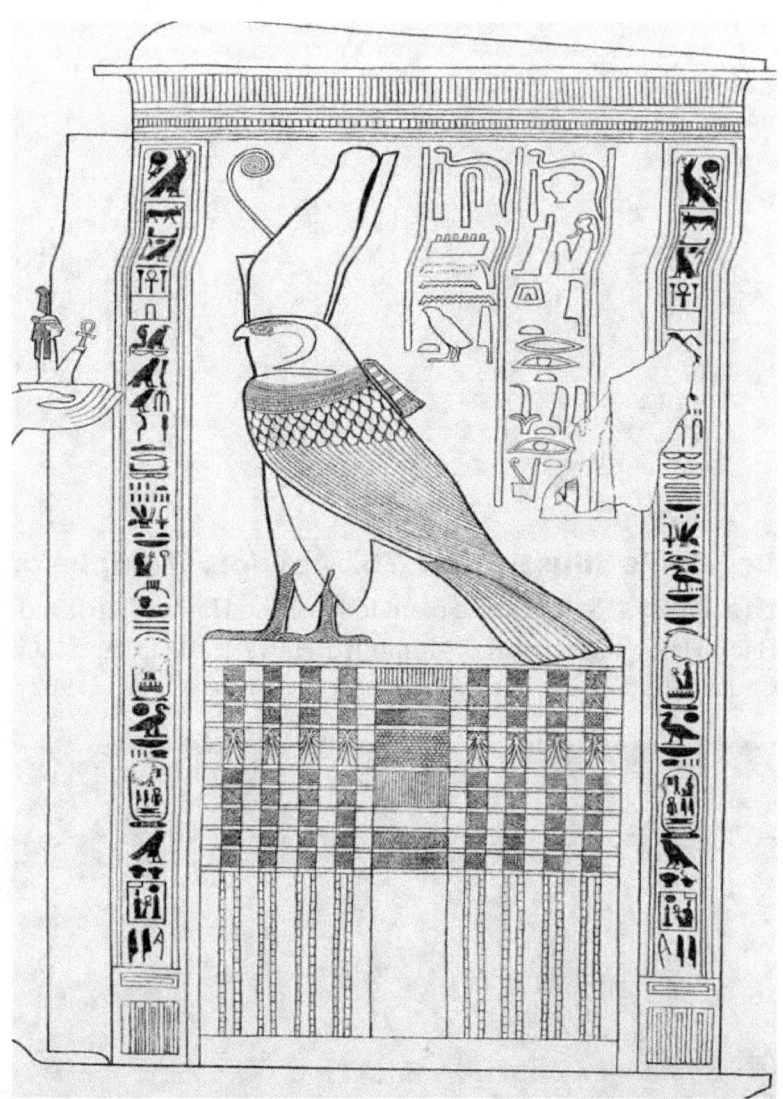

Dr. Ben's Illustration 77. A. St. G. Caulfield's *The Temple of the Kings at Abydos (Seti I)* (1902) **Abydos. Temple of the Kings**. Shrine of the Mummied Hawk. The King offers Ma'at, in the form of his name to the falcon God wearing the Double White and Red Crown.

CELEBRATING DR. BEN-JOCHANNAN

Now the serious first question is: "Why would white (Caucasian) red men be worshipping Gods painted black?" Equally too, another question is, "Why did Murnane not refer to the color of Amon, as Min, being black?" Elsewhere, in the *American Journal of Archaeology* Amon has been described as "so black, he was blue!" Many writers have a tendency to skillfully dance around the question of the race of the Egyptians, particularly when evidence indicates they were black! It's all part of the conspiracy. Much further, when evidence surfaces depicting Egyptians "painted black" the logical explanation given is there were painted black because either they were dead or for the death ceremony. Yet, while no evidence exists to show Egyptians white, the assumption and propagated falsity is that they were white! Again, a very good reason the white writer affirmed to this researcher "The Egyptians were not white" is simply because today men of reasonable intellect know the falsity of a white, Caucasian, Egypt is just that, falsity.

II. Classical Writers

a. **Homer** - Most scholarship seems to date Homer to about 800 B.C. However, this may be incorrect, even though we know he is "credited" with writing the *Iliad* and the *Odyssey*. Several things need to be looked at in relation to dating of Homer and even questioning his originality. First, we are told that Abu Simbel temple of Rameses II has the earliest examples of Greek writing and this writing is dated to the 7th Century B.C. Now, if Homer wrote the *Odyssey* and *Iliad* then it cannot be 800 B.C., as previously thought. Second, Cheikh Anta Diop says, if Homer visited Egypt it had to be in the 8th Century during the time of the Twenty-fifth Ethiopian

Dynasty and much of his descriptions may be representative of later events in Egypt. Interestingly, Murray's Handbook *for Egypt* (1888) informs: "In the Ramesseum, North face of the South East Wall of the 2nd area is a scene of combat that very much resembles what Homer tells us of his Odyssey."

b.   Herodotus 480-425 B.C. - Herodotus visited Egypt around 450 B.C. and wrote the *Histories* devoting Book II *Euterpe* to Egypt. Diop (1989) argued in "Origins of the Ancient Egyptians" in *Egypt Revisited* Edited by Ivan Van Sertima, and quotes the father of history in regard to the Origins of the Colchians: "It is in fact manifest that the Colchidians are Egyptians by race ... several Egyptians told me that in their opinion the Colchidians were descended from soldiers of Sesostris. I had conjectured as much myself from two pointers, firstly because they have black skins and kinky hair (to tell the truth this proves nothing for other peoples have them too) and secondly and more reliably for the reason that alone among mankind the Egyptians and Ethiopians have practiced circumcision since time immemorial." Herodotus says further that the Egyptians have "thick lips, broad noses and are burnt of skin," meaning they are black. Practically everything else Herodotus wrote was accepted as (observed) fact other than that the Egyptians had "wooly hair, thick lips, broad noses and were burnt of skin." Much of what he heard or theorized could be considered conjecture, but his observations cannot be disputed. Naturally, he never said black as compared to what or whom!

c.   Aristotle 384-322 B.C. - Aristotle in his work *Physiognomonica* made a somewhat controversial statement regarding the ancient Egyptians. He says: "The Egyptians and Ethiopians are cowards because they are black" and of the Nordics he said these "whites are also cowards" because they are white. He was, perhaps, seeking to affirm that the middle ground, perhaps a "Mediterranean Race," type was the ideal.

CELEBRATING DR. BEN-JOCHANNAN

Now, while his science of cowards was wrong, for we know as proven by the many wars Africans have fought; however, his description of the Egyptians and Ethiopians is essentially correct. This is one incidence in which this great philosopher and scientist was both wrong and right on the same issue.

d.   Diodorus Siculus of Sicily 63-14 B.C. - Diodorus held to the view that Ethiopians colonized Egypt. Diop says, according to Diodorus: "The Ethiopians say that the Egyptians are one of their colonies, which was led into Egypt by Osiris. They claim that at the beginning of the world Egypt was simply a sea but that the Nile, carrying down vast quantities of loam from Ethiopia in its flood waters, finally filled it in and made it part of the continent. They add that the Egyptians have received from them, as from Author's and their ancestors, the greater part of their laws." Inadvertently Diodorus tells us the origin of Osiris as being Central African!

Dr. Ben's Photo 232. Luxor Temple of Amenhotep III and Rameses II. The Western Colonnade in the Court of Amenhotep III.

FREDERICK MONDERSON

Dr. Ben's Photo 233. Luxor Temple of Amenhotep III and Rameses II. The Processional Colonnade as viewed from the south in the Court of Amenhotep III.

Dr. Ben's Photo 234. Luxor Temple of Amenhotep III and Rameses II. From the West, (outside), colonnades of the Court of Amenhotep III.

CELEBRATING DR. BEN-JOCHANNAN

e. **Diogenes** says of Zeno, founder of the Stoic School 333-261 B.C. that he was "tall and black" and "people called him an Egyptian vine-shoot."

f. **Ammianus Marcellinus** 33-100 A.D. notes the "men of Egypt are mostly brown or black with a skinny and desiccated look." He says further that the Colchians were "an ancient race of Egyptian origin."

g. **Count Volney**, one of the Savants who followed Napoleon to Egypt at the end of the 18th Century, made the following statement regarding the ancient Egyptians from observations of the modern Copts. According to Diop (1989), Volney wrote: "All of them are puffy-faced, heavy-eyed and thick-lipped, in a word, real mulatto faces. I was tempted to attribute this to the climate until, on visiting the Sphinx; the look of it gave me the clue to the enigma. Beholding that head characteristically Negro in all its features, I recalled the well-known passage of Herodotus, which reads: For my part I consider the Colchoi are a colony of the Egyptians because, like them, they are black-skinned and kinky-haired. In other words, the ancient Egyptians were true Negroes of the same stock as all the autochthonous peoples of Africa and from that datum one sees how their race, after centuries of mixing with the blood of Romans and Greeks, must have lost the full blackness of its original color but retained the impress of its original mold. It is even possible to apply this observation very widely and posit in principle that physiognomy is a kind of record usable in many cases for disputing or elucidating the evidence of history on the origins of the peoples …."

III.   To the Mid-19th Century
In a chapter entitled "Modern Falsification of History" Cheikh Anta Dips *African Origin of Civilization: Myth or Reality*

discusses Domeny de Rienzi's contention that: "It is true that back in the distant past, the dark red Hindu and Egyptian race dominated culturally the yellow and black races, and even our own white race then inhabiting western Asia. At that time our race was rather savage and sometimes tattooed, as I have seen it depicted on the tomb of Sesostris I in the valley of Biban-el-Moluk at Thebes, the city of the Gods." Thus, Are Hindus Egyptians? Second, he distances whites from all the other mentioned types. Nonetheless and far reaching, he colors Hindus and Egyptians as red!

This is interesting for if we believe the Egyptians were white and migrated to Africa leaving no evidence of the prototype of Egyptian culture in their place of origin in Western Asia, then have Thebes in Upper Egypt become the "city of their Gods," requires much explanation. Equally, any claim of a western Asian origin of the Egyptians ties them to the white race. However, let us not forget, Nubia and Central Africa was "God's land." Again, the absolutely absurd conclusion is that whites from western Asia considered Africa as their "Gods land!"

Dr. Ben's Photo 234a. Luxor Temple of Amenhotep III and Rameses II. Columns of the Court and Hypostyle as viewed from the west on the outside.

CELEBRATING
DR. BEN-JOCHANNAN

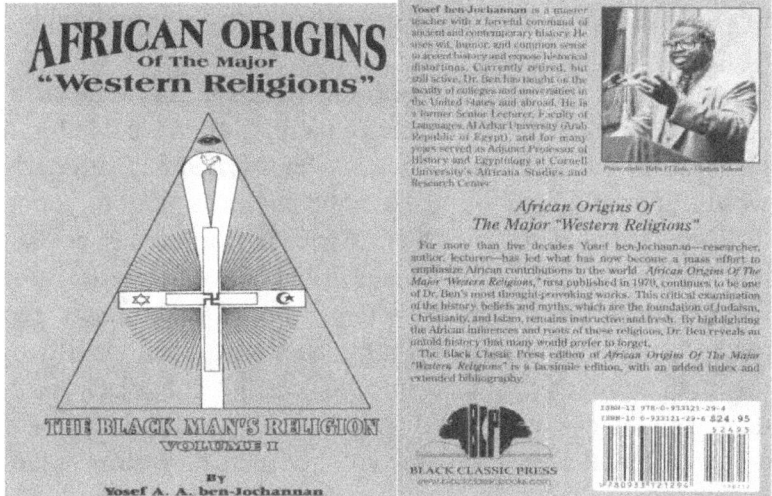

Dr. Ben's Book 15. African Origins of the "Major" Western Religions - The Black Man's Religion - Volume I (1970, 1991)

We should be aware, every people who migrated from one place to the next, retained some reference to their ancestral home. Contrary to popular western prognostication, the Egyptians never associated Mesopotamia or Southwest Asia with their origins. Clearly, this is a modern interpolation. In fact, the record seems to indicate only one reference to origins and is: "We came from the foothills of the Mountains of the Moon where the God Hapi dwells." This area is the plains of the East African mountain range. Inadvertently, he also identified the place of the origin of Osiris also called Hapi, equally a God of the Nile. As Wortham submitted one modern 1825 mummy dissection to prove the ancient Egyptians were Caucasian how then would we regard the ancients Hunefer's and Diodorus contentions as to the origin of Osiris (Hapi) and the Egyptians?

FREDERICK MONDERSON

a. **Jean-Jacques Champollion** the Younger set to work and was successful in deciphering the hieroglyphic script, as we know, in 1822. Within ten years he was dead. However, his extensive work did unleash an interest in antiquarian studies. Diop quotes Champollion from a letter to his brother Champollion-Figeac, who twisted his brother's words, thus helping to bring about the falsification of Egyptian history and the effort to remove Africans from this important part of the African experience. He mentions four groups of people starting with the Egyptians shown with a dark red color. "There can be no uncertainty about the racial identity of the man who comes next: he belongs to the black race, designated under the general term *Nahasi*. The third represent a very different aspect; his skin color borders on yellow or tan; he has a strongly aquiline nose, thick, black pointed beard, and wears a short garment of varied colors; these are called *Namou*. Finally, the last one is what we call flesh-colored, a white skin of the most delicate shade, a nose straight or slightly arched, blue eyes, blond or reddish beard, tall [in] stature and very slender, clad in a hairy ox-skin, a veritable savage tattooed on various parts of his body; he is called *Tamhou*." He wrote elsewhere: "We find there Egyptians and Africans represented in the same way."

Even more striking, Diop argues in comparison with many West African blacks whom he names and finally states: "If the Egyptians were white, then all these fore-mentioned Negro peoples and so many others in Africa are also whites. Thus, we reach the absurd conclusion that blacks are basically whites." Even further, he writes: "On these numerous bas-reliefs, we see that, under the Eighteenth Dynasty, all the specimens of the white race were placed behind the blacks; in particular, the blond beast of Gobineau and the Nazis, a tattooed savage, dressed in animal skin, instead of being at the

CELEBRATING
DR. BEN-JOCHANNAN

start of all civilization, was still essentially untouched by it and occupied the last echelon of humanity."

Dr. Ben's Illustration 96. A Bust of Amenhotep III.

b. **Karl Lepsius** - Diop tells us Karl Lepsius offered a "Canon of proportion" in his *Discoveries in Egypt, Ethiopia* *and the Peninsula of Sinai in the Years 1842-1848* (London: 1852) that denotes: "The proportions of the perfect Egyptian body; it has short arms and is Negroid or Negritian. From the anthropological point of view, the Egyptian comes after the Polynesians, Samoyeds, Europeans, and is immediately followed by African Negroes and Tasmanians. Besides, there is a scientific tendency to find in Africa, after excluding foreign influences, from the Mediterranean to the Cape, from the Atlantic to the Indian Ocean, nothing but Negroes or Negroids of various colors. The ancient Egyptians were Negroes, but Negroes to the last degree."

c. **Garner Wilkinson** – An English nobleman, spent several years in Egypt, particularly Thebes, during mid-19th Century. He did extensive research and produced significant works on the Egyptian culture that is still consulted by experts in the field. Many of the illustrations he copied have now disappeared from their original placement.

IV.   To 1900

a. **Auguste Mariette** – Was of an age when great interest in Egypt very early attracted many scholars from different countries, particularly in aftermath of Napoleon's discovery of the Rosetta Stone and Champollion's decipherment of the language. However, his vision seemed different from most of his age principally bent of antiquities acquisition. Ruffle (1977: 8-9) best puts the man and his time in perspective. "With funds from King Friedrich Wilhelm IV of Prussia, Richard Lepsius made a great survey of the monuments (published in a mammoth twelve-volume work) and collected many objects, which formed the basis of the great Berlin collection. The increasing scholarly interest highlighted the need for orderly and controlled excavation.

CELEBRATING DR. BEN-JOCHANNAN

Auguste Mariette, who was sent by the Louvre to collect antiquities in Egypt, realized this. With the support of the Khedive, he founded the Egyptian Museum and Antiquities Service and became its first director, often pushing through his scientific policies in the teeth of opposition from other European Egyptologists."

"Mariette's concern was matched by the painstaking methodology preached by William Matthew Flinders Petrie, grandson of the explorer of Australia and the first person to hold a chair in Egyptology [in England] – University College, London. This chair had been founded by Amelia Edwards whose un-intentional Nile cruise – she had gone there when a sketching holiday in France was rained off – had filled her with an enthusiasm for Egypt that led her to found not only Petrie's chair but also the Egypt Exploration Fund. Other learned societies were also formed – notably the *Deutsche Orient Gesellschaft* in 1888 and the *Mission Archaeologique Francaise* in 1880, later the *Institut Francais d'Archaeologie Orientale*."

Dr. Ben's Photo 235. Luxor Temple of Amenhotep III and Rameses II. Close-up of the columns of the Hypostyle Hall.

FREDERICK MONDERSON

1. He gives no date for their coming.
2. In the earliest period Lower Egypt was generally desolate with Upper Egypt the principal place of occupation.

Dr. Ben's Photo 236. Luxor Temple of Amenhotep III and Rameses II. From the west, on the outside, colonnades of the Court of Amenhotep III and the Hypostyle Hall to the right.

b. **Brugsch-Bey** – Karl Heinrich Brugsch-Bey in his *Egypt Under the Pharaohs* (London: John Murray, (1881, 1902: 2-3) has argued: "Suffice it to say, however, that, according to ethnology, the Egyptians appear to form a third branch of the Caucasian race, the family called Cushite; and this much may be regarded as certain, that in the earliest ages of humanity, far beyond all historical remembrance, the Egyptians, for reasons unknown to us, left the soil of their early home, took their way towards the setting sun, and finally crossed that bridge of nations the Isthmus of Suez, to find a new fatherland on the banks of the Nile." Many of these

CELEBRATING
DR. BEN-JOCHANNAN

individuals generally argue on speculation and offer no facts to support their contention.

c. **Adolf Erman** – German scholar extraordinaire. It's been argued Erman was probably the only modern who understood exactly what the Egyptians meant in their language. Nevertheless, Charles Finch in "Black Roots of Egypt's Glory" in *Great Black Leaders: Ancient and Modern* (1988: 140-141) states: "As the 19th century wore on, German scholars began applying their meticulous methods of research to the study of ancient Egyptian language. Finding many similarities in words and syntax between Egyptian and the Semitic languages, the Germans unhesitatingly proclaimed Egyptian to belong to this group. As a result, their leading Egyptologists Eber, Erman and Brugsch – concluded that the impetus for Egyptian civilization itself came from a western Asiatic or Semitic source. Like others, they saw in the human figures on the Egyptian monuments – many colored a reddish-brown – evidence of a non-African Mediterranean race. Anthropologically speaking, no such race ever existed, but that did not trouble them overmuch and the term has remained in vogue to this day." Obviously, there was a turnaround because Erman later wrote in *Life in Ancient Egypt* (New York: Macmillan, 1894: 32) confirming: "The inhabitants of Libya, Egypt and Ethiopia have probably belonged to the same race since prehistoric times. In physical structure they are still Africans." Otherwise, he implied they were all white!

d. **Gaston Maspero** – French Egyptian expert has written extensively on the history and culture. However, his take is that the ancient Egyptians were of European origin, who crossed over to North Africa and entered Egypt from the west. What a pity! L'Hote in "Tassili Frescoes" identified Negroes in the Sahara between 7000 and 6000 B.C. Why could these Blacks not be able to enter the Nile Valley from the Sahara but whites could cross over to North Africa from Europe and then follow essentially the same route into the Valley? Nabta Playa Negroes entered the Nile Valley from the west in Upper Egypt, settling in the Aswan Area. However, these new findings were unknown to Maspero. Thus, he may have been right about entry from the west, and, expert that he was, either he suppressed knowledge about Nabta Playa folks or his European migration was based on speculation.

e. William Matthew Flinders Petrie (1853-1942) - The "Father of Egyptian archaeology," did extensive research in Egypt and was one of the most prolific writers of his day, influencing a great many people with his, now considered, racist views. Stuart Tyson Smith in "Race" in Donald B. Redford's Edited *The Oxford Encyclopedia of Ancient Egypt* Vol. 3, (2001: 111) has written: "The origins of the modern conception of race derive from the work of nineteenth-century anthropologists like L.H. Morgan and E.B. Taylor, who developed scientific unilinear evolutionary theoretical models for the development of human beings from Savagery to Civilization. Racial groups were ranked by evolutionary categories, linked to intellectual capacities, based on elaborate cranial measurements; supposedly, this provided causal links between phenotype (observable) traits, mental capacities, and socio-political dominance. This model not coincidentally reinforced the existing European-American domination of third-world peoples with the claim of scientifically objective methodologies based on race and evolution." Even further Smith continued: "The unilinear evolutionary model did influence some early Egyptologists. W. M. Flinders Petrie used it to develop his notion of the Dynastic Race, to explain the rapid development of Egyptian civilization. In part this was based on prevailing models of culture change that emphasized migration as an explanation for cultural change, but, ultimately, racist notions drove the

CELEBRATING
DR. BEN-JOCHANNAN

model. The implication was that Egypt had a white or brown ruling class dominating a native black African underclass who supplied the labor to build Egypt's great monuments. The Egyptological community as a whole never enthusiastically accepted Petrie's model, although the idea persisted through a few enthusiasts. James Henry Breasted echoed the sentiments of most contemporary Egyptologists in seeing the Egyptians as indigenous, but as a brown rather than black race, related to other northeastern Africans. It is interesting to note that the Egyptians became White for a classroom textbook, presumably reflecting the racism of the day. The last serious argument in support of the Dynastic Race theory appeared in Walter Emery's *Archaic Egypt* (New York 1961)."

Dr. Ben's Photo 237. Luxor Temple of Amenhotep III and Rameses II. In Double Crown, Amenhotep III introduces his-self to enthroned Amen-Ra while Sekhmet stands behind the Kings images.

FREDERICK MONDERSON

Dr. Ben's Photo 238. Luxor Temple of Amenhotep III and Rameses II. Amenhotep III gestures before Min, alter ego of Amen-Ra.

f.   Earnest Alfred Wallis Budge - Wallis Budge was Keeper of Egyptian and Assyrian Antiquities at the British Museum and a prolific researcher and writer who worte about *The Gods of the Egyptians*, *The Mummy*, *Egyptian Magic*, and produced an *Egyptian Hieroglyphic Dictionary* (1920), and a

CELEBRATING DR. BEN-JOCHANNAN

whole lto more. Regarding Budge, Finch (1988) states: "Unusual for an Egyptologist, he had conductive extensive research among the peoples of the Sudan and Ethiopia - encountering cultural practices, religious ideas and languages which showed clear and identifiable linkages to ancient Egypt. It became clear to Budge that everything about ancient Egypt could be understood only by reference to Africa; there was nothing fundamentally Asiatic about Egyptian culture. In 1920, in his massive and erudite Egyptian Hieroglyphic Dictionary, Budge, reversing a 100-year trend and his own earlier opinion, classified Egyptian as an African rather than a Semitic language."

Then again, we know the Egyptian religious writings are the oldest in the world. By the First Dynasty, the *Book of the Dead* was a compilation of much earlier works, which means Egyptian writing certainly took some time to develop into that state. How come the people from Asia or wherever they came from never invented Hieroglyphics in their point of origin, nor probably had any writing until they came to the Nile Valley. The answer debunks Brugsch-Bey. Certainly Diop, Arnett and even Winkler (1928) show the development of rudimentary forms of Hieroglyphics in the Upper Nile region dating as early as 6000 B.C. However. while Winkler attributes the early rudimentary hieroglyphs to Mesopotamian origins, Diop sees them as purely indigenous. Toby Wilkinson in *Genesis of the Pharaohs* (2003) attributes these ancient Egyptian markings to a time "1000-years before Winkler's Mesopotamians."

FREDERICK MONDERSON

Dr. Ben's Photo 239. Luxor Temple of Amenhotep III and Rameses II. Amenhotep raises Sistrums to "traveling Amen" (Amon, Amun) who offers Ankh.

Dr. Ben's Photo 240. Luxor Temple of Amenhotep III and Rameses II. The "Two Ladies," *Nekhbet* and *Wadjyt* title of the Pharaoh, standing on Heb.

CELEBRATING DR. BEN-JOCHANNAN

Dr. Ben's Photo 241. Luxor Temple of Amenhotep III and Rameses II. Bust of Amenhotep III as raised relief.

Dr. Ben's Photo 242. Luxor Temple of Amenhotep III and Rameses II. An ear for listening to complaints and requests.

FREDERICK MONDERSON

g. **Canon George Rawlinson**, in the *Story of the Nations: Egypt* (1893: 23-24) wrote: "It is generally answered that they came from Asia; but this is not much more than a conjecture. The physical type of the Egyptians is different from that of any known Asiatic nation. The Egyptians had no traditions that at all connected them with Asia. Their language, indeed, in historic times was partially Semitic, and allied to the Hebrew, the Phoenician, and the Aramaic; but the relationship was remote, and may be partly accounted for by later intercourse, without involving original derivation. The fundamental character of the Egyptian in respect of physical type, language, and tone of thought, is Nigritic. The Egyptians were not Negroes, but they bore a resemblance to the Negro, which is indisputable. Their type differs from the Caucasian in exactly those respects which when exaggerated produce the Negro. They were darker, had thicker lips, lower foreheads, larger heads, more advancing jaws, a flatter foot, and a more attenuated frame. It is quite conceivable that the Negro type was produced by a gradual degeneration from that which we find in Egypt. It is even conceivable that the Egyptian type was produced by gradual advance and amelioration from that of the Negro."

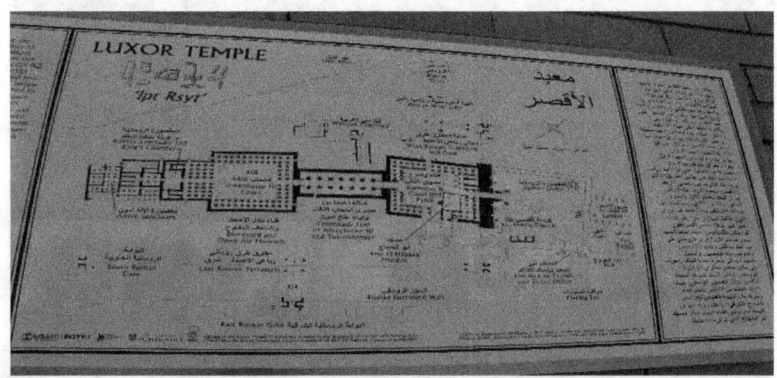

Dr. Ben's Photo 242a. Luxor Temple of Amenhotep III and Rameses II. Plan of the Temple of Luxor, "Ipt Resyt."

CELEBRATING DR. BEN-JOCHANNAN

Dr. Ben's Book 16. The Black Man's Religion Volume II (1970) and a Photo of Dr. Ben. Notice the Doctors Degree, Dr. Yosef ben-Jochannan on the wall above his head to the right.

Dr. Ben's Photo 242b. Luxor Temple of Amenhotep III and Rameses II. Erik Monderson stands in the Peristyle Court of the "Ramessean Front" where statues seem to be coming out from between the columns.

FREDERICK MONDERSON

Two Lectures

The Black Man's Religion
THE MYTH OF GENESIS AND EXODUS, AND
THE EXCLUSION OF THEIR AFRICAN ORIGIN

Volume II

by

Yosef ben-Jochannan

Adjunct Asst. Prof. of History and Religion,
Marymount College, Tarrytown, New York.
Visiting Prof. of History, Africana Studies
Institute and Research Center, Cornell
University, Ithaca, New York.
Adjunct Assoc. Prof. of History, Malcolm-King
College, Harlem, New York City, New York.

Vol. I African Origins Of The Major "Western Religions:" Judaism, Christianity
and Islam [published 1970; second printing 1972, by Alkebu-lan Books Associates]

Dr. Ben's Book 16. The Black Man's Religion, Volume II (1970). The Overleaf of the volume.

Dr. Ben's Photo 242c. Luxor Temple of Amenhotep III and Rameses II. The temple's face, almost completely restored with four standing statues in place.

CELEBRATING DR. BEN-JOCHANNAN

Dr. Ben's Book 16. The Black Man's Religion Volume II (1970). The Dedication of the Volume.

h.   M. le Vicomte J. de Rouge is mentioned in an article in *American Journal of Archaeology*, Vol. 1 (1897: 393-95) where he raises the question of "The Origin of the Egyptian Race" and attempted to "prove the theory of the Asiatic derivation." Emphasizing statues found belonging to the third, fifth and sixth dynasties, he stated: "The types of the faces do not belong to the later Egyptian style, but possess elements of the more refined Semitic organization; and this fact is used by the writer as a proof of the importation of a fully developed civilization into Egypt." Essentially, the article argues there are three theories as to the origin of the Egyptian race: (1) that the entry of the population into Egypt was made by way of Asia, passing through the Isthmus of Suez; (2) that Egypt became occupied by a colony which came in part from Asia, but passed through Ethiopia; (3) that the majority of the Egyptian population had its origin in Africa and passed into Egypt by the west and southwest." This last is a more recent theory which has been in a measure accepted by M. Maspero, and is supported by a large number of students of natural history and of ethnology, while the theory of the Asiatic origin is based on linguistic comparisons and a study of the monuments, especially the primitive monuments of Babylonia."

He says further: "The Egyptians seem not to have preserved any tradition or indication, or even memory, of their foreign origin, for they consider themselves as autochthones, and regard their country as the cradle of the human race." In addition, he argues: "The most ancient monuments discovered up to this time appear to belong to the third dynasty, such as the recently discovered bas-relief of King Sozir; that of Prince Ra-hotpu and of Princess Nofrit, etc. The statues of the two last mentioned royal personages show that the art of sculpture was already in an advanced stage of development, and the types of the faces, with their aquiline noses and thin lips, recall the Semitic race rather than the Egyptian. The great sphinx of Ghizeh, which is perhaps the most ancient relic of Egyptian art, is also anterior to the fourth dynasty." He never says anything more regarding the "Negro features" of the Sphinx.

i. **Edouard Naville**, a Swiss Archaeologist, cleared the two Deir el Bahari complexes. The *American Journal of Archaeology* XVIII (1913: 202) tells Eduardo Naville

CELEBRATING DR. BEN-JOCHANNAN

presented a paper on "The African Origin of Egyptian Civilization" in *R. Arch* XXII (1913, pp. 47-65) that states essentially: "The rise of Egyptian civilization after the Neolithic period was due to conquest by an African people from the South, called Anou. The people who caused the changes when the Thinite period ends and the Memphite period begins may have been Asiatic but they brought in no important new elements, - they merely gave a new impulse to the existing civilization." This means these Asiatics comprised the third and fourth dynasties ruling at Memphis and all they brought were their "pretty white selves." However, Petrie mentioned the founder of the third dynasty was Ethiopian from his features in the Sinai. Notwithstanding, from the images, Snefru of the third and Khufu, Khafre and Menkaure, builders of the fourth dynasty Ghizeh Pyramids, were, by operating definitions, black!

j.   G. Elliot Smith in *The Ancient Egyptians and Their Influence Upon the Civilization of Europe* (London and New York: Harper and Brothers, 1911: 32-39) informs: "Even such eminent scholars as de Rouge, Heinrich Brugsch, and Ebers, among many others, claimed that Egypt derived her language as well as much of her culture and knowledge of the arts from Asia; and Hommel and others went much further, and claimed that the whole Egyptian civilization was Babylonian in origin …."

FREDERICK MONDERSON

Dr. Ben's Book 17. The Black Man's Bible - Volume III (1974).

"De Morgan and his collaborators claim that the Ancient Egyptian language and mode of writing, the importation into Egypt of the knowledge of metals, and of such crafts as brick-making and tomb-construction, and even the fauna and flora

CELEBRATING DR. BEN-JOCHANNAN

of the country in ancient times, all point to Babylonia as the place where the roots of Egyptian civilization should be sought."

"But, under Dr. Reisner's critical analysis of the foundations upon which these speculations were supposed to have been based, practically the whole of the elaborate edifice has tumbled to the ground. As Eduard Meyer has said, "the suggestion that a culture, or even its chief elements, can be derived from another people is unthinkable and historically false: but influences must have been at work, and the Egyptians and Babylonians must have given and taken."

Dr. Ben's Photo 243. Valley of the Kings, Luxor (Thebes). View of the landscape of the Valley where so much history is preserved in Upper Egypt.

FREDERICK MONDERSON

Dr. Ben's Photo 244. Valley of the Kings, Luxor (Thebes). Taftaf used to ferry visitors to the tombs from the ticket entrance.

"Dr. Reisner has proved the indigenous origin of Egyptian civilization in the Nile Valley, and has revealed the complete absence of any evidence to show, or even to suggest, that the language, mode of writing, the knowledge of copper, or the distinctive arts and crafts were imported."

"Schweinfurth argued that the invaders of Egypt – the stereotyped phrase used by so many writers, tacitly assuming as a fact the idea of an immigration into Egypt – came from Southern Arabia (Sabaea or Hadramut), across the Straits of Bab el-Mandeb, thence through Abyssinia and the eastern Desert into Nubia, from which they spread along the banks of the Nile into Egypt …."

CELEBRATING
DR. BEN-JOCHANNAN

"Lortet and Gaillard, the most recent writers to discuss the fauna of Ancient Egypt, protest against the conclusions of Duerst that certain of the domestic animals of Ancient Egypt were brought from Asia; and they tell us that the animals known to have lived in Egypt at the time of the Ancient Empire were all African, that is, local in origin ...."

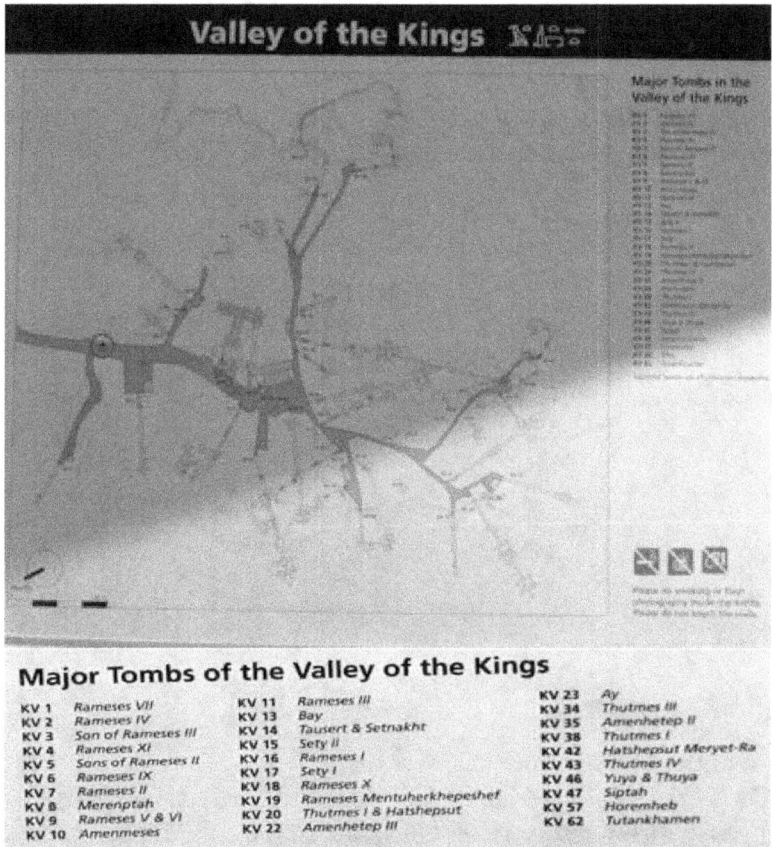

Major Tombs of the Valley of the Kings

KV 1	Rameses VII	KV 11	Rameses III	KV 23	Ay
KV 2	Rameses IV	KV 13	Bay	KV 34	Thutmes III
KV 3	Son of Rameses III	KV 14	Tausert & Setnakht	KV 35	Amenhetep II
KV 4	Rameses XI	KV 15	Sety II	KV 38	Thutmes I
KV 5	Sons of Rameses II	KV 16	Rameses I	KV 42	Hatshepsut Meryet-Ra
KV 6	Rameses IX	KV 17	Sety I	KV 43	Thutmes IV
KV 7	Rameses II	KV 18	Rameses X	KV 46	Yuya & Thuya
KV 8	Merenptah	KV 19	Rameses Mentuherkhepeshef	KV 47	Siptah
KV 9	Rameses V & VI	KV 20	Thutmes I & Hatshepsut	KV 57	Horemheb
KV 10	Amenmeses	KV 22	Amenhetep III	KV 62	Tutankhamen

Dr. Ben's Photo 245. Valley of the Kings, Luxor (Thebes). Map and listing of the Major Tombs of the Valley of the Kings.

FREDERICK MONDERSON

Dr. Ben's Photo 246. Valley of the Kings. An invitation to "Look at the Glory of the Ancient."

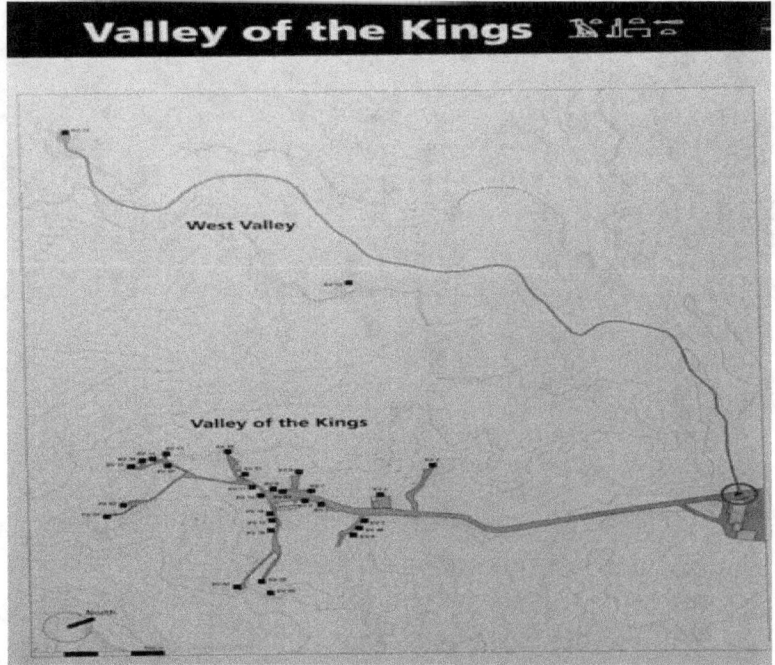

Dr. Ben's Photo 247. Valley of the Kings, Luxor (Thebes). Map showing the location of the principal tombs in the Valley.

Referring to previous statements, and that preceding his book by almost a century, "Blumenbach began the serious study of

CELEBRATING DR. BEN-JOCHANNAN

the physical characters of the Ancient Egyptians. Since then a considerable number of scholars have contributed to the discussion of the significance of the anatomical evidence – in America, Nott, Gliddon, and Meigs might be mentioned as pioneers; in France, Perrier, Pruner, Broca, Quatrefages, Hamy, Fouquet, Zabarowski, Cantre, Lortet, and Verneau have made contributions of varying importance; in German-speaking countries, Carus, Czermak, Virchow, Hartmenn, Emile Schmidt, Stahr, and Oetteking may be mentioned; in England, Bernard Davis, Huxley, Owen, Petrie, Garson, Randall-MacIver, Thomson, Macalister, Karl Pearson and his school of biometricians, Myers and Keith represent some of the outstanding names of those who have written about the craniology of the Egyptians; and last, but by no means least, Italy has added the important and highly suggestive writings of Sergi, Biasutti, and Giuffrida-Ruggeri."

G. Elliot Smith, the anatomist from the University of Manchester examined the mummies and is also the author of "Diffusionist theory" that Egyptian culture spread far and wide influencing many people with its contributions to human civilization development. His book, *The Ancient Egyptians and Their Influence Upon the Civilization of Europe* (1911) is a classic.

Some guides have commented on his bitterness, for, after having examined the mummies, he was ushered from the room without his notes. This may have led to some enmity towards the ancient Egyptians. Nevertheless, he chaired the Committee (1912) (1914) that did the "Report on the Physical Characters."

FREDERICK MONDERSON

V.   To 1950

a.   David Randall-MacIver did a study in 1905 and came to the conclusion that there were two peoples living in Egypt, side by side, Africans and Europeans. There was much discussion about this but it forces us to wonder how the critics in Europe, England especially, could come to agreement on this so later disputed fact.

b.   Arthur Weigall – Young and impetuous, he was an Englishman who first studied with Petrie at Abydos. He wrote a book entitled *Flights into Antiquity* in which he entitled a chapter, "Exploits of a Nigger King," dealing with the XXV Dynasty. The title of this chapter signals his contempt for Africans and thus he would not have seen Egypt as African and black. He is the writer who claimed Rameses II was Syrian. Which begs the question, why would Rameses, in the Battle of Kadesh, call on an African God, Amon, saying his ancestors had worshipped the God for time immemorial, and sought his help at that crucial and challenging time. Imagine a Syrian, Asiatic, calling upon an African God while doing battle in Asia! Further, imagine this same Syrian calling upon and even worshipping an African God whose alter ego, Min, was black! We also know Amon was black. This also questions the contention that Osiris was black because of his role as God of the dead. Weigall also presented a white woman as the Queen of Sheba. Fact is, the straw men arguments fall apart!

c.   James Henry Breasted, pioneering American Egyptologist - Charles S. Finch III again in "The Black Roots of Egypt's Glory" quotes James Henry Breasted who wrote: "Unfitted by ages of tropical life for any effective intrusion among the White Race, the Negro and Negroid people

CELEBRATING
DR. BEN-JOCHANNAN

remained without any influence on the development of civilization."

It is amazing that people of Breasted's hue could write about such significant historical issues with such profound racial venom. Breasted's *History of Egypt, Ancient Records of Egypt, Ancient Times* and *The Development of Religion and Thought in Ancient Egypt* are classic "primary sources of the primary sources" of ancient Egypt. The thought of a German American writing about a people of ancient Africa and could entertain the above quote raises a whole series of questions about intent and influence. We need never forget, Goethe believed, "wherever Germans went, they corrupted whatever culture they found!"

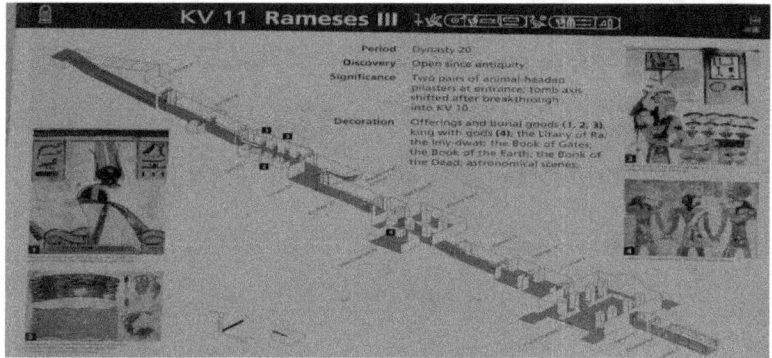

Dr. Ben's Photo 248. Valley of the Kings, Luxor (Thebes). Tomb of Rameses III, the significance of which shows two pairs of animal-headed pilasters at entrance; tomb axis shifted after breakthrough into KV 10. The decoration shows offerings and burial goods, the King with Gods, the *Litany of Ra*; the *Imy-dwat*; the *Book of Gates*; the *Book of the Earth*; *Book of the Dead*; and astronomical scenes.

FREDERICK MONDERSON

Can someone tell me, while writing his *Ancient Records of Egypt* in 1905, by the time Breasted's *Ancient Times* was published in 1916 where he described the Egyptians as "brown people," he did not know Mentuhotep II had "black flesh" even though his statue was discovered in 1898. Perhaps also, the gold of Tutankhamon blinded Breasted to the young king's black skin. In his *Ancient Times* published in 1916, Breasted described the ancient Egyptians as "brown people." However, when he re-issued it in 1935, he only dealt with "the great white race." Some have argued, because Rockefeller gave monies to fund his Oriental Studies Program, this turn-around was the quid pro quo." Again, nowhere does Breasted refer to Mentuhoteps "black flesh."

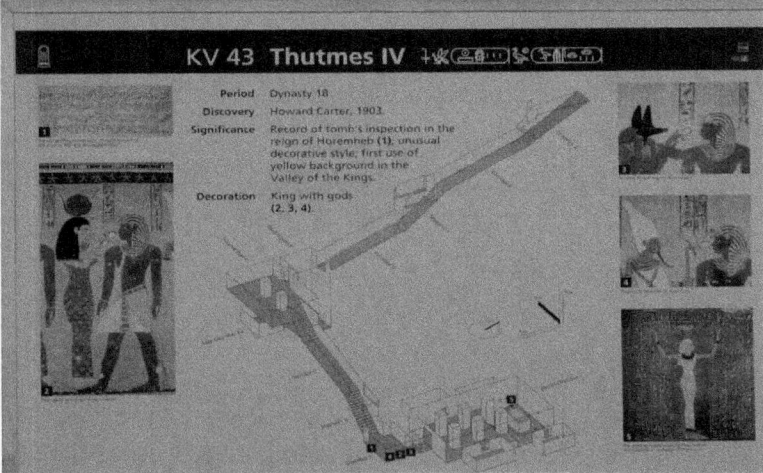

Dr. Ben's Photo 249. **Valley of the Kings, Luxor (Thebes).** Tomb of Thutmose IV whose significance shows a record of the tomb's inspection in the reign of Horemheb; unusual decorative style; first use of yellow background in the Valley of the Kings. The decoration shows the King with Gods.

CELEBRATING DR. BEN-JOCHANNAN

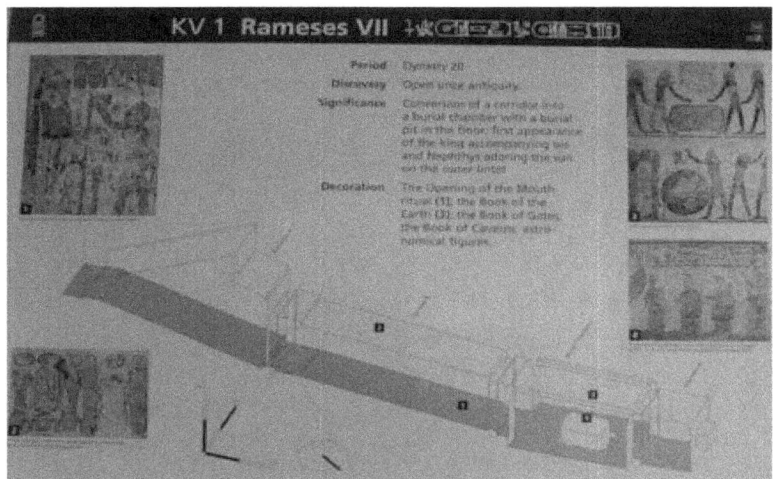

Dr. Ben's Photo 250. Valley of the Kings, Luxor (Thebes). Tomb of Rameses VII whose significance shows conversion of a corridor into a burial chamber with a burial pit in the floor; first appearance of the King accompanying Isis and Nephthys adoring the sun on the outer lintel. The decoration shows the *Opening of the Mouth Ritual*; the *Book of the Earth*; the *Book of the Gates*; the *Book of the Caverns*; as well as astronomical figures.

Nevertheless, it is well known that the resurrection and reclamation of ancient Egypt occurred in the 19th Century and early part of the 20th Century. However, in this period of "The Rape of the Nile" there was a consistent cry about destruction of the ancient culture both by natives and European plunderers seeking treasure and collectibles. Often reports would be made, natives were destroying sites whether for purposes of fuel or in order to secure and sell antiquities to anyone who would buy them. Generally, Europeans who wanted to draw attention to the problem and help to preserve the ancient record made these reports. However, very seldom did the finger get pointed at or identify European plunderers and all that is said is that this or that antique was damaged.

One has to entertain a credible question, with today's hindsight, which is, how accurate is the work of the Breasted's? or, has there been any distortion, omission or exclusion in their work? In the reconstruction of the role of blacks in ancient Egypt, evidence has to be gleaned from fragments and from the honest reports of men of good will, simply because much of racially relevant material has been destroyed in the trampled-over state. However, as more and more meticulous research focus on these fragments, they emerge larger than originally thought, for "truth crushed to the earth shall rise." In this, the work of racist and pseudo-scientific writers and historians are highlighted and the smoke and mirrors they constructed around the historical truth are now being blown away; and the true and marked naked prejudice of their writings and thinking that have misinformed for so long, are finally being blown away. And there they stand, "naked, without clothes" in a world of political and historical correctness.

d.   T. Eric Peet was an Oxford scholar who was part of the Egypt Exploration Fund staff. He was critical of Akhnaton in an article entitled "The Problem with Akhnaton." While doing important work in the reclamation of Egypt, he too had the same false conception that the Egyptians were white! Later he edited a major Egyptian journal and together with Arthur Weigall "experts of the day," helped lay down the false ideas that Egyptians were Caucasians. Imagine, Weigall speaking of Taharka as "a Nigger King!" Disrespectful.

CELEBRATING DR. BEN-JOCHANNAN

VI. The Black Challenge To 2000

a. W.E.B. DuBois began *The Negro* (Oxford University Press (1915, 1970: 140) by affirming Negro blood ran in the veins of the Egyptians, but held they were mulatto! He wrote: "With mulatto Egypt Black Africa was always in close touch, so much so that to some all evidence of Negro uplift seems Egyptian in origin." After writing Black Folks, Thena nd ow (1903) he continued this view in *The World and Africa* but could not fully defend the argument of a black Egypt. Yet, in *The World and Africa* (1946, 1971: 91-92) he quotes Palgrave who says: "As to faces, the peculiarities of the Negro countenance are well known in caricature; but a truer pattern may be seen by those who wish to study it any day among the statues of the Egyptian rooms in the British Museum: that large gentle eyes, the full but not over protruding lips, the rounded contour, and the good-natured, easy sensuous expression. This is the genuine African model; one not often to be met with in European or American thoroughfares, where the plastic African too readily acquires the careful look and even the irregularity of the features that surrounded him; but which is common enough in the villages and fields where he dwells after his own fashion among his own people; most common of all in the tranquil seclusion and congenial climate of Surinam plantation. There you may find also, a type neither Asiatic nor European, but distinctly African; with much of the independence and vigor in the male physiognomy and something that approaches, if it does not quite reach, beauty in the female. Rameses and his queen were cast in no other mold." Such a face flies in the face of those museum displays that misrepresents in catering to please European and American visitors.

FREDERICK MONDERSON

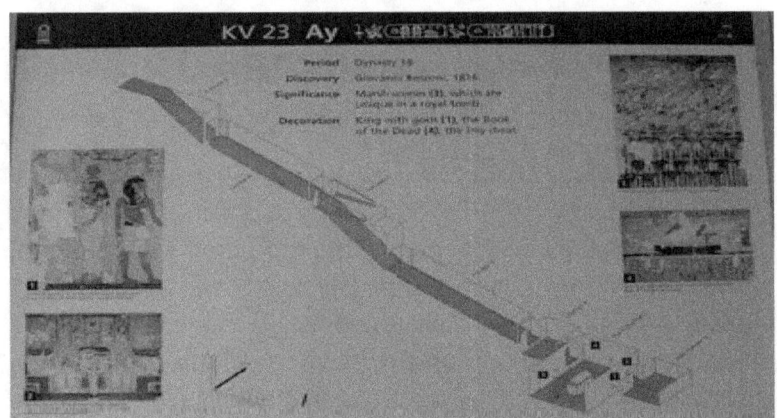

Dr. Ben's Photo 251. Valley of the Kings, Luxor (Thebes). Tomb of Aye is significant for showing marsh scenes which are unique in a royal tomb and the decoration shows the King with Gods; the *Book of the Dead*; and the *Imy-dwat*.

Dr. Ben's Photo 252. Valley of the Kings, Luxor (Thebes). A public tomb scene shows Osiris backed by Isis as the King is introduced to the God by the couple's son Horus in white and red Double Crown.

CELEBRATING DR. BEN-JOCHANNAN

b. **Carter G. Woodson**, the "father of Black History" in *The Mis-Education of the Negro* (Trenton, New Jersey: Africa World Press, 1993: 154) wrote: "We should not underrate the achievements of Mesopotamia, Greece and Rome; but we should give equally to the integral African kingdoms, the Songhay empire, and Ethiopia, which through Egypt decidedly influenced the civilization of the Mediterranean world."

c. **J.E. Harris** (Editor) of *Pillars in Ethiopian History* (Howard University Press) (1981: 6-7) has discussed the work of William Leo Hansberry, who, at Howard University began teaching about Negro Civilizations of Ancient Africa and developed the following courses:

1. **NEGRO PEOPLES IN THE CULTURES AND CIVILIZATIONS OF PREHISTORIC AND PROTOHISTORIC TIMES.** This was a survey course based on the latest archaeological and anthropological findings concerning the Paleolithic and Neolithic cultures of Africa, the pre-dynastic civilization of Ancient Egypt, and relations to the proto-historic and early historic civilizations of the eastern Mediterranean, and western and southern Asia.

2. **THE ANCIENT CIVILIZATIONS OF ETHIOPIA.** This course was a survey from about 4000 B.C., covering the general areas encompassed by the present-day countries of Sudan and Ethiopia. Hansberry relied on Egyptian, Hebrew, and Greek sources as well as archaeological and anthropological data from several

expeditions, including Harvard-Boston Expedition at Kerma, Napata, and Meroe.

(Photo by Al Burliegh Studio, 1/12/70; at Harlem Prep.)

Dr. Ben's Book 18. Extracts and Comments From the Sacred Scriptures of the Holy Black Bible (1974) with a picture of Dr. Ben in Harlem in 1970.

THE CIVILIZATIONS OF WEST AFRICA IN MEDIEVAL AND EARLY MODERN TIMES. This course surveyed the political and cultural development of Ghana, Mali, Songhay and Yorubaland as portrayed in Arab chronicles, and the archaeological and anthropological evidence in English, French and German investigations.

d. Prof. John H. Clarke in John G. Jacksons *Introduction to African Civilization* (1970: 12) says the 19th Century German scholar Arnold Herman Hereen in discussing trade between the Carthaginians, Ethiopians and Egyptians,

CELEBRATING
DR. BEN-JOCHANNAN

"gave more support to the concept of the southern African origin of Egyptian civilization."

Dr. Ben's Illustration 78. Scarabs of Kings and Nobles of the Old and Middle Kingdoms.

FREDERICK MONDERSON

e.   **Yosef A.A. ben-Jochannan** wrote extensively and very early began carrying people to Egypt to experience the monuments while he also meticulously pointed out disparities in reporting by western and American writers. He made sure "the monuments teach!" He made a special effort to point out, in the Cairo Museum the role Gaston Maspero played in shaping the interpretation of ancient Egypt by creating the "Place Cards" of the cases. He particularly pointed to Maspero's determination that Maherpra was "Negroid but not Negro." This was tremendously important because Maherpra papyrus specifically depicts an individual similar to Beethoven whom modern writers describe as Negro!

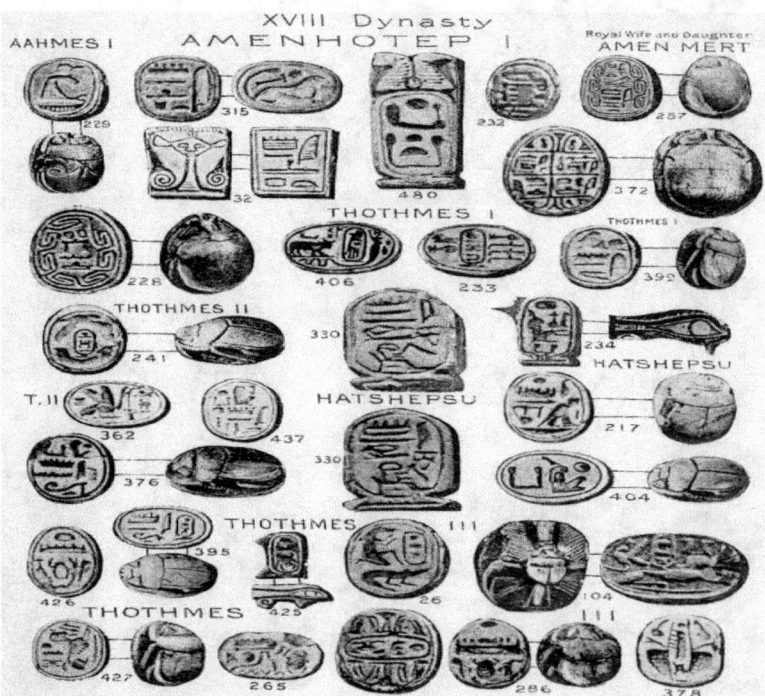

Dr. Ben's Illustration 79. Royal Scarabs of the Early New Kingdom.

CELEBRATING
DR. BEN-JOCHANNAN

Dr. Ben's Illustration 80. Royal Scarabs of Thutmose III of the 18th Dynasty, New Kingdom.

FREDERICK MONDERSON

Dr. Ben's Illustration 81. Royal Scarabs of the 18th Dynasty, New Kingdom.

CELEBRATING
DR. BEN-JOCHANNAN

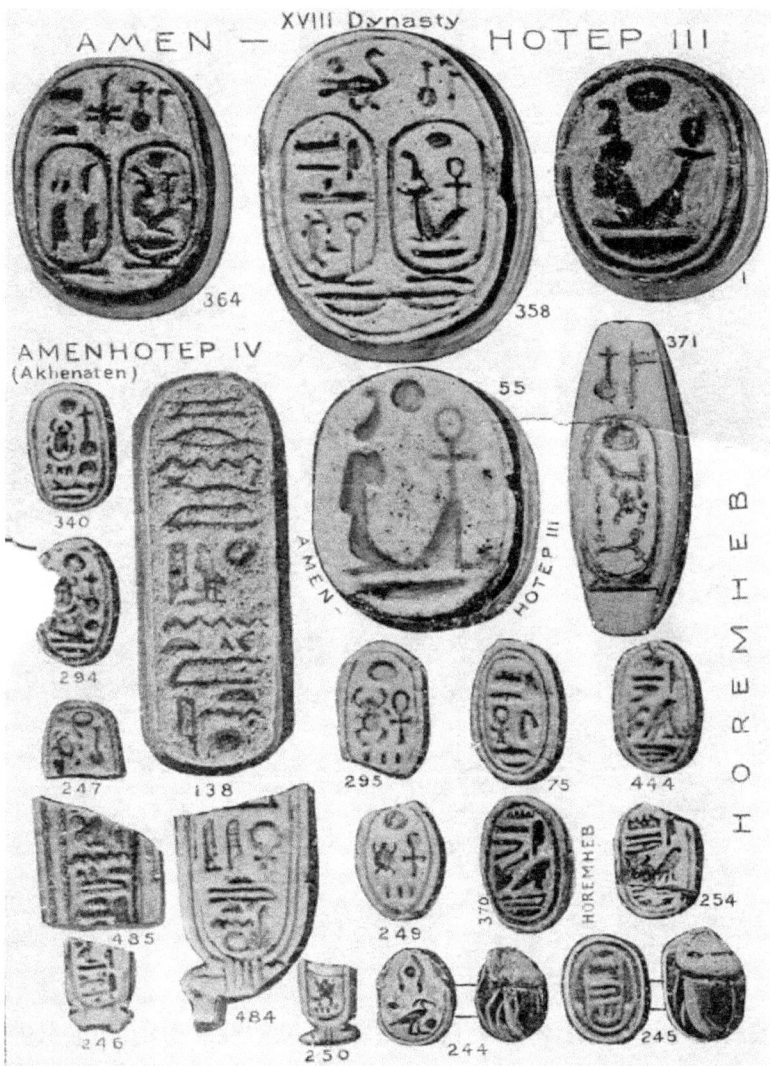

Dr. Ben's Illustration 82. Royal Scarabs of Amenhotep III, Amenhotep IV and Horemheb of the Late 18th Dynasty, New Kingdom.

FREDERICK MONDERSON

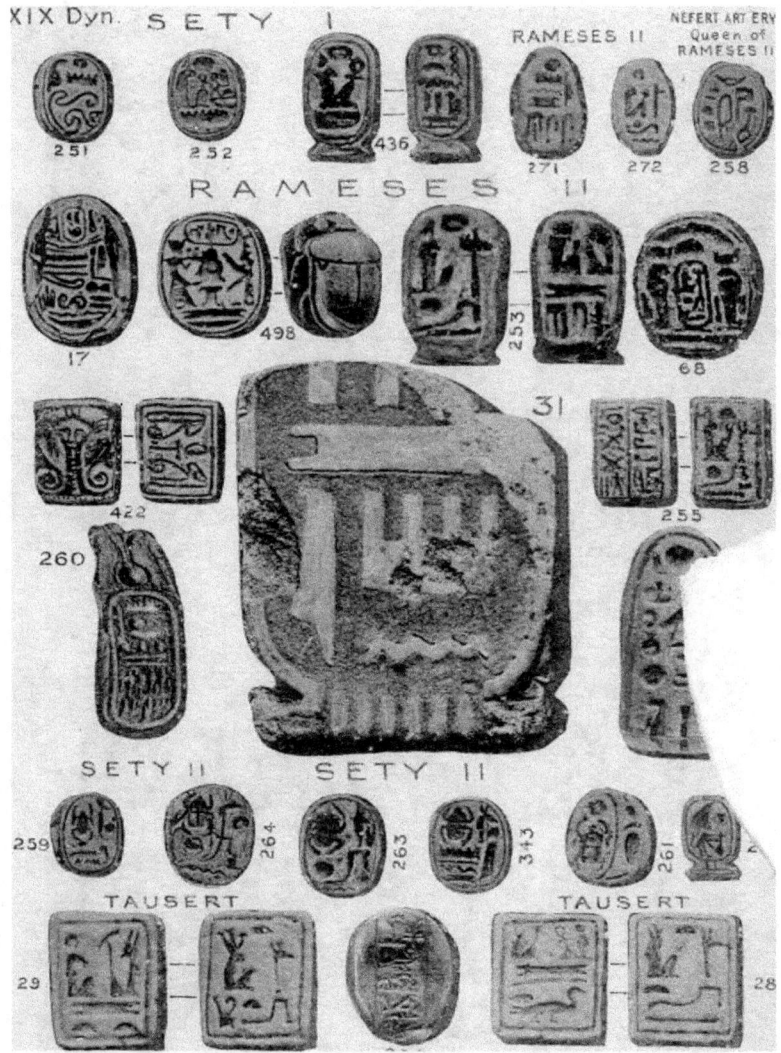

Dr. Ben's Illustration 83. Royal Scarabs of the 19th Dynasty, New Kingdom.

CELEBRATING
DR. BEN-JOCHANNAN

Dr. Ben's Illustration 84. Royal Scarabs of the Late Dynasties.

FREDERICK MONDERSON

Dr. Ben's Illustration 85. Good wishes, mottoes, etc.

f. **J.A. Rogers** in *Sex and Race* Vol. I (1967: 42), echoing sentiments similar to Dips contention that "The true Negro is nothing more than a cigar-store concoction," says

CELEBRATING DR. BEN-JOCHANNAN

essentially Herman Junker, who had written about "The First Appearance of the Negroes in History" *Journal of Egyptian Archaeology* (1921) was mistaken in looking for Negro traits in the graves of 5000 to 3600 B.C. "The Ethiopians, or Nubians, who were described by Herodotus, Diodorus Siculus, Ammianus and others as black and woolly-haired, were Hamites, he declares." Rogers continued: "It is no wonder he did not find any of that type, however, because the kind of Negro created by the right-wing ethnologists is a rarity. It is no more characteristic of the race than the ape-like creature of the bogs that was once used to represent the Irish was true of all Irishmen. Winwood Reade said, 'The typical Negro is a rare variety even among Negroes.' Frobinus says also, "Open an illustrated geography and compare The Type of the African Negro, the bluish-black fellow of the protuberant lips, the flattened nose, the stupid expression, and the short curly hair with the tall, bronze figures from Dark Africa with which we have of late become familiar, their almost fine-cut features, slightly arched nose, long hair .... In other respects, too, the genuine African of the interior bears no resemblance to the accepted Negro type."

Even further, Rogers mentions: "Livingstone said that the Negro face as he saw it reminded him more of that on the monuments of ancient Assyria than that of the popular white fancy." Sir Harry Johnston, foremost authority on the African Negro said: "The Hamite, that Negroid stock which was the main stock of the ancient Egyptians, is best represented at the present day by the Somali, Galla, and the blood of Abyssinia and Nubia. Sergi compares pictorially the features of Rameses with that of Mtesa, noted Negro king of Uganda, and shows the marked resemblance. Sir M.W. Flinders Petrie, famed Egyptologist, says that the Pharaohs of the X Dynasty were of the Galla type, and the Gallas are clearly what are known in our day as Negroes. He tells further of seeing one day on a train a man whose features were the exact living type of a statue of ancient Libya, and discovered that the man was an American mulatto."

Dr. Ben's Photo 253. Valley of the Kings, Luxor (Thebes). Sarcophagus of Thutmose IV.

Dr. Ben's Photo 254. Valley of the Kings, Luxor (Thebes). Gods arrayed on Thutmose IV's Sarcophagus.

CELEBRATING
DR. BEN-JOCHANNAN

Dr. Ben's Photo 255. Valley of the Kings, Luxor (Thebes). Nephthys on the sarcophagus of Thutmose IV.

FREDERICK MONDERSON

Dr. Ben's Photo 256. Valley of the Kings, Luxor (Thebes). Goddesses greeting Pharaoh Thutmose IV.

g.   Ivan Van Sertima in his "Race and Origins of the Egyptians" in *Egypt Revisited* has argued: "The African claim to Egyptian civilization rests upon a vast body of evidence. Some are cultural (ritual practices of the ancient Egyptian can be traced to the African – his totemism, circumcision, form of the divine kingship is distinct from that of the Asian); some are linguistic (Diop demonstrated convincingly at the **UNESCO** debate in 1974 that the Egyptians belonged beyond question to the family of African languages); some indicate a shared techno-complex (the forerunners of mummification and pyramid-building are found south of Egypt in pre-dynastic times). Most important, however, are the physical evidences. The Greeks saw the Egyptians and described the typical Egyptian circa 500 B.C. as dark-skinned with wooly hair. Studies in ancient Egyptian crania by Falkenburger tried to prove that only one-third of the Egyptians were of the classical Negroid type and that most of them were Euro-African or, to use the term invented by Sergi "the brown Mediterranean race" classification. Chatterjee and

CELEBRATING DR. BEN-JOCHANNAN

Kumar in a 1965 study ... analyzed crania from pre-dynastic Egypt and compared them with skulls of the Old Kingdom as well as the much later Middle Kingdom (12th and 13th dynasties) and found that all these skulls in respect to long head, broad face, low orbit and broad nasal aperture have the same characteristic features of the Negroid type."

VII. So Here We Are!

We must affirm, articulate, teach, preach and fight to defend Egypt as African and Negro or black. This is essentially what our intellectual ancestors, researchers, historians, lecturers, writers and activists, who, after their many years, sometimes more than thirty years of research have discovered, as being omitted and distorted regarding the history of the Ancient Egyptians.

VIII. Conclusions

As more evidence is unearthed and equally more Afrocentric scholarship unmasks untruths, distortions and omissions through vigorous analytic examination, the effort of African historiographic reconstruction will not only correct the historical record but also expose the prejudice and vindictiveness involved in earlier writers works. Some years ago, while a student at Oxford University this writer met a black Englishman who, in discussion, told me, "In any debate between a black Historian and a white Historian, the black will always win. All he has to do is to show what white men have been doing all around the world and with any sense of conscience the white man has to back-pedal." Hence, despite efforts to hold back the dawn, unmistakable truths are changing the minds of some while others prefer not to discuss such. They simply skirt around the issues, and with today's knowledge and vision, are ashamed that their mentors, teacher and predecessors had been wrong and prejudiced in reporting the history of black men and women who began humanity along the civilization pageantry of art, architecture, medicine, science, agriculture, astronomy, knowledge, period! It is reassuring to show that despite Breasted's venom, Black men and women have given and continue to give knowledge and enlightenment to all who seek the truth.

IX. References

Brooks, Lester. *Great Civilizations of Ancient Egypt*. New York: Four Winds Press, 1971.

Browder, Anthony. *Nile Valley Contributions to Civilization*. Washington, D.C.: The Institute of Karmic Guidance, 1992.

Clegg, Legrand H. II. "Black Rulers of the Golden Age" in *Nile Valley Civilizations* Edited by Ivan Van Sertima (1985) (1986: 39-68).

Diop, Cheikh Anta. *The African Origin of Civilization*: *Myth or Reality*. New York: Lawrence Hill and Company, (1967) 1974.

_____. "Origin of the Ancient Egyptians" in *Egypt Revisited*, (Edited by Ivan Van Sertima) New Brunswick, New Jersey: Transaction Publishers (1989: 9-37).

Du Bois, W.E.B. *The Negro*. New York: Oxford University Press, (1915) 1973.

_____. *The World and Africa*. New York: International Publishers, (1946) 1971.

Erman, Adolf. *Life in Ancient Egypt*. New York: Macmillan, 1894.

Finch, Charles S. "Black Roots of Egypt's Glory." *Great Black Leaders*: *Ancient and Modern*. Edited by Ivan Van Sertima. Transaction Books, (1988: 139-143).

Harris, J.E. *Pillars in Ethiopian History*. Washington, DC: Howard University Press, 1981.

CELEBRATING
DR. BEN-JOCHANNAN

Jackson, John G. *Introduction to African Civilizations*. Secaucus, New Jersey: Citadel Press, 1970.
Kush, Khamit Indus. *The Missing Pages of "His-Story."* Laurelton, New York: D and J Books, 1993.
Murray, Margaret A. *The Splendor That Was Egypt*. New York: Hawthorn Books, Inc., (1949) 1969.
Perry, W.J. *The Growth of Civilization*. Hammondsworth, England: Penguin Books, 1924.
Rawlinson, George. *The Story of the Nations*: *Egypt*. London: T. Fisher Unwin, 1893.
Rogers, J.A. *Sex and Race*. New York: Helga M. Rogers, 1967.
Van Sertima, Ivan. "Race and Origin of the Egyptians" in *Egypt Revisited*. Edited by Ivan Van Sertima. Transaction Publishers. New Brunswick, New Jersey, (1989: 3-8).
_____. "African Origin of the Ancient Egyptian Civilization" in *Egypt: Child of Africa*. Edited by Ivan Van Sertima. New Brunswick, New Jersey, (1994) 1995.
Woodson, Carter G. *The Mis-Education of the Negro*. Trenton, New Jersey: Africa World Press, (1990) 1993.

Dr. Ben's Photo 256a. Ramesseum, Mortuary Temple of Rameses II. Erik Monderson at the Temple's entrance with Osiride statues and other ruins in rear.

FREDERICK MONDERSON

32. The Conspiracy Against Ancient Egypt
By
Dr. Fred Monderson

I. INTRODUCTION

For centuries an argument has held that the ancient Egyptians and people along the Nile in the earliest antiquity were black and only the moderns with their racism have argued against, proffering a fabricated view. Herodotus and many other ancient writers described the "Colchians, Egyptians and Ethiopians" in the same terms, by today's standards, Black. Some critical scholars have argued that the displacement of "Black Egypt" occurred at the start of the 19th Century. The distinction or process of "removing blacks from Egypt and Egypt from Africa" was begun in the "Age of Hegel" and his contemporaries and continued by many European and American scholars of like mind for much of the 19th and 20th Centuries. This, however, was not the universal European or American view of Egypt. Nevertheless, along with this strategy, the geographical notions of "Middle East" and "Africa South of the Sahara" were created to reinforce the distancing of Egypt from Africa.

Consider, interest in Egypt and Egyptian antiquities had been creeping and began to mount following the discovery of the Rosetta Stone, during Napoleons sojourn in that country, at the end of the Eighteenth Century. This development was at the height of the Slave Trade in Africans to the Americas. Contemporary scholarship of that time went to great lengths to debunk ancient African accomplishments, while glorifying

CELEBRATING DR. BEN-JOCHANNAN

its descent into the inhumane conditions practiced in the institutions of Slave Trade and Slavery. Nonetheless, this "crime against humanity," while perpetrated by Christian Europe, prompted the *Philosopher* Baron de Montesquieu to declare: "It must either be affirmed that we are not Christians or that the Negroes are not men." This was indeed a risky proposition because a great deal of un-Christian behavior was practiced by white legal sanction used to legitimize an inhuman treatment of the African in the institution of New World Slavery! Notwithstanding, critical analysis of that contention and by extension in a comparative manner, if we apply Aristotle's syllogism, a logical tool of analysis, to the U.S. Declaration of Independence of 1776 which says: "We hold these truths to be self-evident that all men are created equal;" we find an inherent contradiction in this statement.

The syllogism has three parts consisting of a major premise, a minor premise and a logical conclusion. If the **Declaration of Independence**, which is today accepted as a true and living document from back then and has not changed, but affirmed all men are created equal while blacks were enslaved in America, then it inherently argued blacks were not men! Now, in that climate of thinking and reality supporting the status quo, it was difficult to credit blacks with being the creators of such a magnificent Egyptian civilization in antiquity. Of course, as early as 1798, the iconoclast Count Volney would not conform and wrote, in essence, the "people we enslave today because of their frizzled hair and sable skin, on the banks of the Nile invented the arts and sciences that govern the universe." Herein then is the contradiction! As a result, all manner of stratagems was resorted to, "to paint this Ethiopian white!" Pardon the pun, but I mean, "Egyptian."

FREDERICK MONDERSON

Dr. Ben's Book 19. A Chronology of the Bible: Challenge to the Standard Edition (1972, 1995).

In the process of historical distortion, the conspiracy against ancient Egypt has long employed a multi-pronged strategy including removal of precious artifacts from the African continent to the other continents, particularly Europe, the Americas and Australia, where principally Europeans live. Following the "naked" and then "enlightened imperialism," another form, "intellectual imperialism" was cloaked in colonialist diplomacy, archaeological excavation and hurried publication of findings, whose interpretations went practically unchallenged, even as well as efforts of preservation of monuments when more artifacts were removed. Brian Fagan has called this operation *The Rape of the Nile*! Coupled with this, destruction of valuable information by unwitting native

CELEBRATING
DR. BEN-JOCHANNAN

and foreign collaborators, and distortion of critical literary, pictographic and artifactual remains were standard practices for much of the Nineteenth Century and quite frankly for much of the Twentieth Century too. As things unfolded, credible critical, constructive commentary was obfuscated in the emerging reservoir of knowledge that began to reach a crescendo, while pandering to a developing Penny Press readership feeding an unquenchable hunger for ancient Egyptian news and artifacts. No one dared challenge the juggernaut of "Pied Pipers" who oftentimes misled others as well as their own people, whether through prejudice even out of sheer ignorance, notwithstanding their purported expertise!

Dr. Ben's Photo 257. Ramesseum, Mortuary Temple of Rameses II (Luxor). Colossal Osiride figures stand before the vestibule to the Hypostyle Hall with its Clerestory.

FREDERICK MONDERSON

Dr. Ben's Photo 258. Ramesseum, Mortuary Temple of Rameses II (Luxor). Front entrance to the Vestibule with the 4 Osiride figures and the Kings head from his colossal statue resting in the foreground.

Dr. Ben's Photo 259. Ramesseum, Mortuary Temple of Rameses II (Luxor). Another view of the structure's ruins from the Court.

Even more important, in the emergence of credible Black scholarship and other literary expressions, a systematic onslaught was made to eviscerate and distort their research

CELEBRATING DR. BEN-JOCHANNAN

findings. *Ipso facto*, Black scholars of note, even their White counterparts, who wrote "correctly" about ancient Egypt were dismissed, their work minutely and infinitesimally analyzed, criticized and ridiculed and marginalized for daring to connect ancient Egypt and Africa and Africans. The purpose and intent of such attacks are clear, because the Afrocentric pioneers in critical commentary attacked the hegemonic pillars of white supremacy and its intended or un-intended historical distortion through inaccuracy, purposely or otherwise bent on elevating Europe and Europeans and denigrating Africa and Africans.

For years fellow students, friends and colleagues have raised the specter of the noses in Egyptian statues that have been broken because they portray a close affinity to the likeness of Nubians and other Africans south of Egypt, in the "Negro mold." Nine out of ten of these noses were destroyed in this manner and this cannot have all been accidental. Without question, many ancient writers have commented on that likeness and Herodotus in particular has said in his work *The Histories*, Book II, *Euterpe*, that the "Egyptians, Colchians and Ethiopians have thick lips, broad noses and are burnt of skin," meaning Black. This was a visual observation on the part of the "Father of history," who was also dubbed one of the earliest anthropologists in history, based on his human, floral and faunal descriptions that are attributed great credibility. This observation, however, came at the "end of Egyptian history." Nonetheless, he was among the people, and wrote about what he heard and saw. As such then, the following quotation is of particular interest for two reasons that will become readily apparent.

John David Wortham in *The Genesis of British Egyptology:1549-1906* University of Oklahoma Press at Norman, (1971: 93) has boldly asserted: "Great progress was made during the nineteenth century in the study of Egyptian mummification. Augustus Bozzi Granville, a physician and a student of Coptic, undertook the earliest nineteenth-century dissection of a mummy at his London home in 1825. From his detailed dissection he correctly concluded that the ancient Egyptians were Caucasians. He also succeeded in clearing up many erroneous ideas about the embalming process. Among the things, he proved the correctness of Herodotus assertion that the ancient Egyptians had, when preparing a cadaver for burial, extracted the pituitary through the nostrils."

The first part is particularly erroneous because in 1992 David O'Connor of the Philadelphia Museum told this writer: "The Egyptians were not white!" Therefore, they were not Caucasian! This is clearly a distortion of the history. Even more important, Wortham asserts that Herodotus was correct in his views about mummification. This was obviously told to him! Naturally, he probably never saw mummification in progress. However, he did observe the people among whom he walked and talked. Yet Wortham refuses to uphold Herodotus eyewitness account that the "Egyptians, Colchians and Ethiopians have thick lips, broad noses and are burnt of skin" meaning black. This, then, is what we call scholarship of convenience. And so, the misrepresentation has continued.

By 1825, just three years after Champollion's decipherment of Hieroglyphics the science had barely evolved, there are questions about the authenticity of the mummy dissected, the conditions under which the study was done and the lack of critical review of the process, challenges the rock-solid founding of "Caucasian Egyptian." That Granville was a student of Coptic is of no consequence for so was Champollion.

The question of omission as well as distortion has also been significant to the controversy surrounding ancient Egypt and, interestingly enough, the whole question is still taboo today.

CELEBRATING DR. BEN-JOCHANNAN

Many have argued the critical nature of the problem and perhaps within another century, Egypt and Egyptian studies will be all white! However, through African scholars, in trail of Diop, et al., and together with the modicum of whites who care, this fight for truth and African historiography reconstruction is far from over!

In a critical retort, the current writer has insisted that all people, black and white, go beyond the nose and be more knowledgeable about the archaeology, anthropology, history, anthropometry, geography, language, biometrics, and use of diagrams, etc. This then raises the stakes in the discussion. Equally, in the disciplines of art and architecture, religion of ancient Egypt, their theosophy, metaphysics and their impact on science, navigation, medicine, and mathematics as well as literature and linguistics, the view from the air or archeoastronomy, all can provide the potent armaments in the battle for ownership of ancient Egypt as research continuously unfolds regarding these ancient Africans.

Dr. Ben's Photo 259a. Ramesseum, Mortuary Temple of Rameses II (Luxor). Erik Monderson sits in the shade with a young Egyptian companion.

Dr. Ben's Photo 260. Ramesseum, Mortuary Temple of Rameses II (Luxor). Close-up of the colossal columns with their closed capitals.

Dr. Ben's Photo 261. Ramesseum, Mortuary Temple of Rameses II (Luxor). Columns and Osiride figures.

CELEBRATING DR. BEN-JOCHANNAN

Dr. Ben's Photo 262. Ramesseum, Mortuary Temple of Rameses II (Luxor). Colossal head of Rameses seated statue.

II. THE NOSE JOB

Recently this writer visited the Metropolitan Museum of Art to observe the Egyptian collection and was impressed by the wonderful display the museum houses. On the other hand, the question of "Nose" caught my attention because several statues seemed to have had their noses broken. Strange it seemed that these statues were made of the hardest, most durable stones and yet the noses were broken. I remember years ago as a student, my professor often said that the "noses were broken because in ancient Egypt in the mummification ceremony the brain was removed through the nostrils." Importantly, one has a tendency to believe one's professors, without realizing either the professor was schooled in another discipline or was ignorant of the facts, though he was teaching the subject. This can happen! Of course, one expects the mummy's nose to be broken but not a statue detached from the mummification process. The statues were made before the corpses demise. Imagine, upon the death of an individual of note, traversing the entire nation, finding every statue made in honor of that individual and breaking its nose, even painting it black! Naturally, one had to do this for every painting and raised and sunk relief portrayal, otherwise the argument easily collapses because the intent is not complete. It seems very probable only statues found were destroyed. Those yet to be discovered and those discovered in an aura of fanfare are not destroyed!

If we argue the exception proves the rule, here's an example of a "nose job." Rosalie David, in *Discovering Ancient Egypt* (New York: Facts on File, 1993, pp. 182-83) presents two photographs of heads whose noses are pointed, but not affected in any manner. The caption to the first reads" "A plaster head from the cemetery at Mallawi (Near Beni Suef), the location of a Roman garrison. The head, originally placed over a mummy, dates to the Roman Period (2nd century AD). Such representations seem to have been in use here for only about eighty years." The second photographs caption reads as follows: "This plaster head of a woman from the cemetery at Mallawi (2nd century AD) depicts the contemporary hairstyle and jewelry of that period, when tomb robbery had led to the custom of representing jewelry on the mask instead of placing it in the tomb." Now, let us again compare another photograph between pages 160 and 161 that reads: "A colossal figure of Nefertari, favorite queen of Rameses II, as the Goddess Hathor. This decorates the façade of her rock-cut temple at Abu Simbel. With the Great Temple, this was rescued by the **UNESCO** salvage campaign." This statue is pretty much preserved but the nose and mouth is disfigured! As I said, one has to wonder if plaster could remain intact over millennia but

CELEBRATING
DR. BEN-JOCHANNAN

granite could be broken and this sets one to thinking, "Is there a conspiracy against Ancient Egypt?"

Case in point. In all probability, nearly all the statues in the Cairo Museum have their noses intact and perhaps only those statues in European and American public display museums have statues with broken noses. The statues discovered in the "Cachette Court" between 1903-04, were placed there by the ancients; who, rightly should have, but probably, did not break noses! In the fanfare of the discovery with every one present, it would have looked suspicious if noses were broken all of a sudden. These statues were delivered to the Cairo Museum as the ancients had placed them! Even further, a good example is made of the "double statue of Neferhotep found in the northern part of the *Wadjyt* under the obelisk of Hatshepsut." This statue is displayed in a photograph at Karnak Temple in the position of how the ancients had placed it. The nose is intact. Therefore, if the argument for the broken nose is upheld, then this statue, *in situ*, should have had its nose broken. This exception does prove the rule and it should also contradict Wortham's one mummy contention in addition to the arguments against his "flawed experiment in 1825!" The mummy of Rameses I in the Luxor Museum has its nose intact.

Dr. Ben's Photo 263. Ramesseum, Mortuary Temple of Rameses II (Luxor). Remains of the statue's left and right foot.

FREDERICK MONDERSON

Dr. Ben's Photo 265. **Ramesseum, Mortuary Temple of Rameses II (Luxor)**. The classic open umbel capitals of the Processional Colonnade.

Dr. Ben's Photo 266. Ramesseum, Mortuary Temple of Rameses II (Luxor). Processional Colonnade and the Processional Way generate great memories.

CELEBRATING DR. BEN-JOCHANNAN

Dr. Ben's Photo 267. Ramesseum, Mortuary Temple of Rameses II (Luxor). Native Temple guide stands before remains of broken columns just above his head.

Dr. Ben's Illustration 86. Karnak. Restoration of the Temple of Amenhotep II on the North/South Axis (left); and, Meydum. Objects – Taurt Amulets, Toilet Articles, Syrian Vases, of the XVIIIth Dynasty.

Consider also only the best pieces were chosen as "gifts" to foreign museums by individuals conducting excavations. It is reasonable to assume, statues of important Egyptians/Kamites

FREDERICK MONDERSON

with "questionable noses" would have been "doctored" before being placed in their cases to justify the professors false or incorrect statement!

In the Metropolitan Museum, I noticed that the noses of statues of earliest Egyptian history, made of granite, one of the hardest of stones, were generally broken in most museum displays, here and elsewhere. In contrast, the noses of sunk and raised reliefs on "Talatat stones" in the Open-Air Museum at Karnak Temple and elsewhere tell a different story. In this regard, Cheikh Anta Diop makes an interesting point in his *African Origins of Civilization*: *Myth or Reality*. He has argued, while statues in museums could be "doctored," the Sphinx, in full view, could not be tampered with as it demonstrates the image of an African, Negro, persona. The best case seems to be that Napoleon's soldiers disfigured the face with canon fire.

Dr. Ben's Illustration 87. The two "Eyes of Horus" on the side of a wooden Coffin.

CELEBRATING DR. BEN-JOCHANNAN

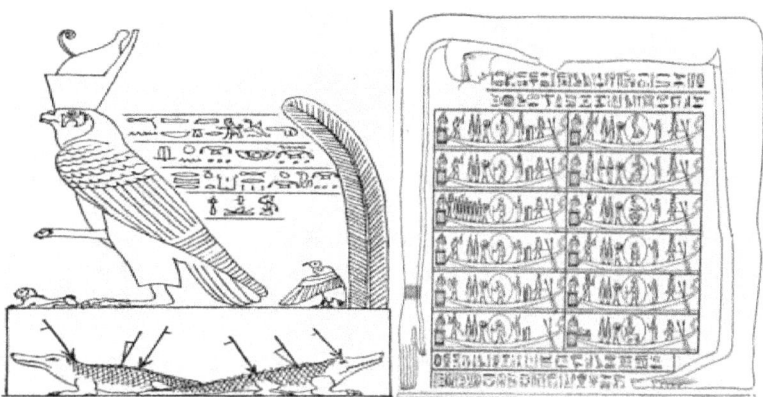

Dr. Ben's Illustration 88. Horus in Double Crown vanquishing Champse (left); and, Dendera. The Goddess Nuit spanning the skies during the 12-hours of the Day, with the divinities of those hours.

To develop our argument further, Gay Robbins, in *The Art of Ancient Egypt* (1997: 24) points out there were two types of stone materials used by Egyptian sculptors. Soft stone consisted of limestone, calcite, sandstone, schist, greywacke and hard stone consisted of quartzite, diorite, granodiorite, granite and basalt. In this, she says: "Stone was the major building material for free-standing and rock-cut temples and

Dr. Ben's Photo 267a. Ramesseum, Mortuary Temple of Rameses II (Luxor). Grated steps past the Osiris figures in vestibule into the ruins of the Hypostyle Hall.

FREDERICK MONDERSON

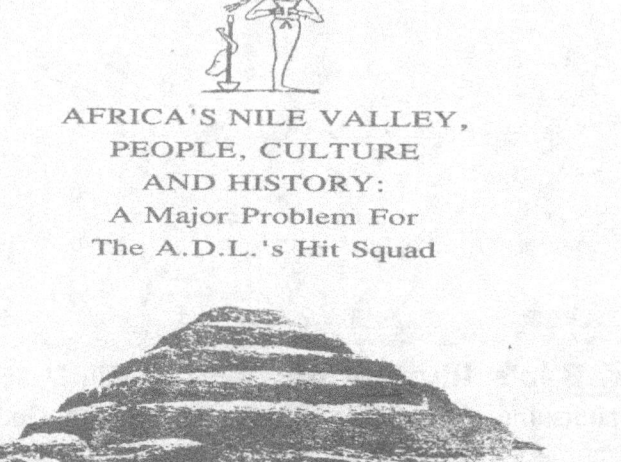

Dr. Ben's Book 20. Africa's Nile Valley: People, Culture and History: A Major Problem for the A.D.L's Hit Squad (1994).

tombs. It was also used to make statues, stelae, offering tables, libation bowls, vessels and other ritual equipment." Even further, Robbins (1997: 24) continued: "Soft stones were usually covered with a thin layer of plaster and painted. Although paint was sometimes applied to harder stones, it would seem that much of the stone was left visible, and that the color of the stone was often chosen for its symbolism. Black stones like granodiorite referred to the life-giving black silt brought by the Nile inundation. Thus, they symbolized new life, resurrection and the resurrected God of the dead, Osiris, who is often shown with black skin. A range of colors

CELEBRATING DR. BEN-JOCHANNAN

– red, brown, yellow, gold – was associated with the sun, so that stones of these colors, such as red and brown quartzite and red granite, carried a solar symbolism. Green stones referred to fresh, growing vegetation, new life, resurrection and Osiris, who can also appear with green skin."

Since the Egyptian religion was essentially solar-based, can their use of red, "associated with the sun," be the reason they painted themselves, generally, red to be identified with this solar phenomenon? Perhaps, and this raises a whole lot of other serious questions.

Nevertheless, as I observed the displays at the Met, I realized that statues or busts or faces of the Graeco-Roman period with rather aquiline noses were intact. What raised a "red flag" is that busts of many of these statues were oftentimes made of plaster, perhaps *Paper Mache*, and were probably so well-preserved because they portrayed European images. On the other hand, Egyptian statues of hard stone that portrayed African images were broken. Imagine plaster thousands of years old being more durable than the hardest stone! If these two mediums were exposed to the elements, then plaster would dissipate in a relatively short time whereas stone would remain, seemingly forever. This got me to thinking! The stone head of Rameses IIs colossal seated statue at the Ramesseum or even the seated one at Luxor's entrance, lying open in the elements for thousands of years have not changed, yet so many concealed stones have been broken or destroyed in some form or fashion!

On the way to the Cafeteria at the Met, I passed through the Medieval European period and noticed statues with the most aquiline noses imaginable, really thin and long, all were well-preserved in these displays. Time did not permit a determination of the nature of the material used. One thing

FREDERICK MONDERSON

seemed certain, the most durable and indurable materials portraying European noses seems to outlast the most durable materials portraying African noses, and one has to wonder whether there was and still is a conspiracy regarding ancient Egypt. That is because, since the argument for the breakage is not credible, when subjected to close scrutiny the argument falls apart. However, there is no question the noses of the most ancient Egyptians differed from those surviving of the Graeco-Roman period and certainly than those of the European Medieval Period when they were very aquiline.

Equally, the noses of many mummies, particularly those of the Kings are not broken in anyway which begs the question of why break the nose of a statue and not the mummy? It seems for the most part, the nose breaking phenomenon was primarily a modern phenomenon. That is, since these pieces comprise museum and other public displays, they are generally "Doctored" to suit a projected view!

Dr. Ben's Photo 268. Luxor. From a balloon, ariel view of sentinels "Hama and Chama" of Amenhotep III that stood before his Mortuary Temple, destroyed in an earthquake.

CELEBRATING DR. BEN-JOCHANNAN

Dr. Ben's Photo 269. Luxor. On-Ground, close-up of the sentinels of Amenhotep III that stood before his Mortuary temple, destroyed in an earthquake.

Dr. Ben's Photo 270. Medinet Habu, Mortuary Temple of Rameses III (Luxor). The Temple as viewed from the air in a balloon.

FREDERICK MONDERSON

III.   THE HAIR

Hair is an interesting topic in ancient Egypt. Yet, it's hardly dealt with in the multitude of books on this subject.

As early as 1905 Randall-McIver commented on the strongly curled hair he found in his study of the cemeteries of El Amrah, an Upper Egyptian pre-dynastic site. We must remember Count Volney's description. It is interesting that not much has been said about hair in Dynastic and Predynastic graves. In the Cairo Museum of Egyptian Antiquities there is a case on the second floor displaying Egyptian wigs. This is a one-of-a-kind exhibit; because to my recollection there are no other displays housing wigs, "Afro-Wigs." In view of the "destruction of Egyptian monuments" this "find" was discovered in the 1881 "Deir el Bahari cache" amidst great fanfare and, as such, was preserved.

Let me add, recently Zahi Hawass has called for a re-evaluation of the identities of all the mummies based on the fact "King Tut was the only king found resting in his unopened tomb." Such a call, however, does not disprove who the other pharaohs are said to be, it is simply an effort to be absolutely clear who they actually are based on the "Tutankhamon yardstick."   Since, Queen Hatshepsut's mummy has been identified through a broken tooth!

Now, all kinds of conflicting deductions have been made regarding the ethnicity and function of the two replica statues placed before Tuts burial chamber. In as much as these statues were placed in this location it may very well be a burial practice to place such figures of the occupant with their respective function in this location. Using Hawass "Tutankhamon yardstick," every other pharaoh may have had such figures as part of the funerary ritual. Being of wood, their tombs not discovered sealed, whether through nature or

CELEBRATING
DR. BEN-JOCHANNAN

malicious intent, these figures could have been destroyed or rotted, in ancient or modern times, because they show the true color of the ancient Egyptians. Let us not forget **UNESCO's** 1974 Conference underscored the **fundamental blackness of ancient Egypt!**

In fact, according to "IMPORTANT ARCHAEOLOGICAL DISCOVERIES IN EGYPT" published in the London *Times* Thursday, August 4, 1881, from Cairo July 24, 1881, regarding the great Deir el Bahari discoveries of New Kingdom monarchs of the above year: "Fifteen enormous wigs for ceremonial occasions form a striking feature of the Deir-el-Bahari collection. These wigs are nearly 2 ft. high, and are composed of frizzled and curled hair. There are many marked points of resemblance between the legal institutions of ancient Egypt and of England. For instance, pleadings must be Traversed, confessed and avoided or demurred to. Marriage settlements and the doctrines of uses and trusts prevailed in ancient Egypt, but the wearing of these wigs was not extended to the members of the legal profession, but was reserved exclusively for the princess of the blood and ladies of very high rank." Yet, they have not shown us any of these brothers, I mean pharaohs, wearing these big Afros! This is because this is the type of hair these royals sported.

Importantly, such a significant find is encapsulated in a simple description. Similarly, as in the case of Wortham above, it was a single sentence before he moved on.

Pardon this digression. In the case of the single study done by Granville in 1825, a number of factors can be considered.

FREDERICK MONDERSON

1. This early in the 19th Century, studies of this type could have been considered "primitive" and not generally done in a scientific setting.

2. The mummy he dissected was probably not of royal lineage. The study was done 3 years after Champollion's decipherment of Hieroglyphics and so the discipline of Egyptology was very young.

Dr. Ben's Photo 271. Medinet Habu, Mortuary Temple of Rameses III (Luxor). Side view of the Temple's "Migdol" entrance.

Dr. Ben's Photo 271a. Medinet Habu, Mortuary Temple of Rameses III (Luxor). Entrance to Hatshep and Thutmose's 18th Dynasty temple.

CELEBRATING DR. BEN-JOCHANNAN

Dr. Ben's Photo 271ah. Medinet Habu, Mortuary Temple of Rameses III (Luxor). Dromos to the Temple's proper entrance with the King smiting enemies before Amen-Ra on the left side of the Pylon and again smiting enemies before Ra-Horakhty on the right side.

3. According to Diop's *The African Origins of Civilization: Myth or Reality*, Champollion's letters to his brother based on his pristine and unprejudiced observations, clearly indicated the Egyptians were African and Black, not Caucasian.

4. Wortham goes from the specific to the general, a sort of "one sparrow, so its summer" supposition.

5. There was probably hardly any "credible criticism" of the study at the time it was done.

FREDERICK MONDERSON

Equally, a similar argument is made for the Old Kingdom seated scribe now in front and center in the Louvre Museum, Paris. This individual is shown with blue eyes; therefore, the argument is made, "See, the Egyptians had blue eyes." Such an argument also goes from the specific to the general. It utilizes deductive as opposed to inductive reasoning. We do know, in many instances, the Egyptians inlaid eyes, with whatever material, depending on the situation. The question never delves into very much, such as Are the eyes of the Louvre Scribe inlaid? Is this statue a fabrication? and so on! That's all part of the omission and distortion syndrome in the conspiracy against ancient Egypt.

Dr. Ben's Photo 272. Medinet Habu, Mortuary Temple of Rameses III (Luxor). Looking past the security individual into the First and Second Courts and into the deep recesses of the Temple.

CELEBRATING DR. BEN-JOCHANNAN

Dr. Ben's Photo 273. Medinet Habu, Mortuary Temple of Rameses III (Luxor). Goddess Sekhmet guards the entrance portal.

Nonetheless, many of the images of the Old Kingdom and later, show people who seem to be wearing "black hair" as opposed to the long flowing type. Case in point. The Nubian lady wearing "Black hair" and coming out of the cow's head in the "Ascent of the Princes" of Rameses II's sons on the south wall of the "Ramessean Front" it seems she wears this type of hair. Nevertheless, when this latter is shown, it seems to be in the form of a wig that is basically a covering of the head. All evidence seems to show, in ancient times, from noble to fellahin all wearing "wigs" of "black hair." The question is, since we are told "Nefertiti was purportedly Syrian" and so white, should she wear a "black" or "white hair" wig?

Notwithstanding, in a final commentary, we turn to H.K.S. Bakry's *A Brief Study of Mummies and Mummification* (Cairo, 1965) where he provides insights on the hair of some New Kingdom pharaohs whose mummies were recovered in the two 19th Century "Caches" discovered at Thebes.

He begins (1965: 21) with Ahmose (Amosis I) of the 18th Dynasty, who reigned c. 1575-1550 B.C. "His body is covered with black resinous material and his hair is rather long, dark brown and curly." Then (1965: 23-24) he gives Thutmose II, also of the 18th Dynasty (1510-1490 B.C.) and states: "The crown of the head is bald, but there is curly hair on the temples, nearly five inches long and dark brown." For Amenhotep II, son of Thutmose III, (1436-1413 B.C.) he states: "His hair is brown and curly like that of his son and successor, Thutmose IV, but Amenhotep has a lot of grey hair on his head." For Thutmose IV (1413-1405 B.C.) he states: "The hair is curly, dark brown and about six and a half inches in length." An issue of note, the black resinous material is a preservative. This has nothing to do with a statue being painted black for the funerary ceremony. We must remember, the deceased hoped to exist into eternity as himself not as someone "painted" differently and be other than himself!

One thing is remarkable and often not commented on. The New Kingdom Pharaohs height varied from five feet to five and a half feet, not generally taller. Thutmose III was 5 feet 1

CELEBRATING
DR. BEN-JOCHANNAN

inch tall! This shows that height is not a principal hallmark of greatness.

Dr. Ben's Illustration 89. Karnak. Discovery of the Statues of Amenhotep IV (Akhenaten).

Dr. Ben's Illustration 90. Karnak. Discovery of the Statues of Amenhotep IV (Akhenaten). Heads of the Statues of Amenhotep IV (Akhenaten).

FREDERICK MONDERSON

Added for further clarification, the following is a 1961 **Publisher's Note** that is appended to Hope (1962: xxi) who wrote nearly two centuries ago about ancient Egyptian costumes: "The ancient Egyptians were descended from the Ethiopians, and while their blood remained free from any mixture with that of European or Asiatic nations, their race seems to have retained obvious traces of the aboriginal Negro form and features. Not only all the human figures in their colored hieroglyphics display a deep swarthy complexion, but every Egyptian monument whether statue or bas-relief presents the splay feet, the spreading toes, the bow-bent shins, the high meager calves, the long swinging arms, the sharp shoulders, the square flat hands, the head, when seen in profile, placed not vertically but obliquely on the spine, the jaws and chin consequently very prominent, together with the skinny lips, depressed nose, high cheek bones, large un-hemmed ears raised far above the level of the nostrils, and all the other peculiarities characteristic of the Negro conformation. It is true that the practice prevalent among the Egyptians of shaving their heads and beards close to the skin (which they only deviated from when in mourning) seldom allows their statues to show that most undeniable symptom of Negro extraction, the woolly hair; the heads of their figures generally appearing covered with some sort of cap, or, when bare, closely shaven. In the few Egyptian sculptured personages, however, in which the hair is introduced, it uniformly offers the woolly texture, and the short crisp curls of that of the Negroes; nor do I know a single specimen of genuine Egyptian workmanship, in which are seen any indications of the long sleek hair or loose wavy ringlets of Europeans or Asiatics. The black streak, which, in the masks or faces carved and painted on the cases of the mummies, is carried from the outside corner of the eye-lids to the temple, seems to denote that anciently, as to this day, the natives of Egypt were in the habit of artificially deepening the hue and

CELEBRATING DR. BEN-JOCHANNAN

increasing the length of their eye lashes, by means of some species of pigment."

If one writer could observe such characteristics, why can't others see the same features? Of all the scientific studies done on the mummies, with all the measurements taken, none have come close to such a description or finding. Does it mean such studies - physical, craniometrical, biological, are for the most part, flawed?

Dr. Ben's Photo 274. Medinet Habu, Mortuary Temple of Rameses III (Luxor). Eight squat decorated columns of the First Court.

FREDERICK MONDERSON

Dr. Ben's Photo 275. Medinet Habu, Mortuary Temple of Rameses III (Luxor). The Gods introduce Rameses III in "Blue or War Crown" to Amen-Ra.

Dr. Ben's Photo 276. Medinet Habu, Mortuary Temple of Rameses III (Luxor). The King's cartouche buried so deep, no one would dare to expropriate or disturb it.

CELEBRATING
DR. BEN-JOCHANNAN

Dr. Ben's Photo 277. Medinet Habu, Mortuary Temple of Rameses III (Luxor). *User-Ma'at-Ra* cartouche of the King who had a habit of making his mark so deep it was futile for others to reuse them.

The name User-Ma'at Ra belonged to Rameses II and a standard Egyptian practice was to choose the name of a revered ancestor and for Rameses III, Rameses II was considered his "spiritual father," though Setnakht was his physical father. Another problem not given much attention is, why paint only wood and not stone, generally if "Black" is associated with funerary practices for Afterlife existence.

IV.   THE STATUES – STONE VERSUS WOOD

a. Stone – This medium was exploited from the earliest times in depicting the Gods, pharaohs and sometimes nobles. All manner of stone, soft as well as hard, was used for sculpture. It is understandable that there would be some

FREDERICK MONDERSON

losses in recovered material but when all of the hardest stone on display in Western and American settings seem to have this problem, one has to wonder about the intent! We must also remember as Gay Robbins pointed out above, stone statues are not painted; the color of the stone is the representative color of the statue. However, wood is painted. It seems the artists went to great lengths to show the people by painting wood to convey an unmistaken message!

As a freshman student in college, we were told the *Ad hominem* argument that is generally fleeting, and upon closer inspection it begins to fall apart, a straw man. For example, one must consider the context of the color of stone or material used in representing the individual depicted. In the late 1970s around the bicentennial celebrations of American independence, the Tutankhamon exhibit toured the United States. Naturally, choice pieces comprised the collection. Significantly, the symbol representative of the boy king was not the famed gold mask, which seems to be on the cover of more books on Egypt and the ancient world than any other single representation. The symbol representing the Tutankhamon exhibit in the United States for that historic tour was the alabaster bust of the young king. Thus, are we to believe, purported while for being alive while painted black for the funerary ceremony? Equally, are non-Egyptians white but Egyptians red? The only white I saw in my many years, of course, excluding the mannequins in the Cairo Airport bazaars, woman in the tomb of Rameses VI in the Valley of the Kings and she certainly did not look Egyptian.

Now, try to remember Danny Kaye's famous children's song, "The Kings New Clothes." In all the hoopla during the parade, people waving, drums drumming, intellectuals, all commenting on how well the suit fitted the king. It stands to reason, perhaps, some of those fat bureaucrats standing and

CELEBRATING DR. BEN-JOCHANNAN

cheering as the king went by probably said to their associates or persons nearby, "the suit looks so good, I must have one!" Fortunately, it was a youngster who saw through the farcical facade that the king was naked!

Now, fast forward to the parade and again all the farcical hoopla and here comes the symbol, that little Black boy is jolted because, not knowing that alabaster is a white material, he opines, the king is white! Shame is cast on American organizers who perpetuated the myth of a white King Tut on the little Black boy, and on so many other little Black boys and girls. This applies even to White boys and girls, scattered across the globe, who never did, or probably would never, see the life-like statue of the boy-king, but would hear of his name, King Tut. They would never know that Tutankhamon had himself represented as similarly a little Black boy. That is the nature of what this essay is all about, **"The Conspiracy Against Ancient Egypt!"**

In the Cairo Museum, the same two life-like black statues of Tutankhamon, with left foot forward in a moving, living position and dressed in kingly paraphernalia; though at the entrance of the gallery housing his treasures, are never really seen and some probably don't care, as visitors rush into the hall to view the gold and other wealth of his funerary furniture.

Just to the right of these statues on a wall are two plaques made of bronze. One shows the young King Tutankhamon colored bronze slaying an enemy and the other, the King in the same material as a sphinx crushing his Nubian enemies who are painted black like the statue. If the Nubians are represented as they are, black; then the King is represented as bronze but he is actually and nonetheless Black. Get the point! Let us not forget, contrary to popular misguided "spin" that the statue was painted black for the funerary ceremony, the king represented himself as he wanted to be seen in the next world and the life-like statues guarding his dead body are exact replicas of himself, dressed in kingly attire. Let us not forget, Zahi Hawass clarified that Tutankhamon is the only king whose identity is certain because his tomb was found intact and the statues are just that. In all probability, similarly painted statues may have been similarly situated before other pharaohs burial chambers and been the victims of the destroyer's hands.

Dr. Ben's Illustration 91. Karnak Temple. From atop the north roof of the Entrance Pylon, a Panoramic view of the Great Court's Taharka Column, the Southern Colonnade and its Sphinxes and entrance to Rameses III's Temple on the North-South Axis, with the Eighth and Ninth Pylons in the rear, further on.

b. Wood – While statues seem to be made from a wide variety of colorful stone material that give no indication regarding the ethnicity of the people represented, it is a whole lot different with wooden statues. First and foremost, because of its nature not too many wooden statues have been recovered

CELEBRATING
DR. BEN-JOCHANNAN

in their entirety showing facial and other features. A valid argument has been made; wooden statues have been "doctored in basements" of western museums. This treatment is not reserved exclusively for wooden statues but also for any artifact that gives credence to the blackness of Egypt, or essentially in the "Negro mold." And, most important, no evidence of "White Egyptians" have been found to deny this fact! It goes without saying that those images that have survived of Black Egyptians, Kings Tutankhamon and Mentuhotep II, Queen Aahmes Nefertari, Thutmose I, etc., "could not be destroyed" because of their prominence or possibly fanfare at the time surrounding their discovery. Despite this, in face of their images, their blackness is still denied through all forms of presented ridiculous arguments. In view of this, one has to give some credence to the notion of a conspiracy against ancient Egypt.

Dr. Ben's Papyrus 11. The Sphinx and the "Three Great Pyramids" on the Ghizeh Plateau.

The Cairo Museum has a room on the second floor housing displays of small wooden statues painted black. Some are

FREDERICK MONDERSON

pharaohs and some are of animals. One particular statue of interest is the black-panther, beside an Amenhotep also painted black. These understandably are "survivors." However, if the panther is painted black to represent its color, then it's a powerful given that the pharaoh represented juxtaposed and similarly painted, is also Black. There are also a great many Osiris statues of wood and painted black in this room. Many of these are housed high above the cases near the ceiling or in some obscure place, and thus, out of sight of the most casual visitor. If we look at all the wooden statues of people or animals, they are either painted or not. The greatest majority of those painted are either in the traditional red or black. If, therefore, any panther, goose, bird or Nubian is painted black and that portrays such, why then would any Egyptian God, king or regular person painted black, not be such.

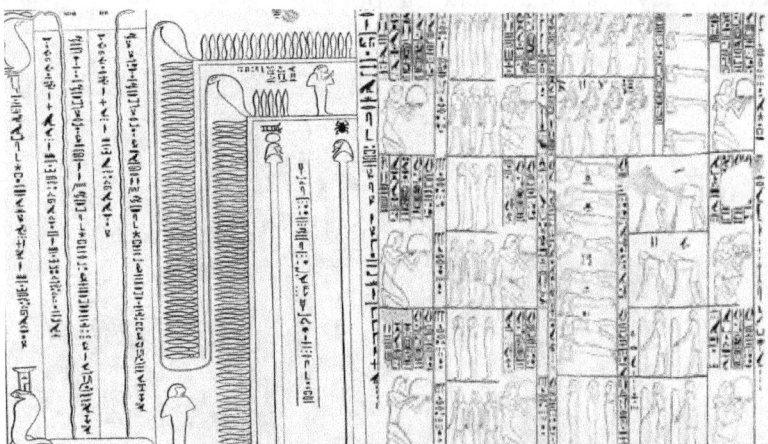

Dr. Ben's Illustration 92. Abydos. Osireion. North Passage, West Wall (left); and, Abydos. Osireion. North Passage, West Wall in Margaret A. Murray's *The Osireion at Abydos* (1904).

CELEBRATING
DR. BEN-JOCHANNAN

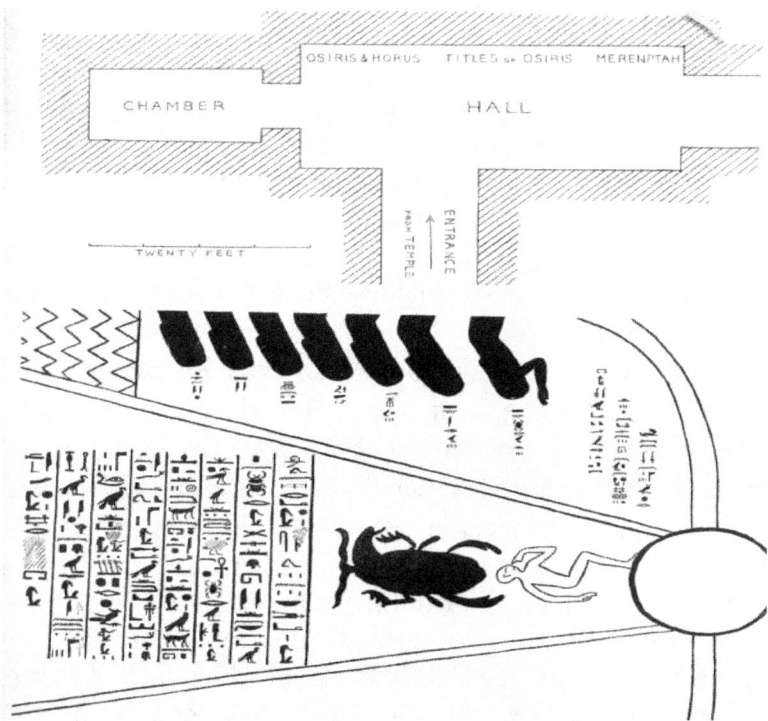

Dr. Ben's Illustration 93. Margaret A. Murray's *The Osireion at Abydos* (1904) Abydos. Osireion. Plan, North Passage. East Wall.

On October 7, 2010 this writer entered the Hall of Tutankhamon on the second floor of the Egyptian Museum as a local guide was addressing a group of visitors. He began by describing the differences between the two statues in that one wore the white crown and the other a cloth headdress. Both headdresses were signs this was indeed a royal depiction. Two things caught the passing observer. First, he said, "The black skin does not mean the king was Nubian." Second, that the statues were guards placed before the Kings burial chamber. Can one imagine, paint a guard black, then dress him in royal attire. Can one also imagine, just before he dies, the king asks his people, "Paint me a different color so I can exist into eternity as a "fake Negro!" How interesting that the statues painted black does not represent the color of the king, yet, nearby on a wall plaque the king is depicted bronze attacking Nubians painted black. Are we to believe black is the color of the Nubians but bronze is the color of the king? Why would statues of the king painted black be considered mere guards yet be wearing crowns of the Upper and Lower Kingdoms?

In another instance, a young Egyptian female guide in the Cairo Museum once told this writer in September 2005, the Pharaoh Mentuhotep II, whose **Heb Sed Festival** statue was found in his temple at Deir el Bahari and painted black, was so "painted for the funeral ceremony." Let's be clear, the **Heb Sed Festival** is about rejuvenation and has nothing to do with the funeral ceremony. When I questioned her about this, she told me her teacher at the American University in Cairo taught her such! Two things are readily apparent here. First, Professors at the American University in Cairo seem to be teaching the strange history of Egypt which their students, acting as guides, are propagating on unsuspecting visitors in their tours. This augurs well with gullible and ill-educated European visitors to the Cairo Museum who choose to see themselves represented in the culture of ancient Egypt. Equally, for the most part, most European visitors never read a book about Egypt before they get there or purchase one while there. One has to wonder about the Professors intent, the fact of misinformation being disseminated in this age and their students or "disciples" perpetuating this false information right there in the heart of the culture. Obviously, in this day and age, she probably did not know of W. Stephenson Smith's *Art and Architecture of Ancient Egypt* (1959), wherein the author says Mentuhotep II had "black flesh." She did not know that by wearing the Red Crown of Lower Egypt, its postulated that the Pharaoh, in all probability, wore the White Crown in another statue not discovered and this had nothing

CELEBRATING
DR. BEN-JOCHANNAN

to do with his death ceremony per se, but represented his kingship over the north and south. After all, in the desert and fertile land contrast, red is desolate and death while black, is fertile and life-giving.

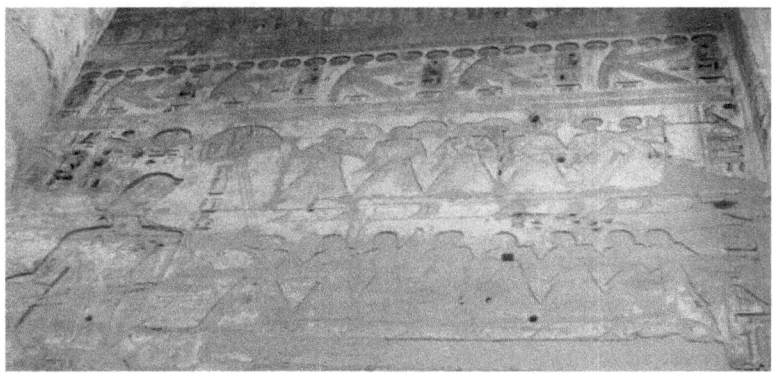

Dr. Ben's Photo 278. Medinet Habu, Mortuary Temple of Rameses III (Luxor). Members of the sacerdotal and social order follow Rameses.

Dr. Ben's Photo 279. Medinet Habu, Mortuary Temple of Rameses III (Luxor). Soldiers on the move.

FREDERICK MONDERSON

Dr. Ben's Photo 280. Medinet Habu, Mortuary Temple of Rameses III (Luxor). The King, in his car, leads his horse at a gallop.

Equally and important too, there are too few Black Egyptian Guides in the Museum, who could give a different view than the false one presented to visitors by the young lady referred to above. I noticed one such person on my October 7, 2010 visit to the Museum.

Pressing the young lady further, and mentioning that Osiris was often represented black, she said "I have never seen Osiris painted black!" Imagine being a guide in the Cairo Museum and never seen Osiris painted black. There are many examples on papyrus and in wooden statues. Just then I realized she had an agenda. As a guide she did not know Osiris was known as the "Great Black!" Interesting, the people who argue vehemently and inclandestine against the Afrocentrists have never taken on the likes of this young lady or recanted their falsity, nor have they challenged professors the likes of John David Wortham. This may simply be that these preachers of falsity uphold and vehemently defend the false notion that the Egyptians were Caucasians, coming from South-West Asia!

CELEBRATING DR. BEN-JOCHANNAN

Once again, the people who argue in this vein, that the deceased was colored black for the death ceremony seem to forget that in the designation "Red Land, Black Land," red stands for the desert and its deathlike appearance while black represents life and regeneration. Osiris the God of the Dead is generally portrayed as black or even green but hardly red, and certainly not white, even though he was dead. This is because he represented rebirth or life and the best example of this is black. Additionally, when the God says to the king, "I give you the Black Land," does he mean he does not give him that part of Egypt referred to as the Red Land comprising 96 percent and the Black Land 4 percent. Or, is it that the God meant he gave pharaoh the whole land that is representative of the people, as Theophile Obenga says (2004), the "black land" refers to the country and black people!

V. IMAGES

Queen Aahmes-Nefertari was the founder and ancestress of the 18th Dynasty and in the portrait in the British Museum she is shown as a "Coal Black Ethiopian." She married her brother, Aahmes, as was customary at that time. If she was black, then it goes without saying that her brother was also black and so must have been her father and mother. If their parents are considered, so too must have been the other brother Kamose who led the expulsion of the Hyksos following his father Sekenenra's death in the fighting. Let us still not forget, these people were Thebans from the south or Upper Kingdom and not from the Delta or north or Lower Kingdom where their racial origin could be an issue. Afterall, in "Egyptian Religion," Flinders Petrie wrote, "The 17th Dynasty, coming from Nubia, held Thebes as its capital….!"

FREDERICK MONDERSON

This family relationship is underscored in **"THE ROYAL MUMMIES OF DEIR-EL-BAHARI."** *The Academy* 35 No. 891 (June 1, 1889: 383-384) as indicated: "Among other genealogical emendations, Prof. Maspero makes out Queen Aah-hotep (the famous Queen Aah-hotep of the Boulak jewels) to be the wife, not of Kames, as hitherto believed, but of Sekenen-Re, and the mother of both Kames and Aahmes I."

Please appreciate the humor here in this example. On one occasion the respected Dr. Yosef ben-Jochannan was giving a lecture. At the end, during the question-and-answer period, a lady came over and complained to the Brother about her son. She is quoted as saying: "Dr. Ben, I don't know what to do about this boy, he is the black sheep in the family!" Dr. Ben responded appropriately: "Well lady, you are black, your husband is black, and so what type of sheep do you expect to have?" Therefore, if Sekenenra and Aah-hotep (Tetisheri) produced a "black sheep" in Nefertari, then what type of ewe and ram were they? Ha. Ha.

Sometimes we run into pertinent information without marking the appropriate reference and later this poses a problem. I do remember encountering a 19th Century reference in the British Journal *Academy* of a report done by Prof. Sayce. Wherein he says he entered a tomb of a nobleman and the occupant is shown in a painting on the wall worshipping Tuthmose I painted black! This revelation never seemed to be repeated sufficient times and is a classic example of the omission creating distortion in this subject. Just as this piece of critical information is omitted from subsequent records, it stands to reason that other information just as critical is often also omitted, perhaps destroyed because it challenges the myth of a white Egypt. Hence, we must adhere to Dr. Ben's dictum, as researchers "Get the oldest information and work from there!"

CELEBRATING
DR. BEN-JOCHANNAN

Dr. Ben's Photo 281. Medinet Habu, Mortuary Temple of Rameses III (Luxor). Uraei above signifying this is a Temple with a Son of Ra cartouche above and even higher black smoke from the time villagers used fire in the Temple.

Dr. Ben's Photo 282. Medinet Habu, Mortuary Temple of Rameses III (Luxor). Rameses in the traditional pose of smiting Egypt's enemy. Notice the heads of the Egyptians of that age as they have been defaced. "You do the math!"

FREDERICK MONDERSON

Dr. Ben's Photo 283. Medinet Habu, Mortuary Temple of Rameses III (Luxor). Foreigners bowing in the King's presence.

A subject that needs to be discussed more frequently regards the four figures in the tomb of Rameses III, 20th Dynasty, that is akin to that of Seti I, New Kingdom Monarchs of the 19th and 20th Dynasties.

The following is presented in Murray's Handbook *for Egypt* (1888: 483-485) and provides a description of the "Tomb of Rameses III," No. 11, in the Valley of the Kings, commonly called *Bruce's* or *The Harpers' Tomb*. "This tomb was discovered by the English traveler Bruce, hence one of its names. The other appellation is derived from the famous picture in one of the chambers of the men playing the harp. The execution of the sculptures is inferior to that in No. 17 [Seti Is], but the nature of the subjects is more interesting."

CELEBRATING DR. BEN-JOCHANNAN

Dr. Ben's Photo 284. Medinet Habu, Mortuary Temple of Rameses III (Luxor). Thoth "watches the King's back" and as he pours a libation and incenses, he is again protected by hands of significance.

Dr. Ben's Photo 285. Deir el Medina. The Theban Triad of Khonsu, Mut and enthroned Amon-Ra (left); and, Amon enthroned with Mut at his rear. Notice the God's Black color!

FREDERICK MONDERSON

Dr. Ben's Photo 286. Medinet Habu, Mortuary Temple of Rameses III (Luxor). Rameses stands behind Khonsu and behind Khonsu and Mut.

SCULPTURE –
Tomb of Rameses III.

"This tomb is much defaced, and the nature of the rock is unfavorable for sculpture."

"The subjects in the first passage, after the recess to the right, are similar to those of Seti's and are supposed to relate to the descent to Amenta. The figure of Truth, and the other groups in connection with that part of them, is placed in a square niche. The character of the four people in the first hall differs slightly from those of the former tomb."

CELEBRATING DR. BEN-JOCHANNAN

"Four Blacks clad in African dresses, being substituted instead of the Egyptians, though the same name, Rot, is introduced before them."

"A. The entrance hall opens to the light of day. B - The hall from which the religious processions started. C and D contained altars where prayers were recited as the processions passed. In the hall E were the four barks and which often played so conspicuous a part in the processions. The chamber F was a laboratory for the preparation of perfumes. In G, the consecrated products of the earth used in the ceremonies were collected. H and I were for offerings and libations. J was the treasury of the temple. In the chamber K, the vestments were deposited with which the statues of the Gods were draped. Prayers were recited in the chapel L. The court M was used for the collection of offerings and the limbs of the victims slaughtered at the sacrifice. N was another place for deposit, and in O, P, and Q, the king consecrated special offerings. The walls of the corridor R were used for the sculptured pictures representing the motif of the temple. S, the chamber where Isis was consecrated to Osiris. T, the chamber consecrated to Osiris. U was sacred to Osiris-On-Nophris, who restored youth to his body and imparted vigor to his limbs. In the chamber V the work of resurrection was completed. In X, and Y, Hathor was worshipped. The chamber Z is the axis of the temple, and the principal divinity was adored there under the most comprehensive titles. Lastly, in the chambers, A, B, C, D, a special worship is paid to Pasht, considered as the fire that vivifies; to Horus, considered as the light which has conquered darkness, and the terrestrial Hathor." After Mariette in B.L. Wilson's "The Temples of Egypt" 1888.

Regarding distortion and omission as a method for falsifying history we are quite aware that among arguments, one holds the Egyptians did not know of the arch! They probably did not

FREDERICK MONDERSON

know of McDonalds! Every time I'm in the rear of the Ramesseum I question whether the structures of storehouses I'm seeing is an arch and am I the only one who has seen this structure though it's been there for ages. As if that is not enough to dispel this argument, the following is a 19th Century reference of **EGYPT EXPLORATION FUND**. *The Academy* 44 No. 1104 (July 1, 1893: 17-18) "**The Excavations at Dayr el Bahari**" which states inter alia: "The western door leads to a long hall, with well-preserved sculptures of gigantic proportions, showing Hatasu and Thothmes III making offerings to Amon. Next to it is an open court limited on the north by the mountain, on the east by the remains of a chamber with columns. From that court one enters into a small rock-out chapel, the funeral chapel of Thothmes I. The ceiling, well painted in blue with yellow stars, is an Egyptian arch." This description predates the previous statement since Hatshepsut is of the 18th Dynasty and Rameses is of the 19th Dynasty. Let's also note Garstang depicts the "emergence of the Arch" as early as the Third Dynasty. We hear the same falsity about the Zodiac as being a foreign importation and so on as the Conspiracy against Ancient Egypt continues but "Truth crushed to earth shall rise."

Even more important, Ptah the Creator God was a pygmy from central Africa. Are we to believe the ancient Egyptians were foreigners to Africa, Caucasian from the Caucus on the Russian steppes, and notwithstanding, their creator, one of their highest Gods, came from Central Africa? Hathor was Sudani, according to Budge. Oftentimes Amon or other Gods are described as being exceedingly happy when they come from "Gods Land," Africa proper. This reminds of Taharka welcoming his mother, Queen Isis, from Ethiopia, after he had succeeded to the throne during the 25th Dynasty. Will someone please tell Wortham that the Gods of the "Caucasian

CELEBRATING DR. BEN-JOCHANNAN

Egyptians" came from "Gods land," in Black Africa! We are also told in the literature, after Ra made the world and two principal Gods, the first people he made were Nubians. See how the cookie crumbles or the house of cards tumbles!

VI.   THE STUDIES

Many studies are done to prove the "non-African" nature of the ancient Egyptians. More correctly, these studies are done to "prove the Caucasian origins of the Egyptians;" just as extensive studies were done in the 19th Century to prove man originated in Europe! But this was to no avail. In the nineteenth century a great many studies were done about the Egyptians but none really proved conclusively that they were White! A good example of one such study pertained to: "**THE ROYAL MUMMIES OF DEIR-EL-BAHARI**." *The Academy* 35 No. 891 (June 1, 1889: 383-384).

"It was during the summer of 1886 that Prof. Maspero resigned his Egyptian appointment; and the opening of the royal mummies closed his official labors. On June 1, in the presence of the Khedive and a select company of Egyptian and foreign notabilities, the mummies of Rameses II (XIXth Dynasty) and Rameses III (XXth Dynasty) were formally un-bandaged. Next followed, on June 9 the un-bandaging of Sekenen-Ra (XVIIth Dynasty) and Aahmes 1 (XVIIIth Dynasty); and subsequently, during the interval which elapsed between the arrival of M. Grebaut and the departure of Prof. Maspero, the rest of the Deir-el-Bahari Pharaohs, with the single exception of Amenhotep I, were duly opened. Each body in succession was carefully unwrapped and measured by Prof. Maspero, M. Bouriant, M. Insinger, and Dr. Fouquet, assisted by M. Mathey in the capacity of chemical analyst. These measurements, which are calculated on the French metrical system, give the lengths of the hand, foot, arm, forearm, etc.; various diameters of the skull; the circumference of head, shoulders, and waist; the length of the orbit of the eye, and the distance between the two orbits; the width of the mouth, length of nose and chin, circumference of pelvis, facial angle, etc. etc.; all having been twice taken and verified. Even the position of the orifice of the ear has been noted, and one learns with no little interest that, in at least one instance – e.g., that of the Princess Sit-Kames - this orifice is parallel with the root of the nose and somewhat above the line of the eye, precisely as we see it represented in Egyptian statuary."

Dr. Ben's Photo 287. **Deir el Medina**. With Thoth at his back, Rameses incenses and pours a libation to the Theban Triad of enthroned Amon-Ra, Mut and Khonsu with his image behind them.

CELEBRATING DR. BEN-JOCHANNAN

Dr. Ben's Photo 288. Medinet Habu, Mortuary Temple of Rameses III (Luxor). Looking out from the inner recesses of the Temple beyond the Second Court.

Dr. Ben's Photo 289. Medinet Habu, Mortuary Temple of Rameses III (Luxor). The Temple proper where the roofed Hypostyle Hall and Sanctuary were located, much before their collapse under the weight of the village that covered it.

FREDERICK MONDERSON

Seriously, I don't think any other race of people have been so microscopically studied as the black race to disprove them black! Even more, another quote is appropriate here.

Dr. Ben's Book 21. *African Origins of the "Major" Western Religions: The Black Man's Religion*, Volume II (1970, 1991).

"The King Ra Kha-em-Uas, whose name, at all events in this form, is unknown, is identified by Prof. Maspero with Rameses XII, the contemporary and predecessor of Her-Hor, and by M. Grebaut, with Rameses IX. Among other genealogical emendations, Prof. Maspero makes out Queen Aah-hotep (the famous Queen Aah-hotep of the Boulak jewels) to be the wife, not of Kames, as hitherto believed, but of Sekenen-Re, and the mother of both Kames and Aahmes I. He also, with infinite skill, based on an exhaustive study of a vast number of scattered inscriptions, reconstructs the framework of the XXIst Dynasty - thus, for the first time, presenting a satisfactory solution of one of the most difficult problems in Egyptian history."

CELEBRATING
DR. BEN-JOCHANNAN

Besides the repetition here, two things should be mentioned here. First, all this measurement and even the great Maspero could not indicate that, whatever said, Queen Aah-hotep and King Sekenen-Re produced Kames and Aahmes I, but give us no color of these personalities. Yet, Queen Aahmes-Nefertari who is akin to that group is pictured as a "Coal Black Ethiopian." So, what does this make her brothers and father and mother? Unfortunately, there was no "Diop Detective" to challenge Maspero and his associates and their findings. But, of course, there was Emile Amelineau, whose comments after he had found "Osiris tomb," showed Maspero fumbling or bungling the issue and making that great m an appear not so!

Second, all the above measurements, notwithstanding, when Prof. Diop asked for a miniscule piece of the mummies to do his own study to show that they were black, he was denied. Still, he was able to secure some specimens elsewhere for his studies. Such meticulous research as Dr. Diop had done was instrumental at the **1974 United Nations Conference on Egypt** that affirmed the **"fundamental blackness"** of ancient Egyptian civilization!

VII.   THE WRITINGS

I.   THE ANCIENTS

Homer, one of the earliest writers of Europe refers, in the *Iliad*, to the Greek Gods and their connection to Ethiopians "Jupiter today, followed by all the Gods Receives the sacrifices of the Ethiopians" and again, "Yesterday to visit holy Ethiopia Jupiter betook himself to the ocean shore."

FREDERICK MONDERSON

In his *Histories*, Book II, *Euterpe*, Herodotus stated: "The Colchians, Egyptians and Ethiopians have broad noses, thick lips, woolly hair, broad noses and are burnt of skin." On the other hand, G. Mokhtar in the official report of the 1974 United Nations Conference on the Nile Valley, as given in *Ancient Civilizations of Africa* Vol. II (London: Heinemann Educational Books, Ltd., 1981, p. 68) states, in replying to Prof. Vercoutter's question of how precisely Herodotus had defined the Egyptians as Negroes Dr. Cheikh Anta Diop responded: "Herodotus referred to them on three occasions in speaking of the origin of the Colchians, in speaking of the origin of the Nile floods, and in discussing the oracle of Zeus-Amon." Even further, Kamit Kush in *The Missing Pages of "His-Story"* (1993: 54) quotes Mokhtar (p. 62) that, "Professor Diop went on to speak of the evidence provided by ancient written sources, pointing out that Greek and Latin Author's described the Egyptian as Negroes. He referred to the testimony of Herodotus, Aristotle, Lucian, Apollodorus, Aeschylus, Achilles, Tacitus, Strabo, Diodorus Siculus, Diogenes Laertius and Ammianus Marcellinus."

John D. Baldwins *Pre-Historic Nations* (Harper and Brothers, New York: 1898, p. 276) as quoted in Indus Kamit Kush's *The Missing Pages of "His-Story"* (p. 47) wrote: "Diodorus Siculus adds to his statement that the customs, religious observances, and letters of the ancient Egyptians closely resembles those of the Ethiopians, the colony still observing the customs of their ancestors." There were no Asian ancestral customs in Egypt.

Xenophanes, an Ionian by birth, wrote according to Bertrand Russell, *A History of Western Philosophy* (New York: Touchstone Books, Simon and Schuster, 1972, p. 40) as quoted in Kamit Kush (p. 46), "The Ethiopians make their Gods black and snug-nosed; the Thracians say theirs have blue eyes and red hair." This view was also echoed by Dr. Victor

CELEBRATING DR. BEN-JOCHANNAN

Robinson in *The Story of Medicine* (New York: Albert and Charles Boni, 1936, p. 38) again quoted by Kush who states: "… the Gods of the Ethiopians are swarthy and flat-nosed; the Gods of the Thracians are fair-haired and blue-eyed." The Gods of the Egyptians were no different and this forces us to question Wortham's contention that the Egyptians were Caucasians, and if so, why would they worship Black Gods?

Dr. Ben's Photo 290. Dendera, Home of Goddess Hathor. Dromos to the First Pylon and into the Court the Pronaos or Hypostyle Hall with its massive engaged columns with Hathor Heads and free-standing decorated columns within.

Dr. Ben's Photo 291. Dendera, Home of Goddess Hathor. The Mammisi where the God was born with its varied columns.

FREDERICK MONDERSON

Dr. Ben's Photo 292. Dendera, Home of Goddess Hathor. Close-up of the engaged columns at the entrance or Pronaos or "Outer Hypostyle Hall," with uraei at top (bottom) of the screen entrance. Notice how every one of the Goddess faces are defaced because of her African features.

II. THE MODERNS

Count Volney in *The Ruins of Empire* (1791) (1833: pp. 16-17) noted: "There a people, now forgotten, discovered, while others were yet barbarians, the elements of the arts and sciences. A race of men now rejected from society for their sable skin and frizzled hair, founded on the study of the laws of nature, those civil and religious systems which still govern the universe."

George Glidden in *Ancient Egypt*: *The New World*, (New York: J. Winchester, 1843: p. 59) stated: "The advocates of the African origin of the Egyptians cling to the superior antiquity of the pyramids at Meroe, as a proof of the origin of civilization in Ethiopia, and its consequent descent into Egypt

CELEBRATING DR. BEN-JOCHANNAN

...." While not subscribing to this view himself, he states the "advocates" were Champollion Figeac and Rosellini, the Italian.

Herein is an important conundrum facing people who insist on the "Caucasian" origin of the Egyptians. Great store is given to the work and efforts of Herodotus and Champollion but when they say the Egyptians were Black nobody pays any attention. How sad!

a. Wilhelm Hegel - While contemporary with our time, Prof. Jacob Carruthers has quite eloquently pointed out how Hegel had not only removed Africa from being a part of history but also began the process of removing Egypt and Egyptians from Africa. Obviously, Hegel was probably not aware or unconcerned about Jean-Jacques Champollion's description of the ancient Egyptians and other Africans and the level of their cultural accomplishments alongside his comparison of the accomplishments of, as he said, "our ancestors" or the "Blond beasts." Strange, that the notion of "our ancestors" as they refer to Europeans in this work is equally incorrect when European writers refer to the ancient people of the Nile Valley as "our ancestors." Ideas die hard and as such we have the debacle that now pervades the discipline of the history of the Nile Valley cultural experience. Again, let's not forget Goethe's statement about how Germans corrupt other people's culture!

b. Samuel Cartwright - was described as "the banana skin physician," who equally, was an apologist for slavery in the ante-Bellum south. His book, *Slavery and Ethnology* was published in 1857, that epoch-making year and decade when Dred Scott was enshrined on the wrong side of American history and jurisprudence. In that work, Samuel Cartwright

FREDERICK MONDERSON

wrote: "The Nilotic monuments furnish ample evidence that blacks (Negroes) were slaves along the banks of the Nile from time immemorial." What did he know? He probably never heard of Champollion the Younger or read his reports. His work had scant; if any referents; was certainly not scientific, and most assuredly was apologetic for slavery. In critique of contemporary European and American thought, the philosopher Immanuel Kant insisted, people, "act as if your work or words can become a universal axiom." However, these arguments have a tendency to fall apart upon closer scrutiny and revelation of new and sometimes even older information. Need I say more!

c. The distinguished **Gaston Maspero** certainly did little to dispel the distorted misinterpretation of this aspect of a discipline he was so versed in. His Cairo Museum Place Cards in the display cases shaped the interpretation of the exhibits to this day. His description of the 19th Dynasty Nobleman Maherpra as being "Negroid but not Negro" has gone a long way to color the misinterpretation and misrepresentation of the ethnology of the ancient Egyptians. Since Maspero falls between Augustus Bozzi Granville and John David Wortham and the latter claims "Egyptians were Caucasian" and the former that Maherpra was "Negroid not Negro," could we then conclude the Nobleman was a "Negroid Caucasian." Or, should we entertain Cheikh Anta Dips statement that "we reach the absurd conclusion that Negroes are basically whites."

CELEBRATING
DR. BEN-JOCHANNAN

Dr. Ben's Photo 293. Dendera, Home of Goddess Hathor. The 23 crowns of Ancient Egypt.

Dr. Ben's Photo 294. Dendera, Home of Goddess Hathor. Native Egyptian Guide "Shawki" Abd-el-Rady with flashlight greets counterparts in the Goddess sacred space.

FREDERICK MONDERSON

Dr. Ben's Photo 295. Dendera, Home of Goddess Hathor. The 23 crowns on a column in the Hypostyle Hall.

Dr. Ben's Photo 295. Dendera, Home of Goddess Hathor. Native Guide Shawki Abdel Rady and Carmen on the Dromos after an exciting visit to the Goddess' temple.

CELEBRATING
DR. BEN-JOCHANNAN

Dr. Ben's Photo 296. Dendera, Home of Goddess Hathor. The Goddess (left); and, her husband Horus (right) wearing the Red Crown.

It's strange that of all the untold numbers of books written about ancient Egypt so little ever address the real facts of the case as it is raised in this selection. Such vivid descriptions are made about these ancient Egyptian Africans, but they seem so couched in misleading language it's hard to locate them.

FREDERICK MONDERSON

A case can be made to compare different writers on the same topic. I use as an example, Beethoven, the German musical genius, whom it was argued, had "Moorish" blood implying he was Negro, African or had what we would call African-American features. Authorities differ on the "racial Origin" of this musical great. Writing in *Sex and Race* vol. III, J. A. Rogers (1944: 306) supplies *Notes on Beethoven* showing: "Beethoven was German and because his portraits are usually shown with a white tone and abundant hair nearly every one thinks of him as white." Rogers' beliefs on Beethoven's color are based on commentary supplied by the musical genius biographers that are included here as follows. Fanny Giannantonio del Rio writes, "mulatto;" May Byron "swarthy;" Alexander Wheelock Thayer "Negroids;" Frederick Hertz "Negroids;" Brun old Springer "Negroids;" Brun old Springer "negro;" Emil Ludwig "dark."

Why then would these writers use different words to describe the same person who is considered "Negro?" It's the same with Maspero's definition of Maherpra that others may call the nobleman "Negro." We must remember the declaration, "We came from the foothills of the Mountain of the Moon where the God Hapi [Osiris] dwells!!!" Also, let us consider all attempts to locate the ancient Egyptians are based on speculation. Yet, one seated scribe's statue with inlaid eyes out of thousands of such workers; one dissected mummy out of millions done by an Englishman in an age when Britannia ruled the world and perpetuated slavery of Africans, enshrining "white supremacy." Still, they disregarded the monumental sphinx and Hunefer's pinpointing not only the Egyptians origins but also that of Hapi (Osiris) in "Gods land."

To continue, two things are also raised in the following. First, in **EGYPT EXPLORATION FUND. THE**

CELEBRATING DR. BEN-JOCHANNAN

EXCAVATION OF THE TEMPLE OF QUEEN HATASU AT DEIR-EL-BAHARI. *The Academy* 45 No. 1137 (February 17, 1894: 153-154).

Luxor: Jan. 10, 1894.

We are told: "So far, the main finds of the latter class have been beads, scarabs, and figurines, made of the famous blue-glazed ware. Good Demotic and Coptic *Ostraka* are frequent, and there is much refuse from rifled mummy pits of the XXIInd Dynasty. Some coffins and mummies have been found lying loose among the upper layers of *debris*: one fine case belonged to Namen-Kenkhet-amen, a relative of Osorkon II and Takelothis; another contains a very finely rolled mummy, for whose reception it was not originally intended; a third is early Coptic, and shows on the front of the outer cloth representations of wine and corn in the hands, while below is the sacred boat of Osiris and over the heart a swastika." This must shock Hitler's master race theorists as well as that erudite German school beginning with Hegel! So here we have ancient African use of this master-race symbol eons ago. The patron saint of Germany, a black African general, also wears this symbol.

Secondly, and this is significant because Dr. ben-Jochannan often told us the people were colored red by the henna plant. It states here in the above reference: "The last toilette of some royal ladies of the XXIst Dynasty was, for instance, most elaborate, the wrinkles caused by the process of mummification being filled up with some kind of enamel, the skin colored with ochre, the cheeks and lips rouged, and false eyes introduced under the shriveled and half-open lids; thus, giving a horribly life-like appearance to the faces, as shown in the auto-type illustrations from Herr Brugsch's photographs."

FREDERICK MONDERSON

The ochre here is the Henna plant. Imagine the numerous individuals in the Rekhmire (Rekhmara) tomb, working, all dead, are they painted red with Henna? The "false eyes," are they reminiscent of the "Louvre Scribe who has blue eyes?" Or, are they painted red as the "chosen people" in association with a solar deity?

Even further, elsewhere in East Africa, the anthropologist Mary Leakey and her husband Louis between 1935-1951 (*Nile Year* 6175-6191) discovered and catalogued 186 rock-painting sites. This extensive gallery supplied 1,600 individual scenes, over a 500-square-mile area in Tanzania. Through Mary Leakey's (1983: 86) work, "Tanzania's Stone Age Art," we are helped in understanding an archaeological study of man's distant past in Africa, that brings to us the startling conclusion: "Those long-ago works of art tell us, for example, that Stone Age man in Africa wore clothing, had a variety of hairstyles, hunted, danced, sang, played musical instruments, and may even have known the secret of fermenting spirits."

Dr. Ben's Illustration 94. Drama of the Funeral with the boat trip, dragging of the Bier to the place of internment then the ceremony at the gravesite.

CELEBRATING
DR. BEN-JOCHANNAN

Dr. Ben's Illustration 95. Adolf Erman *Life in Ancient Egypt* (1894) - Another example of ancient Peoples including, from left to right, Egyptian, Libyan, Asiatic and African.

Dr. Ben's Illustration 96. Adolf Erman *Life in Ancient Egypt* (1894) - Wearing different crowns from left to right, the King in different dresses and without and with sandals, presents a miniature Sphinx; prepares to incense and pours a libation; and offers two jars of ointment.

FREDERICK MONDERSON

The interesting point is, for these early East African painters, in many respects similar to those of the Tassili artists, painting materials were of principal concern. Their choice of colors is interesting for, "the predominant red was made from ocher, which is derived from iron ore. Black probably came from manganese, and bird droppings may have provided the basis for the white." So even these peoples removed from Egypt loved "predominant red." Many figures, even those represented by the Tassili frescoes show red in their paintings. Are we to believe these people are also Egyptians? In October, 2014, *The New York Times* mentioned discovery of a "paint factory" in South Africa dated to 107,000 years. These people mixed "red paint" as in a "paint pot and brush." At Nabta Playa, Black African people were painted with red color!

Dr. Ben's Illustration97. Rameses II makes an offering before Goddess Nephthys.

CELEBRATING
DR. BEN-JOCHANNAN

Dr. Ben's Photo 297. Dendera, Home of Goddess Hathor. Horus and Hathor in the Crypt.

Dr. Ben's Photo 297a. Dendera, Home of Goddess Hathor. Ceiling drama as the Gods parade in the heavens.

FREDERICK MONDERSON

Dr. Ben's Photo 298. **Dendera, Home of Goddess Hathor**. Hathor in two different attitudes.

Dr. Ben's Photo 298a. Dendera, Home of Goddess Hathor. More ceiling drama as the Gods parade in the heavens.

CELEBRATING DR. BEN-JOCHANNAN

Dr. Ben's Photo 299. Dendera, Home of Goddess Hathor. Once again, Hathor enthroned in yet two more and different attitudes.

Another significant point is developed from the following quote. Budge (1969, II: 22-23) explained how: "The worship of Amen-Ra was introduced into Nubia by its Egyptian conquerors early in the XIIth Dynasty, and the inhabitants of that country embraced it with remarkable fervor; the hold which it had gained upon them was much strengthened when an Egyptian viceroy, who bore the title of royal son of Cush, was appointed to rule over the land, and no efforts were spared to make Napata a second Thebes. The Nubians were, from the poverty of their country, unable to imitate the massive temples of Karnak and Luxor, and the festivals which they celebrated in honor of the Nubian Amen-Ra, and the processions which they made in his honor, lacked the splendor and magnificence of the Theban capital; still, there is no doubt that, considering the means which they had at their disposal, they erected

Dr. Ben's Photo 300. Dendera, Home of Goddess Hathor. Powerful symbols of Hathor worship.

CELEBRATING
DR. BEN-JOCHANNAN

Dr. Ben's Photo 301. Dendera, Home of Goddess Hathor. Horus as a falcon in all his glory.

temples for the worship of Amen-Ra of very considerable size and solidity. The hold which the priesthood of Amen-Ra of Thebes had upon the Nubians was very great, for in the troublous times which followed after the collapse of their

FREDERICK MONDERSON

power as priest-kings of Egypt, the remnant of the great brotherhood made its way to Napata, and settling down there made plans and schemes for the restoration of their rule in Egypt; fortunately for Egypt their designs were never realized." So, whatever happened to these Egyptians since they were so different from the Nubians? Why have they vanished? Also, if "fortunately for Egypt their desires were never realized" is true, what are we to say of the Persian, Assyrian, Greek, Roman, Christian, Arab, and all others.

Equally, we are also told from inscriptions at Abu Simbel Temple of Rameses II, of 200,000 or so soldiers who rebelled against Psammetichus settled in Nubia, in that age, Ethiopia. So where are these foreigners in Nubia? I mean these red Egyptians who were so different from the African Nubians! In anthropometrical studies done by Myers, he claims no difference between ancient and modern Egyptians. Yet, the above two groups of Egyptians settled among the Nubians and we see no difference today. No less significant, Egypt, at the crossroads of the ancient world was conquered by Hyksos, Persians, Assyrians, Greeks and Roman as well as infused by various peoples as conquered slaves, then the Muslim invasion of 640 and the Mamelukes and all other foreign conquerors as the French, English, and everyone else who came, invaded and without question certainly did damage to the culture. Thus, that there is no difference between the ancient and modern Egyptians is a laughable conclusion.

CELEBRATING DR. BEN-JOCHANNAN

Dr. Ben's Illustration 98. The Temple of Luxor, after Restoration by Gnauth, Chief Commissioner for Public Buildings in Adolf Erman's *Life in Ancient Egypt* (1894).

Kush quotes W.E.B. DuBois in *The World and Africa* (New York: International publishers, 1965, p. 106) who wrote: "We conclude, therefore, that the Egyptians were Negroids, and not only that, but by tradition they believed themselves descended not from the whites or the yellows, but from the black peoples of the south. Thence they traced their origin, and toward the south in earlier days they turned the faces of their buried corpses."

Even more, when the statue identified as the "Sheikh el Beled" was discovered, arguments were made that the ancient and modern Egyptians were so alike there was no change, despite the many centuries of admixture Egypt underwent. In a parallel case, with the significant incursions of these "different Egyptians" who moved into Nubia how come they are not distinct from the other Africans? We know Sesostris left an army in the Caucus who were the Colchians and that element is pronounced in that environment today. Hannibal had an army in Italy for two decades and this affected the population of southern Italy, Sicily, for millennia to come. Therefore, perhaps we can ask how really different were the Egyptians from the other Africans south of Egypt? Prof. Diop's simple explanation is that the Egyptians painted themselves red so as to be distinguished from other Africans. They could not foretell the modern conception of race and racism and the impact it would have on people relationships. The only answer seems it's all part of the Conspiracy against Egypt.

VIII. ARGUMENTS FOR ORIGINS

The arguments for origins and ethnicity of the Egyptians have principally centered on external influences and *ipso facto* they could not be black. The last half and particularly the last quarter of the 19th Century witnessed a full court press of theories of the origins of the Egyptians that were primarily based somewhat on linguistic evidence coupled with migration factors that for all but the seasoned linguist seems convincing. However, the substantive cultural features such as architecture, the earliest significant culture manifestation in any societal development seem lacking in the places of supposed Asiatic origins. In a modern comparison, the Australians of today possess cultural affinity that links them with England and British culture; so too do the Americans. Germans, Italians and many who migrated to America brought and have retained their cultural connections with their ancient homelands. However, the foreigners who supposedly migrated and advanced Egyptian civilization have not left any significant cultural remains of their homeland. Nor do we see similar remains in their place of origins, especially in the Southwest Asia and European Caucasus. Yet still, these

CELEBRATING
DR. BEN-JOCHANNAN

spurious ideas have persisted, been preserved in mothballs and trotted out ever-so-often, despite the fact that reputable scholars are not "Concerned with physical origins but cultural accomplishments." However, there is clear evidence of Central African ideas and motifs and even contemporary survivals linking modern Africa with their ancient antecedents in Egypt. Yet, these are not given the consideration they deserve.

Dr. Ben's Photo 302. Dendera, Home of Goddess Hathor. Entrance to the Chapel of Goddess Nuit (Nut).

FREDERICK MONDERSON

Dr. Ben's Photo 303. Dendera, Home of Goddess Hathor. On the ceiling of Goddess Units chapel, she gives birth to the sun on the morning and swallows it up at night.

Dr. Ben's Photo 304. Dendera, Home of Goddess Hathor. Double winged sun-disk with uraei with disks on the architrave to the Goddess chapel.

CELEBRATING DR. BEN-JOCHANNAN

Dr. Ben's Photo 305. Dendera, Home of Goddess Hathor. Relief of Goddess Hathor.

IX. CONTEMPORARY VIEWS

The contemporary approach is one of "don't ask, don't tell," as it relates to the race of the ancient Egyptians; yet, modern books, despite the avalanche of recent research are tremendously sanitized that "the issue is really a non-issue." We ought not to forget Dr. ben-Jochannan's admonition. "Get the earliest research material and work from there," as it falls upon us as participants in African historiographic reconstruction to do what we must to set the record straight.

The African world is awake and its scholars are seriously challenging the misrepresentations, distortions and omissions systematically implanted by pseudo-scientists, racists and all who are ignorant of the fact of the glorious role Africans have played not only in Africa but globally. Clearly history has to be and is being rewritten placing Africa in her respectful place at the head in the order and narrative of humanity's global and triumphant experience.

X. References

Bakry, H.K.S. *A Brief Study of Mummies and Mummification.* Cairo: 1965.
Diop, Cheikh Anta. *The African Origin of Civilization*: *Myth or Reality*. Brooklyn, New York: Lawrence Hill Book Co., (1955) 1974.
Herodotus. *The Histories*. Translated by Audrey de Selincourt. New York: Viking Penguin, Inc. (1954) 1972.
Kush, Indus Kamit. *The Missing Pages of "His-Story."* D and J. Books, Inc., Laurelton, New York: 1993.
Robins, Gay. *The Art of Ancient Egypt*. Cambridge, Massachusetts. Harvard University Press, 1997.
Smith, W. Stephenson. *The Art and Architecture of Ancient Egypt*. Boston: Museum of Fine Arts, 1959.

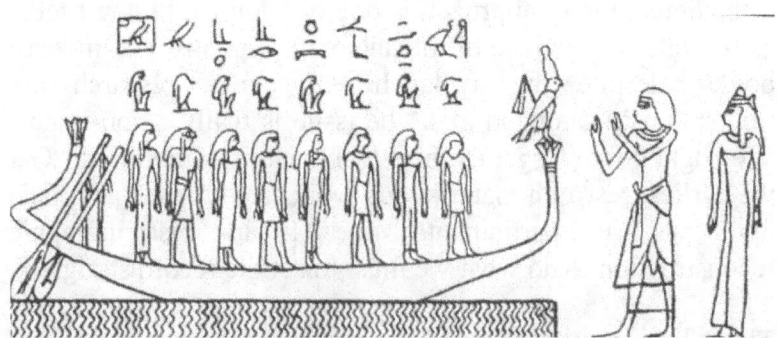

Dr. Ben's Illustration 99. The Deities Shu, Tefnut, Geb, Nuit, Osiris, Isis, Horus, and Hathor in the Barque of Ra.

CELEBRATING
DR. BEN-JOCHANNAN

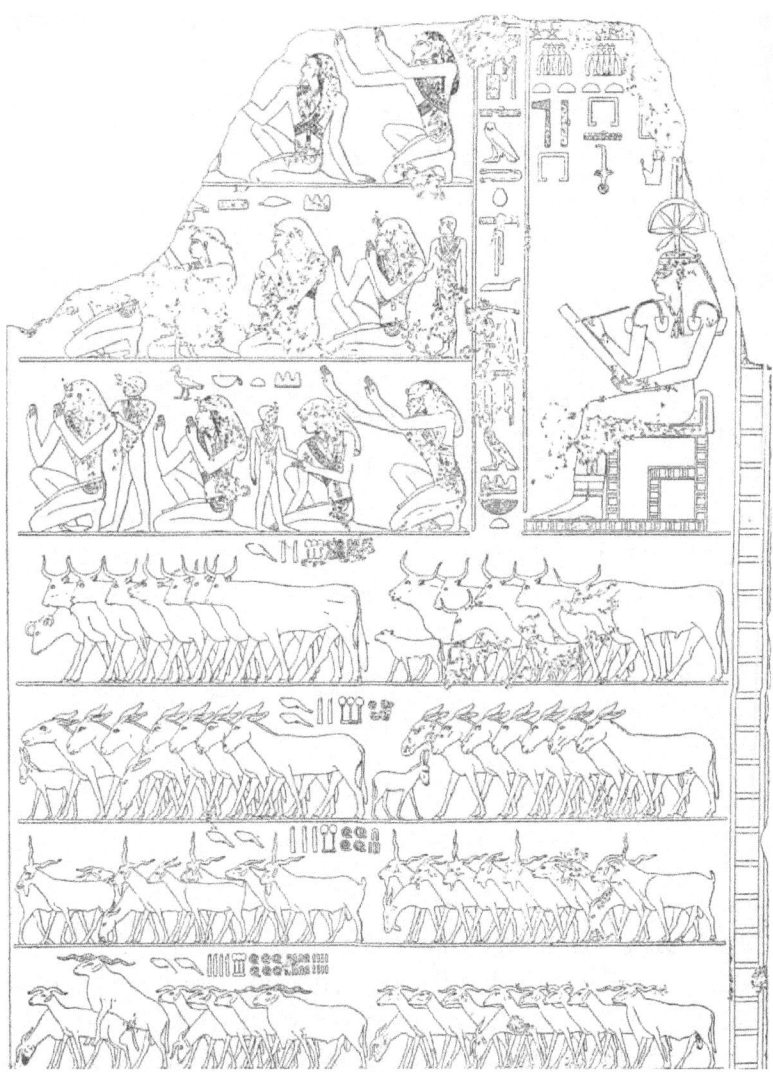

Dr. Ben's Illustration 100. The Goddess Seshat takes record as cows, asses and goats are assembled. To the left at the bottom, notice a Ram having his way!

FREDERICK MONDERSON

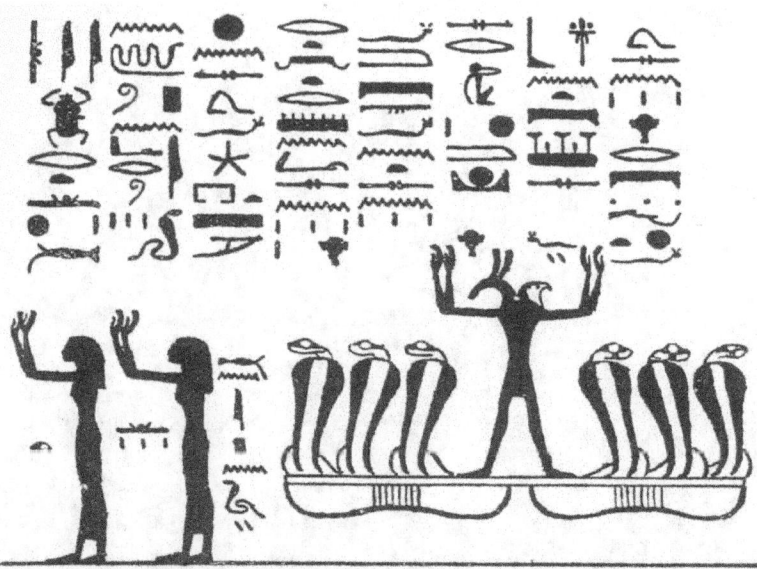

Dr. Ben's Illustration 101. The double-headed God – Horus and Seth combined - from the Sarcophagus of Seti I of the 19th Dynasty, now in the Soane Museum.

Dr. Ben's Illustration 102. Adolf Erman (1922) - A 19th Dynasty scene of the Drama in the Heavens, Gods in their Barques, and enthroned deities wearing White and Red Crowns. If this is predynastic mythology, does this mean these crowns preceded Narmer as Upper Egyptian symbolism? More important, Tum, Set and Horus wore the Double crown and they preceded Narmer. This lends to the view, the White, Red and Double Crown, worn by the Gods were made in heaven and stands to reason, first manifested in Upper Egypt.

CELEBRATING DR. BEN-JOCHANNAN

Suggestions for Further Reading

ben-Jochannan, Yosef A.A. *Black Man of the Mile and His Family*. New York: Alkebu-Lan Publishers, 1972.

_____. *Africa: Mother of Western Civilization*. New York: Alkebu-Lan Publishers, 1970.

_____. *African Origins of the "Major" Western Civilizations*. New York: Alkebu-Lan Publishers, 1971.

Bernal, Martin. *Black Athena*. 2 Vols. New Brunswick, New Jersey. Rutgers University Press, 1987.

Carruthers, Jacob H. *Mdw Ntr: Divine Speech*. New Jersey: Red Sea Press, 1995.

_____. *Intellectual Warfare*. Chicago: Third world Press, 1999.

De Graaf-Johnson, J.C. *African Glory*. Baltimore, MD.: Black Classics Press, (1954) 1986.

Diop, Cheikh Anta. *Civilization or Barbarism*. Brooklyn, New York: Lawrence Hill Books, (1981) 1991.

_____. *Pre-Colonial Black Africa*. Westport, Connecticut: Lawrence Hill and Co., 1987.

_____. *African Origins of Civilization: Myth or Reality*. Brooklyn, New York: Lawrence Hill Book Co., (1955) 1974.

_____. *The Cultural Unity of Black Africa*. Chicago: Third World Press, (1959) 1987.

FREDERICK MONDERSON

Dr. Ben's Photo 306. Dendera, Home of Goddess Hathor. Decorated ceiling reached by decorated column with Hathor Head capitals and Abacus.

Dr. Ben's Photo 307. Dendera, Home of Goddess Hathor. Thoth and Horus baptize the Pharaoh before he enters the Temple.

CELEBRATING DR. BEN-JOCHANNAN

Dr. Ben's Photo 308. Dendera, Home of Goddess Hathor. In a crown of horns, disk, feathers and with uraei with disks, pharaoh offers Ma'at as his name to the Goddess backed by Horus with a youngster in the foreground in Double Crown.

DuBois, W.E.B. *The Negro*. New York: Oxford University Press (1915) 1970.
Finch, Charles S, III. *Echoes of the Old Darkland*. Decatur, Georgia: Khenti, Inc., (1991) 1996.
_____. *The Star of Deep Beginnings*. Decatur, Georgia: Khenti, Inc., 1998.
Jackson, John. *Introduction to African Civilizations*. Secaucus, New Jersey: The Citadel Press, 1970.
De Graaf, Johnson, J.C. *African Glory*. Baltimore, MD.: Black Classics Press, (1954) 1986.

FREDERICK MONDERSON

Karenga, Maulana and Jacob Carruthers. *Kemet and the African Worldview*. Los Angeles: University of Sankore Press, 1986.
Kush, Indus Khamit. *The Missing Pages of "His-Story."* Laurelton, New York: D and J Books, 1993.
Rogers, J.A. *World's Great Men of Color*. 2 Vols. New York: Macmillan, 1972.
_____. *Sex and Race*. 3 Vols. New York: Helga Rogers, 1967.
Van Sertima, Ivan. *Nile Valley Civilizations*. Journal of African Civilizations, Inc. New Brunswick, New Jersey: Transaction Publishers, (1985) 1986.
_____. *Egypt: Child of Africa*. New Brunswick, New Jersey: Transaction Publishers, (1994) 1995.
_____. *Egypt: Revisited*. New Brunswick, New Jersey: Transaction Publishers, 1989.
_____. *Great African Thinkers: Cheikh Anta Diop*. New Brunswick, New Jersey: Transaction Books, (1986) 1987.
_____. *Great Black Leaders: Ancient and Modern*. New Brunswick, New Jersey: Journal of African Civilizations, 1988.
_____. *Blacks In Science: Ancient and Modern*. New Brunswick, New Jersey: Journal of African Civilizations, Ltd., Inc., 1983.
_____. *Black Women in Antiquity*. New Brunswick, New Jersey: Journal of African Civilizations, Ltd., Inc., ((1984) 1986.
Williams, Chancellor. *Destruction of Black Civilizations*. Chicago: Third World Press, 1970.
Woodson, Carter G. *The Mis-Education of the Negro*. Trenton, New Jersey: Africa World Press, (1990) 1993.
_____. *The Education of the Negro*. Brooklyn, New York: A and B Books Publisher, (1919).

CELEBRATING DR. BEN-JOCHANNAN

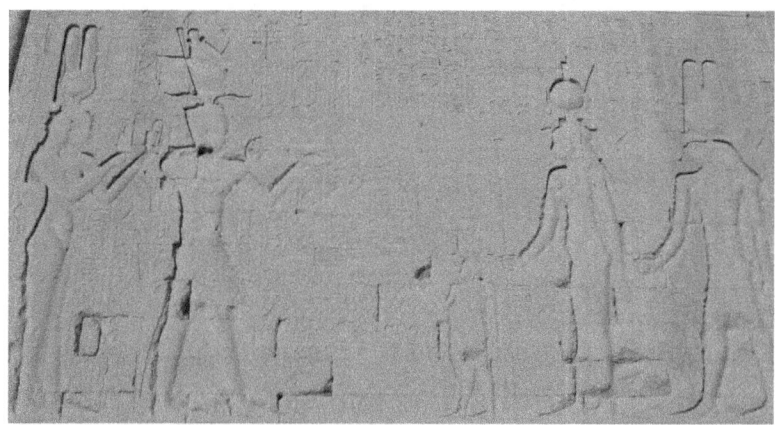

Dr. Ben's Photo 309. Dendera, Home of Goddess Hathor. Wearing a Double Crown with horns and backed by his queen holding a sistrum and making a presentation, Pharaoh prepares to incense Hathor as Isis with Horus at her rear and their son in foreground.

Dr. Ben's Photo 310. Dendera, Home of Goddess Hathor. While Pharaoh offers flowers, a youngster rattles a sistrum to enthroned Hathor and Horus in Double Crown.

FREDERICK MONDERSON

Dr. Ben's Photo 311. Dendera, Home of Goddess Hathor. As the Queen offers two vessels and two youngsters in Double Crown and Osiris Crown Hathor as Isis sits enthroned between Khnum with the instrument for longevity and "watching her back!"

33. Comparing EGYPTIAN Chronology

(Dr. A.A. ben-Jochannan *Black Man of the Nile*, 1972)

(William Murnane The *Penguin Guide to Ancient Egypt*, 1983)

Predynastic 6000-3200 B.C. 5000-3300 B.C.	Predynastic
Badarian .... 5000-4000 B.C.	Badarian
Amratian	Amratian 4000-3500
(Naqada 1) Gerzean .... 3500-3300 B.C.	Gerzean

CELEBRATING
DR. BEN-JOCHANNAN

(Naqada I and II)   (Naqada II)
                                   3300-3050 B.C.

Archaic Period   Archaic Period
3200-2780 B.C.   3050-2686 B.C.

Old Kingdom 2780-2270 B.C.   Old Kingdom 2613-2181
2780-2270 B.C.   2613-2181
First Intermediate Period   First Intermediate Period
2270-2100 B.C.   2181-2040 B.C.

Middle Kingdom   Middle Kingdom
2100-1675 B.C.   2040-1782 B.C.

Second Intermediate Period   Second Inter. Period 1675-
1600 B.C.   1782-1570 B.C.

New Kingdom 1600-1090 B.C.   New Kingdom 1570-1070

Third Intermediate Period   Third Inter. Period
1090-527 B.C.   1070-713 B.C.

Late Period   713-332 B.C.   Late Period 527-332 B.C.

Graeco-Roman Period   Graeco-Roman Period
332 B.C.-640 Period   332 B.C.-395 A.D.

The **Comparing of Egyptian Chronologies** is designed to give the reader some insights into how scholars have viewed this important subject. The dates presented here represent those of the "Short Chronology," whereas at the end of the 19th Century the "Long Chronology" was in vogue. The "Long Chronology" moves certainly the earliest period back by nearly two thousand years. However, the period from the New Kingdom onward is generally more stable for it coincides with other "Middle Eastern" dates of societies on the move. Nevertheless, we should not be unmindful that some scholars have argued use of the "Short Chronology" is more political for it synchronizes with Mesopotamian dates. Notwithstanding, the two scholars works chosen above is contemporary, though Murnane is newer than ben-Jochannan and is the generally accepted working model among most scholars today.

Dr. Ben's Illustration 103. The Sacred Barque of Amon hoisted in the time of Thutmose II at Karnak. When the Temple was rebuilt later, Seti I placed his Prenomen on it.

CELEBRATING
DR. BEN-JOCHANNAN

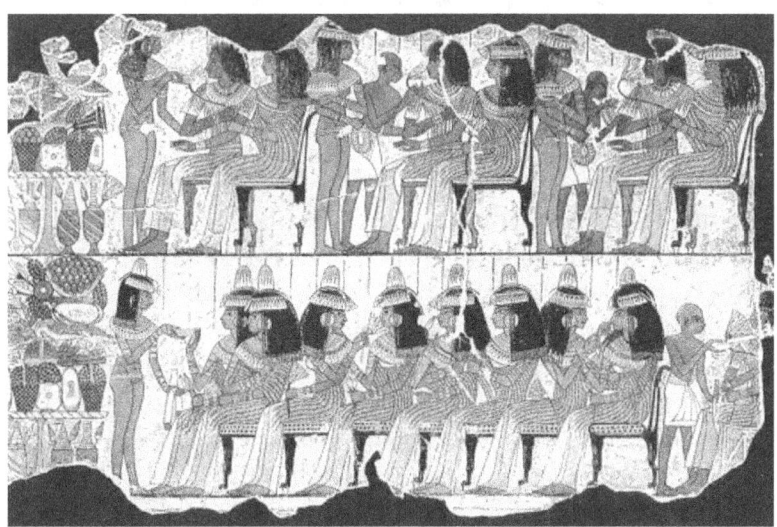

Dr. Ben's Illustration 104. A wall picture from a Theban tomb in the British Museum shows Egyptian ladies at a Feast.

Dr. Ben's Illustration 105. Inspection of Herd of Oxen as presented to tax officials.

FREDERICK MONDERSON

34. THE MAGIC OF KING TUTANKHAMON BY DR. FRED MONDERSON

The magic of King Tut is again on display in New York City as the world continues to be amazed at the wealth of the most famous monarch of all time. However, the most striking difference between this display and the one some 30 years ago is the singular piece symbolizing the exhibition. Seldom in an exhibit, a single piece could so define the experience and can generate such discussion because of its controversial nature and the overall implications of the broader issue its a part of.

Reflecting on the previous exhibit, it is not surprising in the aftermath of bi-centennial independence celebration of 1976, the mini-series *Roots* had swept the nation and it became fashionable to look to ones ancestral heritage. Underlying the glitz and hoopla was the unmistaken and packaged reality we were dealing with the slave heritage of an entire people. After all, as depicted, Alex Haleys ancestral heritage began c. 1750 of our era and no thought was given to any historical or cultural connection of African people earlier than that date. Therefore, when the King Tut exhibit opened in 1979, the symbolic piece chosen to represent the boy king was an alabaster bust. While not expressly stated, the "**three card Monte con** perpetuated against all viewers" is that King Tut, by all accounts looked liked a white person, when in fact this was not so, only the composition of the stone was white. Malcolm X in his demonstrated wisdom has always affirmed "They know how to put it." Only the most astute individuals saw through the scheme and raised the question of distortion in the representation. Naturally, the apologists who perpetuated the misrepresentation denied such was the intent.

CELEBRATING
DR. BEN-JOCHANNAN

Notwithstanding, the visual imagery of the intended falsity was registered and it has remained part of the more elaborate grand scheme of falsely claiming the ancient Egyptians were white, or as Wortham states, they were "Caucasian." We know recent examination of the mummy, determination of his parentage and computer simulated reconstruction of his skin and facial features produce a "brown skinned" youth, easily at home in Harlem, New York City.

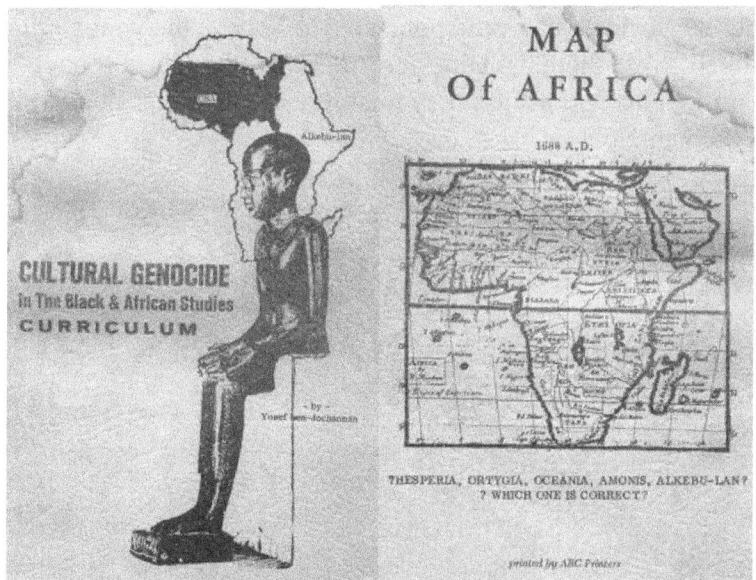

Dr. Ben's Books 22. CULTURAL GENOCIDE in the African American Studies **CURRICULUM** (1976).

This time around the exhibitors chose a bust depicting a "brown skinned" individual, not inconsistent with the computer model. Yet, in all this, the attraction has always been the jewelry and associated wealth the young king took to his grave. John H. Clarke, Professor Emeritus, Hunter College,

FREDERICK MONDERSON

CUNY liked to say "Tutankhamon was a minor king who got a major funeral." Yet, the "swicheroo" of the exhibits symbol says nothing about the king being a young black boy, certainly by Americas standards. That is, at the rate of the current "switcheroo," in another 30 years time when Tut returns to New York, perhaps then the two black replica statues guarding his burial chamber may be chosen as symbol. Then again, unless we remain intellectually vigilant, promoters may still foist on us the belief the statues were painted black for the funeral ritual. This too is falsity! It is a poor rational explanation that denies King Tut was a young black king. This way, young black boys and young black girls in this country and the world over, would not be led to believe the young king looked like them. Shame on individuals who propagate historical falsity because they misrepresent to the black as well as the white public.

Dr. Ben's Photo 312. Dendera, Home of Goddess Hathor. Beauty of the Hieroglyphics.

CELEBRATING DR. BEN-JOCHANNAN

Dr. Ben's Photo 313. Dendera, Home of Goddess Hathor. Beauty of the Hieroglyphics.

Dr. Ben's Photo 314. Dendera, Home of Goddess Hathor. Beauty of the Hieroglyphics.

FREDERICK MONDERSON

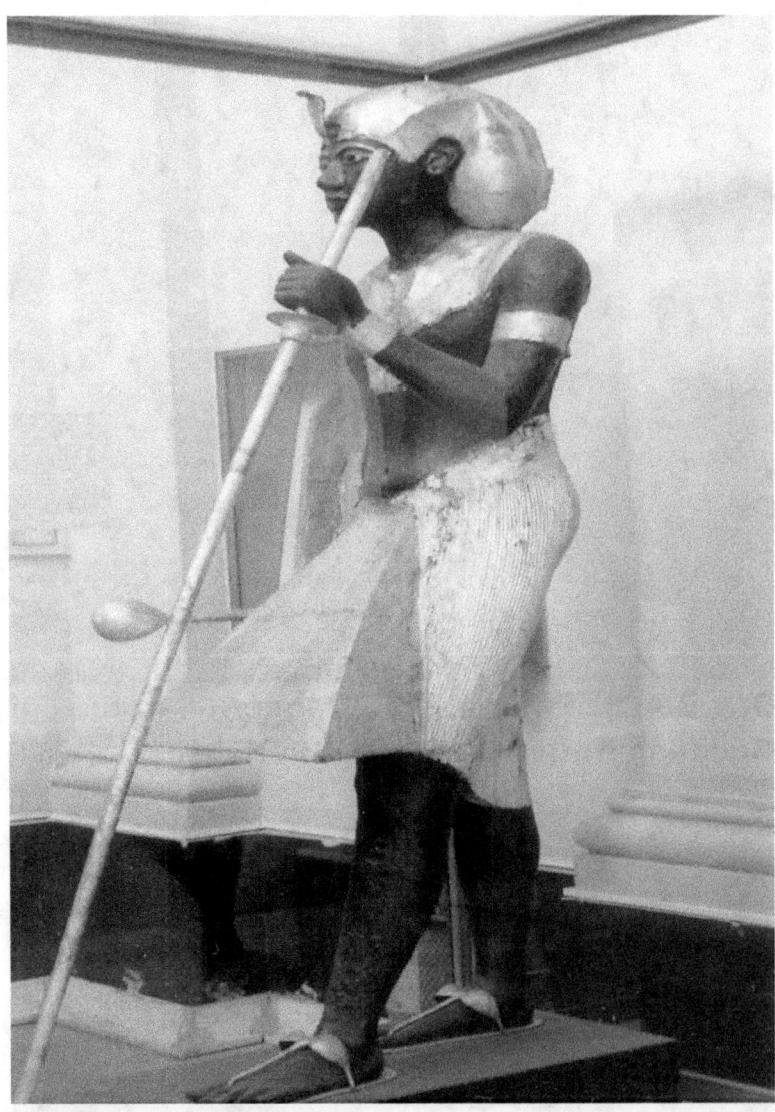

Dr. Ben's Photo 315. One of two life size replica statues of King Tutankhamon that stood guarding the burial chamber in his tomb and now in the Cairo Museum.

CELEBRATING DR. BEN-JOCHANNAN

The controversy of Tutankhamon is encapsulated in the whole question as to who were the ancient Egyptians and the reason for not using the alabaster bust, purportedly a white Egyptian; yet, in todays research potential environment, such misrepresentation cannot stand the critical scrutiny. Hence, after the challenge and struggle and switch, the status quo holds to the ridiculously absurd conclusion the ancient Egyptians were now "brown, white Egyptians." Nevertheless, to get a better appreciation for King Tut, one has to have an understanding of his parentage and the dynasty from which he hails.

The 18th Dynasty launched the New Kingdom after the expulsion of the Hyksos and its foundress Aahmes-Nefertari, mother of Amenhotep I and grandmother of Tuthmose I, is pictured in the British Museum as a "coal-black Ethiopian." In another context, the Distinguished Professor Dr. Ron Daniels has argued, not until the Atlantic Slave Trade has race been a factor in peoples relationships. Dr. Chancellor Williams in his *Destruction of Black Civilization* has postulated the theory of Asian penetration of ancient Egypt through the "marriage route." What this represented actually, in the power dynamics of ancient nation states relationships, marriage was one way of creating and cementing alliances. Essentially, it was about culture, trade and economics. Race was a mute issue.

In the 19th Century, creation and propagation of racial theories to justify enslavement of non-white peoples, particularly the African, at the time down trodden, brutalized and debased from the ghastly slave trade and slavery, Wilhelm Hegel and others "took Egypt out of Africa and Africans out of Egypt." In this fabrication of history the myth of a Caucasian Egypt was born. Whereas, no evidence existed of a "white Egyptian." Thus the newly created "Red Race" theory got lots of mileage. Under intense scrutiny, the "Red Race" was obfuscated in a "Brown Race" rather than a "Black Race." Yet, for example, in 1916 when the American Egyptologist James Henry Breasted published his *Ancient Times* he described the ancient Egyptians as a "Brown Race." Reissuing this work in 1935, scholars state the Rockefeller Foundation gave him millions of dollars to establish an Egyptological school at the University of Chicago. Then he changed his tune and spoke of the "great White Race" of Egyptians. Sad to say, generations have been fed this falsity. Yet, the propagators of a "white Egyptian" theory rather vehemently attack others who argue to the contrary as they themselves continue to confuse their constituency lost in the fabricated malaise.

Without a doubt, as Europe and America have denuded the non-white world of its great repository of artifactual remains, it is not far-fetched to conceive the perennial hoax perpetuated against black and white audiences whether purposely or through inundated ignorance.

Countering the contention, Dr. Cheikh Anta Diop, in his *African Origins of Civilization: Myth or Reality*, has masterfully demolished the theories of white as well as Asian origins of the ancient Egyptians. Equally, he has exposed the deceitful falsification of the historical record and his work stands as a bulwarked fortress against the falsity of a "white Egypt," while simultaneously attacking the "pillars of white supremacy" by exposing the lengths to which devious minds could conceive such elaborate schemes of falsification to mislead.

Toward the end of the 18th Dynasty, Amenhotep III whose reign climaxed a "golden age" of Egypt, began a co-regency with his son Amenhotep IV. Soon the old king retired to a palace called Malcata with his wife Queen Tiy and their son assumed the throne. The very beautiful Tiy, a Nubian, was well liked by her husband and enjoyed an elevated status and

CELEBRATING
DR. BEN-JOCHANNAN

came to exert much influence on both him and their son. Some scholars believe she introduced both to the sun worshipping Aten religion that came to play a significant role in the young kings rule. In the perennial claim of early scholars particularly Arthur Weigall, that significant rulers were Syrian and that Tiys parents Huya and Thuya were such, the initial source, the nucleus of Aten worship, the temple Gem Aton, was discovered in Nubia.

Dr. Ben's Photo 316. Bronze plaques depicting the boy king grasping a lion by its tail and as a sphinx trampling his enemies, Africans to the south of Egypt. If their color is as represented, then the kings is just as black and not painted for the funerary ritual!

Nevertheless, a short time after assuming leadership of the nation, Amenhotep IV changed his name to Akhenaton (Akhenaten) and decreed the new God Aton (Aten) disk of the sun should be paramount and all others must be subservient. This revolutionary action caused consternation in the nation because from time immemorial the people had set great store in the traditional Gods.

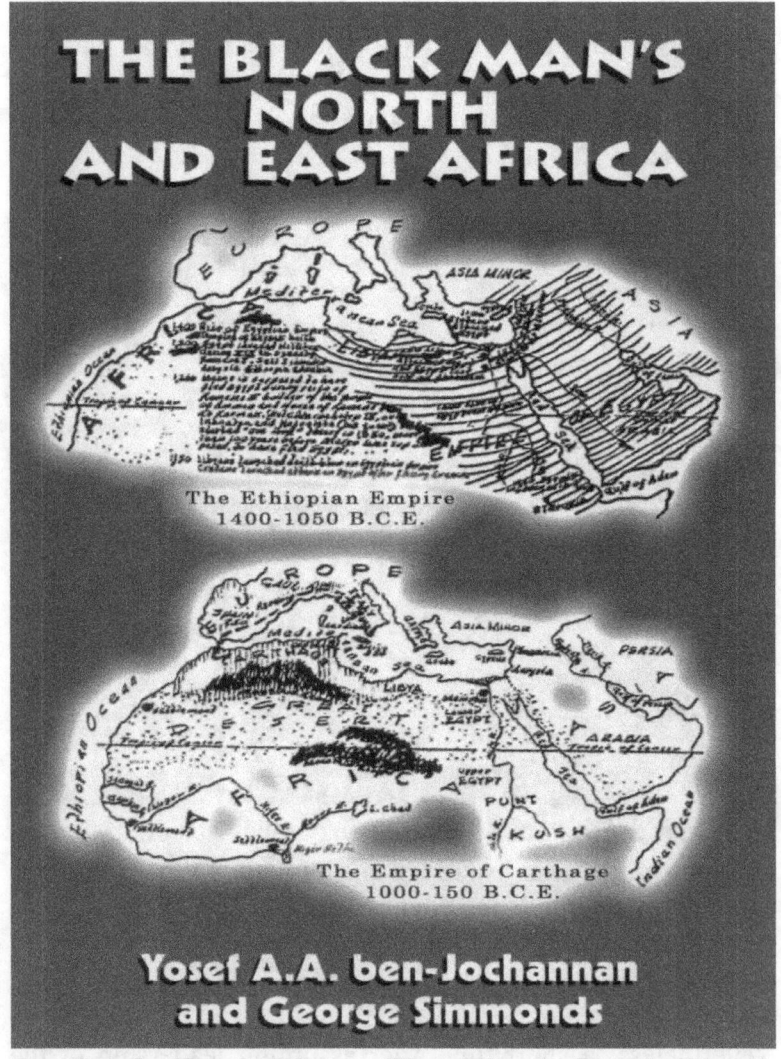

Dr. Ben's Book 23. The Black Man's North and East Africa (1984).

CELEBRATING DR. BEN-JOCHANNAN

The king built a temple to the Aten at the national temple at Karnak, home of the God of the empire, Amon-Ra. Soon he found himself uncomfortable at Karnak, having to walk the gauntlet of Amon-Ra worship paraphernalia to get to his temple.

As if imbued with a new divine inspiration the young king personally drew up the plans for the new city and temple, began praising his new God, composing poetry in praise of his deity, and instructing artists in new forms of artistic representation. Then he turned with a vengeance on Amon-Ra. He decreed everywhere Amon's name was found on monuments in the records, etc., it was to be expunged and replaced with that of the Aton.

The principal reason for his removal to Amarna is, since every city, nome, temple owed its very existence to a particular God, for Thebes and its Karnak temple to reject Amon was to renounce its very existence. Nevertheless, rather than peacefully lay the foundation for worship of the Aten, the sun, Akhenaton, Ikhnaton, unleashed violence against his competitor and the Amarna heresy disrupted the soul of the nation. The king had married the beautiful Nefertiti who bore him six daughters. Some scholars have argued she ruled in his stead upon his death or disappearance. Notwithstanding, being a foreigner she was not considered a legitimate heir and a succession of rulers followed. First, his brother Smenkhare ruled and he was soon followed by Tutankhaton, Akhnaton's son by another wife.

The behind the scenes manouvering that occurred upon Tutankhatens assumption of the mantle of leadership, insisted he agree to forego Aten worship, return the nations capital to Thebes, restore the nation God Amon-Ra and his worship at

FREDERICK MONDERSON

Karnak and equally change his name from Tutankhaten to Tutankhamon. In this Restoration, Amons adherents wreaked havoc on the remaining vestiges of Aton worship, destroying the city of Amarna and the Sanctuary of his God the Aten. Tutankhamon did much to restore the primacy of Amon by building at Karnak, Luxor, erecting the Restoration Stele as well as statues of Amon and Mut in front of the Sanctuary. Evidence indicates he and one of Amenhoteps daughters were married, lived merrily but soon he died from some infection suffered as a result of an accident. At his death, the Prime Minister Aye assumed the throne and officiated at Tuts burial.

Ayes strategy was to restore legitimacy to the throne, restore Amons primacy and close the horrible chapter in the nations history. He too was followed as pharaoh by General Horemhab, Commander of the national army. Horemhab dismantled Akhnaton's temple in the Fourth Court at Karnak and any other structures he erected there. To hide the stones of a solar deity, which could not be sullied beyond the temple walls, he constructed the Second Pylon and stuffed them therein. Ending the 18th Dynasty, Horemhab chose Rameses I as his successor, beginning the 19th Ramesside Dynasty, who completed the Pylon and so got credit for its construction.

Evidence seems to indicate to fill the Court between the Second and Third Pylons, Horemhab conceived of the hypostyle halls wings to flank the Processional Colonnade Amenhotep III had constructed beyond the Third Pylon. Amenhotep III also built a similar colonnade at Luxor. However, there is a remarkable distinction between the two colonnades. The Karnak colonnade has 12 massive columns while the Luxor one has 14. There is a similar Processional Colonnade at Soleb in Nubia that served as the prototype of his later erections at Karnak and Luxor. Rameses I began the magnificent hypostyle structure, Seti I completed it and began its decoration that was completed by Rameses II.

CELEBRATING DR. BEN-JOCHANNAN

Dr. Ben's Illustration 106. Inspection of the flocks of Geese and of their Herdsmen by a High Official.

The Ramesside pharaohs of the 19th and 20th Dynasties proved Amons greatest adherents. Seti I did much restoration work, removing Atons name and reinserting Amons with his alongside. Seti I built his extraordinary temple to the ancestors at Abydos, home of Osiris, the resurrected God of the dead. It is unique in that it is dedicated to 7 deities; the Osiris triad of Horus, Isis and Osiris; the three great Gods of the Empire, Amon-Ra, Ra-Horakhty and Ptah; and Seti himself, deified. Several unique features of this temple include a lateral appendage seemingly added after the original temple was built. Behind the temple is the Osireion. Not only does the Osiris Temple at Abydos contain the finest reliefs surviving from the New Kingdom, but in the appendage is located the Corridor of Kings. Here is found, *in situ*, the *Abydos Tablet*, a list of cartouches/Shennus or ovals listing 76 kings from Narmer to Seti I. Five of cartouches are left blank because Seti felt their owners had transgressed against the monarchy and therefore the state. The names are Hatshepsut, the first female

FREDERICK MONDERSON

who ruled as king, very early in the 18th Dynasty. She built a temple greater than her ancestor Mentuhotep II at Deir el Bahari; built a tomb in the Valley of the Kings after having prepared one in the Valley of the Queens; wore male clothing; and sported a beard. The other names are those of Amenhotep IV or Ikhnaton, Smenkhare, Aye and Tutankhamon, all associated with the Amarna heresy.

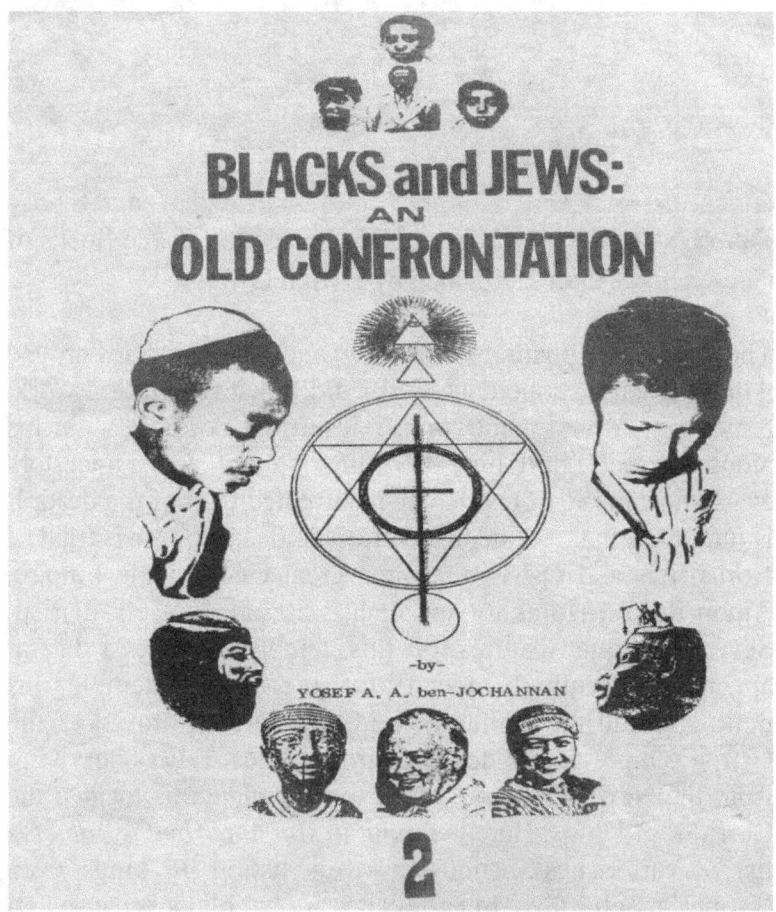

Dr. Ben's Book 24.   Blacks and Jews: An Old Confrontation (1985).

CELEBRATING DR. BEN-JOCHANNAN

The Englishman Howard Carter was part artist, part archaeologist who had been working in Egypt since the late 1890s. Perennially searching, he made a few insignificant discoveries at Thebes. For nearly two decades in the new century, Lord Carnarvon underwrote his efforts for a share of any discoveries. He discovered the tomb of Tutankhamon in November, 1922, while riding his horse in the Valley of the King. The horse's hoof actually fell into a hole and voila!

The *American Journal of Archaeology* XXVII (1923: 76-78) wrote accordingly about "The Tomb of Tutankhamon," that it is considered: "the most important royal tomb excavated in recent years, and contains objects of unique interest and value. Its situation is just below the tomb of Rameses VI. From the outer door found by Mr. Carter a flight of sixteen steps and a sloping passage led to a door in the east wall of a chamber of twenty-five feet long, twelve feet wide, and about nine feet high. The longer axis of the chamber is north and south, at right angles to the passage. The north wall is a partition wall, and contained a blocked-up door, indicating that beyond it was the actual burial chamber. On either side of this door were found wooden statues of the king. The body and limbs of each of these were painted black, while the headdress, skirt, and sandals were covered with gold leaf.

In the west wall an irregular opening, made by ancient robbers, allows a glimpse of a confused mass of tomb-furniture in an inner chamber. The outer room itself had been robbed of objects of precious metals, probably not long after the death of the king but the other furnishings were not much disturbed, and include an elaborately carved and ornamented royal chair or throne; three great state couches of gilded wood, three chariots, musical instruments, pottery and alabaster vases, boxes of clothing, boxes of preserved venison, mutton, duck, etc. Folded sheets, which were at first thought to be papyri, proved to be napkins. Among objects of special artistic interest is a wooden box covered with fine miniature paintings of hunting scenes: the pursuit of gazelles, wild asses, ostriches and hares is represented. A footstool is significantly inlaid with a row of figures of captives and prisoners. The largest chariot, which is semicircular in form and opens at the back, is of wood covered with gold leaf with delicately embossed decorations and exquisite inlaid designs in carnelian, malachite, lapis-lazuli, blue glaze and alabaster. At each corner is a small inlaid circle enclosing the sacred eye of Horus. These eyes are inlaid in blue, black and white. The inner surface of the chariot is of plain gold with large embossed cartouches of the king and his queen under the royal vulture which has wide, up-spreading wings."

"The edges of the chariot and the hand-rail around the top are covered with red leather, but the bottom, which was also of leather, has fallen away. Between the rail and the body in front are small-carved figures of Semitic captives. This is the largest Egyptian chariot known, and was doubtless used by the king and queen on state occasions. A yoke, which went across the necks of the horses, was found with it. Still more important than the chariots is a bust, perhaps representing the young queen, exquisitely carved in wood and covered with a thin coating of plaster. The figure has on its head a crown similar to that designed by Akhnaton for his queen. This is painted yellow to represent gold."

CELEBRATING DR. BEN-JOCHANNAN

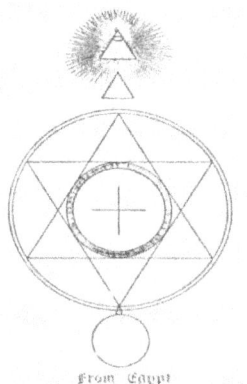

"It has the *uraeus* over the forehead. The face and neck are brownish yellow and the eyes and eyebrows black. The arms of the figure were intentionally cut off at the shoulders, but the body, which is draped in a white robe, extends far as the waist. The features show the soft expression characteristic of the artists of Akhnaton, whose daughter the figure may represent. The nostrils are finely carved, the lips are clear-cut and full, and the cheeks and chin round and youthful. The figure is an

FREDERICK MONDERSON

important work of art. On February 16 the burial chamber was opened and found to contain a gilded canopy almost filling the room. Within this was a second canopy enclosing the sarcophagus. Adjoining the burial chamber was another room full of chests, works of art, etc. The tomb lies so low that it is not free from damp, and some of the objects, which have been found in it, will need special care to prevent disintegration. In the work of clearing the tomb the discoverers are assisted by Dr. A. M. Lythgoe of the Metropolitan Museum and other Egyptologists. (A. E. P. Weigall, Philadelphia *Evening Bulletin*, Jan. 20-Feb 12, 1923.")

Dr. Ben's SIGNS AND SYMBOLS OF ALKEBULAN (1985).

American Journal of Archaeology XXVIII (1924: 84) continued its commentary on the Tomb of Tutankhamon, discovered by Howard Carter in 1922. Following all the excitement at the tombs first opening, it was closed and later reopened with Howard Carter beginning a systematic cataloguing of the precious contents. The *Journal* noted: "The two large wooden statues of the king, which stood on either side of the door which leads from the antechamber to the burial chamber, have been carefully packed and removed. To facilitate the removal of the elaborately constructed series of shrines, which enclose the sarcophagus of the king, it has been necessary to take down the wall between the antechamber and the shrine. The fresco on the inner face of the wall, though not of special interest, has been preserved. From the narrow space between the wall of the sepulchral chamber and the outermost shrine a considerable number of interesting objects have been recovered: wine jars; eleven black paddles; an inlaid royal staff; gilt emblems of Anubis. The great outer shrine, which is of wood, elaborately ornamented with designs in gold and in blue faience, has been dismantled. Within this shrine was a linen pall, supported on a wooden frame, and ornamented with

CELEBRATING
DR. BEN-JOCHANNAN

gold rosettes. This originally concealed the next inner shrine, but was in a state of partial disintegration, and had to be removed with great care."

Such antiques with historical and cultural relevance had to be preserved with great care and it became a significant task of the discoverers and those concerned to protect these valuables for posterity. Not only would these artifacts serve historical, cultural, and artistic purposes, it allowed those in the field of preservation to also be a part of preserving such evidence for posterity.

The *American Journal of Archaeology* XXVIII (1924) continued that: "Some valuable objects were removed from the space between the first and second shrines, including a gold staff and a silver staff, each surmounted by a statuette of the king. The second shrine is of wood covered with gold; and the doors are ornamented with representations of the king in acts of adoration. Within this, a third and a fourth shrine have successively been revealed. The decorations of the inner shrine are said to be more sumptuous and of finer quality than those of the outer shrine. The problem of removing without injury the parts of these structures has presented grave mechanical difficulties; but these have been so far overcome that in January the stone sarcophagus of the king was disclosed within the fourth shrine: and in February the granite cover was raised. Beneath a pall was found the gold case, which contains the mummy of the king, resting on a couch of a form, which resembles that of the couches discovered in the outer chamber. Adjoining the sepulchral chamber to the east is another room, containing an elaborate shrine in which it is expected that the canopic jars of the king will be found. Much funeral furniture is heaped up in front of and at the side of this shrine. At the present writing the investigation of the tomb has been halted by a disagreement between the excavators and the archaeological service of the Egyptian government."

Beyond the many tests, exhibits, commentary and speculation, Dr. Zahi awass, Supreme Head of the Antiquities Council in Egypt made an even more important comment showing Tutankhamon's continued influence some 88 years after his tombs discovery. According to Dr. Hawass, since Tutankhamon was the only king whose mummy was found in an intact, unopened tomb, we have no question about his identity. However, this realization creates the need to seek to determine the true identity of every other pharaoh because, not found in their original resting place, their names were determined from associated paraphernalia. All this, with the exception of Queen Hatshepsut whose identity has been confirmed through an elaborate system of tests and a missing tooth found nearby. Nevertheless, the treasure found in King Tuts tomb which constitutes his magic, of which a miniscule portion is included in the New York exhibit, echoes Prof. Clarke's contention what asked about African burials. He responded, "We put them away nicely!"

Dr. Ben's Illustration 107. Feast, with Musicians and Dancing Girls supplying the entertainment.

CELEBRATING DR. BEN-JOCHANNAN

35. IMMORTAL Distortions and Omissions in Ancient Egypt

Oftentimes scholars would argue the history of Egypt is incomplete because we dont have sufficient information, despite all we have. Yet still, and further they argue, we only have 15% - 20% of the information we should have. Even more, many, pardon I use the term right wing scholars to this day postulate the view, the ancient Egyptians were: (1) Caucasian people; (2) they came from South-west Asia; (3) they were Semitic; (4) they migrated to Africa bringing a high level of civilization; (5) they ruled over an indigenous people, elevating their mental faculties and social and artistic abilities without whose paternalistic blessings they would have remained at the level of brutes. Some critical scholars have labeled this mentality "The Hamitic Hypothesis" which essentially argued "Any evidence of a high culture found in Africa was brought there by people of a white morphology;" (6) *Ipso Facto* whites comprised the ruling elements of the society and blacks were slaves comprising the lowest echelons of the society who did all the work under white supervision; (7) the Egyptians were red-skinned whites and their women were lighter skinned because they did not go in the sun; (8) evidence of blacks in the higher echelons of the society are so painted for the funeral service; (9) the fundamental basis of Egyptian language is Semitic; (10) the migrating whites brought their art, architecture and industry to the Nile Valley and founded the civilization that developed there; (11) the migrating whites or Semites came from the Caucus region; (12) the cultural history of the Nile Valley traveled from North to South; (13) agriculture developed in Southwest Asia around 8000 B.C.E. and entered the Nile Valley around 4500 B.C.E., and thence elsewhere to Africa; (14) the Egyptians never developed the arch; (15) the Zodiac is a foreign importation into Egypt; (16) the Sphinx is the image of Khafre, builder of the second great pyramid at Ghizeh; (17) a young female guide in the Cairo Museum told this writers Group, Mentuhotep II was painted black for the funeral ceremony and she had never seen Osiris painted black; (18) the zero is an ancient Mesopotamian invention; (19) Julius Caesar is credited with developing the Leap Year he introduced into Europe; (20) until very late in its history as evidence indicates the Egyptians developed the use of iron.

Dr. Ben's Photo 317. Dendera, Home of Goddess Hathor. Nile God and Goddess bringing fruits of the land.

CELEBRATING
DR. BEN-JOCHANNAN

Dr. Ben's Photo 318. Dendera, Home of Goddess Hathor. Nile God and Goddess bringing fruits of the land.

Naturally, this enumerated list is a paltry sum in the long history of falsity that has colored, misrepresented and ossified the foundations, teachings and misrepresentation of ancient Egypt in presentations, books, reports and museums contributing to the present-day confusion in the discipline.

Dr. Ben's Photo 319. Dendera, Home of Goddess Hathor. Nile Gods bringing the fruits of the land.

Dr. Ben's Photo 320. Dendera, Home of Goddess Hathor. Nile Gods and a Goddess bringing the fruits of the land.

CELEBRATING DR. BEN-JOCHANNAN

Dr. Ben's Photo 321. Dendera, Home of Goddess Hathor. Nile Gods bringing the fruits of the land.

Dr. Ben's Photo 322. Dendera, Home of Goddess Hathor. Nile Gods and a Goddess bringing the fruits of the land.

FREDERICK MONDERSON

Dr. Ben's Photo 323. Kashida Maloney, of Brooklyn, New York, strikes a pose in Egypt.

CELEBRATING DR. BEN-JOCHANNAN

36. BLACK EGYPT AND THE STRUGGLE FOR INCLUSION
By
Dr. Frederick Monderson

Recently Hollywood has again imprinted upon the minds of young people with their films on Egypt, which include *The Mummy*, The Mummy Returns, *The Scorpion King* as well as the Disney productions of *Prince of Egypt* and particularly *Tarzan*, with his legacy in Africa, which now did not have any Africans in it. In olden times, *The Ten Commandments*, *The Mummy* and several versions of *Cleopatra*, to name a few, have left indelible impressions on the minds images regarding the people of Egypt. Equally too, *National Geographic Magazine* has done extensive writings on Egypt. More importantly, however, seeing these movies and reading *National Geographic Magazine* will not tell our people the ancient Egyptians were black! We must consider this distortion and omission as false representation! Many of the books, particularly those written by European and European-American writers today are so sanitized they give no inclination that the Egyptians were black people in North-East Africa along the banks of the River Nile.

For my Egyptian enlightenment I am indebted to Dr. Yosef ben-Jochannan, who in his admonition reminded me "When doing research on Egypt, get the oldest materials and work from there." This is because of the need for a reference point in view of modern Egyptological teachings. Importantly, however, many new books are so devoid of constructive reference to the role of black people in Egypt; there is need for vigorous re-writing, or certainly more critical analysis of their content, particularly with what we now know as history manifests itself. None of these books purposely propagate the fact of Queen Aahmes-Nefertaris blackness, despite her portrait in the British Museum that depicts a "coal-black Ethiopian" wearing the fashion of the times, white, red and blue, 1500 years before Christ and 3500 years ago. This Black Queen is the ancestress of the 18th Dynasty. She was deified and worshipped along with her son Amenhotep I, in their own temple at Thebes, on the West Bank and regarded as patrons of the mortuary area. His son, Thutmose I is the father of Queen Hatshepsut who ruled as pharaoh. When challenged for being an "uppity woman" who ruled as pharaoh, Hatshepsut underscored her relationship to Aahmes-Nefertari, the Black Queen and Goddess, her great grand-mother.

Dr. Ben's Photos 324. Colorful image of Horus as a hawk or falcon, some say peligren falcon, wearing the White resting on Red Double Crown. Notice the size of his claws.

CELEBRATING DR. BEN-JOCHANNAN

Dr. Ben's Photo 325. **Abydos**, Home of God Osiris. Entrance to the Temple with its famed 42 steps.

The modern historical record is replete with distortions and omissions. In 1898 the temple and tomb of Mentuhotep II, founder of the 11th Dynasty and the Middle Kingdom, was discovered and then cleared from 1903-1906 at Deir el Bahari, Thebes. In this structure scholars found King Mentuhotep dressed in Heb Sed festival attire wearing the Red Crown as symbolic of King of Lower Egypt. The assumption is there was another statue with the king wearing the White Crown as King of Upper Egypt. However, what was significant for the ethnicity of this monarch is he was painted black. This surviving statue was then moved to the Museum of Egyptian Antiquities in Cairo, where it still rests. Importantly, this temple was described in the major archaeological and news media as being the only surviving Middle Kingdom temple and the oldest temple discovered at Thebes andexcavate between 1903-1906. However, no one said anything about the kings color. It was 1959 when W. Stephenson Smith of the Boston Museum of Fine Arts in his *Art and Architecture of*

FREDERICK MONDERSON

Ancient Egypt stated, did say Mentuhotep had "black flesh." Thus, for more than half-a-century the great Egyptological scholars of Europe and America did not notice nor comment on this fact. In retrospect, how could we trust the accuracy of their other pronouncements?

In 1922, one hundred years after the decipherment of Hieroglyphics, Howard Carter discovered the intact tomb of King Tutankhamon, the boy king. There was such a great stir about this fabulous find, because of the wonderful treasures contained in his tomb. Still, two life-like wooden statues of the king were painted Black and stood guard over the burial chamber. Today, these are at the entrance to the Hall of Tutankhamon in the Cairo Museum. People by-pass them unnoticeably in their hurry to view the wonderful treasures he carried to the next life. In 1978-79, the King Tut exhibition toured the United States and the symbol of that display was an alabaster bust of the boy king. Alabaster is a white marble-like material. How appropriate to show this picture or image of the young African Pharaoh. No one would suspect in this "switcharoo!" All the major cultural institutions in the United States accepted the bust as symbolic of the kings representation. I dont think there was any objection, except perhaps by knowledgeable African-Americans who understood the distortion and fraud being perpetuated. However and interestingly enough, it was a fraud being perpetuated against the white public who was forced to accept a distorted view, in this and in so many instances.

It is my opinion and belief that the true color representation of kingly persons can only be viewed in wooden statues. These statues are the only ones painted, while others of stone or metal reflect the color of the material being used! This is significant because inasmuch as so little artifacts have survived and then the need to understand what may possibly have been destroyed for their de-facto link to Black ethnicity

CELEBRATING DR. BEN-JOCHANNAN

of the Egyptians, everything is suspect. We must not forget that the remains of ancient Africa are scattered throughout the capitals of Western Europe, Canada, the United States and Australia. As such then, there is so much "culture in captivity."

In *Destruction of Black Civilization: Great Issues of a Race 4500 B.C. to 2000 A.D.*, Chancellor Williams wrote about the record being distorting to show that despite Dynasties beginning with black founders they end up being pictured as white. This is particularly true of the 18th Dynasty. There is a statue of Seti I in the British Museum that is made of wood. Even the untrained eye could detect this statue of the son of Rameses I, the founder of the 19th Dynasty and father of Rameses II, seemed willing to depict a Black Pharaoh. There is a considered belief many such pieces are "doctored" in the "Basement" of institutions willing to be in complicity with this historical distortion. Perpetuating such a fraud is to deny Rameses II, "the Great" would be Black and so too the 19th Dynasty. Which brings us to the 20th Dynasty and last but not least, the 25th Dynasty?

There is talk that Egypt is building the world's largest museum to house some of its wonderful collection. Many things could be displaced, misplaced or certainly replaced. However, there is one case in the Cairo Museum, on the second floor where wooden statues are housed. Here there are small wooden statues of pharaohs painted Black alongside a particular statue of a leopard also painted Black. Now, if there is no connection between these wooden pieces it is hard to fathom. However,

FREDERICK MONDERSON

there is a question of whether they will be placed again in such close proximity when the new museum is opened.

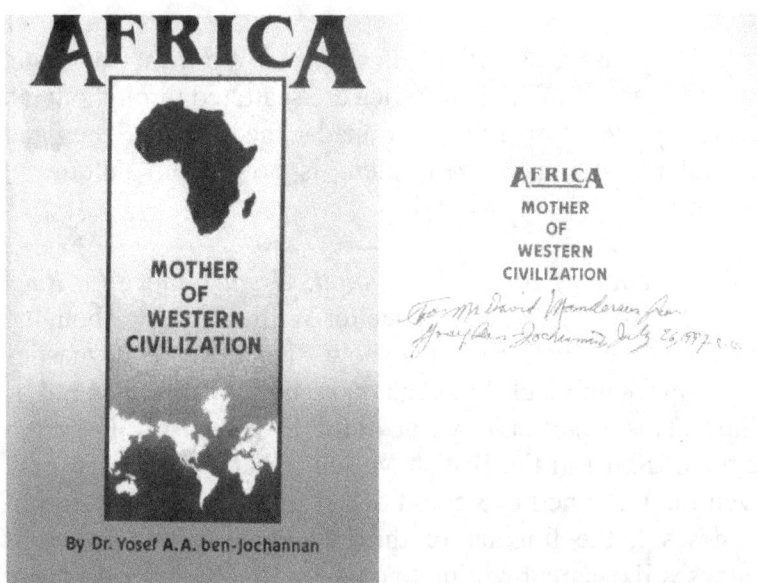

Dr. Ben's Book 25. Africa: Mother of Western Civilization. This is a revised version of the already presented First Edition also signed by the Author.

In the 19th Century several European explorers visited and reported from all over Egypt and these appeared in some of the credible journals or newspapers of that age. An issue of the Academy in the 1880s mentions the discovery of a tomb of an official of King Thutmose I of the 18th Dynasty. Here the official is pictured in his tomb praying to a statue of Thutmose I, painted black. This is lost to history and despite the numerous books being written today none contain any reference to this. Such a statue reinforces the blackness of the 18th Dynasty. In this era another such tomb records a black image of Osiris. Cheikh Anta Diop in *African Origin of Civilization*: *Myth or Reality* and *Civilization or Barbarism*: *An Authentic Anthropology* has shown how Egypt has been

CELEBRATING DR. BEN-JOCHANNAN

falsely represented. Underscoring the intellectual professionalism Diop brought to his studies, Clegg's "Black Rulers of the Golden Age" in Van Sertimas *Nile Valley Civilizations* has showed us Dr. Diop relied on "anthropology, iconography, melanin dosage tests, osteological measurements, blood groupings, the testimony of classical writers, self-descriptive Egyptian hieroglyphs, divine epithets, Biblical eyewitnesses, linguistic and various cultural data in support of his opinion regarding the ethnicity of the ancient Egyptians." In fact, Diop shows, the ancient Gods and Goddesses Apis, Min, Thoth, Isis, Hathor, and Horus, all were black. So too was Amon the great God of Thebes during the Middle and New Empires. Equally too, in *African Origins*, Diop quotes Herodotus that in Egypt the "Natives are black with the heat." Even further, regarding the Greek oracle at Adelphi, Herodotus said: "By calling the dove black they [the Dodonaceans] indicated that the woman was Egyptian." Diop further said Strabo wrote "Egypt founded Ethiopia" and that Diodorus also noted "Ethiopia founded Egypt." Either way we are dealing with the same people, the same cultural roots!

Even further, elsewhere in his *Physiognomonica*, Aristotle, in his search for the mean wrote: "Egyptians are cowards because they are black." So too were northern Europeans cowards because they were white! The Greeks are the mean in between. Aristotle was wrong about their courage but right about their color.

If we start with the ancient scholars, historians and priests, Herodotus, Manetho, Diodorus Siculus, Strabo, and even Aristotle and Lucan, all agree the ancient Egyptians were black. Herodotus said the "Colchians, Ethiopians and

FREDERICK MONDERSON

Egyptians" were Negroes with "Broad noses, thick lips, wooly hair and had burnt" or black "skin."

Even more, when we look at the works of such brilliant scholars as Cheikh Anta Diop, the Senegalese "Pharaoh," *The African Origin of Civilization: Myth or Reality, Civilization or Barbarism: An Authentic Anthropology, The Cultural Unity of Black Africa*; Theophile Obenga's *Ancient Egypt and Black Africa* and *African Philosophy: The Pharaonic Period* 2780-330 B.C.; then, Ivan Van Sertimas *Egypt: Child of Africa, Egypt Revisited*, and *Nile Valley Civilizations, Great African Thinkers: Cheikh Anta Diop*; then Yosef ben-Jochannan's *Black Man of the Nile and His Family, Africa: Mother of Western Civilization, African Origins of the "Major" Western Religions*, and *Abu Simbel to Ghizeh: A Manual and Guide Book*; and Fred Monderson's *10 Poems Praising Great Blacks for Mike Tyson* and *Seven Letters to Mike Tyson on Egyptian Temples, Where are the Kamite Kings, Research Essays on Ancient Egypt, Temple of Karnak, Hatshepsut's Temple at Deir el Bahari, Egypt: Essays on Ancient Kemet, Who Were the Ancient Egyptiians? Let's Liberate the Temple*, etc., the reader gets the full dimension of the issues, problems and solutions.

Therefore, the work of reclamation and rectification of Africa and African roles in ancient Egypt must continually be stressed, for the young should never allow their history to be systematically and continually distorted. They must continue to assert and defend Egypt as African. The reason is not because the valuable antiquities of this wonderful heritage are in captivity in western collections and museums. The reason is that we must not acquiesce in the pernicious and false position that there is no history of Africa, only a history of Europeans in Africa. Africa has a long, rich and culturally diverse and enlightening history. She first spoke through Ethiopia, the Nile Valley and Egypt. We must continue to

CELEBRATING DR. BEN-JOCHANNAN

affirm that Egypt was a black civilization, as it was peopled by black Africans for most of its duration, and to trust the work of our redemptive black scholars, researchers and historians who for many years in their careers have grappled with the questions of distortions and omissions and now have given us the tools to continue the fight for African historiographic reconstruction. Diop said the history of Africa cannot be fully told without the inclusion of Egypt. The African scholar who refuses to deal with Egypt is either a neurotic or ill-educated. We must teach and defend Egypt as African and therefore black. Egypt was a black civilization!

Dr. Ben's Photo 326. **Abydos, Home of God Osiris**. Left side pillars of the entrance to the Temple.

FREDERICK MONDERSON

Dr. Ben's Photo 327. **Abydos**, Home of God Osiris. Right side pillars of the entrance of the Temple.

Dr. Ben's Photo 328. On the Nile River, Kashida Maloney of Brooklyn, New York, in deep contemplation about the significance of the monuments, the trip, etc.

CELEBRATING DR. BEN-JOCHANNAN

Dr. Ben's Temple Site Ticket (Board) 8. Abydos. Seti I's Temple to God Osiris.

37. RED – COLOR OF THE GODS
By
Dr. Fred Monderson

More and more, new and dynamic research is blowing away the smoke that clouded interpretation of the ethnological basis of ancient Egypt, grossly misinterpreted to falsely represent Europe, Caucasians, as the creators, originators of a culture steeped in African ethnicity, symbolism, motifs, spirituality and demographic factors. Despite their significant work in archaeology, anthropology, biometric and related fields, it now seems these scholars' efforts in rush to interpret, publish, and propagate through publications, lectures, displays and fund-raising, were fueled by the desire to falsely portray Europeans not Africans as the culture's architects. We know, history is a subject that seeks to include as much credible evidence as possible; to paint a complete picture of any historical phenomenon, but when, upon close examination of information now deemed grossly inaccurate, whether through distortion or omission, fueled by racist notions, it forces future researchers to not simply offer a corrective but question the original motive and intent of such interpretation. This has been the case in Egyptological research over the past two centuries and though currently in vogue, its being vigorously challenged by new and ground-breaking Afrocentric research.

A recent work entitled *Black Genesis* (2011) by Thomas Brophy and Robert Bauval argued Black Africans inhabiting a region west of Southern Egypt, Nabta Playa, were likely the forerunners of the pharaohs. These scholars offer archaeoastronomical evidence and sculptured and artistic remains that depict these black people practicing stargazing, calendar creation, mathematically positioning stones to map the heavens and were viewed and seriously considered as laying the foundation of what we today know as science. The area of this early African culture nucleus was also teeming with game and flourishing agricultural practices that benefitted from heavy rainfall in the region, trapped in lakes after torrential down pour. When finally, the rains subsided and the area desiccated, not being able to support a thriving community of both agricultural and pastoral practices, the people migrated to the Nile Valley, settling in the region south of the vicinity of Aswan and Elephantine Island. The new research shows the rise, development and decline of this cultural phenomenon has been dated anywhere from 20,000-3500 B.C.

Evidence has revealed these Africans of that luscious desert region, among other practices were pastoralists. From these endeavors they originated religious worship of the Cow Goddess. We know the "Great Mother" of the universe has been shown as a cow probably because of the nourishment gained from this animal that provided milk, blood, meat, leather and more. Interestingly, the Goddess Hathor of Egyptian mythology and religion has been depicted as a cow. It ought not to be forgotten, a popular theme of Egyptian mythology and religion, "the many moods of Hathor," depicts

CELEBRATING
DR. BEN-JOCHANNAN

the Goddess as a cow, in fact, seven cows in different attitudes assisting the mummy. One such depiction survives in a small room or chapel at Medinet Habu, Mortuary Temple of Rameses III, in the temple proper, the Sanctuary area. We know of the mythological depiction of "Hathor coming out of the hills of Deir el Bahari" and also an image on a wall depicts Hatshepsut in her temple there, drinking at the udders of the "Cow Goddess Hathor." Equally, it's been clearly stated by E.A. Wallis Budge, noted British Keeper of Egyptian and Assyrian Antiquities of the British Museum and a prolific Egyptological researcher and writer who places the "origin of Hathor in the Sudan." His characterization of the Goddess as "Sudani" is not in conflict with the time and people of Nabta Playa that Bauval and Brophy have credited with migrating to the Nile and laying the foundations for pharaonic Egypt. "The many moods of Hathor" show generally the Goddess in her relationship to the mummy on it journey to the next world.

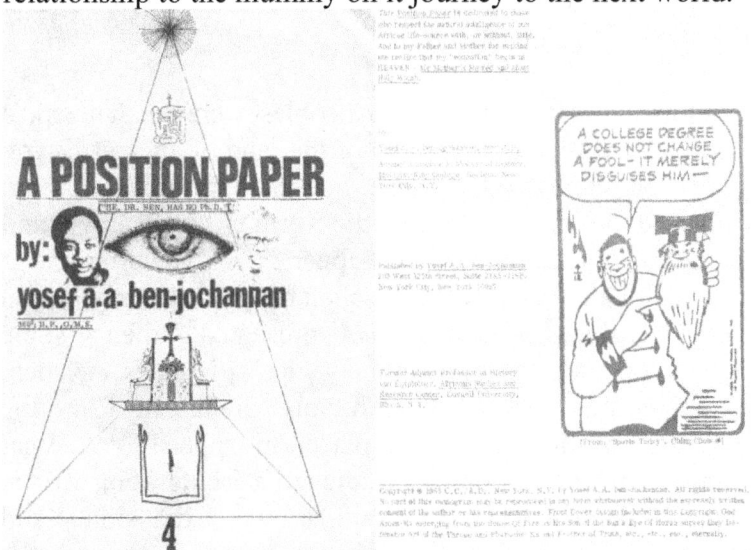

Dr. Ben's Book 26. A POSITION PAPER: "He Dr. BEN, HAS NO Ph.d!" (1985).

FREDERICK MONDERSON

Various sources credit the early Egyptians with being pastoralists. Others describe them as a "boat people." While some skeptical scholars have tended to accept any such designations, they choose to ascribe such descriptions to a migrating people from South-West Asia, whom Wortham described as "Caucasian." In addition, the "father of Egyptian archaeology," W.M. Flinders Petrie had proposed a theory of a "New Race in Egypt" under the assumption, they originated outside of Africa. Yes, but they won't consider south of Egypt. However, realizing many of Petrie's pronouncements were driven by racist assumptions of European supremacy, led by the British of course, but under intense scrutiny his migration views were discounted. Rejecting his findings, detractors argued for an indigenous nature of the Egyptians. Amidst several indigenous theories, scholars insisted on a North/South dichotomy of two races, one dominating the culture then the other. Still, this reasoning originally argued for predominance of the North since this area was nearer the Mediterranean and Sinai Peninsula culture clusters.

By allowing such a view, two peoples were recognized, a black and a white, as occupiers of the land of ancient Egypt, one predominating in the North, one in the South. Naturally, this placed the white element in the North or Lower Egypt and the black element, the South or Upper Egypt. Nevertheless, it is a hallmark of Egyptian scholarship that only when incontrovertible evidence is presented then some consideration is given the argument such articulates. As such, not being able to eliminate the black element from the equation, *ipso facto*, they were placed in Upper Egypt. What is further incontrovertible, for the greatest duration of the cultural development, consolidation, expansion and perpetuation of the Egyptian miracle, Upper Egypt was the driving, creative force of innovation and experimentation as the preponderance of monumental evidence left in the physical

CELEBRATING
DR. BEN-JOCHANNAN

geography show. Much of this is unequivocally proven in the architecture, art, religion, transport mechanisms and science accomplishments whose remains adorn cultural and academic institutions throughout the world were generally acquired from the Southern Upper Egypt.

Dr. Ben's Papyrus 12. The **Register** or division of the illustrated frame was an important artistic invention where multiple scenes can be represented in a single image.

In regard the "Boat people" theory, it seems reasonable to argue, people in a riverain culture would more likely be "boat people" than migrating wanderers crossing a desert region to an unknown land. We should be reminded; the black inhabitants of Nabta Playa, west of the Nile in the Upper Egyptian region were on the move by c. 3500 B.C. arriving thereabouts in the vicinity south of Aswan, Elephantine Island, the First Cataract region possessing millennia of accumulated scientific knowledge. It is also not coincidental that Bruce Williams of the University of Chicago discovered among that institutions artifactual "holdings," evidence of the world's earliest monarchy resident at Qustol in Nubia/Upper Egypt. Ivan Van Sertima identified this culture as the Kingdom of Ta-Seti. We must also recognize in those remote times, political

FREDERICK MONDERSON

boundaries, borders, were not as clearly delineated as we understand such today.

Nevertheless, the outstanding motifs of this discovery involved a Nile boat, enthroned pharaoh wearing the White Crown, a Serekh atop a palace façade and an incense burner, etc. These features were dated approximately 3400 B.C., some 200 years before we see such pharaonic paraphernalia in Egypt at 3200 B.C. Still, it is more palatable to associate these cultural accomplishments to the early "scientists" of Nabta Playa rather than migrating Caucasians who never arrived in Egypt, if they ever did, any sooner than 2500-2400 B.C., a thousand years later! Dr. Diop credits the first Caucasians, the Hyksos, as arriving following the Middle Kingdom, c. 1800 B.C. Notwithstanding, all that has gone before, scientists recently discovered, in a cave in South Africa, evidence that Stone Age man had tools as well as "pottery and mixed ocher paint more than 107,000 years ago." This fascinating discovery of an ancient "paint factory" workshop of the Middle Stone Age raised a number of interesting and intriguing questions relating to then, now and the years in-between.

Dr. Ben's Photo 328a. Abydos, Home of God Osiris. Erik Monderson stands before the Osireion at rear of the Osiris temple with the desert in the background.

CELEBRATING DR. BEN-JOCHANNAN

Dr. Ben's Photo 329. Abydos, Home of God Osiris. Seti incenses enthroned Horus in Double Crown.

Dr. Ben's Photo 329a. Abydos, Home of God Osiris. Seti prepares to incense and pour a Libation to enthroned Horus as Ra-Horakhty.

FREDERICK MONDERSON

Dr. Ben's Photo 330. **Abydos, Home of God Osiris**. In Blue or War Crown, Seti incenses and pours a libation before enthroned Horus.

CELEBRATING
DR. BEN-JOCHANNAN

Dr. Ben's Photo 331. Abydos, Home of God Osiris. An extraordinary scene of Seti in full "battle dress" of Double Crown lined with uraei, neck-laced, bearded, in apron and see-through long flowing dress and holding scepter and ankh with a tail, approaches and gestures to Anubis sporting implements of his power within his shrine as he offers "Life" to the nostrils of the King.

FREDERICK MONDERSON

Dr. Ben's Photo 332. Abydos, Home of God Osiris. Wearing a headdress with uraei and tassel with uraei and disk surmounted by horns, disk, feathers, uraei and disks above and below the horns, bearded, neck-laced with armbands and bracelets, embroidered short kilt, and holding a bird, Seti kneels to receive truncheon and life from enthroned Amon-Ra while enthroned Khnum has "got his back" with life and laying on the hand!

It is common knowledge sometime between the Old and New Stone Age man began to transform his habits and his thinking. The only thing is, while Europe was given prominence in researching this area of interest, scholars did not focus much on this transformation unfolding in Africa because the initial research was done in Europe to prove the primacy of Europeans to other peoples on the face of the earth. Let us not

CELEBRATING DR. BEN-JOCHANNAN

forget, as this line of inquiry unfolded in the 19th Century especially, Europe had transitioned from its imperialist practices of "naked imperialism" of the Slave Trade and "New World" conquest to one of "enlightened imperialism" with the ramifications of colonialism and "intellectual imperialism" that developed there from. As Prof. John H. Clarke pointed out and it must never be forgotten, "The people who preached racism, colonized history" and in so doing, "Europe colonized the worlds knowledge." The resulting arrogance of power pitted "European powers" against each other scrambling for colonial territory around the world in general and Africa in particular, and this competition carried them to the precipice of self-annihilation resulting in the First World War and later World War Two.

Nonetheless, the image we came to associate with Stone Age man is that he was a hunter and gatherer. That is, men hunted and women gathered or foraged for edible foods among growing victuals. At that time his food supply was considered 90 percent meats and 10 percent Agri-vegetation. In time he developed seed culture and his food changed to 10 percent meats and 90 percent Agri-produce. In the division of labor dichotomy, men manufactured tools for the hunt while women tended the family and foraged for edible produce. In disposing of seeds, women accidentally discovered agriculture. As this process unfolded, also through the "Oasis theory" animals became domesticated and all parties settled down in change from nomadic to sedentary existence.

FREDERICK MONDERSON

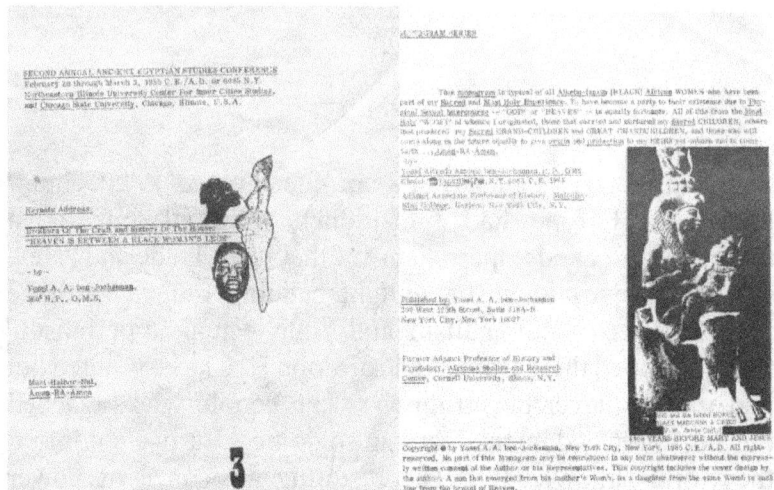

Dr. Ben's Book 27. "Brothers of the Craft and Sisters of the House : Heaven Is Between A Black Woman's Legs" (1985).

As their social consciousness developed, humans first inhabited natural covers or ravines and caves. Then they later built shelter. Growing culturally, they created sites for various functions. There were "butchering sites" where game was cut up; "workshop sites" or "floors" where tools were crafted and repaired. At "ceremonial sites" certain rites were celebrated and at "burial sites" the dead were disposed of. In "home bases," having retired for the day and with chores completed, tools of the hunt repaired, man sat by the fireside and began to plan for the next day's hunt, "speculate and philosophize." Those with artistic abilities began to paint using the walls of the cave as a canvass. A popular theme was game of the hunt fueled by the belief if such was drawn on the cave walls this may aid in a successful hunt the next day. In North, South and East Africa particularly, evidence remains of Stone Age artists at work. It is interesting that some sites were visited by different generations of artists who used the same "canvass," never erasing but painting over the same surface. It is,

CELEBRATING
DR. BEN-JOCHANNAN

however, not certain if particular sites were chosen because of the natural smoothness of the "canvass," the religious or sacred nature of the spot or a superstitious belief painting on that site would bring luck in the hunt. One more important observation can be made of these early artists is that they took liberty in representing their subjects giving them size, legs and loops not actually in their physiogamy. Again, on one particular canvas with giraffe head and horns of wild sheep and other figures, the "expedition discovered 12 superimposed layers painted during a period of perhaps 2,000 years." To this revelation L'Hote (1987: 191) reasoned: "It is not known why different artists used the same locations. Some sites may have offered a better painting surface than others or held special religious importance. Perhaps the act of painting filled a ceremonial function more important than the artwork itself."

Dr. Ben's Photo 329. Abydos, Home of God Osiris. Seti presents a golden necklace to a defaced enthroned deity.

FREDERICK MONDERSON

Dr. Ben's Photo 333. Abydos, Home of God Osiris. In the Osiris shrine, Thoth with double scepters each sporting uraeus wearing red and white crowns individually, offers "life" to Osiris.

CELEBRATING DR. BEN-JOCHANNAN

Dr. Ben's Photo 334. Abydos, Home of God Osiris. On the same plane with Osiris and wearing red and white Double Crown and holding triple scepters Horus pours a libation from 3 vessels before the great God in his shrine as he wears a crown of disk and feathers on horns supporting four uraei with disks and feathers, and four hanging uraei with disks and with uraeus on his crowns brow with tassel hanging down, Osiris holds his crook and whip while the four sons of Horus stand atop a shrine of *Ma'at*.

FREDERICK MONDERSON

Dr. Ben's Photo 335. Abydos, Home of God Osiris. Isis in Queen Mother Crown with uraei surmounted by Double Crown and holding *Heh* symbol for eternity, seems to be offering her jewelry to Seti.

In the article, "In African Cave, Ancient Paint factory Pushes Human Symbolic Thought Far Back," a science writer, John Noble Wilford, for *The New York Times* dated Friday, October

CELEBRATING
DR. BEN-JOCHANNAN

14, 2014, p. A 14 notes, "These cave artisans had stones for pounding and grinding colorful dirt enriched with a kind of iron oxide to a powder, known as ocher. This was blended with the binding fat of mammal-bone marrow and a dash of charcoal. Traces of ochers were left on the tools, and samples of the reddish compound were collected in large abalone shells, where the paint was liquified, stirred and scooped out with a bone spatula." Even further, the article added, "archaeologists said that in the workshop remains they were seeing the earliest example of how emergent Homo sapiens processed ocher, one of the species first pigments in wide use, its red color rich in symbolic significance. The early humans may have applied the concoction to their skin for protection or simply decoration, experts suggested. Perhaps it was their way of making social and artistic statements or other artifacts."

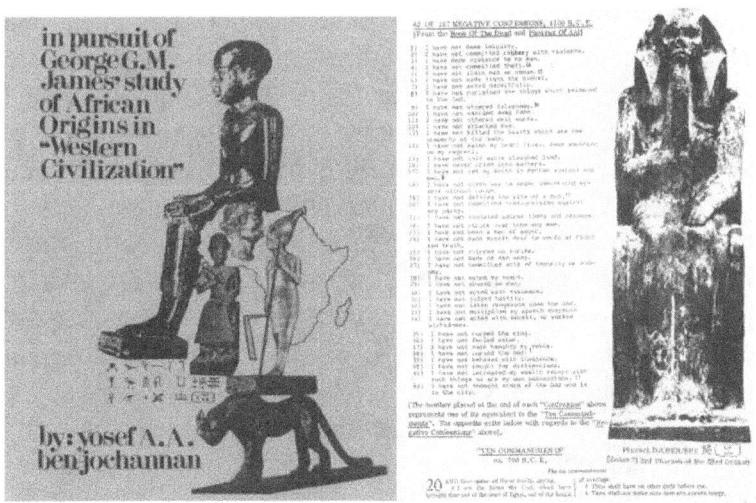

Dr. Ben's Book 28. *In Pursuit of George G.M. James' Study of African Origins in "Western Civilization"* (1980).

FREDERICK MONDERSON

This is interesting, for we know the ancient Egyptians colored themselves red and this generated a great deal of commentary. Dr. Cheikh Anta Diop, a great proponent of the view that the ancient Egyptians were Black Africans argued the Egyptians painted themselves red so as to be distinguished from other Africans. Equally, Dr. ben-Jochannan pointed out Nubians, ancient and modern, also painted themselves red. In fact, modern Nubian brides, he explained, paint themselves red with the Henna Plant. However, wanting evidence that the Egyptians were white men, proponents of this theory began emphasizing the ancient Egyptians as a race of "Red, white men."

All such designations were intended to remove the discussion from its true nature because Antiquarian Societies in Europe fell in love with Egypt; government, museum and private collections of Egyptian artifacts in Europe and America abounded; academics and lecturers spread the word to a public gullible in accepting unquestioned evidence from experts and willing to see their cultural heritage in an ancient setting, accepted the prevailing view; while books, discussions and even movies began to reinforce the view of a white Egypt; and, as no credible and sustained critique of a "Caucasian Egypt" challenged the accepted norm, falsity, distortion and omission reigned. Today, as new evidence begins to chip away at the false notions, this forces us to remember "old ideas die hard" and that people threatened by new information are victims of cognitive dissonance.

CELEBRATING DR. BEN-JOCHANNAN

Dr. Ben's Book 29. AXIOMS AND QUOTATIONS OF YOSEF BEN-JOCHANNAN (1982).

Dr. Ben's Book 29. *AXIOMS AND QUOTATIONS OF YOSEF BEN-JOCHANNAN* **(1982)**.

FREDERICK MONDERSON

From the Stone Age to ancient Egypt the color red has had a magnetic attraction, perhaps because of its brightness, like gold as the sun. The color gold was considered God-like. When the poor could not take gold into afterlife, they carried objects painted gold. However, not being able to paint themselves golden, red became the next most logical color considering its history. It is therefore understandable the ancient Egyptians would paint themselves red since they considered themselves special and in addition their relationship with the Gods may also be emphasized. This seems even more reasonable. What is even more significant, they were not the only people to utilize the brightness of red. Dr. Yosef ben-Jochannan pointed out that modern Nubians still paint their young brides with the henna plant, making them red. Equally, if the modern Egyptians are supposedly no different from the ancient Egyptians why do they not continue this ancient tradition, yet the modern Nubians do continue such.

Dr. Ben's Photo 336. Abydos, Home of God Osiris. Isis watches Seti's back as he stands before enthroned Ra-Horakhty.

CELEBRATING DR. BEN-JOCHANNAN

Dr. Ben's Photo 337. Abydos, Home of God Osiris. With Isis as Hathor behind enthroned Osiris, Seti offers a plant and pours a libation to the God, while at right the king receives ankh and Heh from enthroned Ra-Horakhty.

Dr. Ben's Photo 337a. Abydos, Home of God Osiris. With Isis at his rear and holding the Heka Scepter, Seti receives emblems of power from enthroned Horus

FREDERICK MONDERSON

Dr. Ben's Photo 338. Abydos, Home of God Osiris. Clad in lion skin, Seti stands before and salutes Osiris.

Now, continuing the use of red from the South African natives of Kolombo in that early age, *The New York Times* of February 1972 mentions a "43,000-year-old Mine discovered in Swaziland," the world's earliest in South Africa. Before

CELEBRATING DR. BEN-JOCHANNAN

Present, means you have to discount 2000 years of the current era (41,000 B.C.), in which residents were mining hematite, a form of oxide used for metallurgical purposes but also be part of the paint factory supply. This discovery raised an even more serious issue, that of agriculture. Years ago, when Prof. John H. Clarke of Hunter College of C.U.N.Y. was asked about the significance of this find, his comments were: "If people were mining a form of iron oxide at this time it meant they had had a large population. To feed such, they had to have begun practicing agriculture" which threw this whole issue into contention since agriculture was thought to have been discovered in South West Asia c. 8000 B.C., spreading throughout Africa after 4500 B.C.

The magazine **Science** reported in 1982 there was evidence of Nile Valley farming of wheat, barley, lentils, beans, fruits, vegetables, etc., at 16,500-14,500 B.P. (14,500-12,500 B.C.). Elsewhere evidence in **Man** indicated Upper Nile catch basins revealed mealing stones for grinding wheat dated at c. 11,000 B.C. This takes us off message but it certainly fuels questions about entrenched interpretation of issues that point to and question the role of Africans in generating Egyptian civilization.

Louis and Mary Leakey were extraordinary archaeologists who made the world take Africa seriously by first discovering *Zinjanthropus Boisie* dated at 1.75 million years old. Then Mrs. Leakey made discoveries of footprints she dated at a "firm date of 3.25 million" years. However, Mrs. Leakey made another significant contribution by discovering and cataloguing more than two thousand Stone Age sites in East Africa depicting fresh and outstanding Stone Age Art. Much of both members of this team's work was reported in *National Geographic Magazine*. In discussing paints, Mrs. Leakey's

FREDERICK MONDERSON

"Tanzania Stone Age Art" (1983: 86) not only mentions the colors Stone Age man used but confessed "Their choice of colors is interesting for: the predominant red was made from ocher, which is derived from iron ore. Black probably came from manganese, and bird droppings may have provided the basis for the white." In the Sahara the Frenchman Henry L'Hote made significant discoveries at Tassili and he too identified these people as black, Negroes and their art was also predominantly red based. Like so many areas in Africa, the art of Nabta Playa was also red based!

Dr. Ben's Papyrus 13. Before a "**Table of Offerings**," Queen Nefertari, wife of Rameses II, offers two jars to enthroned Goddess Hathor wearing horns and disks.

One of the arguments for the origins of the ancient Egyptians put forward by another Frenchman Gaston Maspero is that people from the west, in the Sahara, migrated to the Nile but these were Europeans who may have lived on the North African Mediterranean shore. Two things are clearly evident here. The first is confusing as the European proponents for an external origin of the Egyptians have held, they came through

CELEBRATING DR. BEN-JOCHANNAN

the Isthmus of Suez, through the Horn of Africa and even through the Nubian Desert, all in the East and Upper Egypt. All this, in an age of global white supremacy, colonialism and imperialism when justification for European dominance was the order of the day! Hence, anything African was not considered thinkable.

Second, the new information was not available when the "law" was being laid, ossifying the falsity in the minds of men. It stands to reason, if red was a predominant color in art in South, East, West, Central, then why not in North-East Africa? It is not farfetched to think they were all connected. To argue otherwise, be careful, the men in white jackets may be lurking! Meanwhile, with the ancient Egyptians, symbolism and symbolic logic were the orders of the day in practically every field of expertise and experience, especially in terms of intellectual expression. Thus, use of red to symbolically paint or beautify is not a stretch of the imagination; for, when considering the precedent for decoration of the body as a symbolic expression, such practices extended more than 107,000 years in several parts of Africa. To not associate the Nile Valley Africans with this phenomenon but to claim these people were "red Caucasians" not only flies in the face of logic but is downright stupid and racist. This is one example of the falsity African historiographic reconstruction seeks to address.

FREDERICK MONDERSON

Dr. Ben's Photo 339. **Abydos, Home of God Osiris**. In Blue Crown with tassel, Seti incenses and pours a libation to enthroned Ra-Horakhty.

CELEBRATING DR. BEN-JOCHANNAN

Dr. Ben's Photo 340. Abydos, Home of God Osiris. In Blue or "War Crown," Seti presents his name as *Ma'at* (defaced) to Osiris.

38. CELEBRATING IVAN VAN SERTIMA
By
Dr. Fred Monderson

In ancient Egypt, the king celebrated his *Heb Sed Festival* of rejuvenation after 30 years of rule, which was a significant achievement then, as is any such lengthy accomplishment, now. Its public knowledge, when Dick Clark, the TV personality, celebrated 30 years of New Years "Rocking Eve," this was greeted with much hoopla and congratulatory accolades from print, radio and television media; emphasizing

FREDERICK MONDERSON

his longevity and how significant this milestone really was. Granted this was so! However, after Gil Noble the public service news reporter reached the same milestone with his TV Show, **LIKE IT IS**, ABC, Channel 7, New York, moved to cancel this program. Fortunately, the community and such groups as **CEMOTAP** under the distinguished leadership of Dr. James McIntosh and Sister Betty Dopson dispatched a forceful rebuke in defense of this important program. Both sides recognized the significance and ramifications of the public service message this important show presented, as demonstrated by the interest generated over the longevity of its duration. As a result, the Gil Noble show continues today telling it "**Like It Is**" and now he has an international audience.

Dr. Ben's Photo 341. **Abydos, Home of God Osiris**. Entrance Pylon to Rameses IIs Temple at Abydos.

CELEBRATING DR. BEN-JOCHANNAN

Dr. Ben's Photo 342. Abydos, Home of God Osiris. Left side Gateway decoration of Rameses II's Temple at Abydos showing the King offering a vase to enthroned Thoth (left) and right, he presents to Osiris while the Sun Disk sporting uraei and ankhs hovers over the Kings head and his cartouche is evident.

This April 2009, marks the 30th Anniversary of the *Journal of African Civilizations* founded by Dr. Ivan Van Sertima of Rutgers University. This writer, historian, anthropologist, teacher, humanitarian and scholar extraordinaire has produced ground-breaking scientifically based, accurate and historically truthful, research monogams depicting people of African ancestry, as subjects not objects of historical phenomena. Van Sertimas initial emphasis has been on Blacks in ancient Egypt and expanding into a historical "catch-basin funnel" to include Africa and the Diasporas involvement in science, mathematics, medicine, metallurgy, aerodynamics, linguistics, building, agriculture, and most importantly, history.

FREDERICK MONDERSON

Dr. Ben's Photo 343. Abydos, Home of God Osiris. Right side Gateway decoration of Rameses II's Temple at Abydos showing the enthroned King with God Thoth standing behind him and both defaced.

Through the work of this visionary with enormous potential, that quintessential organ, the *Journal of African Civilizations*,

CELEBRATING
DR. BEN-JOCHANNAN

became a major source in Egyptian, African and African-American history. Undaunted by criticisms, the *Journal's* coverage expanded to give agency to enormously credible scholarship. Its content was well researched and provided laudable credence to an enormous body of scientifically based, factually revealing information on Africans in Africa, Europe, Asia, and the Americas. This ground breaking approach and its results made the world stand up and take notice of significant Black contributions across the wide spectrum of knowledge, from ancient through modern times. In view of these amazing revelations, one has to wonder how credible non-African scholarship had not been able to make the same discoveries and reported such. Naturally, this new information, once revealed by the *Journal of African Civilizations*, was thereafter put to tremendous scrutiny to authenticate its findings. This was expected for much of these new revelations threatened the pillars that supported the foundations of a questionable world history whose structural integrity, it has now come to be known, propagated the false notion of all the history thats printed to fit, rather than all the history fit to print. Therefore, kudos goes out to Dr. Ivan Van Sertima, a pioneer who deserves qualitative recognition for the legacy he bequeathed. His steadfast and consistent ferreting out important cultural data, placed African people at the nucleus of knowledge advancing the cause of humanitys progress along the historical continuum. In this he struck a major blow to global white intellectual supremacy!

FREDERICK MONDERSON

Dr. Ben's Photo 344. Abydos, Home of God Osiris. Native Egyptian Guide Abdel Rady, "Shawki the Black," explains the significance of Rameses *Son of Ra* Cartouche or Shennu, in his Temple at Abydos.

Dr. Ben's Photo 345. The Ghizeh Plateau. Two of the Great Pyramids as seen from Sphinx Road out side of Mena House Garden Hotel.

CELEBRATING
DR. BEN-JOCHANNAN

Dr. Ben's Photo 346. The Ghizeh Plateau. View of the Sphinx as guardian to Khafra's Great Pyramid with the bee-hive of visitors who come to see this wonder.

Dr. Ben's Photo 347. The Ghizeh Plateau. The Pyramid of Khufu, denuded of its outer casing.

FREDERICK MONDERSON

The *Journal of African Civilizations* began as a Quarterly that was ground-breaking in its revelations as a tremendous reservoir of factual information; and this contributed to its success in appeal for academic and grass-roots support. The present writer was glad to have purchased the first two gold-covered issues in 1979; that in their own-right consisted of "gold-loaded new and revolutionary information." The standards of his unparalleled scholarship, impeccable in their nature, copious nature of his sources, not only stunned but attracted a reading public ecstatic with the new and high level of quality historical recordings. This organ never let-up as the vision and focus of its creator masterfully commanded the academic and intellectual stage of knowledge. This new approach at African historiographic reconstruction sought to correct distortions and include omissions within the corpus of African and African-American history, science and culture, systematically manipulated by pseudo-scientific writers and historians from Europe and America who, for one reason or another could not countenance the significance of Dr. Van Sertima prodigious production.

As with all such iconoclastic work, Dr. Van Sertimas scholarship was naturally subjected to the most intense scrutiny to check and challenge his findings; but, alas, his scholarly approach and ferreting techniques were unparalleled. Thus, he was able to produce such remarkable results that have withstood the vicissitudes of pernicious challenges to his integrity and the impeccable nature of his scholarship.

As an intellectual visionary, this outstanding iconoclastic scholar thus unleashed a cascading avalanche of scientific revelations, that coupled with his lectures, shattered prevailing falsity regarding African history which struck a blow against the falsity of global white supremacy. **NASA** recognized the potency of his work and welcomed his unparalleled scientific

CELEBRATING
DR. BEN-JOCHANNAN

scholarship. His scholarly ground breaking, *They Came before Columbus* (1976, 2003) is a seminal work in African and African-American history detailing Africans in the Americas before Columbus. The irrefutable revelations heralded the reservoir of knowledge Van Sertima unleashed in the masterful presentations later produce in its metamorphis from Journal to consistently voluminous and scholarly work in monograms.

With Ivan Van Sertima as Editor, the *Journal* boasted an Editorial Board consisting of Godfrey C. Burns, MD; Leonard Jeffries Jr.; John Henrik Clarke; Edward Scobie; Legrand Clegg II; and Clyde-Ahmad Winters. Sylvia Bakos was Art Editor and Sandra Schell, Secretarial Assistant.

The East Coast Board consisted of Godfrey C. Burns, MD; Ida Lewis; Gil Noble; John A. Williams; Leonard James. The West Coast Board comprised Legrand Clegg II; Asa Hillard; Clara Mann. Mid-West consisted of Ismay Ashford; Celeste Henderson; and Roger K. Oden; while New England and South were Willard R. Johnson and Ernest Withers, Jr., respectively.

This tremendous brain thrust was a dynamo that encouraged and supported Dr. Van Sertima as he blazed the trail of remarkable revelations changing the whole dynamic of historical discussion regarding African peoples contributions to the advancement of knowledge.

FREDERICK MONDERSON

Dr. Ben's Photo 348. The Ghizeh Plateau. The Summit of Khafra's Pyramid.

Dr. Ben's Photo 349. The Ghizeh Plateau. From the wall of a Hotel Room, two Goddesses lay hands on a Queen.

CELEBRATING DR. BEN-JOCHANNAN

As an example, Volume 1, No. 1 April, 1979 of the *Journal of African Civilizations* consisted of:

Section 1: EARLY EGYPT

"Early Egypt: A Different Perspective"
Excerpts from WABC-TV documentary "Tutankhamun: A different Perspective" produced by Gil Noble, with John Henrik Clarke and Josef Ben-Jochannan.
Cheikh Anta Diop and Freddie L. Thomas: "Two Philosophical Perspectives on Pristine Black History" – James G. Spady.
"The Black Image in Egyptian Art" – Jules Taylor.
"Ancient Cataclysmic and Tectonic Change: Their Impact on the Peopling of Egypt" – John A. Williams.

Section 2: EARLY AFRICAN SCIENCE

"Editorial Introduction" – Godfrey C. Burns, M.C.
"Complex Iron-Smelting and Prehistoric Culture in Tanzania" – Peter Schmidt and Donald H. Avery.
"Namoratunga: The First Archeoastronomical Evidence in Sub-Saharan Africa" – B.M. Lunch and L.H. Robbins.

Section 3: EARLY AMERICA

"They Came Before Columbus: New Developments and Discoveries" – Ivan Van Sertima
"Mandingo Scripts in the New World– Part I" – Clyde-Ahmed Winters.

FREDERICK MONDERSON

"The First Americans" – Legrand Clegg II
Biographical Note on Contributors.

Journal of African Civilizations Vol. 1, No. 2 November 1979

Editorial: Ivan Van Sertima

Section 1: AFRICAN SCIENCE

"African Astronomy"
"African Astronomy: African Observers of the Universe: The Sirius Question" – Hunter H. Adams III.
"African Mathematics"
"The Yoruba Number System" – Claudia Zaslavsky
"African navigation"
"Traditional African Watercraft: A New Look" – Stewart C. Mallory.
"African Metallurgy"
"Independent Origins of East African Iron-Smelting" – Clyde-Ahmed Winters

Section 2: "African American Science and Invention"

"Black Americans in the field of Science and Invention" – Robert C. Hayden.
"Lewis Latimer, Bringer of the Light" – John Henrik Clarke.
"African Americans in Science and Invention: A Bibliographical Guide" – John Henrik Clarke.

CELEBRATING DR. BEN-JOCHANNAN

Dr. Cheikh Anta Diop was so impressed with the path Dr. Ivan Van Sertima had undertaken; in the second issue of the *Journal*, he wrote a letter to the Editor, detailing his observations regarding the mummy of Pharaoh Rameses II. The mummy of this "Great" king was in a state of decay and was rushed to Paris to undergo "corrective surgery" to stem its deterioration. The Senegalese, Cheikh Anta Diop was the only black African scholar of sufficient Egyptological proficiency permitted to be part of the reconstruction team. This inclusion enabled him to observe and report "New World Tobacco" was found in the intestines of Rameses II. In the revealing tradition of the *Journal*, Dr. Diop, himself a researcher of tremendous potential, theorized and postulated the view, Rameses II of the 19th Dynasty, 13th Century Before Christ, had dispatched seafarers to the New World who brought back tobacco which he smoked before he died. Much ink was spilled to prove it was "Old World Tobacco," but to no avail. Thus, Dr. Diop through the auspices of Dr. Van Sertima's *Journal* proved Africans were in the Americas nearly 2800 years before Columbus. Much of this, however, was in keeping with Dr. Van Sertima's contention that *They Came before Columbus*. Hence, Dr. Diop's postulation added to Van Sertima's arguments for Africans in America before Columbus.

This incredible scholar was therefore able to begin and produce a tremendous body of scholarly work including the following:

Blacks in Science: Ancient and Modern. New Brunswick, New Jersey: Transaction Books, 1983.
Black Women in Antiquity. New Brunswick, New Jersey: Transaction Books, (1984) 1985.
Nile Valley Civilizations. Journal of African Civilizations, (1985) 1986.

FREDERICK MONDERSON

African Presence in Early Europe. New Jersey and London: Transaction Books (1985) 1996.
Great African Thinkers: Cheikh Anta Diop. New Brunswick, New Jersey: Transaction Books, (1986) 1987.
Great Black Leaders: Ancient and Modern. New Jersey: Transaction Books, 1988.
Egypt Revisited. New Jersey: Transaction Books, 1989.
African Presence in Early America. New Brunswick, New Jersey: Transaction Publishers (1992) 1995.
Egypt: Child of Africa. New Brunswick, New Jersey: Transaction Books, (1994) 1995.
Early America Revisited. New Brunswick, New Jersey: Transaction Publisher, 1998.
African Presence in Early Asia. New Brunswick, New Jersey: Transaction Publishers (1985) 2004

The above sources indicated here do not exhaust that outstanding scholars prodigious production of a reservoir of knowledge that now arms the young, teacher and student engaged in rectifying the role of African people in the intellectual development of humanitys cultural and historical legacy and social accomplishments. Such an outstanding production places Dr. Van Sertima on par with the likes of Dr. Yosef A.A. ben-Jochannan, Dr. John Henrik Clarke, Dr. Molefi Asante, Dr. Carter G. Woodson and J. A. Rogers. For this we give praise to a great African-American mind whose name will forever echo in the pantheon of Black heroes and be remembered as arming his people for the challenges to their intellectual and cultural integrity and accomplishments. For this enormous gift of Africa to the world, we say, **God Bless and Thank God for Dr. Ivan Van Sertima**.

CELEBRATING
DR. BEN-JOCHANNAN

Dr. Ben's Photo 350. Sakkara, Home of the Step-Pyramid. the Step-Pyramid from a distance.

Dr. Ben's Photo 351. Sakkara, Home of the Step-Pyramid. The entrance facade of the Enclosure Wall.

FREDERICK MONDERSON

Dr. Ben's Photo 352. **Sakkara, Home of the Step-Pyramid**. Pathway through the world's earliest colonnade.

CELEBRATING
DR. BEN-JOCHANNAN

Dr. Ben's Photo 353. Sakkara, Home of the Step-Pyramid. Luis Casado stand before the world's earliest colonnade, reconstructed.

Dr. Ben's Photo 354. Sakkara, Home of the Step-Pyramid. Erik Monderson stands on steps in the Great Court with uraei on the cornice of a wall.

FREDERICK MONDERSON

39. INTELLECTUAL EXPRESSION FOR HUMAN AND SOCIAL PROGRESS
By
Dr. Fred Monderson

Assessing the literature of the period of struggle to acquire rights in America, it seems some of the greatest Black minds put forth their best efforts to acquire the greatest gains made in civil and social rights. Thus, for some analysts, today's intellectual contributions pales in significance as ships without rudder, making donuts out there while never making port for falsely assuming we have arrived. While we can rightly attribute progress in the struggle for human, civic, political and all forms of equality to peaceful direction on the part of a great many people, the force of African intellectual expression can never be underestimated. While the African, and by extension, African-American has been credited with the gift of *Nomo*, it's no question that thought precedes orality and action. Hence, we must pay tribute to the intellectual expressions that have galvanized the people to effectuate positive action to challenge and correct inequities in the American process and social order, as objection to the oppressor's machinations.

Recently in the 2008 presidential campaign, Hillary Clinton challenged Barak Obama for using words, and then accused him of plagiarizing their origins.

Words are like the wind, free! However, the uses to which they are put actually tell the story. Words have a tendency to galvanize and stir to action the people who for whatever reason have resigned themselves to their condition.

CELEBRATING DR. BEN-JOCHANNAN

A great American once said, "My people picked cotton in the South and unless you marked you place of origin, you ended up doubling back," so he suggested we return to the source, the beginning. In this case, it's the intellectual origins of African thought. In this instance, it's very apropos we begin at the beginning, and the best place for this journey is certainly the chalkboard of early African thought in the Nile Valley, ancient Egypt, benefitted tremendously from "Mother Africa's" second oldest daughter, Ethiopia.

The earliest, uncensored and unadulterated, religious literary expressions are the so-called "Pyramid Texts" of the Fifth and Sixth Egyptian dynasties. These words of such tremendous metaphysic and spiritual power begin with: "Rise Up, O Teti, thou shall not die." Imagine, this early in time words that challenged the unconquerable abyss of death was spoken by ancient Africans. Never before or since have words of such potency been uttered! Not surprising, they were issued forth from the intellectual incubator of the African mind. Of course, we are not unmindful of the earlier pronouncements of the Third Dynasty multi-genius Imhotep who said: "Eat, drink and be merry, for tomorrow we die." Of course, while its origins are not clearly delineated, the admonition: "Man, know thyself," may very well be attributable to this early African well-spring of creative expression and other equally accomplishments in architecture, medicine, administration and poetry.

The great African philosophers teach us:

THE BOOK OF KAKIMNA. - A TREATISE ON MANNERS IN THE TIME OF THE KINGS HUNI AND SNEFRU OF THE THIRD DYNASTY.

FREDERICK MONDERSON

"I am sure of being respected. A song that is right opens the stronghold of my silence; but the paths to the place of my repose are surrounded by words armed with knives against the intruder, no admittance except to those who come alright."

"As a glass of water quenches thirst, as a mouthful of vegetables strengthens the heart, as one good takes the place of another good, as a very little takes the place of much, he who is drawn away by his stomach when he is not on the watch is a worthless man. With such people the stomach is master. However, if thou sittest down to eat with a glutton, to keep up with him in eating will lead afar; and if thou drinkest with a great drinker, accept in order to please him. Do not reject the meats, even from a man repugnant to thee, take what he gives thee, and do not leave it; truly that is disagreeable."

THE PRECEPTS OF PTAH-HOTEP

I. "The prefect Ptah-Hotep says: O God over the two crocodiles, my lord, the progress of time brings old age. Decay falls upon man and decline takes the place of novelty. A new misery weighs him down each day; the sight grows dim, the ears become deaf; the powers are constantly falling. The mouth is silent; speech is wanting, the mind flickers, not remembering yesterday. The whole body suffers. That which is good becomes bad, taste departs. Old age makes man miserable in every way; the nose is stopped, breathing no longer from exhaustion. In whatever position, this is a state (?) of.... (?) .... Who will give me authority to speak that I may tell him the words of those who have heard the counsels of former times? The majesty of this God says: "Instruct him in the speech of former times. This it is that constitutes the worth of the children of the great. Whatever makes souls calm

CELEBRATING DR. BEN-JOCHANNAN

penetrates him who heeds, and what is thus told will not produce satiety."

II. "Arrangement of good words," as a means of instructing the ignorant in the knowledge of the choice of good words. There is profit to him who will listen to this; there is loss to him who will transgress them. He says to his son: "Be not proud because of thy knowledge; converse with the ignorant as with the scholar; for the barriers of art are never closed, no artist ever possessing that perfection to which he should aspire. But wisdom is more difficult to find than the emerald; which is found by slaves among the rocks of pegmatite."

III. "If thou hast to do with a disputer while he is in his heat, and if he is superior to thee in ability, lower the hands, bend the back, do not get into a passion with him. As he will not permit thee to spoil his speech, it is very wrong to interrupt him; that shows thou art not able to be quiet when thou art contradicted. If, then thou hast to do with a disputer while he is in his heat, act as one not to be moved. Thou hast the advantage over him, if only in keeping silent, when his speech is bad. Better is he who refrains, says the audience; and thou art right in the opinion of the great."

Dr. Ben's Photo 355. Sakkara, Home of the Step-Pyramid. Four pairs of feet belonging to statues, more than likely Gods.

FREDERICK MONDERSON

Dr. Ben's Photo 356. Sakkara, Home of the Step-Pyramid. Ptah stands beside two other defaced images.

Dr. Ben's Photo 357. Sakkara, Home of the Step-Pyramid. Part of the surviving ruins in the *Heb Sed* Court.

CELEBRATING
DR. BEN-JOCHANNAN

Dr. Ben's Papyrus 14. Pharaoh Tutankhamon fires an arrow from his charging chariot as he strikes a wild turkey and his hunting dog pursues the game!

Dr. Ben's Photo 358. Sakkara, Home of the Step-Pyramid. Sign indicating tombs available for visiting and colossal image of Ptah-Hotep.

FREDERICK MONDERSON

"If thou art wise, take care of thy house, love thy wife purely. Fill her stomach, clothe her back; these are the cares (to give) to her body. Caress her, fulfill her desire, during the time of thine existence; it is a kindness which honors its master. Be not brutal; consideration will lead her better than force, this is her breath, her aim, her gaze. This establishes her in thy house; if thou repellest her, it is an abyss. Open thine arms to her for her arms; call her, show her thy love."

"Do not disturb a great man; do not distract the attention of the busy man. His care is to accomplish his task, and he strips his body for love of the work. Love for the work they do brings men to God. Therefore, compose thy face, even in the midst of trouble, so that peace may be with thee, when agitation is with ... these are the people who succeed where they apply themselves." XLIV

"Do that which thy master tells thee. Doubly good is the precept of our father, from whose flesh we come forth. May what he tells, be in our hearts; do for him more than he has said and satisfy him wholly. Surely a good son is one of the gifts of God, a son doing better than he has been told."

In his **Atlanta Compromise** speech, Booker T. Washington urged both Blacks and Whites in the South, to "cast down your buckets." Marcus Garvey said: "When I looked around for Africa's Men of Big Affairs, I could not find any. So, I created, titled nobility as Duke of the Nile, Count of the Congo, Black Cross Nurses" and so on.

W.E.B. DuBois insisted, a "talented Tenth," should lead the nation.

While Martin Luther King, Jr., gave his "I have a Dream" Speech, he also insisted, let me tell you, "Why we can't wait."

CELEBRATING DR. BEN-JOCHANNAN

Minister Louis Farrakhan in 1995 called for "one million Black men on the great lawn in Washington, D.C."

Dr. Khalid Mohammed insisted: "The million youth will march down Lenox Avenue," while, Congressman Charles Rangel responded, "There will be no hate in my Harlem."

On October 24, 1997, on the Podium at the Million Women March in Philadelphia, one of the speakers uttered: "We are here, one million strong, in support of the brothers who marched in Washington, two years ago."

Dr. Ben's Photo 359. Memphis Museum, Home of God Ptah. Clossal statue of Rameses II, transported for export to England but abandoned on the spot and in time a structure was built around it comprising the crux of the museum.

FREDERICK MONDERSON

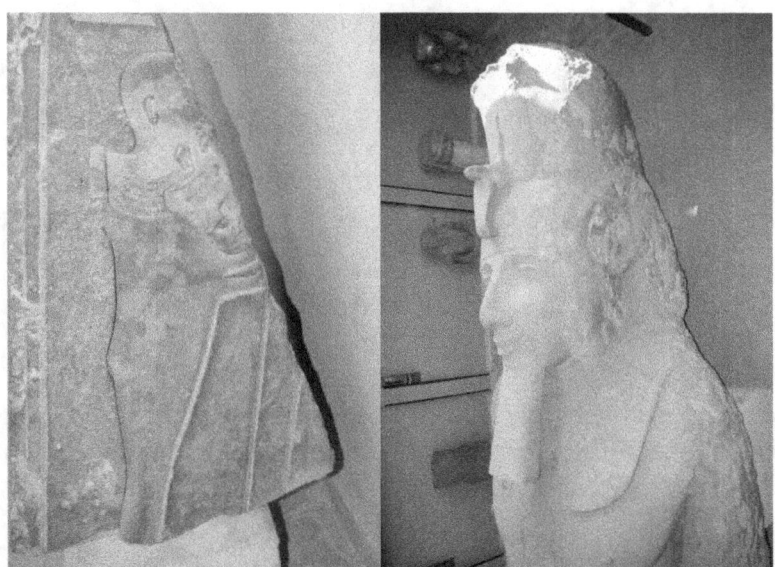

Dr. Ben's Photo 360. Memphis Museum, Home of God Ptah. Image of Ptah, considered a bald-headed pygmy and the Rameses II statue viewed erect.

40. THE GOLDEN AGE OF WEST AFRICA

By
Dr. Fred Monderson

Introduction

The middle age of African history comprised the Medieval Sudanic empires of Ghana, Mali and Songhay that accomplished all the characteristics of civilization. In those areas considered the bedrock of African high-cultural experience and development, viz., economics, politics, and culture, the accomplishments were tremendous. However, while cultural developments are important, geography has also been significant in shaping the emerging culture of this

CELEBRATING
DR. BEN-JOCHANNAN

expansive sub-continent. For example, the Western Sudan and the Sahara are curious environments. Evidence indicates in earlier times the Sahara was very fertile, teeming with game and had many rivers, supporting a significant population. Importantly, however, in *African Glory*, J.C. De Graaf-Johnson, informs the Roman occupation of North Africa decimated the wildlife of this region. Leopards, lions and elephants once roamed this area and have vanished. He mentions 3,500 animals killed in 26 games given by Emperor Augustus Caesar, to amuse the people of Rome. Pompey, Roman general and Emperor, slew 600 lions, 315 being males. Julius Caesar killed 400 lions in the shows he gave. Warfare also bears some fault. Nevertheless, more animal and plant-life were destroyed by man than by other geographic or climatic factors; aiding desertification of the region since.

Dr. Ben's Photo 361. Cairo Museum of Egyptian Antiquities. The Distinguished Auguste Mariette looks over the grounds and towards the building's entrance of the wonderful institution he helped inaugurate.

FREDERICK MONDERSON

Dr. Ben's Photo 362. Kashida Maloney of Brooklyn poses beside replicas of the two statues of Tutankhamon, while a native Egyptian looks on.

We know culture is the most viable and vital dynamic of any civilization. In examining regions beyond the Nile Valley, we find evidence of tremendous growth. Bernard Fage mentions fragments of coal found at Jos, in West Africa, radio-carbon dated at "greater than 39,000 years." These dates range from the Middle Stone Age to the New Stone Age, showing man in West Africa using fire some forty thousand years ago. These dates are not far-fetched for the *New York Times* reported discovery of an iron-ore mine in South Africa dated to 43,000 years ago. However, whether Jos, Nigeria and sites in the Sahara were continuously occupied is difficult to tell. Nevertheless, Nok culture does show occupational stratification at 3500 B.C., 2000 B.C., 900 B.C. and 200 A.D. It is therefore considered a "transitional" culture, from stone to metal workings.

Basil Davidson's *Lost Cities of Africa*, mentions the Frenchman L'Hote's discoveries in the Sahara at places occupied by "Negroes" from the earliest times. Producing

CELEBRATING DR. BEN-JOCHANNAN

"beautiful and sensitive realism in art," these Africans originated naturalistic human portraiture very early, laying the cultural foundations for later West African Sudanic art with its religious and spiritual dynamics. We must be cognizant, however, beyond Greece and Rome, comparatively speaking, in the ascendancy of the Glorious Age of West Africa, much of Western and Central Europe had not yet completed their emergence from a barbaric past.

The history of the Western Sudan is recounted by Islamic scholars chronicling the rise and expansion of Medieval states, where success of these empires was due to trade, good government and strong armies. Islam played a pivotal role, helping and yet destroying Ghana, aiding Mali and was a factor in Songhay's rise and destruction. Accomplishments were made in higher education, where literacy flourished and scholars produced academic manuscripts; while philosophy, law, astronomy, mathematics and medicine were taught at the Universities of Sankore, Djenne and Timbuktu. The *Tarikh as-Sudan* and *Tarikh al-Fattah* as primary sources recount the history of *Bilad es-Sudan* "land of the Blacks," during this period. Art was primarily supported by the state and royalty; and so blended African conventions and social needs with Islamic ideas. Still, despite the importance of the large states, the Western Sudan has no uniform art style.

Economic factors played a pivotal role in this agricultural region influenced by the desert, the Sudanic belt, the forest region, the Niger River Valley and the Atlantic Ocean to the westward. The area supported sedentary hoe farming, with millet, maize and rice as staples. To support industrial activity two sets of craftsmen, blacksmiths and professional jewelers, dominated the work of base and precious metals. Gold of Western Sudan became legendary. E.W. Bovill's *The Golden*

FREDERICK MONDERSON

Trade of the Moors mentions large gold production as late as start of the sixteenth century. By this time, however, much of the gold trade was diverted to the Atlantic coast after the destruction of Songhay. Still, estimates show "gold from the Gold Coast was accounting for an amount that has been estimated at about one-tenth of the total world supply at that time." This was an immense total from one state or region.

International, regional and local markets developed from the trans-Saharan trade. In these markets one could find cloths, thread, straw hats, mats and calabash bowls. Much of this was decorated with geometric and other patterns. Craftsmen worked in glass beads, did leather work and made iron hoes. The book trade was lucrative. Gold, however, characterized the "Golden Age of West Africa."

From the time of Ancient Ghana, the Trans-Saharan trade exported some 9 tons of gold annually. Much of this was in the form of well-worked jewelry and coins of gold. Goldsmiths worked with twisted thread and ingots, using a variety of art forms. Weapons were of iron and copper. However, royal weapons were made of gold. Goldsmiths made bracelets, rings and necklaces. The state awarded "toe rings" of gold, for bravery. The sword scabbard of the royal interpreter and instruments of the king's musicians were made of gold. Ceremonial sabers, lances and arrow quivers were made of gold. Also, trappings of horses and royal dinner plates were made of gold. Royal dogs were leashed in gold.

The forest region provided an abundance of wood for smelting metals and sculpturing. Jean Laude's *The Arts of Black Africa* describes tools of sculptors as "various types of adzes, broad-axes, chip axes, hollow chisels, and double-edged knives." They used "leaves for polishing the finished sculpture and special palm-oil preparations for obtaining an artificial patina." Natural ingredients were used for colors as kaolin for

CELEBRATING
DR. BEN-JOCHANNAN

white, charcoal for black, and sometimes ochre for red and yellow.

Dr. Ben's Photo 363. Cairo Museum of Egyptian Antiquities. Rameses between Ptah and Sekhmet (left) and an engaged statue of a King (right).

Ghana

Medieval Ghana filled a transitional gap in the civilizations of Africa. In fact, many West African peoples as the Akan of Ghana have legends of migrations from the Nile Valley. They believe in the divine death and birth of the founder of the royal lineage. There are similarities in the ram's religious symbolism in Egypt, Kush and much of West Africa. The figure 8, as a religious symbol "suggests life, death, and rebirth forever repeating itself." Lastly, the West African concept of time is viewed cyclically and not lineal as in Europe. These cultural traits show an eastern connection with the upper reaches of the Nile River. In fact, the migration was fueled by invading Assyrian and Persian forces attacking peoples of the Nile Valley. Equally, the eclipse and fall of Kush, miseries of dynastic strife and the search for wealth are other factors in the early population shift. Importantly, advances in iron smelting at refineries of Meroe, Napata, Ethiopia, transformed cultural standards and ways of life. Ghana therefore benefitted from resulting demographic and cultural migration, fueled by technological advances of this early period.

Scholars differ on Ghana's beginnings, though consensus believes Soninkes were the founders of the state, while the Sisse clan supplied rulers of the state. They provided kings, governors of provinces and the principal political officials. The Kante clan, on the other hand, provided the artisans who worked in metals as blacksmiths, goldsmiths and silversmiths. Other clans also worked in agriculture, animal husbandry, boat building and the manufacture of clothing.

In 722 Al Fazari called Ghana the "land of Gold," while Al Masudi the "land of gold beyond Sijilmasa." In the 9th century, Al Hamadhani described Ghana as a "country where gold grows like plants in the sand in the same way as carrots do, and is plucked at sunset;" and Ibn Hawkal thought the ruler of Ghana "the wealthiest of all kings on the face of the earth on account of the riches he owns and the hoards of gold acquired by him and inherited from his predecessors since ancient times." In the 11th century Al Idrisi and Al Bekri wrote descriptions of Ghana, while Al Bekri commented on the gold of Ghana and the lucrative system of taxation utilized by the government, noting "all gold nuggets found in the kingdom were reserved for the king, only gold dust being left for the people." Also, the "king owns a nugget as big as a stone,"

CELEBRATING DR. BEN-JOCHANNAN

weighing about thirty pounds. Gold came from the mines of Fulme and Bambuk in the forest regions. However, while the king of Ghana did not seek to ascertain this source of gold, much later, the kings of Mali and Songhay annexed the lands of the forest and claimed ownership of the mines.

Ghana was famous for sustaining a trans-Saharan trade in gold for salt and utilizing an elaborate system of taxation. According to Al Bekri, "for every donkey load of salt that enters the country, the king takes a duty of one gold dinar and two gold dinars from everyone that leaves. From a load of copper, the kings due is five mitquals and from a load of other goods ten mitquals."

Sijilmasa to the north and Awdaghost to the south were the rendezvous and market center destinations for the caravan trade across the Sahara. Exploiting the "silent trade," made Ghana rich and powerful. Gold miners of the forest exchanged gold for salt in the "**silent trade**." Yet, while gold made Ghana rich and powerful, it also contributed to its decline. Ghana was destroyed by fanatical Muslims in search of gold in 1076. Therefore, Ghana's reign of 1000 years was ended one decade after William the Conqueror invaded England, ending its "Prehistoric Period." It should be pointed out, while much of Pre-Norman English history is partly mythical or unrecorded, that of the states of the Western Sudan are factual.

Mali

Sundiata Keita was born a cripple who overcame his handicap and became the 12th King of Mali, ascending the throne in 1234. Within twenty-one years, he turned the tiny vassal state into the powerful and flourishing Empire of Mali. Three factors are credited with his rise and the growth of Mali. The first is the favorable or central location of his state. Second, the unsettled political conditions of the time of transition in the Western Sudan was a factor. Third, his courage, wisdom and ability to overcome adversity and rally his people to greatness was a personal character trait.

Sundiata Keita was also an able administrator who understood the significance of gold of the Sudan and importance of the trans-Saharan trade. He quickly conquered the gold producing regions of Bure and Bambuk to the south. Thus, while Ghana never actually controlled the gold producing regions, Mali had control over them before Sundiata's death. The empires boundaries were extended to the north. He exploited the agricultural base of the Niger River Valley, introducing cultivation and weaving of cotton. In 1255, he died after laying the foundation for the Empire of Mali and providing it with a flourishing capital.

Within a century, the Mali Empires four main towns, Jenne, the capital Niani, Timbuktu, and Gao, had become thriving commercial centers of the Western Sudan. In 1353, Ibn Khaldoun, an Arabic scholar and traveler, reported seeing a caravan of merchants from the east with 12,000 loaded camels heading for Mali. At an estimated 300 pounds per camel, the volume of trade staggers the imagination. This volume of merchandise needed security guaranteed by a large and effective army. This force in turn provided the political stability that attracted the merchants who paid the taxes to conduct business in this Golden Age of West Africa.

Mansa Musa, king of Mali, while making his pilgrimage to Mecca in 1325 so impressed the contemporary Middle Eastern region, the price of gold declined for some time due to the wealth his entourage splurged in their stay. Naturally, his fabled wealth and generosity attracted Muslim intellectuals, architects, administrators and artisans who wanted to return to

CELEBRATING
DR. BEN-JOCHANNAN

Mali and work for his administration. During that same 14th Century, another king of Mali, Abu Bekr, sent ships across the Atlantic to the "New World," almost a century and a half before Columbus' voyage. It's been indicated only one such ship returned from what would later become America.

Dr. Ben's Papyrus 15. King and Queen offer flowers to enthroned Hathor while the lady also rattles Hathor's favorite instrument, the sistrum; while, to the right, Pharaoh offers life in his left hand while the Goddess reciprocates with her necklace.

Songhay

Songhay next rose to prominence with a monarchy and continued the system of government. The empire was divided into four regions and each headed by a Viceroy. The Army had a Commander-in-Chief. There was a Council of Ministers who advised the Government headed by the king. Officers of the government included a Chief Tax-Collector, Finance

FREDERICK MONDERSON

Minister, Minister of Foreigners, Minister of Property, and Minister in Charge of Rivers, Lakes and Fisheries. Judges administered the courts impartially. One of its greatest rulers was Askia Mohammed.

In *Black History*, Norman E.W. Hodges credits Askia Mohammed with some remarkable innovations. He came to the throne in 1491 by a coup d'état. He presided over "establishment of schools, a uniform system of weights and measures, the improvement of taxes and credit procedures, reorganization of the armed forces, the promotion of more foreign trade, and the creation of an effective governmental administrative network throughout the land." Lastly, Muslim law based on the Koran, became the basis for administering justice in the state.

In essence, towards the end of the Sixteenth Century, Songhay grew powerful from the stability of a mixed economy. This consisted of farming, fishing, and cattle raising. The trans-Saharan trade was still important. Songhay was also successful in uniting against rivals. Throughout the land security was enforced and political stability reigned. Intellectual activities flourished at Sankore University. Islam as the state religion competed with traditional African religious systems.

In 1591, Songhay was attacked by an Islamic force from Morocco, who introduced guns into the Western Sudan. Still, Songhay's demise is blamed for both internal and external factors. Importantly, however, firearms changed the nature of African warfare and weak leadership of Africans also hurt Songhay.

CELEBRATING DR. BEN-JOCHANNAN

Dr. Ben's Photo 364. Cairo Museum of Egyptian Antiquities. Kashida Maloney of Brooklyn stands beside a head of Hathor on the Grounds of the Cairo Museum.

Results of the Moroccan conquest saw Muslim marauders refusing to replace the governmental structure they destroyed; demise of the army and disruption caused by the war affected the important trans-Saharan trade; the Moroccans disregarded the level of cultural sophistication attained in literacy. Destruction of Songhay began in 1591 ending two millennia of West African cultural and civilization growth in culture, government and economics. Literacy and learning had

FREDERICK MONDERSON

progressed to a high level until discontinued. This began a downward spiral leading to Atlantic influence and the slave trade that further decimated Africa and Africans.

Flyer of Dr. Ben's Educational Trip to Egypt in 1997 and the itinerary.

41. HONORING A GIANT
BY
DR. FRED MONDERSON

CEMOTAP attracted a tumultuous turnout at the Dr. Robert Johnson Life Center, to honor and celebrate the 72nd birthday of Dr. Leonard Jeffries, historian, scholar, activist, author, healer, on Saturday, January 24, 2009, at 2: 00 pm.

Sister Betty Dopson did the Welcome; Sister Yvonne Hill, the Prayer; Dr. James McIntosh asked "Who is this African Man and Why do we Honor him?" Brother James Smalls, "A Tribute from a Spiritual Son;" and Dr. Leonard Jeffries himself, offered a Blessing of the Food by the Honoree.

CELEBRATING DR. BEN-JOCHANNAN

After the Introductory Music by Mark and the Music Messengers, Birthday tributes were offered by Attorney Alton Maddox, Dr. Adelaide Sanford, Sister Frederica Bey and Brother Gil Noble. After a music interlude, and collection of gift envelopes, Sister Viola Plummer boasted: "I roasted him five years ago." Then there were highlights of "My life with Leonard" by his wife Dr. Rosalind Jeffries, and then the Honoree offered "Thank you my friends."

Dr. James Macintosh, Master of Ceremonies, provided a glowing and well-deserved tribute to Dr. Leonard Jeffries that set the stage for a night of great praise and earnest outpouring of love, respect and accolades for a giant and great warrior chieftain. In referring to his subject, he began by saying: "Marcus Garvey said Men in earnest are not afraid of consequences." Then he quoted Claude McKays poem "If We Must Die."

This literary classic of the Harlem Renaissance appropriately epitomizes the condition and struggles of the great one who never shied away from great engagements. The poem reads:

"If we must die, let it not be like hogs
Hunted and penned in an inglorious spot
While round us bark the mad and hungry dogs
Making mock at our accursed lot.

"If we must die, O let us nobly die
So that our precious blood may not be shed
In vain; then even the monsters we defy
Shall be constrained to honor us though dead!

"O kinsmen we must meet the common foe!
Though far outnumbered let us show us brave
And for their thousand blows deal one death blow.

FREDERICK MONDERSON

"What though before us lies the open grave
Like men well face the murderous, cowardly pack
Pressed to the wall, dying, but fighting back!"

Then Dr. Macintosh quoted the English poet Rudyard Kipling who believed "Even a broken clock is correct two times every day;" before he glowingly synopsized why he was honoring and supporting Dr. Jeffries.

"If you can hear the truth you've spoken
Twisted by knaves to make a trap for fools
Or watch the things you gave your life to broker
And stoop and build 'em up with worn-out tools

"If you can meet with triumph and disaster
And treat those two imposters just the same
If you can fill the unforgiving minute
With sixty seconds worth of distance run
Yours is the Earth and everything that's in it
And which is more, you'll be a Man my son."

Saying that Kipling and his types have had to recognize Dr. Jeffries was a man, is the reason **CEMOTAP** was honoring this giant, celebrating his 72nd birthday.

Even more, MacIntosh offered some important reasons why Jeffries could be considered for the honor are: "Not just because he rose out of the Newark Public School system; not because he became President of his graduation class at Sussex Avenue School; or graduated with honors from Barringer High school; not because he graduated from Lafayette College (in Easton, Pennsylvania), or joined operation crossroads, or lead trips to Senegal; not because he left law school to get the background in Political Science that he would need to serve

CELEBRATING DR. BEN-JOCHANNAN

his lifes mission; not because he married Nana Essie Abibio, Queen Mother of Education, Development and Social Services of the Edina Traditional Area in Elmina; not because he has travelled back and forth to Africa 40 times (actually 100 times); or has been building a hotel for our people on the motherland; or taught thousands of students in and out of the class room about mother Africa and the greatness of African Civilization. Not because he has nurtured other giants such as Brother James Smalls; not because he has loyally supported U.A.M. Brother Alton and Sister Leola Maddox during their bleakest hours; or helped Dr. John Henrik Clarke establish the African Heritage Studies Association. Or that he has helped set up the Black Studies Program at San Jose; not because he has lectured at Harvard, Yale and First World Alliance. He was being honored, not because he was installed as the Division Chief of Agogo, Ghana; not because he fought to change the curriculum of NYC schools or did so many other great things. But, we honor him because he is a man who has stood for African people; because he represents the very best of what it means to be an African man, a complete man with the kindness and humility for his people and possess a fierce warrior spirit for any who would harm his people. This is why we celebrate Dr. Jeffries."

Prof. James Smalls confessed about the influence Dr. Jeffries has had on the evolution of his cultural consciousness, from his days as a student at City College and up to today. Prof Smalls said, he learned from Dr. Jeffries the importance of economics, politics and culture. Then he added, "your culture is at the core of your spirituality. African spirituality is its most profound attribute." Looking at the audience, he reminded them as to the reason they were in attendance: "Youre here because you see God in him. His spiritual-beingness. True revolutionaries exist in the spirit." Then he admonished them,

FREDERICK MONDERSON

"You must restore your spiritual religiosity. If you can't kill the African spirit, you can't kill the African revolution."

Next it was Regent Dr. Adelaide Sanford who gave a tremendously glowing tribute emphasizing the gentle, creative, omnipotent power of Dr. Jeffries, the author of a portion of the **Curriculum of Inclusion** that told the African-American story. He has a nobility of spirit, great magnanimity, majesty, dignity, pride, is an extra-dimension of the creator, centered on the reality of who we are. He is also brilliant, gracious in the face of confusion, steps over the debris, and rises from the ashes. Then she turned to the audience and confessed, "I be loving you!"

Gil Noble of **Like it Is**, likened Dr. Jeffries to someone mirrored in Dr. Martin Luther Kings declaration that, "A man can't ride your back, unless its bent." He confessed, in his day, no Black History was taught in school so he had to learn Black History from those like Dr. Jeffries. Therefore, he was there to salute the honorees sojourn on this planet.

Alton Maddox exclaimed Dr. Jeffries, "Takes the burden off of us." Thus, "We will celebrate Dr. Jeffries birthday every year this month, on the 19th. Fredericka Bey, visiting from New Jersey, was equally eloquent in her praise of the man who has given so much.

Sister Viola Plummer spoke to Dr. Jeffries of, the "African spirit you embody. The African-ness that made you who you are – never to bow down."

Dr. Rosalind Jeffries explained some aspects of her life with Leonard. Upon their marriage, she confessed of not being prepared for sharing her husband with the struggle. She had no preparation for what to expect. Yet, she boasted, "I got a giant,

CELEBRATING
DR. BEN-JOCHANNAN

genius, magnanimous man, possessing a tender streak; tender, loving, full of absolute truth. He lives on the cutting edge of things and this is dangerous." Jokingly, she continued, "He did not want to be born. They used forceps to pull him out. He is a genius and Godly being."

Finally, it was Dr. Leonard Jeffries turn to address those who came to acclaim him. He began by pointing to Wade Nobles dictum: "Power is the ability to define reality and to have other people accept it as if it was their own." Then he opened up, "We are the creation. It was an African victory. African primacy created the evolution of society. The cradle of civilization. There were no Europeans in the origins; no Europeans in evolution; no Europeans in civilization." Then he explained the role of the Ethiopians who comprised the 25th Egyptian dynasty and were the only kings who ruled the entire distance of the Nile Valley. He too took that journey of 1000 miles of glory from Khartoum to Cairo for the "Nourishment of the mind. This is what sustains me," he confessed. Finally, he informed "My wife is my rock and my best friend."

Dr. Ben's Photo 364a. Cairo Museum of Egyptian Antiquities. The Ben-Ben stone.

FREDERICK MONDERSON

42. PRAISE OF DR. BEN
Historical Overview

Dr. Yosef Alfredo Antonio ben-Jochannan is a well-respected elder, historian, Egyptologist, author, publisher and speaker who was never afraid to take an individual, idiosyncratic point of view and defend it irrespective. Dr. Ben told us, "I took Egypt to challenge white supremacy." He shined the light for many of us to see and encouraged the acquisition of knowledge. Throughout his career, Dr. Ben emphasized Egypt/Kemet is a black civilization and whatever whites found there were latecomers to Egypt after the Middle Kingdom following the Hyksos invasion. He challenged distortion, omission and misrepresentation of the culture. He also paid a price from both black and white interests. We know the status quo would like to eliminate people like Dr. Ben from the consciousness of young people, but we will not have it! For this I say:

Prehistory

The Paleolithic Period lasted from about 300,000 to 25,000 years ago. It comprised the Lower, Middle and Upper Periods. This is called the Old Stone Age. The Mesolithic is called the Middle Stone Age. Where we see Homo erectus, early man, begin the use of more sophisticated stone tools. Let us not forget, Zinjanthropus Boise, "near man" had been a tool using being dated at 1.75 million years old. Paleolithic Sites included Merimde, the Faiyum, Kharga Oasis, and Thebes where Hand-axes were found dating to more than 200,000 years. Kom Ombo was also a Paleolithic site. In the Paleolithic Period man used bifacial flint tools, hand-axes and choppers. He began learning to use bone tools.

CELEBRATING DR. BEN-JOCHANNAN

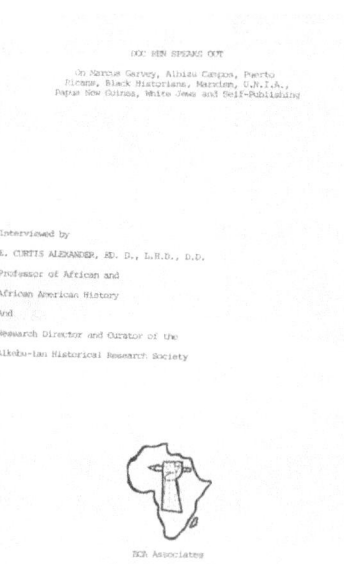

Dr. Ben's Book 30. "Doc Ben Speaks Out - Interview by E. Curtis Alexander" (1982).

The Mousterian Period is contemporary with the Middle to Upper period and more sophisticated hand tools, hand axes, emerged. We also see early burial of man and feelings of family living. Paleolithic tools of the Mousterian Period were flint, antler, ivory, lance-heads, knives and microliths, or very tiny tools of stone particularly. By the Mesolithic Period the bow and arrow emerged with arrow-heads of flint and later stone. We see carvings of various animals.

A big change occurred in the history of man between the Mesolithic and Neolithic Periods. The Neolithic Period began about 10,000 B.C. The Neolithic Age is characterized by sedentary beginnings as he began to settle down. This is marked by the birth of food production. In the Paleolithic Period, man's food supply was characterized as 90 percent meats from the hunt and 10 percent Agri-vegetation. The big change was him settling down in communities, growing crops, domesticating animals and pursuing a more systematic burial of his dead. We see early containers for grain, use of sickles and evidence of winnowing grain. Equally too, we see the emergence of division of labor and specialization of function. There is evidence of ivory combs, needles, and manufacture of points and knives.

Three major cultures emerge in Neolithic Egypt. These are the Badarian, Amratian and Gerzean or Naqada I and II. This period is Proto-dynastic. The Badarian is named after El-Badari, the site where Flinders Petrie did his **Sequence Dating**. At El-Badari there were ivory figurines, some religious significance. There are cosmetic palettes. Jewelry is made of shells, turquoise, and much burnished pottery. Trade seems to have developed in this period. The Amratian Period is named after El-Amrah and Merimde where we first see beehive huts. There was a shrine for the local God. People are seen hunting. A woman sits at a loom. There is a figurine of a dancing lady. The bird lady figurine in the Brooklyn Museum comes from El-Amrah. The earliest mother Goddess figurine comes from this site that is transitional to the Gerzean culture. Gerzean – was characterized with white incised pottery with a ripple pattern. This culture produced the first incised pottery with people and animals. We see also a double-shaped type of pottery, as well as black-topped pottery, with red burnishing of various designs.

The Nagada site, which together with el Gerza characterizes the period, is located in Upper Egypt. Petrie did his Sequence Dating at Nagada. A tomb from Gebelein shows the earliest representation of boats and the first clear figures on pattern. Linen from Gebelein is one of the oldest found. The Gerzean pottery represents variety in pottery form, design and use of material. Some were in regular mud, stone and even alabaster.

CELEBRATING DR. BEN-JOCHANNAN

Whether red, black topped, designed, we see great sophistication in the pottery. Some pottery changed to votive offerings. Rock carvings show use of bow and arrows with kilts as garments. The Dog Palette in the Louvre depicts mythical animals.

By this time the Nomes were beginning to be delimited with 22 in the south and some 20 in the north. Those in the South were clearly delineated while the exact boundaries of the north were still being worked out. There is much fighting for domination that ends in formation of dynastic period. There are many battle scenes with much pictographic representation. The Scorpion King is shown as Horus. Other predynastic kings and animal guises are shown. The most distinguishing thing to emerge here is the Register, a method of representing art that seems to separate the chaos of predynastic from the order of the dynastic period, ushered in by Narmer the conqueror from the south.

Much evidence from this period comes from Hierakonpolis and Abydos. Many battle scenes depict the process of unification. King Scorpion is seen on a Macehead from Hierakonpolis. He is shown opening a new canal with scenes of defeated enemies. He is depicted wearing a white crown, symbol of the south. There is much controversy regarding the kings Narmer, Menes and Hor-Aha. We know Narmer married a queen from north, Lower Egypt, to solidify the unification. This brings us to the end of the Pre-historic Period.

FREDERICK MONDERSON

Discoveries at Qustol in Nubia or Ethiopia.

The discoveries at Qustol in Nubia show the paraphernalia we associate with Kingship, such as White Crown, enthroned pharaoh, sailing boats, palace façade, Horus bird, incense burner that we see in Egypt at around 3100 B.C., evident in Nubia some 200 years earlier.

Writing was well developed by this time and much research, particularly since Post-World War II has shown Upper Egyptian origins of the writing developed from local flora, fauna and human motifs. Diop, Arnett and others have shown the rudimentary development of the writing in cliffs along the upper areas of the Nile. Mathematic was also highly developed

Dynasties:

The Archaic Period, Dynasties I and II, is important for the formative beginnings of government, religious expression, establishment of the military, trade patterns, burial of the dead, etc. The most reliable record of the kings of Egypt is the Tablets listing the order of these rulers. The **Palermo Stone** begins with the predynastic kings and been commented on by Josephus, Eusebius and Manetho. The **Turin Papyrus** is now a fragmented relic in the Turin Museum. The **Tablet of Karnak** was removed in 1864 by Prisse D'Avennes to the Louvre. At that time, it listed 64 kings though only 48 were legible. The **Tablet of Abydos** is one of two such sources still in its original place. It lists 76 kings from Menes or Narmer to Seti I. Five of its cartouche names of kings are blank. We will get to this later. Its companion, the Second Abydos List, from the Temple of Rameses II at Abydos is now in the British Museum. The tomb

CELEBRATING DR. BEN-JOCHANNAN

of an Old Kingdom noble named Roy preserved the **Sakkara List** of a small number of kings resides in its place of deposit. While the nation's capital was administered from Memphis, the kings were buried at Abydos during the Archaic Period's first two dynasties. When Memphis remained the Capital city, new kings changed to being buried at Sakkara.

We know the Old Kingdom was a Period of Creativity, establishing the form of government, religious worship, building of Pyramids, emergence of Pyramid Texts and much more, with Memphis as the Capital. Trade flourished, river navigation and transportation of large stone became perfected. The art of medicine made great strides, particularly to treat injuries from principally building in stone and in whatever military ventures the pharaohs engaged in. The Priesthood emerged as a powerful body that perpetuated the religious philosophy of the God King, conducted religious worship and oversaw the cult of the dead. In time they became very powerful, a state within the state, king makers or king breakers.

The Pyramid Texts buried in the tombs of fifth and sixth dynasty pharaohs represent the earliest writings that mapped-out the fundamentals of Egyptian religious beliefs. This is one of the highlights of Dr. Ben's work. As some of you may know, Dr. Ben is an anthropologist, historian, engineer, and he also taught religion. His problem with the "Major Religions" is that not only did they come after this great flowering of African religious thought, while the Pyramid Texts remain unchanged for some 5000 years, the 2500 years of the Bible has seen many, many revisions that still has not changed the negative representation of the African in its content.

FREDERICK MONDERSON

Let me review some of the first Dr. Ben has enlightened us about Egypt.

1. The first tunnel was dug during the Old Kingdom to create a passageway between the two great pyramids.

2. The first representation of a moving image shows a hound running after a gazelle during the Old Kingdom.

3. There were 70 pyramids built in Egypt. He taught us about the **silt pyramid**, the **natural pyramid**, the **step pyramid**, and **true pyramid**. There was also a **bent-pyramid**.

4. He showed the prominence of women in ancient Egypt/Kemet. Dr. Ben put the black woman on a pedestal. Narmer's queen was given prominence. His son Aha built a large tomb at Abydos for his mother. Women transmitted divine genes. Peseshet was a "Lady Director of Lady Doctors." That's why I named my grand-daughter Jayde after her.

5. Imhotep was the first physician to step out of the mist of history. He came from an architectural family; his father was an architect and presumably his grandfather.

6. Quarrying and transportation of large stone was greatly developed.

7. The practice of medicine and dentistry had reached unprecedented levels.

Middle Kingdom – The Middle Kingdom was a period of Unification, Consolidation, Reorganization,

CELEBRATING DR. BEN-JOCHANNAN

Expansion and Cultural flowering, following the collapse of the Old Kingdom that had ushered in the First Intermediate Period. The Kings Intef and Mentuhotep united the country and provided the wherewithal to transition the form of government, nature of the military, schools of art and thought, religious practice, building techniques and much more. The temple of Mentuhotep at Deir el Bahari is a masterpiece of Egyptian architecture that transitions from the Old Kingdom to New Kingdom architectural techniques.

Egyptian town life leaves practically no records. Only tombs and cemeteries have evidence of the people's existence. Tombs were profusely illustrated with scenes of the dead, evidence of the *Coffin Text*, a continuation of the *Pyramid Texts* of the Old Kingdom which was later replaced by the *Book of the Dead* or *Book of Coming Forth by Day*, the *Per Hru*.

Language was highly developed during this time. In fact, the language for most of the later period is based on Middle Egyptian.

The New Kingdom saw the expulsion of the Hyksos invaders and development of Imperial adventures with prominence of Thebes, home of Amon Worship, temple and tomb construction and arts and crafts representing the full repertoire of the culture. Reorganization of the military aided warrior pharaohs to go abroad, conquer peoples and places, bring back wealth and enslaved peoples to help build and enrichen the temples and ipso facto, the Priesthood who continuously praised Amon-Ra who had been so good to his adherents. Science, art, medicine, transportation, trade, quarrying, astronomy and astrology reached unprecedented heights in the New Kingdom.

FREDERICK MONDERSON

Late Period: Various peoples invaded and conquered Egypt.

Ethiopians – Piankhi, Shabaka, Taharka

Greeks and Romans – Temples at Edfu, Esneh, Kom Ombo, Isis and Kalabsha were built during this period.

II. What is the proper attire/behavior in the Temple?

Dr. Ben has always insisted on a particular dress code and mode of behavior when visiting any temple in Egypt. That is to say, no short shorts and any such attire. He frowned on European visitors who enter the holy places practically naked as if sunning themselves. He advised against entering the Sanctuary, "Holy of Holies," the most sacred place in the temple. Only the Pharaoh or High Priest, he insisted and reminded, could enter this place where the God rested.

The Shabaka Proscription was made against some people who plotted a murder in the temple. As such, he advised, be on your best behavior, think only positive thoughts and look, learn and enjoy your visit. Before you go, it's advisable that you read as much as possible so what you see on the monuments will be more easily instructive and understandable. Get yourself a good camera and lots of film, 20-25 rolls. Enjoy your pictures and boast about what you saw! One of the Axioms of Dr. Ben has been, "Only the documented sources are what determine the interpretation of the subject." Writing always played a significant role in the development of religion and as far as is certain, Egyptian religion is older than the dynasties.

CELEBRATING DR. BEN-JOCHANNAN

When it comes to the writing there is clear evidence, contrary to 19th Century European scholarship with claims of Asiatic and Indo-European and Semitic origins of the Egyptian language, Diop, Arnett, even Winkler have shown there is clear evidence of the emergence of writing in Upper Egypt and Nubia in the caves on the high ridges of the Nile. The flora, fauna, geography and people provided the basis for the language stock. However, while Winkler believes this was the work of Mesopotamians, Diop has shown it was indigenous and he connected the early language to other African languages. Even Wallis Budge, in his massive *Hieroglyphic Dictionary* reversed himself and pronounced Egyptian an African rather than Asiatic language.

Now, since we know mathematics was already developed by the First Dynasty and a coherent body of religious doctrines were available by the Old Kingdom, it's safe to say centuries of preparation went into this development. For example, we know the earliest evidence of Greek writing is found at Abu Simbel and dated to the fifth century. Homer wrote his *Iliad and Odyssey* and this has been dated, with some stretch to the eighth century. Some have tried to argue these events go back centuries before they were written down. Are we to believe such ideas as the pyramid texts did not take centuries to become coherent in its evolution, thus stretching the origins of writing back into the fourth millennium?

Bases of knowledge – Thoth, scribe of the Gods is also the inventor of writing as well as astronomy, measurement, music and other forms of knowledge. His female counterpart was Seshat, Goddess of building.

FREDERICK MONDERSON

Dr. Ben's Photo 365. **Erik Monderson**, "Going up to the Spirit in the Sky," "Going up to the Spirit in the Sky," while climbing the stairs to the **Tombs of the Nobles**, Aswan, Egypt in 2018.

43. INDEX

Abdul, Brother – 11, 385, 420, 436 (Photo)
Admonition to Dr. Fred –
Aldred, Cyril – 116, 119, 124

CELEBRATING DR. BEN-JOCHANNAN

Allam Schafik – 90
    Life in Ancient Egypt
Allen, James Exhibit – 733
Archaeological Survey of Egypt – 351
Archaeological Survey of Nubia – 351
Aristotle – 199-200, 204, 474, 529, 582, 649
    Physiognomonica
Asante, Molefi – 107, 206, 224, 344, 691
Bacon, Sir Francis – 71
Baedeker – 402-403
    (1929) *Guide to Egypt*
Bakry, H.K.S. – 554
    (1965) *A Brief Study of Mummies and Mummification*
Baldwin, James – 195
    "Civilization lies first in the mind."
Baldwin, John D. – 451, 582
    (1898) *Pre-Historic Nations*
Barney – 62, 163
Bauval and Brophy – 175, 276, 280, 281, 284, 285, 290
    295, 357, 654, 655
    (2011) *Black Genesis*
Beethoven – 178, 196, 360, 468, 514, 590
ben-Jochannan, Dr. Yosef – 2, 4, 7, 8, 48, 60, 62, 63, 65, 66, 71, 72, 74, 78, 79, 80, 81, 82, 99, 107, 150, 151, 161, 163, 206, 217, 219, 227, 229, 242, 246, 266, 323, 324, 326, 329, 330, 331, 333, 384, 402, 416, 420, 421-22, 425, 468, 514, 570, 591, 605, 616, 643, 650, 669, 670, 671, 688, 691, 722

BOOKS
    (1981) *Black Man of the Nile and his Family*
    (1978) *Our Black Seminarians and Black Clergy without a Black Theology: The Tragedy of Black People/Africans in Religion Today*

FREDERICK MONDERSON

(1990) *The African Called Rameses ("The Great") II and The African Origin of Western Civilization*
(1981) *The Alkebu-Lanians of Ta-Merry's "Mystery System" and the Ritualization of the Late Bro. Kwesie Adebisi*
(1989) Abu Simbel to Ghizeh: A Guide Book and Manual
(1970) *Black Man of the Nile*, (later) *Black Man and His Family* (1989)
Dedication
Table of Contents
(1983) *We the Black Jews: Witness to the "White Jewish Race" Myth*
(1978) *Tutankhamon's African Roots Haley, Et. Al., Overlooked*!?
(1971) *Africa: Mother of Western Civilization*
(1976) *The Black Mans or the "negros" bicentennial year of ??? from 1619-20 to 1976 C.E.: Black Mental Illness and The Bicentennial* Volume 1
(1976) *Influence of Great Myths of Contemporary Life, or The Need for Black History in Mental Health and the Bicentennial* Volume II
(1978) The Saga of the "Black Marxists" versus the "Black Nationalists" A Debate Resurrected
Dedication
(1975) *Understanding the African Philosophical Concept Behind the "Diagram of the Law of Opposites"*
(1980) *They All Look Alike! All*!!!
(1970) *African Origins of the Major "Western Religions": The Black Man's Religion* - Volume I (1991)507
(1970) *The Black Man's Religion* Volume II (1970) and a Photo of Dr. Ben. Notice the Doctorate Degree, Dr. Yosef ben-Jochannan on the wall above his head to the right

CELEBRATING DR. BEN-JOCHANNAN

(1974) *The Black Man's Bible - Volume III*
(1974) *Extracts and Comments From the Sacred Scriptures of the Holy Black Bible* (1974) with a picture of Dr. Ben in Harlem in 1970
(1992) *A Chronology of the Bible: Challenge to the Standard Edition* (1995)
(1994) *Africa's Nile Valley: People, Culture and History: A Major Problem for The A.D.L's Hit Squad*
(1970) *African Origins of the Major "Western Religions": The Black Man's Religion* Vol. II (1991)
(1976) *Cultural Genocide in the African American Studies Curriculum*
(1984) *The Black Man's North and East Africa*
(1985) *Blacks and Jews: An Old Confrontation*
(1971) *Africa: Mother of Western Civilization.* This is a revised version of the already presented First Edition also signed by the author (1988)
Table of Contents
Dedication
(1985) **A POSITION PAPER: "He Dr. BEN, HAS NO Ph.d"** (1985)
(1985) *Brothers of the Craft and Sisters of the House: "Heaven Is Between A Black Womans Legs"*
(1980) *Pursuit of George G.M. James Study of African Origins in "Western Civilization"*
(1982) *Axioms and Quotations of Yosef Ben-Jochannan*
(1982) *Doc Ben Speaks Out*: Interviewed by E. Curtis Alexander

Bernal, Martin – 208
(1987) *Black Athena* Vol. 1

Black Woman – 60, 82, 98, 161, 728,
Bolden, Tonya – 97
    The Book of African American Women
Boswell – 205
    Life of Samuel Johnson –
E.W. Bovill – 156, 707-708
    (1932) *Golden Trade of the Moors*
Breasted, James H. 4, 156, 175, 225, 260, 356, 487, 504, 505, 506, 508, 526, 624
    (1905) *Ancient Records of Egypt*
    (1907) *A History of Egypt*
    (1932) *The Development of Religion and Thought in Ancient Egypt*
    (1916) *Ancient Times*
    (1934) *The Dawn of Conscience*
British Museum – 95, 223, 260, 359, 360, 407, 488, 509, 569, 623, 644, 647, 655
Brooks, Lester – 457, 459
    (1971) *Great Civilizations of Ancient Africa*
Browder, Anthony – 128, 206, 448
    (1992) (1995) *Nile Valley Contributions to Civilization*
Browne, Charles Farrar (1934-1867) – 100
Brugsch-Bey, Karl Heinrich – 468, 484, 485, 489, 497, 591
    (1902) *Egypt Under the Pharaohs*
Budge, E.A.W. – 4, 87, 172, 221, 223, 360, 488, 489, 576, 597, 655, 731
    Book of the Dead
    Papyrus of Ani
    (1926) *Cleopatras Needles*
Burton, Sir Richard F. – 332
    The Kasidah of Haji
Cadogan – 470
    (2002) *Cairo, Luxor, Aswan*
Cairo Museum of Egyptian Antiquities – 226, 260, 396, 404, 428, 514, 539, 548, 563, 566, 568, 586, 638
Cartwright, Samuel – 585-586

CELEBRATING DR. BEN-JOCHANNAN

(1857) *Slavery and Ethnology*
Carruthers, Jacob – 9, 206, 362, 385, 414, 585
    (1984) *Essays in Ancient Egyptian Studies*
    (1995) *Mdw Ntr: Divine Speech*
    (1999) *Intellectual Warfare*
Champollion, Jean Jacques – 126, 130, 360, 362, 407, 462, 480, 585, 586
Chapel – 57, 142, 248, 253, 366, 393, 404, 447, 577, 578, 657
    "Red Chapel" 147
    "White Chapel" 147
Choc-Full-O-Nuts – 62, 164
Chronology – 211, 228, 327, 336, 369, 618
Churchward, Albert – 195, 198, 211
    (1924) *Signs and Symbols of Primordial Man*
Clarke, Dr. John Henrik – 9, 68, 74, 79, 107, 163, 176, 178, 182, 196, 199, 206, 207, 229, 233, 324, 448, 451, 512, 619, 636, 662, 674, 686, 687, 688-689, 690, 691, 719
    (2004) *Who's Betraying the African World Revolution*
    (1970) *Introduction to African Civilization*
Clarke, Robert – 182, 214
    (2005) *An Order Outside Time*
Confucius – 178
Congreve, William (1670) – 101
Crowns – 48, 566, 666
Daniels, Ron – 186, 623
David, Rosalie – 538
    (1993) *Discovering Ancient Egypt*
Davidson, Basil – 4, 156, 449, 706
    Africa in History
Delaney, Martin – 3
Denon, Count Vivan – 157, 329
De Rouge, M. Le Vicomte – 495
    (1897) "Origin of the Egyptian Race"219,
Diodorus – 154, 359, 451, 475, 479, 521, 582, 649,
Diogenes – 477, 582

FREDERICK MONDERSON

Diop, Dr. Cheikh Anta – 62, 107, 178, 199, 206, 216, 218, 219,
    222, 227, 231, 256, 257, 273, 284, 343, 357, 451, 459,
    463, 464, 468, 473, 474, 475, 477, 480, 481, 489, 524,
    526, 535, 542, 581, 582, 602, 606, 609, 612, 648, 649,
    650, 651, 658, 669, 688, 690, 691, 726, 730, 731
    (1974) *African Origins of Civilization: Myth or Reality*
    (1978) *Cultural Unity of Black Africa*
    (1982) *Civilization or Barbarism*
Dopson, Betty – 99, 154, 679, 716
DuBois, W.E.B. – 3, 98, 107, 205, 509, 601, 611, 702
    (1915) *The Negro* (1970)
    (1930) *Black Folks Then and Now*
    (1946) *The World and Africa*
Dunmoodie, Curtis – 62, 163
Egypt Exploration Fund – 348, 351, 508
Egyptian Research Account Production – 348, 351
    Graeco-Roman Branch – 349, 351
Egyptian mummy – 230
Emery, Walter – 487
    (1961) *Archaic Egypt*
Erman, Adolf – 113, 119, 260, 485, 526, 593, 601, 608
    (1894) *Life in Ancient Egypt*
Fagan, Brian – 351, 463, 530
    (1975) *Rape of the Nile*
Fage, Bernard – 411, 706
    History of West Africa
Finch, Charles – 206, 211, 485, 489, 504, 526, 611
    Echoes from the Old Darkland
    Star of Great Beginnings
    (1988) *Great Black Leaders: Ancient and Modern*
Foreign Exchange – 420, 433
Frazier, James – 157
    The Golden Bough
Frost, S.E. – 367
    (1947) *History of Education*
Garvey, Marcus – 3, 61, 73, 83, 98, 205, 230, 325, 332, 343,

CELEBRATING DR. BEN-JOCHANNAN

    702, 717
    Philosophy and Opinions
Gentleman's Magazine – 356
Geography of the Gods – 222, 272, 347
Glidden, George – 584
    (1843) *Ancient Egypt: The New World*
Groves, C.P. – 156
    The Planting of Christianity in Africa
Guides, Native – 11, 106, 431, 439, 503, 568
    Farouk – 11
    Shawki – 11
    In the Museum – 226
Haiti, respect for – 186, 264, 268, 298, 299, 300, 306, 307, 308, 310, 311, 312, 313, 315, 316, 317, 318, 320, 321, 462
    University of the Haitian Academy – 311, 313, 316
Haitian Revolution – 186, 462
Harris, J.E. – 511
    (1981) *Pillars of Ethiopian History*
    (1972) *Africans and Their History*
Hatshepsut – 44, 47, 54, 55, 56, 84, 95, 135, 139, 145, 170, 226, 263, 360, 396, 437, 439, 445, 470, 539, 548, 576, 629, 636, 644, 650, 655
Hawass, Zahi – 263, 280, 281, 360, 548, 562, 636
Hecataeus of Abdera – 359
Hegel, Wilhelm – 204, 343, 460, 528, 585, 591
Herodotus – *The Histories* (1972)
Hieroglyphic history – 623
Higgins, Sir Godfrey – 265
    (1836) *Anacalypsis*
Hill, Yvonne – 716
Hyponex – 84
Homer – 152, 473, 474, 581, 731
    Iliad and Odyssey
Hope (1961) – 556

FREDERICK MONDERSON

Howells, William Dean – 101
Hunefer, Papyrus of – 195, 468, 479, 590
"Hunter School" of **CUNY** – 79, 163, 227, 619, 674
Hypostyle Hall – 48, 106, 129, 137, 140, 141, 145, 146, 242, 242, 390, 391, 394, 398, 402, 404, 416, 422, 425, 428, 443, 445
Ideal man – 740
Immaculate Sisters – 18
Imhotep – 35, 61, 88, 169, 178, 291, 292, 440, 444, 446, 696, 728
Imperialism – 4, 68, 196, 227, 342, 530, 662, 676
Isfit – 191, 192, 205, 255, 367, 377, 410
Jackson, John – 127, 205, 512, 527, 611
    (1970) *Introduction to African Civilizations*
James, George G.M. – 157, 199, 200, 202, 204
    (1954) *Stolen Legacy* (1976)
    Parts of the Soul
James, Dr. Leonard – 5, 6, 62, 204, 206, 352, 448, 686
    Marilyn James – 62
Jeffries, Leonard – 2, 9, 83, 156, 230, 686, 716, 717, 718, 719, 720, 721
Jeffries, Rosalind – 717
Jeffries, M.D.W. – 4, 156
Karenga, Maulana – 107, 175, 182, 183, 184, 188, 192, 195, 206, 210, 343, 362, 364, 367, 368, 369, 374
    Kemet and the African Worldview
    (1984) *Selections from the Husia: Sacred Wisdom from Ancient Egypt*
    (2006) *Ma'at: The Moral Ideal in Ancient Egypt*
    (1990) *The Book of Coming Forth by Day: The Ethics of the Declaration of Innocence*
"Kash" – 99, 386
Kush, Indus Kamit – 112, 128, 136, 152, 154, 157, 158, 175, 325, 449, 450, 582, 583, 601, 606, 709, 710
    (1993) *The Missing Pages of "His-Story"*
    (1983) What *They Never Told You in History Class*

CELEBRATING DR. BEN-JOCHANNAN

Leakey, Louis and Mary – 212, 592, 674,
Leo Africanus –
Lepsius, Richard – 260, 360, 481, 482
Leuzinger, Elsy – 156
    The Art of Africa
Lewis, Dr. and Mrs. – 7, 8, 23, 167
Lewis, J.H. – 23
    The Biology of the Negro
Library of Congress – 9, 178, 183
Lucy or *Denk Nesh* – 8, 63
Ma'at's Principles – 182
Maddox, Alton – 719, 720
McIntosh, Dr. James – 717, 718
Maherpra – 431, 514, 586, 590
Malcolm X – 4, 207, 352, 618
Malek, Jaromir – 295
    (1980) *Cultural Atlas of Ancient Egypt*
Manetho – 359
    A History of Egypt
Mann – 242
    (93) *Sacred Architecture*
Marcellinus, Ammianus – 477, 582
Mariette, Auguste – 126, 360, 482, 483, 575
    Maspero, Sir Gaston – 113, 195, 218, 233, 260, 278, 329, 345, 360, 431, 468, 485, 486, 496, 514, 570, 577, 580, 581, 586, 590, 675
Massey, Gerald – 127
    A Book of the Beginnings
Meredith, George – 100
Mertz, Barbara – 94
    Temples, Tombs and Hieroglyphics
Monderson, Dr. Frederick with Dr. Ben –
    Photo – 65
Meyer, Edouard – 499
Montesquieu – 529

FREDERICK MONDERSON

Spirit of the Laws
Mummy – 356, 357, 655
    Rameses II's Mummy – 231, 690
    Granville, Bozzi – 232, 261, 289, 534, 550
    Movies – 291, 643
    Queen Hatshepsut – 439, 548
    Tutankhamon's – 636
Murnane, William – 470, 473, 6164
    (1983) *The Penguin Guide to Ancient Egypt*
Murray, John – 474, 572
    (1888) *Handbook for Egypt*
Murray, Margaret – 94, 123, 131, 133, 454, 455, 456
    (1949) *The Splendor that Was Egypt*
    Seven Wonders of the World – 456, 457
    (1931) *Egyptian Temples*
Nabta Playa – 69, 175, 280, 285, 286, 288, 357, 486, 594, 654, 655, 657, 658, 675
Names of Africa – 8, 152, 198, 326
NASA – 686
Naumann, Professor – 451
Naville, Edouard – 260, 496
    (1913) "Origin of Egyptian Civilization"
Negative Confessions – 5, 75-76, 174, 197, 252, 254, 255, 307
Nkrumah, Kwame – 62, 334
Noble, Gil of **LIKE IT IS** – 679, 720
Nobles, Wade – 199, 206, 721
Obenga, Theophile – 107, 206, 468, 469, 569
O'Connor, David – 463, 534
Opet Festival – 56, 403, 404, 439
"Panel Discussion" – 166, 266
Papyrus of Hunefer – 195
Parks, Gordon – 178
Patterson, David (Governor) – 17
Peet, T. Eric – 72, 260, 508

CELEBRATING DR. BEN-JOCHANNAN

Perry, W.J. – 343, 453
    (1924) *The Growth of Civilization*
Petrie, W.M.F. – 4, 135, 149, 170, 175, 187, 210, 218, 225, 257, 260, 273, 289, 292, 343, 350, 483, 486, 487, 497, 503, 504, 521, 569, 656, 724
    (2001) *The Oxford Encyclopedia of Ancient Egypt*
Plummer, Sister Viola – 99, 717
Poem – 188, 332, 334, 717
    Amon-Ra – 36
    Karnak – 47
    Ptah – 26
    Ra – 18
Posener – 117
    Dictionary of Egyptian Civilization, 456
Precession – 210, 285
Prices for the Monuments – 440
Price of the Trip – $3999.00
Psalms – 178
Ptah-Hotep – 189, 349, 363, 371, 385, 409, 414, 415, 697, 701
Pyramids – 92, 134, 169, 219, 345, 404, 446, 450, 457, 584, 728
Randall-MacIver – 743, 548
Rawlinson, Canon George – 219, 492
    (1893) *Story of the Nations: Egypt*
Reymond, E.A.E – 7843
    The Mythological Origin of the Egyptian Temple
Reisner, Dr. – 500
Rev. McNair – 266
Robbins, Gay – 464, 544, 560
    (1997) *Art of Egypt*
Robinson, Dr. Victor – 583
    (1936) *The Story of Medicine*

FREDERICK MONDERSON

Dr. Ben's Photo 365a. Shawki Abdel Rady, Luis Casado and their Driver on route to Beni Hasan and Amarna.

Rogers, J.A. – 62, 196, 205, 520, 521, 527, 590,
    (1944) *Sex and Race*
Rosellini, Professor –
Russell, Bertrand – 582
    (1972) *A History of Philosophy*
Sarton, George – 360
Scobie, Professor – 17, 686

CELEBRATING
DR. BEN-JOCHANNAN

Shafer, Byron E. – 236
    (1998) *Temples in Egypt*
Shaw and Nicholson – 125
Simmonds, Prof. George –237
Skinner, Otis (1901) – 84
Smith, G. Elliot – 343, 453, 454, 497, 503
    (1911) *The Ancient Egyptians*
Smalls, James Prof – 716, 719
Smith, W. Stephenson – 222, 260, 356, 431, 465, 566, 645
    (1959) *The Art and Architecture of Ancient Egypt*
Snowden, Frank – 156
    Blacks in Antiquity
Steindorff and Seele – 260
    When Egypt Ruled the East
Strabo – 152, 154, 359, 582, 649
Temple – 12, 106, 35
Temples, Types of –
    Abu Simbel – 71, 96, 216, 226, 386, 391, 428, 434, 473, 538, 600, 650, 731
    Abydos – 134, 252, 257, 289, 399, 421, 422, 423, 445, 629, 726, 727, 728
    Beit Wali – 392
    Deir el Bahari – 135, 246, 351, 356, 439, 440, 429, 445, 464, 465, 496, 548, 549, 566, 630, 645, 650, 650, 655, 729
    Edfu – 139, 147, 148, 392, 394, 396, 397, 424, 425, 428, 443, 445, 730
    Esneh – 392, 398, 399, 428
    Gerf Hussein – 392,
    Kalabsha – 147, 391, 730
    Karnak – 11, 12, 20, 27, 40, 47, 49, 54, 56, 95, 106, 136, 138, 139, 140, 225, 242, 246, 385, 402, 404, 416, 420, 421, 428, 436, 437, 439, 440, 470, 539, 542, 562, 597, 627, 628, 726
    Kom Ombo – 147, 392, 393, 394, 424, 428, 434,

FREDERICK MONDERSON

722, 730
Luxor – 6, 7, 12, 125, 128, 139, 146, 221, 226, 260, 261, 273, 332, 367, 402, 404, 416, 421, 424, 428, 438, 439, 440, 539, 554, 628
Philae – 359, 438, 440, 444
Ramesseum – 174, 246, 348, 404, 439, 440, 474, 545, 576

Ten Commandments – 216, 291, 643
Tourist Police – 408, 421
Trinity, Egyptian – 126, 316, 320
UNESCO "fundamental blackness of ancient Egypt" – 259, 524, 538
Valley of the Kings – 12, 96, 439, 440, 445, 560, 630
Van Sertima, Dr. Ivan – 62, 107, 125, 206, 231, 256, 259, 263, 357, 474, 524, 526, 649, 650, 657, 680, 682, 685, 686, 690, 691, 692

(1999) *Egypt Revisited*
(1979) *Journal of African Civilization*
(1976) *They Came Before Columbus*

Volney, Count –208, 454, 477, 529, 584
(1791) *Ruins of Empire*

Waddell's *Manetho* – 156
Wainwright, G.C.W. – 225
"The Origin of Amun"
Weigall, Arthur – 260, 504, 625, 634
(1925) *Flights into Antiquity*
White, J.E. Manchip – 93
Ancient Egypt: Its Culture and History
Wilford, John Noble – 668
(October 14, 2011, p. A14 *The New York Times*) – "In African Cave, Ancient Paint Factory pushes Human Symbolic Thought Far Back"
Wilkinson, Garner – 482
Wilkinson, Toby – 357, 489
Williams, Bruce "Qustol" discovery – 256, 260, 288, 451, 657
Williams, Chancellor – 205, 219, 227, 313, 623, 647

CELEBRATING DR. BEN-JOCHANNAN

(1976) *Destruction of Black* [African] *Civilization*

Dr. Ben's Photo 365a. Erik Monderson and Dad, Dr. Fred Monderson, stand before Memphis Museum's alabaster Sphinx.

Wilson, Robert Forest – 112

FREDERICK MONDERSON

(1924) The *Living Pageant of the Nile*
Woodson, Carter G. – 4, 62, 98, 107, 205, 511, 527, 691
    (1993) *The Mis-Education of the Negro*
Wordsworth – 100
Wortham, John David – 232, 261, 262, 273, 280, 356, 463, 479, 533, 534, 539, 549, 551, 568, 576, 583, 586, 619, 656
    (1971) *Genesis of British Egyptology*

Dr. Ben's Photo 365b. Erik Monderson and a group of young Egyptians pose on stairs to the Sphinx on the Ghizeh Plateau in 2018.

www.ingramcontent.com/pod-product-compliance
Lightning Source LLC
Chambersburg PA
CBHW061947300426
44117CB00010B/1251